The Concise Encyclopedia of

ROMANTICISM

The Concise Encyclopedia of
ROMANTICISM

Francis Claudon

CHARTWELL
BOOKS, INC.

Translated by Susie Saunders

Published by
CHARTWELL BOOKS, INC.
A Division of **BOOK SALES, INC.**
110 Enterprise Avenue
Secaucus, New Jersey 07094

Copyright © 1980 Editions Aimery Somogy, Paris

ISBN 0-89009-707-0

Printed and bound in the GDR.

Contents

The Romantic Movement

The term 'Romantic' applies to the vast movement which, as early as the 18th century, called the all-pervading Humanism and Reason into question, at the risk of destroying the ancient foundations of classical civilisation. No field or country escaped its influence. In Europe, it was the driving force of spiritual life, philosophy, the arts, society and mores, and the social and political revolutions of the time. Its influence spread to every discipline, and its history was so complex that to attempt a coherent study is a mammoth task. This Encyclopaedia is an attempt at synthesis.

Definition of the term

The adjective 'romantic' predates the use of the noun 'Romanticism'. In French, it was initially confused with 'romanesque', from the Italian 'romanzesco' and already noted by Cotgrave in 1611. English did not adopt the term 'romanesque' until much later, to describe Saxon or Norman architecture and art. The English usage of 'romantic' was then adopted on the continent. The word derived from tales of chivalry and the romances of the troubadours and thence, in a broader sense, came to signify whatever, in landscape or in ruins, was evocative of the naivety of the old romances. This is the sense in which John Evelyn used it in his *Diary* as early as 1654 when he wrote of a 'very romantic place' near Bath: similarly Pepys in 1666 described a castle as 'the most romantic in the world'. In these early examples, the adjective 'romantic' evokes the realm of the imagination. From the outset, Romanticism had strong links with the irrational.

In 1674, Rymer, in his translation of Père Rapin's *Reflections on the Poetry of Aristotle*, applied the adjective to the poetry of Pulci, Boiardo and Ariosto. This brings us to the other basic connotation of the term: that of freedom from rules, freedom to apply fantasy. Furetière, in 1690, spoke only of 'romanesque' meaning 'of romance' or that which is unbelievable. Pope in his description of Windsor Castle and Addison describing Chevey Chase at the beginning of the 18th century, both used the word 'romantic' to convey the savagery and eerie attraction of what they saw. The term was then applied to Christian names: Goldsmith in *The Vicar of Wakefield* (1776) found new names like Olivia 'romantic', while in Germany Wieland chose the name Amandis to be the title of one of his works.

From then on, the adjective passed into everyday language. In England, James Thomson, Thomas Warton the Younger and many others used it to evoke *rêverie* and mystery, while in Germany and France the word was widely used. In the last quarter of the 18th century, Rousseau wrote in his *Rêveries d'un promeneur solitaire* 'the shores of the lake of Bienne are wilder and more romantic than those of the lake of Geneva' and Letourneur, in the preface to his translation of Shakespeare, wrote in 1776 that 'one should not only read and meditate on Shakespeare in the heart of a town. To understand him, the reader must wander through the countryside … climb to the peak of rocks or mountains and from there look out over the vast sea and fix his gaze on the airy and *romantic* landscape of the clouds. Then he will feel Shakespeare's true genius, the genius that paints everything, that animates everything.'

In 1801, Sebastien Mercier in his *Néologie ou Vocabulaire des mots nouveaux* distinguished between 'romanesque', which he disdained and considered 'false and bizarre', and 'romantic' which he favoured because 'you can feel it but you cannot define it'. In 1802–1803, Sennancour entitled a now famous fragment of *Oberman* 'De l'expression romantique et du ranz de vaches' (a Swiss pastoral tune): in this case, neither the place nor the feeling it evokes is 'romantic', but an abstract art (music) and the sensation of melancholy and nostalgia induced by it. He even used the name 'Romanticism' to designate not a literary movement, which had yet to emerge, but the quality, in Nature, of that which is romantic. Furthermore, in his *Dictionnaire des Beaux-Arts* (1806), A.L. Millin advised that the French language, which had no equivalent for it, should imitate English and German and use the epithet 'romantiqüe' in painting as well as literature.

Although the adjective 'romantisch' appeared rather late in Germany, initially to designate the Gothic and mediaeval, it was rapidly adopted in the fields of literature and criticism. In the last decade of the 18th century, F. Schlegel started to use the term 'romantic poetry' in a historical sense, to mean mediaeval poetry, as well as the poetry of impulse and fantasy. As early as 1801, A.W. Schlegel drew a clearer distinction between Romantic and Classical literature. Tieck, writing in what he claimed to be the new style, called his 1801 poems *Romantische Dichtungen*. Schiller subtitled his play *The Maid of Orleans* (1802) *'eine romantische Dichtung'*, to indicate its links with the world of chivalry. From then on, the word was established, to the point where Goethe protested at the use of the Romantic/Classical distinction in a polemical literary sense. He would have liked, initially at least, to limit the meaning of the word to 'mediaeval', 'miraculous' or even 'Christian'. It was only later that he gave it a different connotation in his famous diction: 'Classical' - healthy, 'Romantic' - unhealthy.

It was from German that Madame de Staël drew the usage of the term which was to prevail in France during the last years of the Empire. In *De l'Allemagne*, she wrote the famous statement that was soon to provoke a great literary debate: 'I here consider classical poetry to be that of the ancients and romantic poetry to be that which in some way derives from the traditions of chivalry' and in chapter XI of the second volume, she added: 'The name "Romanticism" has lately been introduced in Germany to designate the poetry, originating from the songs of the troubadours, which is born of chivalry and Christianity … The distinction for us is not between classical and romantic poetry, but between the imitativeness of the one and the inspiration of the other.'

It is from this work by Madame de Staël (as well as from German) that the Italian language was to borrow the adjective 'romantico' in around 1815, although at first it was used only to describe a literary trend. That trend had its platform in the *Conciliatore*, in which Monti, Foscolo and Visconti advocated the use of the word 'romanticismo', adopted as a noun by Stendhal when he wrote *Racine et Shakespeare*, to designate the new literature. Shortly afterwards, the same word appeared in Spanish and in other languages. It is, however, worth noting that in English, which had created both the term and its usage, the word continued for some time to be evocative of a legendary past and of a fantasy world. It was only in the late 19th century that the word 'Romanticists' came to denote a school of poets, whereas the term

Caspar David Friedrich *Chalk Cliffs on the Isle of Rügen*

'Romantics' had passed into common parlance, referring to Germany, France, Italy, Spain, Poland etc. In Scandinavia, the term 'neo-romantic' ('nyromantisk') was used to distinguish the new literary concepts from their mediaeval models and sources. But, almost everywhere, in addition to its literary meaning, 'romantic' retained its connotation of that which is poetic, dream-like and individualist. In 1816, as the literary debate started to rage, Saint-Chamans stated in *l'Antiromantique*: 'All I see is that the Classicists are material and the Romantics are spiritual.'

From then on, the term did not evolve further, becoming part of the vocabulary of literature and criticism.

Pre-Romanticism

The term Pre-Romanticism usually serves to identify a trend which was first apparent in the middle of the 18th century. It was a reaction against the Age of Reason, and against an intellectuality which favoured comprehension at the expense of sensitivity. It heralded a new climate which celebrated the world of imagination and dreams.

The first theories of pleasure and emotion are to be found in the works of the 18th century philosophers. It was in fact a priest of the Society of Jesus, Père André, who provided perhaps the best analysis of the primacy of the senses.

The aesthetics of Stendhal, the Christian poetry of Chateaubriand, and Balzac's morality were developments of these principles. The Romantic vindication of passion, and of the immorality of love (for which, curiously, the Germans, Byron and Pushkin were reproached), were a part of this revolutionary primacy of feeling and pleasure. Even in the graphic and pictorial arts, the imperious domination of passion, as formulated nearly a century before its time by the Abbé Du Bos in his *Refléxions critiques sur la Poésie et la Peinture* (1718), became an accepted principle.

The writings of Joseph Addison (1672–1719), in his famous series in 'The Spectator' on *The Pleasures of the Imagination* are indicative of this new wave of sensitivity:

'By greatness, I do not mean only the bulk of any single object, but the largeness of a whole view, considered as one entire piece. Such are the prospects of an open champaign (flat) country, a vast uncultivated desert, of huge heaps of mountains, high rocks and precipices, or a wide expanse of waters, where we are not struck with the novelty or beauty of the sight, but with that rude kind of magnificence which appears in many of these stupendous works of Nature. Our imagination loves to be filled with an object, or to grasp at anything that is too big for its capacity. We are flung into a pleasing astonishment at such unbounded views and feel a delightful stillness and amazement in the soul at the apprehension of them ... But if there be a beauty or uncommonness joined with this grandeur, as in a troubled ocean, a heaven adorned with stars and meteors, or a spacious landscape cut out into rivers, woods, rocks, and meadows, the pleasure still grows upon us, as it arises from more than a single principle.'

This is reminiscent of the vast lonely spaces of Chateaubriand's America and the torrid and frozen vistas of *Oberman*; the same awesome empty spaces are to be found in Blechen, Carus and Schinkel, and the same magnificent skies in Constable, Turner and Corot. A new taste, as well as a new aesthetic language, was taking shape: it gave a new face to Nature as rediscovered by the 18th century.

In England, Nature provided inspiration for James Thomson (1700–1748), William

Jean-Auguste-Dominique Ingres *Ossian's Dream*

Collins (1721–1759), and Thomas Gray (1716–1771), while new themes, characteristic of a nascent Romanticism, appeared in the poetry of Thomas Chatterton (1752–1770), William Cowper (1731–1800) and William Blake (1757–1827). Nonetheless, they were still no more than isolated cases. They were no more conscious of their precursory role than were James Macpherson (1736–1796) when he wrote *Ossian*, or Goethe when he wrote *The Sufferings of Young Werther*, the works that were to be the inspiration for the whole Romantic movement.

The German Pre-Romantic era was undoubtedly more homogeneous. The *Sturm und Drang* movement, which took its name from Klinger's work (1752–1794), and men like Bürger (1747–1794) and Herder, who refused to consider reason as the main instrument of knowledge but preferred intuition and sensitivity, were in a way the heralds of Romanticism. Goethe and Schiller were in the same position, but they soon took fright at the breadth of the nascent movement and retreated into a more conservative vision.

Unlike England and Germany, France did not really have any great Pre-Romantic poets, apart, perhaps, from Chénier. The novel, on the other hand, was of great importance, dominated from very early on (Defoe's *Robinson Crusoe* dated from 1719) by the power of Nature and the supremacy of the rights of the individual over social rules and conventions (Rousseau's *La Nouvelle Héloïse* dates from 1761, *Paul et Virginie* by Bernardin de Saint-Pierre from 1787). Nature's hold was evident in fields other than that of literature: the painting of 'views' was a genre born in the last decades of the 18th century, though it was still dominated by Classicism. According to Watelet, the term 'view' applies to 'the portrait of a site that has been drawn from Nature ... The category of views extends to cover an infinity of specific subjects. The sea, a cottage, an unusual terrain, rocks, all of these are called "views" ... They provide great artists with relaxation.'

Fragonard, Hubert Robert and the Vedutists in 18th century Italy paved the way for Corot's Italian series, the views of the Austrian Empire by Koch and Gurkh, the paintings of Bonington, Turner and Cotman in England, and Cole and Sachse in America.

But while the 18th century depiction of Nature was purely descriptive and static, dominated by Reason, the Romantics were to imbue it with their sensitivity, their feelings of nostalgia and sometimes their spiritual confusion when faced with the immensity of the elements.

National Romantic movements

The Romantic movement as a whole drew on all the new trends and the individuality of each of its precursors.

Nevertheless, it is as difficult to speak of a single Romantic movement as it is to attempt to define it in time or space. None of the major crises or the great revolutions experienced in the West broke out in all countries at the same time. They were not experienced in the same way, nor did they follow identical courses, as each country reacted differently to the same stimuli because of its national characteristics, political, social and historical background, and aspirations.

Obviously Romanticism could not have had the same repercussions in countries as different as France, at the time of the Revolution, the Napoleonic wars and the Restoration of the monarchy, and a divided Germany, or the various parts of occupied Italy.

Sometimes, even within a country, there were contradictory trends. It is paradoxical that an absolute aesthetic emerged from such diversity. Unlike French Classicism or the Renaissance, the early Romantic movement had no clear conception of its aims, no considered poetic inspiration, no schools, no synchronised international movement. In literature, although Sainte-Beuve wrote of *Chateaubriand et son groupe littéraire*, Chateaubriand was in every sense an isolated figure. A group like the one formed by Coppet, which might be considered as the most organised and the most conscious of a sense of history, was deprived of all influence due to political circumstances. In Great Britain, the literary revival began in Scotland with the all but folkloric poets. Although it was a time of Revolution, the minds most affected by that revolution were, in the fields of art and literature, Neo-Classicists. Even authors who were philosophical and political innovators such as Chénier, Hölderlin and Schiller, based their ideas upon a return to the model of Antiquity. The plastic and pictorial arts, though they drew inspiration from dramatic subjects, were often obsessed with hierarchies and balance, composition and design. Chénier is close to Canova, as Raynouard is to David. Their rigorous metrics, cold elegance and perfect plasticity have none of the colour, enthusiasm and spontaneity that to today's observer would have suited their subject matter and the historical moment. *The Young Captive* and *The Tarentine Girl* by Chénier and Canova's *Psyche* share the aesthetic of Antiquity. Chateaubriand, in his *Lettre à M. de Fontanes sur la campagne romaine*, seems to cry out for Vernet, Hubert Robert, even David, to illustrate his ideas.

Even more paradoxical is the fact that a movement which set such store by enthusiasm, by the heart ruling the head, and by a brotherhood of the arts, should have seen the light of day amid squabbles between schools and in specialists côteries. It is a striking fact that in Germany, the theoreticians of the power of music and of the irrational were men of letters and science. The author of *Hymns to the Night* was an engineer, a minerologist. Wackenroder and Tieck, who were the first to write ecstatic praise of the new ideals in music, had only known the music of Reichardt, Zelter and Gretry. The different circles which, at Jena, Heidelberg and Berlin in turn, established the great German Romantic school, were composed of intellectuals who still admired Weimar Classicism. Jena, with the Schlegels, was a place for experimentation in structures and ideas, rather than a source of perfected works; it housed more philosophers than poets, more philologists and historians than imaginative spirits. In Heidelberg, lyricists like Armin and Brentano are found alongside the Grimm Brothers, who were grammarians, folklorists and lexicologists; Creuzer, whose *Symbolics* attempted to synthesise the myths and religions of Antiquity; and with Görres, the doctrinarian of national resistance to France.

In France, somewhat later, it was equally difficult to find a homogeneous circle or a purely artistic group. The 'Romantic Party' of journalists were opposed by other journalists, leading to press quarrels between *Débats* and *Le Spectateur littéraire* – academicians against aristocrats. The opposing claims and grievances were all so vague (as proved by this definition in *Minerve Française* in 1818: 'The main characteristic of Romantic literature (is) to express the new order of ideas and feelings, born of new social groupings') that the public entertained serious fears for the sanity of their men of letters.

Conversely, the true Romantic artists like Nodier or Lamartine did not involve themselves in theoretical wranglings. If Fontaney is to be believed, the Arsenal salon was more of a setting for poetry reading and musical recitals than the enclave of a faction. Later on, *chez* Jacques Deschamps in the *Conservateur littéraire* group of 1820, an exchange of views took place from which no doctrine emerged. *Chez* Délécluze, from 1821 on, politics rather than literature were discussed, and there was a preoccupation more with art and theatre criticism than with poetry or fiction. When the battle opened up in 1823, it remained all but incomprehensible to the general public, such was the technical nature of its disputes: the proper meanings of words, the Three Unities of the theatre, metrication and so on. For a long time, the circles that surrounded Hugo, Vigny and the Globe group were far better known for their political stand-points than for their literary tendencies. It is obvious that the movement could not have spread in France in the same way as it did in Germany. In Germany the precursors of Roman-ticism were much bolder by far, whereas in France they were hampered by childish squabbles between different salons and circles, by polemics about form and by rival influences.

Nor was it any different in the spheres of the fine arts and of music. The opposition between Ingres and Delacroix which, after the event, came to symbolise the battle of Classi-cists against Romantics, appeared at the time to be a personal quarrel with the Institut as its underlying cause. In the field of music the situation was similar: a reading of Berlioz's *Mém-oires*, leaves the impression that the composer's setbacks in the competition for the Grand Prix de Rome were not so much caused by aesthetic considerations as by 'bargaining' between the professors of the Conservatoire. When Berlioz finally received the prize, in July 1830, it was for his 'conversion to healthy doctrines'. In Italy, the Milanese Romantic movement asserted itself primarily as a political force, so much so that the Austrians deported Pellico and harassed Foscolo and Berchet, while Manzoni remained at liberty and Canova and Rossini were officially fêted.

Thus, not only was the Romantic movement neither homogeneous nor coordinated, but, more important, its novelty was not clearly perceived, not even by those most closely con-cerned with the movement. In the history of Romanticism, there was little or no agreement between either men or principles, no continuity between its beginnings and ends. This pro-found and influential aesthetic renewal was born in disorder, confusion and paradox.

It remains true, nevertheless, that despite their heterogeneity, the Romantic movements stemmed from a common ideological root, interpreted and nourished by each of them in different ways.

The sense of passing time

It was in the 18th century that a sense of the irrevocable passing of time became preva-lent; it was evident in the love of ruins (Hubert Robert and Diderot), the feeling for history and legend (Ossianism and the cult of Shakespeare), and for dreams (Fuseli, Goya, Rousseau and Novalis). This sense of time provided, paradoxically, both continuity and contrast. It is hard to see a great deal in common between the ruins painted by Hubert Robert and those depicted in the poems and drawings of Victor Hugo. Yet both owe their poetic inspiration to ruins, the sense of time past, and a love of Antiquity, and owed their inspiration to Winckelmann's archaeological investigations and the discovery, in around 1755, of Herculaneum and Pom-peii.

Similarly, it seems quite natural that, for Chateaubriand, for example, the thought of the fall of Rome and of all that was beautiful in Humanism and Classicism should have engen-dered a hatred of life and fed a growing 'mal du siècle'. The taste for Gothic and for the Middle Ages (typically Romantic if one is to believe Madame de Staël) was a product of the 18th century. Even before its rediscovery by historians and Romantic poets, the Gothic vault was a symbol of classic sentimentalism (epitomised in Walpole's novels). Kenneth Clark wrote that 'with the help of a ruined ogive, the admirer of Young's *Nights* could contemplate himself as a work of art'. The members of the *Sturm und Drang* movement in Germany were the first to express great admiration for Strasbourg Cathedral. The young Goethe extolled the ogive in 1772, well before the classical column. Gradually, but inexorably, the 18th century moved away from the conception of time as circular or static towards a perception of irreversible time. This concept of time also gave rise to the Hellenism of the Weimar group and of Ingres, to English and French Palladianism, to the heroic Romanism of David, to the love of ruins and tombs and to Ossianism and the Neo-Gothic.

There was thus a continuity in moral and aesthetic philosophy and poetic vision between these two centuries, which are more usually contrasted than compared.

The metaphysical value of Nature

But Romanticism did not confine itself to temporal escapism: it also needed to escape in space. Like the traveller in Liszt's *Années de Pèlerinage*, painters were to evoke in landscape a sense of their own melancholy and dreams. A landscape painting was not necessarily a direct representation of a site, but was composed of chosen elements selected for their meaning and value. The paintings of Caspar David Friedrich and Philipp Otto Runge provide the best illustration of this, but it applies also to the work of Turner and Corot. The painting must, necessarily, be of a secluded place, a place at once a hermitage and Elysium, a kind of 'refuge for a day to await death', as Lamartine wrote in *Le Vallon*. Senancour and the English Lake poets found refuge in such places; there Schumann's *Prophet-Bird* sand and *Solitary Flowers* grew.

Hubert Robert *Roman Ruins*

Many Romantic painters saw the site as blend of soft curves set around meadows or pools. Even so, the hills, hedges or forests that protected it from the world could not always adequately convey its unreality. So a reminder of the past was added to the scene – a ruin or a Gothic cathedral; we catch a glimpse of misty sky through the branches of a tree, or the sea in the distance, blurring into the horizon. As well as memories and the promise of rest, the landscape might also include the figure of the dreamer as he stands motionless in contemplation or is engaged in activity reminiscent of bygone times, like Millet's peasants. The presence of these figures underlines the suspension of time. Often, the choice of muted grey tones or an indefinite twilight setting serves to reinforce this feeling of the temporary nature of life. The presence of tombstones and cenotaphs in the heart of these landscapes invites the spectator to reflect upon the destiny of Man as no more than a straw in the wind.

Exoticism and revolt

Another important influence was the attraction of the vast open spaces of the New World (*Atala*, 1801), and the exoticism of Spain, the Orient and Greece which inspired Delacroix to paint *Greece expiring under the ruins of Missolonghi* and *The Massacre at Chios*; Hugo to castigate Turkish oppression in *Les Orientales*, and Byron to give his life at Missolonghi. Artists thus gave concrete support to the cause of Hellenism and its national struggles, while at the same time they changed the direction of their art in a militant and picturesque sense. The attraction of the exotic was accompanied by a yearning for the ideal place, free from all tyranny. Romanticism contained the elements of revolt, in metaphysical terms as well as socially and politically. The Romantic movement had much in common with the revolutionary movements, in that it expressed the dissatisfaction of the individual with the established power structures, and his yearning for the divine, the infinite or simply for change.

The first half of the 19th century saw the combined effects of two revolutions: the French Revolution and the Industrial Revolution. These fundamental revolutions provided an entirely new setting for social movements and insurrections, unrelated to the experiences of previous centuries. Authority versus liberty, tradition versus freedom and individualism were notions that were applicable to politics as well as to art and literature, and fuelled the most heated of debates in all countries until 1848. They concerned, for example, personal freedom and freedom of action: many countries followed the French lead in abolishing serfdom; the Romantics fought personally for the abolition of black slavery; the Napoleonic Code was introduced, though not without opposition; and Mancunian liberalism became economic dogma. Political life seemed to resign itself to opposition to the powers of the state and to the rights of the citizen. The same was true of the form of government: different peoples in turn obtained their own constitutions and recognition of their nationhood, if not their independence. The concept of nationhood was at the hub of everything and it was a Romantic and revolutionary concept.

The cause of the Risorgimento, or of Italian unity against Austria and the forces of the Holy Alliance, was the foundation stone and the cement of Italian Romanticism. Without national inspiration and hope of revival, its literature would simply not exist. Its most remarkable products drew the very reason for their existence from the Risorgimento. A novel like Manzoni's *Promessi Sposi* is Romantic both in form and in ideology: because it imitated Walter Scott, it appeared to be new in form: but its novelty also served a political purpose in that it described, vividly and historically, the revolt of the inhabitants of Milan and of the poor people against the oppression of the aristocracy and the Spanish. The lyricism of Leopardi, say, may not seem, a priori, to have anything to do with ideology: but feelings of world weariness and dereliction find an excellent point of application in the fact that the illness of the young poet prevented him from taking part in the struggle and caused his bitterness and conviction that he was wasting his life.

On the other hand, in a literature like that of Austria, the pessimism and the patriotism of Grillparzer, the 'Weltschmerz' of Lenau, the apparently superficial wit of Stifter or Nestroy, must be seen in relation to the ideological oppression exerted by an anachronistic political system. Literature expressed the historical malaise and the dulling of reason.

In Germany, however, the cause of unity and nationhood brought like minds together: all the Romantics of the Heidelberg and Berlin circles were united in their reflections upon the mission of Prussia and the nature of German art.

Coincidences of art and thought

Architecture and furnishing, music and philosophy – not one discipline remained oblivious to the new ideological commitment: the 'neo' style of building; the so-called 'Gründerjahre' designs in furniture; Nietzsche and Wagner; all would be inconceivable without reference to nationalist values. In the socio-political sphere as well as in art, in each form of expression and almost every theme and technique, there was a clear link between Romanticism and revolution. F.R. de Toreinx wrote in 1829 that 'the banner of Romanticism bore a triple motto: political, religious and literary freedom'.

The Revolution of 1789 opened the corridors of power to the bourgeoisie. Its corollary was belief in progress, liberalism and revolution in every field. Normally, such a society might have been seduced by tangible qualities and given birth to a form of realism. The very opposite was true. Art turned away from still life; if portrait painting flourished, it paid scant attention to physical resemblance or psychological characteristics. The person sitting for David, Ingres, Lawrence or Goya wanted above all to see his own symbol, his social rank reflected on the canvas. He was not averse to a certain precision of detail on condition that that detail drew attention to his position and his wealth. The pose or posture was all important, because it symbolised power and influence. The person took second place to the personage.

Those who had just acquired power also naturally sought to remodel the environment according to their own vision, and thus town planning was re-directed along political lines. Haussmann was to provide the supreme expression of this, but there were other, earlier, examples. In Paris or in London, total transformation was unthinkable, so only certain areas were rebuilt. But in the United States where everything was new, possible and legitimate for a nation that had just been born, they dreamed of the cities of the future. The plans that the architect L'Enfant drew up for the capital to be, Washington, conformed in their scale and symmetry to the American ideal: an ordered, magnificent yet habitable city. The creation of new monuments in Europe can be attributed to the same socio-politico-economic origins: stations, parliaments, theatres, department stores, parks and mansion houses. In the event, their style was less important than their *raison d'être* and their position. They were monuments to the dominant ideology.

Perhaps this explains why it is so difficult to arrive at a definition of a Romantic style of architecture. On the one hand, the rather confused aesthetic of the time imposed its requirements: a love of times gone by, a return to the past – to Antiquity, the Middle Ages and the

Henry Fuseli *The Nightmare.* 1802

Gothic – all brought about a strangely disparate style with no real unity, its different element cohabiting but not always integrating well with one another. On the other hand, those fo whom order and reason were the basis of art, saw architecture as a form of rational expression since it projected perfect geometry upon space. This was the direction taken by Ledoux, Soane and Gilly, who sought to create buildings whose beauty lay in their perfection of volume, harmony of mass and balance of structure. But these monuments, by their very nature, had to be functional and required new techniques and research. This is one of the reasons why Labrouste enthusiastically used iron and glass for the construction of the Bibliothèque Sainte-Geneviève in 1845. Bourgeois ideology invited art to celebrate power, its own political, economic, intellectual and social power.

Interior decoration was more coherent. Germany and Austria invented an intimate bourgeois style, *Biedermeier*, that was stripped of pathos but pleasant and comfortable. The corresponding style in France was 'Louis-Philippe'. The latter cohabited with the Empire style which was still popular, although its fortunes were varied. The cult of the hero, inspired particularly by Napoleon, went hand in hand with the triumph of the people: it is best illustrated in Victor Hugo's *Châtiments*, Beethoven's *Eroica Symphony*, *Liberty guiding the People* and *The Battle of Taillebourg* by Delacroix. Legend, mainly Greek or Roman, was added to depictions of national and contemporary history: *The Funeral of Patroclus* and *Napoleon distributing the Eagles* by David are related to Makart's frescoes, the cycles of Moritz von Schwind. Turner, in his *Battle of Trafalgar*, resembles Rude, David and Géricault. Even when art was not so explicitly directed or solicited by power, it found ways of glorifying strength: the legendary strength of the ancient heroes, Goya's rebels, Delacroix's *Faust* or the brutal ugly strength of the bourgeois, who reigns in Daumier's work. All of it was clearly, albeit remotely, based on the revolutionary explosion of 1789. By its insistence on expressiveness and intelligibility, on rationality and pomp, Romantic art conveyed the needs and demands of a newly established power. The growing confidence of that power should perhaps be seen in relation to the gradual decline of a particular kind of Romanticism. The Romanticism of strength and of secular revolution was to die out with the troubles of 1848.

More clearly than pictorial art or architecture, literature expressed the changes in the dominant ideology. In *Racine et Shakespeare*, Stendhal admitted that 'le romanticisme' was the acceptance of a modern sensitivity born out of the torments of 1789. He was not the only man, nor the first, to express this view. Even writers who had had royalist leanings, either through inclination or personal bitterness like Chateaubriand and Goethe, or through the influence of their families like Vigny, Kleist and Arnim had no desire to return to the pre-1789 order of things. Madame de Staël stated in her *Considérations sur la révolution française*, published in 1818, that the new literature was the logical consequence of the political cataclysm. And Hugo, in his preface to the *Nouvelles Odes* in 1824, added these words to a profession of legitimist faith: 'The literature of today may be to some extent a result of the revolution without being an expression of it ... The new literature is real. And what does it matter if it is the result of the revolution? Is the harvest less beautiful because it ripened on the slopes of the volcano?'

Nonetheless, the fact remains that the themes and poetic expression of literary Romanticism are to a large extent based on revolution.

It was above all a revolution of form, which found its justification, with some hindsight, in the political revolution. Drama was presented as the theatre of the future in contrast to neo-Racinian tragedy, as anachronistic as the absolute power of the monarchy. The novel, at the hands of Stendhal and Dickens, became a battering ram with which to bring down the ramparts of affected aristocratic literature. Lyricism blossomed spontaneously into epic verse and political and philosophical poetry (Shelley, Lamartine, Heine). There followed a revolution of themes and sentiments, reinforced by the liberation of metrication and vocabulary: war, the Napoleonic adventure, the struggles for national liberation and heroism, all inspired

Eugène Delacroix *Greece expiring on the Ruins of Missolonghi*

the poets of 1813 in Germany, and Polish, Russian, Italian and Spanish poets. Finally, there was a revolution of style: history (Michelet, Carlyle), criticism (Schlegel, Hazlitt), moral and political philosophy (particularly the German *Naturphilosophie* and Italian Risorgimentism) benefited directly from the new ideology. It is summed up by Hugo's polemical but striking dictum: Romanticism is 'the revolution in literature'.

Philosophy

Romanticism was not only evident in artistic style or a series of social and economic upheavals; it was also a new way of thinking. With hindsight, this new mode of thought seems to have evolved entirely in the German domain and one can safely say that German philosophy, with all its various streams, was the leading philosophy of the Romantic movement.

In fact, although there was a Romantic school of thought in France, expressed in the utopian socialism of Blanqui, Proudhon, Fourier and Saint-Simon, and in England by Adam Smith and Robert Owen, it had neither the continuity nor coherence of the German doctrines. Echoing the words of Moses Hess, it could be said that France worked in the field of revolution, England in the field of economics, and Germany in the field of theoretical invention.

Romantic philosophy originated in the metaphysics of Kant. The distinction between the nomenon and the phenomenon established that the thing in itself (Ding an sich) is unknowable, since the mind of man makes him no more than the legislator of Nature by virtue of his innate faculties (a sense of space and time, an understanding of causality, reality, substance and unity). The possibility of perceiving a coherent representation of the world does not alter the fact that the world as it is in itself is not the world as reflected in the human mind. Here is the measure of human greatness: man builds his world by organising his knowledge; but herein also lies the proof of the mysterious and ideal nature of the world. Romantic ideology is an ideology of the irrational because it must first find, as in Kant, the rational proof of its own abstraction. *Mal de vivre*, the pain of living, could from that point onwards be a theoretical position. Kant adopted the same view with regard to morality. Nothing, outside man himself, can decide for him what his choice as a free man should be. No external or superior law may govern him; his dignity is embodied in his rational freedom to want things for their own objective qualities, in other words, in submission to the categorical imperative. This was a true 'Jacobite' morality: all men are free and equal, individualism is laid down as an objective principle, subjectivism and sentiment are seen as rational necessities. Kant was the first philosopher to endow confused values and nascent revolutionary ideas with a theoretical justification.

Fichte, Kant's disciple and successor, whose major work was *Wissenschaftslehre* (Doctrine of Science), re-affirmed more energetically still that reality was no more than a construction in man's mind, and passionately refuted the idea that the thing in itself could limit human intelligence of it. Fichte saw man in the role of a conqueror – one of the characteristics of Romanticism. Knowledge and action, intellectual effort and moral progress were all assigned to a single messianic goal.

This metaphysical sublimation of voluntarism and universality, and rejection of the notions of the hereafter and transcendancy, could not but appeal to a revolutionary century. Fichte, who was interested in Nature only in as far as man acted upon it and realised himself through it, summed up the aspirations of 18th century philosophers, and paved the way for all ideologies of action. Goethe, Schelling and Hölderlin had each arrived in their own way at a similar view of Nature from a historical standpoint, and it was a view shared by Novalis, the Schlegels and the Grimm brothers (Fichte and Schelling had both taught at Jena). Schelling adopted Fichte's theory with enthusiasm and pursued it much further, and in his wake came a host of fascinated young minds who shared the same inchoate dream: that drama is unfolding at the heart of the universe, discord exists at the heart of unity, but from it springs the principle of life and the source of hope. One has to start from Nature to find the self, because everything is in perpetual evolution. That evolution can only be born of a struggle of Nature and life, which is the source of diversity and development. If the organism were to become insensitive to the assaults of Nature, it would mean certain death, since struggle and movement are the very essence of life. Unity of knowledge, faith and will should be the supreme goal of Man.

With Hegel, the dialectical relationship between subject and object gave a cloak of theory to the idealistic individualism elaborated by Kant and Fichte. Hegel was a philosopher of history, of its contradictions and resolutions; he was the perfect theoretician for a movement that was essentially historical. If Romanticism represented progress, relativity and revolution, then it could not but find its theoretical justification in Hegelian dialectics. According to Hegel, the truth of the world is to be found in its history, which is constantly changing and developing. The intellect is history, as it mixes variable proportions of the rational and the irrational, necessary and accidental, sense and non-sense. This brief outline of the idealism and historicism of Hegel's philosophy suffices to show how much it was in tune with the time, and how it came to be seen, by an intellect as critical as that of Marx, as representative of all the ambition and the ambiguity of Romantic thought.

Schopenhauer provided a systematic philosophical formulation for that most famous of Romantic traits, world-weariness. He was certainly not the most synthetic thinker of the Romantic movement, but probably best represents the excesses of Romanticism. Nietzsche and Wagner were not mistaken when they saw in him the tragic impasse into which such a mind could be led.

In his major work, *The World as Will and Perception*, Schopenhauer suggested, even in the title, that the world is a cerebral phenomenon – an attitude typical of his time. The world becomes fact to us if perception of it derives from the constitution of our mind, and it is supported not by thought, but by the immutable root of human life: the will. Neither conscience nor thought are cardinal realities, but phenomena that derive from the will, the only true absolute. Man uses his intelligence in the service of his will, the better to protect his precarious existence from destruction. Death is but an illusion of the world of phenomena. The individual dies, but the species lives on. If we cease to question the place, time, reason and outcome of things, we can bring our intellect to grasp an intuition of pure form.

Thus architecture transformed ideas of height, weight and cohesion into intuitive notions, while in sculpture and painting, especially historical painting, the theory found its most individual expression. Music objectified the will itself: 'Melody expresses the intimate history of the selfconscious will: the secret life of the human heart, its ebbs and flows, its joys and its sorrows.' Music moves us because the feelings which it evokes are universal, because, more than any other medium, it brings a sense of calm and release to the spirit. We know what great store Nietzsche and Wagner set by this definition. Philosophical ethics, too, were striving to achieve release, seeing life as only effort and pain. The one real sin is to cling to one's individual life, which is seen as the most fundamental selfishness. Only death, suicide, pity and revolt are rational and useful attitudes.

Thomas Lawrence *Portrait of Princess Lieven*. c. 1820

There were other thinkers whose theories had some basis in Romanticism. In the work of Marx, for example, although he was constructing a realist philosophy based on dialectical and historical materialism, the messianic background to his theory of revolution is evident: it is as if the passionate impulses of his youth were born again in his mature years. Nietzsche, on the other hand, took Schopenhauer's pessimism and attempted to graft on to it a vision of the hereafter. The initial friendship between Nietzche and Wagner, witnessed by the admirable pages about *Tristan and Isolde* in Nietzsche's *The Birth of Tragedy*, were a confirmation of the Romantic foundation of such a position. Nietzsche later renounced both Wagner and the

23

illusion of art, but his feeling of despair in the face of human values has its echoes in Romanticism too. In *Also Sprach Zarathustra*, the philosopher seeks salvation in the will to power and the emergence of the Superman; and this ultimate vision is strongly Romantic.

Dreams and the Romantic soul

'Each epoch of human thought can be sufficiently deeply defined by the relationship which it establishes between dreams and waking life' wrote Albert Béguin in *L'Ame romantique et le rêve* ('The Romantic Soul and the Dream'), published in 1939.

It was Béguin who demonstrated the extent to which the Romantic movement renewed the awareness of dreams and the importance they attached to it. For the generation born in Germany around 1800, states of unconsciousness or ecstasy dictated by the hidden self, were ranked as revelations of reality.

That unreal world was by nature a feminine one. The official status and relatively conventional role of the woman in the bourgeois ideology of the time might have been expected to dampen effusive sentimentality, yet Woman was worshipped and praised above all else. She was the sensitive wife and mother in Schumann's *Love and Life of a Woman* (from Chamisso's poems); and the loyal and tearful fiancée of Ludwig Richter's engravings, or those of Moritz von Schwind. But she was also the woman of the world who entertains, and is entertained, like the famous Madame Récamier who was painted by David in her salon at Abbaye-aux-Bois.

At the same time, a whole Romantic mythology of womanhood was developing, and was echoed in the arts, especially in literature. Poets invented language anew to sing the praises of the beloved woman, and to invoke the woman of their dreams. Their passions, real or imaginary, were revealed in broad daylight, without any shame, and so was their suffering. For women were also the cause of pain: the theme of the 'femme fatale' was born of the Romantic age and was later successfully taken up by the Symbolist movement. The term applies equally to the woman-vampire as to Carmen the flirt and to the diabolical Cecily in *The Mysteries of Paris*. For Velleda, the witch patriot of Chateaubriand's *Martyrs*, and her sister Norma from Bellini's opera, love becomes a criminal passion. There were the Amazons: Kleist's Penthesilia, Stendhal's Mathilde de la Môle; and the women who symbolised chastity and death: Salammbô, Esmeralda of *Notre-Dame de Paris*, Nodier's heroines, and the beautiful exotic creatures loved by Gautier, Heine, Baudelaire, Barbey d'Aurevilly; a whole repertory of female characters walked straight out of the Romantic imagination.

Throughout the Romantic movement, there was a constant recourse to dreams. It might be a sleeping dream which took on aesthetic or metaphysical significance, as in Hoffmann's *Elixirs of the Devil* or Nerval's *Daughters of Fire*; or it might be a flow of emotionally charged images, as in Hugo. Then again, dreams might, as in the tales of Tieck and Grimm, draw on the sources of ancestral memory, which provided the poetic and mythological imagination with such riches. Some dreams were haunted by ghosts, as in Arnim and Hoffmann; others in visualised the gates of Paradise, as in Novalis and Brentano. They could be the channel by means of which God delegated His solemn warnings, as in Novalis and Eichendorff; or, for Jean-Paul Richter and Victor Hugo, they could reveal Man's earthly roots plunging into the bountiful heart of Nature. In every field, Romanticism drew its substance from dreams.

The cult of the dream should not be regarded as a mere psychological device. German Romanticism did not set out only to describe the laws of the mind: it postulated the existence of a magical realm that could be perceived by art through the interpretation of dreams. The outpourings of Jean-Paul Richter's characters in the midst of Nature; the strange significance taken on by objects and beings in Hoffmann's world; the symbolic values that Novalis and Nerval tried to find in the languages of science, figures, sensations and images, all make reference to a presentiment of a world of the soul beyond the world of the senses. Thus Romanticism became a form of escapism into a world beyond its own. Reality was so well disguised that it is not clear whether the poet was searching for himself through his characters or whether, through their adventures, he was offering his own soul to the reader. The Romantic artists all had a sense of belonging to two worlds: the external, visible world, and the internal world of the soul and of dreams. A kind of memory recalled the time when the soul was at one with the harmony of Nature; poetry had to evoke that time, and it did so by means of the myth.

The first myth was that of the soul. Whereas classical doctrine divided the being into faculties and essences, there was a fervent belief in the early years of the 19th century in an inner core, the soul. Sennancour wrote about the soul in the *Libres Méditations*, in which he attempted to synthesise evangelical spirituality and illuminism. It was the soul that Sternbald, the hero of Tieck's novel, tried to evoke when he 'often sees his life as a dream and is at pains to convince himself that the objects which surround him are truly real'. The figures in the paintings of Friedrich and Carus were gazing into the soul, as they turn their backs to look at the luminous horizon. Sometimes, in the heat of some exceptional moment, as, for example, when Oberman completed his ascent of the Dent du Midi, or when Sophie von Kuhn appeared to Novalis, the music of the soul blotted out the din of the world. It was these blessed moments that the artist sought to immortalise in his creation.

The second myth was that of the unconscious. The poet in search of avenues to his soul began to believe that dreams, ecstasy and all those states that transcended normal human limitations brought him closer to the very essence of himself. But within this myth lay perilous temptations: what had once appeared as a path to the light could become an open door on to the abyss. Hugo and Arnim's poetic and graphic terrors are glimpses of panic.

The third myth is that of poetry, which was considered to have magical qualities. The poet devoted himself to it, without fully realising its implications but with the conviction that something totally pristine would emerge from its rites: to the Romantic, the poet is a seer.

Black Romanticism

The Romantic soul was not always dignified by dreams or filled with charming sentiments. It sometimes expressed itself in exasperation and morbid exaggeration. What Mario Praz called 'black Romanticism' can be summed up in three words: flesh, death and the Devil. Pleasure became confused with pain, beauty with horror. A Medusa's head, glimpsed in the half-light of the Musée des Offices, fascinated Shelley and a whole generation of Romantic artists after him. Novalis in his *Fragments of Psychology* asked why it was that cruelty should originate in sensual pleasure, and why the relationship between sensuality, religion and cruelty had not been more closely studied. Baudelaire was to become the chief theoretician of this strange alliance, but the principle had been recognised earlier. In Keats' *Ode on Melancholy* are expressed the ideas that 'beauty must die' and that sadness must accompany beauty and happiness. Chateaubriand bears witness to this in a passage from *Mémoires d'Outretombe*: '... and yet the tragic chant of the axe-blows in the distance, filling the air with funeral solemnity, was secretly in tune with the happy beating of my heart'. As for Victor Hugo, he wrote in one of his sonnets: 'Death and Beauty are two profound things.... Two sisters equally terrible and equally fertile.'

As a result, or perhaps as a result of the revival of Christianity, Satan was the god of black Romanticism. Satan appeared in person in the Faust legends and in all the tales of fantasy from Bürger to Erckmann-Chatrian, by way of Poe and Gogol, but his creatures are also present – demons and witches, ghosts, will o'the wisps and vampires. A list of all the manifestations of the Devil would be long indeed. He inspired secondary literature as well (Béranger's *The Devil's Daughter*, Maturin's *Melmoth*); the epic poem (Hugo, Vigny, Shelley); the poetry of Byron (*Cain, The Vision of Judgment*); Lermontov (*The Demon*), opera (*Freischütz, Hans Heiling*) and painting (Delacroix).

When considering the exponents and examples of black Romanticism, it is impossible not to include Goya. His realism of caricature, his cruelty, attraction to violence and the grotesque, and the presence of demons and witches in his paintings, from *The Disasters of War* and the *Caprices* to his *Royal portraits*, all make his work the most striking expression of this aspect of the Romantic movement, pursued to the extremes of horror.

Francisco Goya *The Third of May 1808*

Eugène Delacroix *The Death of Sardanapalus*. 1827

Survivals of Romanticism

Just as it is difficult to ascribe a precise date to the birth of the Romantic movement, so it is vain to attempt to pinpoint its end.

Some authorities place it around 1850. But, far from dying out at any given date, the movement lived on, feeding artistic streams that would have been inconceivable without it.

In music, for instance, it is recognised that Romanticism continued to be an influence until the end of the 19th century. There was no 'realist' or 'naturalist' music. Wagner, who epitomises the most advanced form of Romanticism both technically and from a chronological point of view, laid the groundwork for the emergence of Debussy, Mahler, and Schoenberg. Symbolism, and all other, even more revolutionary musical trends, proceeded from Romanticism. They even became confused with it, as is evident in *Parsifal*, which dates from 1882: its theme, spirit and language appear increasingly to us today to augurs the future.

In architecture, the Neo-Gothic did not reach its apotheosis until the second half of the century: Viollet-le-Duc published his *Dictionnaire raisonné de l'architecture française du XIe au XVIe siècle* in 1864, the Rathaus in Vienna was built in 1883, and the construction of the Parliament in Budapest stretched from 1883 to 1902. At the same time astonishing Romano-Byzantine or Byzanto-Gothic pastiches, such as the Sacré-Coeur in Paris and Notre-Dame de Fourvière in Lyon, were appearing.

The lyricism which had been one of the fundamental characteristics of early Romanticism remained all but unchanged during the second half of the century, in the European Symbolist movement.

Thus, although the Romantic movement is usually considered to have flourished between 1810 and 1850, in fact it covered a far longer period. Already in gestation during the 18th century, it continued until the very end of the 19th, manifesting itself in different ways according to different disciplines and countries. If the Pre-Romantic movement was apparent mainly in painting and letters, the Post-Romantic era was concentrated in the realms of music and literature.

So the dominant figure was that of 'Romantic man': he was to be found both before 1800 and after 1850, and doubtless more recently still. The concepts of freedom, brotherhood and revolution, whatever connotations they may have today, were inherited from the Romantic movement and all the subsequent great trends in art and politics would be inconceivable had Romanticism never existed.

Romanticism and The French Revolution

'All the sickness of the present century stems from two causes: the nation which has experienced 1793 and 1814 carries two wounds to its heart. All that was is no more; all that will be is not yet. Do not seek elsewhere the secret of our ills.' (Musset – *Les Confessions d'un enfant du siècle*)

It is in some ways impossible to understand the Romantic movement unless it is seen in the light of the French Revolution. It would be a mistake, however, to think of them in terms of cause and effect. Ideas that were mooted during the Revolution had already been mooted many years before: they were not suddenly and spontaneously born of the events of 1789, but had come slowly and gradually to maturity. The Revolution was harbered in the mind well before it took place. But the transformation of institutions was the necessary condition for the development and systematisation of those ideas. The symbolic value of the fall of the Bastille contributed towards giving Romanticism the face by which we know it. It is thus appropriate to refer to a 'substantial link between Romanticism and the Revolution'.

The French Revolution was a catalyst, a detonator. It gave unity of expression to the various emotions of individualism and revolt which had manifested themselves during the second half of the 18th century and were expressed in the Romantic literature of different countries. Yet, as Blanchot wrote, 'it is not to the revolutionary orators that the Romantics go for lessons in style, it is to the Revolution in person, to language made history, which is manifested in events'.

From 1789 to 1815, Europe was ravaged by war. France looked for allies in the battle against her enemies and at the same time exhorted nations to liberate themselves from the yoke of tyranny and to overthrow conservative powers. But revolutionary propaganda and incitement to revolt did not last very long. The wars of the Empire, which professed less noble motives, became purely and simply wars of conquest. From then on, there was a rapid decline in the first wave of enthusiasm that the march of revolutionary armies had engendered in Europe.

However, in the years immediately following the Revolution, all enlightened minds in Europe looked towards France and towards what could still pass for the triumphant victory of freedom. Thus the 'societies' or reading-room clubs that had been formed in Germany be-

Hubert Robert *Demolition of the Bastille*

tween 1780 and 1790 and which, in 1791, were placed under police surveillance by imperial edicts, were very well informed about the situation in France. Well before the Revolution, there was barely masked hostility to the privileges of rank and birth in Germany. In such circles the leading French newspapers as well as the great German magazines were to be found.

At this time, the *Allgemeine Literatur-Zeitung* (the Jena literary journal) with its print-run of two thousand copies, was attempting to spread awareness and knowledge of the political works written about the Revolution, while the *Berlin Monthly Review* was inviting both adversaries and supporters of the issue of human rights to submit articles 'which clarify the discussions of the Constituent Assembly on the subject of the declaration of the rights of man and the re-organisation of France' (Droz, *Germany and the French Revolution*).

Among this cultured company, the poets and writers of the time reacted with open enthusiasm. Klopstock (later received as an honorary French citizen by the Constituent Assembly) retracted the severe negative judgement he had passed on the French by dedicating an ode to the Etats Généraux. F. Schlegel wrote in the *Athenäum* – the review which he edited with his brother – that 'the French Revolution, Goethe's *Meister* and Fichte's *Doctrine of Science* are the three great events of the age'.

It was a 'revolutionised' age. In Tübingen, a bust of Liberty was erected to celebrate the fall of the Bastille and placed under a canopy, flanked by the busts of Brutus and Demosthenes. Three young men, friends and fellow-students at the seminary, planted a 'tree of liberty' on the outskirts of the town. Their names were Hegel, Schelling and Hölderlin. Kant, so punctual that they used to set their watches by him, rushed out of his house early when the French Revolution was announced to hear the latest news. Goethe himself, in the verses of *Hermann and Dorothea*, wrote a celebration of the Revolution and of the hopes placed on it by a whole generation:

> 'Who could possibly deny that his heart lifted up within him, that it did not beat with a pulse that was more pure in a breast that was freer, when the first rays of the new sun rose in the sky, when he heard of the rights of men, that were common to all, of such exalting freedom and such laudable equality!'

In England, the Revolution had a great influence on Coleridge, Southey and Wordworth, who were young men at the time. In July 1790, Wordworth and his friend Robert Jones set out on their first journey to France – but did no more than cross it to get to the Alps. What they saw there did not surprise or impress them overmuch, as Wordsworth admitted later: 'If I was not as delighted at the first great outburst as might have been expected of my youth, it was because events seemed to follow the ordinary course of nature and to be a blessing that had been but deferred.'

Coleridge, battling against the prevailing attitude of hostility towards France, espoused the cause of the Revolution. Southey, during the same period, professed republican sentiments in short pieces and in long dramatic poems, while Burns, who invested the Revolution with all his hopes of finally seeing a fairer system of social equality, wrote in *The Tree of Liberty*:

> 'For Freedom, standing by the tree,
> Her sons did loudly ca', man;
> She sang a sang o' liberty,
> Which pleased them ane and a', man.
> By her inspired, the new-born race
> Soon drew the avenging steel, man;
> The hirelings ran – her foes gied chase,
> And banged the despot weel, man.'

Those with a spirit of curiosity and adventure made the trip to France. Many of the Germans who went to Paris returned home full of enthusiasm, if they returned home at all. There was a fairly large German colony in France at the time and some of its members served as correspondents for German newspapers.

But favourable reaction to the Revolution was far from unanimous. Apart from the fact that the masses were often quite indifferent to it, voices were raised in opposition, and that of Edmund Burke was among the loudest. He saw himself as the interpreter of the revolutionary and conservative forces: in *Reflections on the Revolution in France* he saw the Revolution as no more than a vulgar affair of financial speculation. It was, according to him, a mere 'war between the old interests of the nobility and the new interests of money'.

In France, the first Romantics – the young Vigny, Lamartine and Hugo – were of an avowedly monarchist persuasion. But after 1830 most of these writers evolved towards a humanitarianism that professed pity for the miseries of the people and the sufferings of oppressed nations. Hugo's *Les Misérables* comes to mind, as do the novels of Balzac and *Mysteries of Paris* by Eugène Sue.

Hegel, one of the most incisive minds of his time, showed what a vast movement the Revolution was, when he singled out of an apparently incoherent mass of facts the universal essence of the phenomenon which, during his youth, took place before his eyes:

'Ever since the sun has been in the sky and the planets have turned around it, we have not

Patriotic refrains France, late 18th century

seen man use his head as a base, that is to say, starting with the idea and building reality according to it (…). So this was a magnificent sunrise; all thinking creatures celebrated this era. A sublime emotion reigned in those days, enthusiasm of the spirit made the world tremble; it was as if at that very moment we had arrived at a real reconciliation of the divine and the worldly.' (*The Philosophy of History*)

Nationalism went hand in hand with Romanticism, and the different forms it took in the various European countries produced what can be called a Romantic literature. For this reason it is necessary to understand something of the nature of a phenomenon as general and at the same time as disparate as nationalism, and to have some idea of the political and social situation in Europe at the beginning of the 19th century.

The Revolution, the wars of the Empire, the rising glory of Napoleon and its subsequent decline were markers in the troubled period from 1789 to 1815. The Congress of Vienna, by bringing together the powers that constituted Europe at the time, attempted to put an end to such international agitation.

Under the patronage of Metternich, an international police force was formed to infiltrate organisations that might threaten the newly re-established order. Potential conspirators were to be hunted out and denounced, in the interests of peace. This peace was the more fragile because the various governments, while conscious of the fact that they had done nothing to advance the cause of aspiring nationalist movements, had paid scant attention to the integrity of different states when they carved out the new map of Europe.

Countries which had had higher expectations of the revolutionary wars, like Ireland and Poland, were disappointed. For them, the Revolution seemed a source of certain emancipation. In fact, Prussia regarded it as support in its struggle against the ambitions of its neighbours, Austria and Russia. As for the Irish, their struggle merely continued, when their country was invaded by the armies of France.

The general discontent, mainly caused by the economic and social conditions of the time, erupted in revolutionary outbursts in Spain and Naples (1820), Greece (1821), and France and Poland in 1830.

The two great national struggles which captured the imagination of the day and became symbols of independence and liberty were those waged by the Irish and, especially, by the Greeks. Although Ireland failed to wrest its independence from England, the mass movement led by Daniel O'Connell was then going through a period of intense activity and its organisation was to serve as a model for movements in many other countries. But it was the Greek fight for independence that so profoundly affected the young Romantic generation.

These various nationalist movements found their spokesmen in poets and writers like Novalis and Schlegel in Germany, Leopardi in Italy, and Mickiewicz in Poland. Nationalism had become an international phenomenon.

Each nation saw itself as the one best able to liberate the others. As Benedetto Croce said: 'Even the hegemony or primacy claimed on behalf of such or such a nation by Fichte and others in favour of the German people, by Guizot and others in favour of the French people, by Mazzini and Gioberti in favour of the Italian people, by yet others in favour of the Polish people or the Slavs in general, that hegemony was the outcome of a theory that presented it as a right and a duty to be a leader of all peoples, an originator of civilisation, of human perfection and of spiritual grandeur' (*History of Europe in the 19th century*).

The young generation in Germany had welcomed the French Revolution with enthusiasm. But very soon, under the influence of Burke and also that of Joseph de Maistre and Bonald, it was to turn away from it. It turned towards a concept of nationhood based on notions such as that of race or of what Herder called the '*Volksgeist*': the unconscious creative force of a people which is manifest in its language, popular songs, legends, customs and laws. Some of the proponents of this theory developed a myth of the origins of the race which presupposed, as Hegel wrote 'the existence of a primitive people from whom all science and art originated.' This was the ancient German race, which had bravely withstood the invader. The character of Arminius and the Germania of Tacitus were the sources of literary inspiration for this myth.

The end result, notably in the work of Novalis, was a kind of political mysticism. The notion of a social contract was utterly alien to it, and love and friendship were seen as the only bonds between the individual and society. All that was needed to cement the unity of the nation was loyalty to the King and Queen and the love their subjects bore them. Such a society had probably never existed, except perhaps in the Middle Ages, according to Tieck and Wackenroder. The Middle Ages were a favourite and idealised period of history which fascinated both Schlegel and Novalis.

It was a time when a great number of different schools of thought proliferated, of which the jurist Savigny's School of Historical Law was the most erudite.

We should not look for an ideological foreshadowing of Nazism in the Romantic movement, although one might be justified in thinking that Nazism had some ties with the most reactionary tendencies of German Romanticism. In a divided nation, searching for its cultural identity and its national unity and under threat of invasion as well, it was inevitable that the notions held dear by some Romantic theoreticians, like those of *Volksgeist* and *Volkstum*, should find fertile ground.

Of course, the situation of Nazi Germany was not the same as that of Germany at the time of the French Revolution. But in this century as then, it was a Germany in economic and social crisis, a Germany humiliated by the Treaty of Versailles, forced to pay reparation to her neighbours and deprived of avenues to the outside world. So the great Romantic themes could not help but fall on attentive ears: the idea that the German language derived from a fundamental language – *Ursprache* – of which traces still remained; the theory of the unconscious origin of the nation and the contribution of irrational elements in its formation; and the faith in the civilising mission of a chosen people.

Nevertheless, this was only one of the many aspects of Romanticism, and one that was closely linked to a certain period of German history: we should guard against a generalisation of its effect. If, as the German historian Ernst Nolte wrote, Hitler's true enemy was 'Freedom oriented towards the infinite', then the idea and sentiment of that freedom, which Romanticism inherited from the French Revolution, would place the Romantic movement in a context diametrically opposed to Nazism.

Painting

Romantic painting was more of a movement than a 'school': it involved the transposition into art of a new conception of Man and nature entirely different from that which had been prevalent in the preceding centuries.

These new ways of thinking accompanied a radical evolution of society which would bring the bourgeoisie to power and represent, in painting as well as politically, socially and economically, the abandonment of the cult of Reason which had dominated a Latinised Europe, fed on Classical art and culture. In England and Germany a new sensitivity sprang up which had its roots in a much earlier time.

In France it was accepted, notably by Soufflot in 1741, in his famous *Mémoire à l'Académie de Lyon*, that Gothic architecture had its merits. There was interest, evident in the work of Pelloutin, Jacques de Brigant and La Tour d'Auvergne, in the monuments of mythology and Celtic poetry. It was the beginning of an infatuation with the past that was to assume a variety of forms and directions in different countries.

At the same time, the framework of life was being transformed. The garden 'à la française', with its classical precision, gave way to the English garden which imitated nature. The path of this return to nature had been paved by Jean-Jacques Rousseau who, as early as 1750, in his *Discours sur les Sciences et les Arts* and in *Emile* gave new foundations to culture and education. In art, the landscape, which had only been deemed acceptable when it was peopled, as by Poussin, with nymphs, satyrs or mythological characters, was accepted in its own right. In France, Georges Michel in Paris, and Bruandet and Lantara in the forest of Fontainebleau, claimed kinship with the Dutch landscape painters and already appear at the end of the 18th century as precursors of Romanticism.

But between the time when early signs of Romanticism are evident and the Romantic period itself, the classical ideal, reacting against the fussiness of the late baroque and rococo styles, found new life in Neo-Classicism. This return to the sources of Antiquity was advocated both by Lessing, who had recourse to Sophocles and Aristotle, and by the painter Raphael Mengs in Rome who denounced French art as futile, and defined the canons of an ideal of Beauty in accordance with the theories of the archaeologist Winckelmann and who, when he saw the excavations at Herculaneum, Pompeii and the temples of Paestum, was inspired by Greek art and saw in it the perfect example of the artistic ideal.

After him, the Frenchman Laugier, and the Italians Milizia and Carlo Lodoli were to lay down the rules of a linear art, applied in architecture by Juvara in Piedmont and Vanvitelli in the kingdom of Naples for Italy, by Bélanger and Ledoux in France and by William Chambers and Henry Holland in England.

Jacques-Louis David *Saint Roch interceding with the Virgin.* 1780

In painting, Neo-Classicism dominated in Rome. Vien headed the French and his disciples were David, Clérisseau and Zubleyras, while Germany was represented by Mengs, Angelika Kaufmann and Wilhelm Tischbein; Italy by Pompeo Batoni and Marco Benefiale; while the Scotsman Gavin Hamilton and the American Benjamin West were also present. The tenets of Neo-Classicism were also defended by Valenciennes and Quatremère de Quincy, but their doctrinaire teachings were soon to be stifled by the evolution of society and the upheaval of mores that followed the French Revolution and the wars of the Empire.

In France, at the time of Louis XVI, the painter Vien led the Neo-Classic movement. A good example of his work is *Marchande d'amours* (1763, Fontainebleau): the subject, if she had been treated by Fragonard or Boucher, would have been vested with an uneasy sensuality, whereas here we find only a charming and modest grace, a demeanour of chaste reserve. The same is true of *Saint Theobald giving Saint Louis and Marguerite of Provence a Basket of Flowers*, presented at the Salon of 1774 and kept in the reserve of the Château de Versailles: its simplicity is still pure Neo-Classicism. Yet one can sense a new tendency taking shape in *Love fleeing from Slavery* exhibited at the 1789 Salon (Toulouse Museum) which makes a pair with the *Marchande d'amours* but which, painted twenty-five years later, had abandoned simplicity in favour of movement and expression. The painter had turned away from the model of Antiquity.

The same evolution manifested itself in some of Vien's disciples, such as Peyron, whose Neo-Classicism was coloured by Romanticism when at the end of his life he painted the *Death of Général Valhubert* for the 1808 Salon.

It was during this period that the French Academy in Rome was reformed by d'Angivilliers with Vien as its Director. He took with him David, Peyron and Bonvoisin, and they were joined the following year by J.-B. Regnault who won the Prix de Rome for his *Diogenes visited by Alexander* (Académie des Beaux-Arts). Vien demanded a rigorous programme of work from his pupils which consisted, notably, of studies of male nudes treated with no thought for the lyrical or the decorative but from the single point of view of the light.

In two of these studies that have survived (Musée de Cherbourg and Musée de Montpellier), David used a light reminiscent of Caravaggio and in his *Saint Roch interceding with the Virgin* (1780, Musée des Beaux-Arts, Marseille), he applied the principles of the new school: the Virgin is still influenced by Italy and Classicism, while the subject (the tragic great plague of Marseille which left thousands dead in 1720), the dynamic construction of the scene in the shape of a pyramid, and above all the plague victim lying in the foreground of the painting, augur the work of Gros and Géricault.

Difficult as it is to define Romanticism, the ins and outs of the movement, the influences to which it was subject, its received ideas and underlying tendencies, and the interdependence or conflict that existed between painters, the fact is that most of the Romantic painters studied in Rome, that international laboratory of Neo-Classicism, and that their love of Antiquity and their desire to set themselves up in opposition to the existing order resulted in the fact that almost all of them started out as Neo-Classicists. They were, however, to break away, each after his own fashion, as part of the constant evolutionary process in the development of the arts. There is some justification in the view that in some ways, Romanticism represented the terminal phase in the evolution of Neo-Classicism, itself a reaction against the Baroque, which was itself the terminal phase of the evolution of the Renaissance and of mannerism. Thus David's style when he painted the *Funeral of Patroclus* (Dublin Museum), the most ambitious work to emerge from his sojourn in Rome, exhibited at the Salon of 1781, is reminiscent of the Baroque, but his clarity of narrative and form in some way marks the transition to Neo-

Classicism evident in his *Equestrian Portrait of Count Stanislas Potocki* (Warsaw Museum) and in his *Belisarius* (Musée de Lille) which was considered at the time to be his masterpiece and is one of the high points of French art of the late 18th century.

This work, with its startling intensity of garish light and deep shadows, is witness to all that David had learnt at the French Academy in Rome. It was to become even more apparent in his *Andromache Mourning the Death of Hector* (Ecole des Beaux-Arts, Paris). David's contemporaries were very sensitive to the pain of this weeping woman seated at the foot of the rigid corpse of her husband, as they were also moved by the scenes which he was to depict during the following years: *The Oath of the Horatii* (1785), *The Death of Socrates* (1787), and *Brutus and his Dead Sons* (1789), where everything contributed to magnify virtue, stoicism, and the duties of the individual towards society. Other artists of the same period, Jean-Baptiste Regnault for example, dedicated themselves to the same search in the field of style as well as subject matter. This was apparent in his *Descent from the Cross* and his *Deluge* (Musée du Louvre), which was to inspire Girodet. This canvas, with its subtle and delicate use of colour, is witness to the personality of an artist who was rather unfairly forgotten in spite of the originality that was later evident in his work. His *Judgement of Paris* (Detroit Museum) and the *Io* painted in 1827 (Musée de Brest) show how Regnault, after having been influenced by the style of Caravaggio, turned towards Rubens, his Neo-Classicism happily married to a Romanticism which appeared in the spirit as well as in the form of his work.

If David's fellow students adopted his principles to a greater or lesser extent, his pupils conformed to his techniques and style. He had the good fortune to teach a group of particularly gifted pupils who were to be the originators of a radical transformation of art in France. This transformation was directly inspired by Raphael and by Greco-Roman art in its reliance on a thorough knowledge of the human body and of linear perspective. Apart from the quest for historical truth, it advocated life-sized figures modelled in relief and grouped on the same plane, surrounded only by those elements essential to the action and with the unity of the composition assured by all emotion focussing on one single point.

Perhaps the most gifted of his pupils and the first to assimilate his style was Jean-Germain Drouais, whose *Marius at Minturnae* (1786, Musée du Louvre) was considered one of the masterpieces of French Neo-Classicism, while his *Return of the Prodigal Son* (1782, Church of Saint-Roch, Paris) was still much influenced by Peyron.

Second to Drouais, it was Girodet who, before he was even twenty years of age, was considered David's best pupil. Anne-Louis Girodet, known as Girodet-Trioson, was awarded the first Grand Prix in 1789 for *Joseph Recognised by his Brothers* (Ecole des Beaux-Arts, Paris). In the same year, he painted *Deposition from the Cross* (Church of Montesquieu-Volvestre, Haute-Garonne) in which the religiosity was of a very Romantic nature and which prefigured the *Entombment of Atala* in 1808 (Musée du Louvre).

Girodet, who was also a writer and theoretician, is one of the painters most representative of the first generation of the Romantic movement. A talented portrait painter (*le Général Beauchamps, Cathelineau*) but also a painter of history (*Napoleon receiving the Keys of Vienna*, 1808 *The Cairo Revolt*, 1810, Musée de Versailles), his nature can be seen at its most profound in *The Deluge* (1806, Musée du Louvre) and *The Shades of Heroes who died for their Country, received by Ossian into Odin's Paradise* (1802) which he had been commissioned by Napoleon to paint for Malmaison: this tumultuous and frenzied allegory, with its surrealistic spirit, symbols, ghosts eagles, and naked women, found favour with Napoleon but was not appreciated by most of his contemporaries.

Until the time of the Revolution, there was only one means by which painters could become known and achieve distinction. That was to be admitted to the Académie which was under the control of the Superintendent of Buildings, a post held during the period in question by d'Angivilliers. The award of prizes and nominations for prizes were not without their share of intrigue, since the officials of the Académie were all-powerful. David, who had three times failed in the competition for the Prix de Rome before he obtained it in 1774, bore the Académie a persistent hatred and roundly criticised its teaching. When the Commune des Arts was created in 1790, it demanded the dissolution of the Académie and from 1791 onwards the new-found freedom to exhibit at the Salon multiplied two or three fold both the number of exhibitors and the number of works shown. The evolution of morals and customs brought in its wake an identical evolution in the choice of subject matter. 'Grand' painting, deprived of royal and religious commissions, declined in favour of styles that had been adjudged minor: portraiture, the genre scene, and landscape. Gérard, who had not been able to sell his *Belisarius* from the Salon of 1795, nor his *Psyche and Eros* from the Salon of 1797, turned quite naturally to portrait painting.

Regnault was one of the most famous painters of the Revolution, but David stood above the rest: he unfortunately never completed his *Oath of the Jeu de Paume*, and his *Death of Le Pelletier* is now known to us only through copies but his two bravura pieces from this troubled period have survived: *The Death of Bara* (1794, Musée Calvet, Avignon) and *The Assassination of Marat* (1793, Musées Royaux des Beaux-Arts, Brussels), which is regarded as his masterpiece. Deputy to the Convention, influential member of the Committee of public instruction, he was a great organiser of revolutionary festivals. A member of the *Montagne*, he voted in favour of the death of the king. A friend of Robespierre, he became a member of the Committee of general security, signing the orders for a great number of arrests.

Imprisoned briefly after 9 Thermidor, he resumed his career as a painter as soon as he was released, dividing his time between portrait painting and *The Rape of the Sabines*, which he completed in 1799 (Musée du Louvre). He greatly admired Bonaparte, became his official painter and depicted scenes from his career, from *Napoleon crossing the Alps* in 1801 to *Napoleon distributing the Eagles* in 1810 (Musée de Versailles) by way of *The Coronation of the Emperor* in 1806 (Musée du Louvre).

His taste for contemporary and Napoleonic history did not prevent him from depicting themes from Antiquity: *Leonidas at Thermopylae* in 1814, *Sappo, Phaon and Eros* in 1809, *Apelles painting Campaspe in front of Alexander* in 1814, and *Mars disarmed by Venus and the Graces* in 1824.

David, who represented the first generation of the Romantic movement in France, was, like most of his contemporaries, a complex character. He was attached to Neo-Classicism but his temperament was passionately Romantic. These two tendencies cohabited and alternated according to his choice of subject. He dominated the whole of his era. Landscape painting, which had hitherto been disdained, threw off the yoke of conventions and devoted itself to representing nature without the use of artifice. Jean Pillement, who until then had painted only 'composed' landscapes, did not hesitate, in the course of his travels, to paint scenes that struck him as picturesque – Alpine glaciers for example – at a time when nobody was yet interested in mountains. At the time of the Revolution, Louis Moreau and de Machy were painting churches that the patriots had started to demolish and Georges Michel, Bruandet and Lantara were popular.

These three artists, who were independents, deserve to be considered as precursors of Romanticism in the same way as Crome, Bonington and Constable are regarded as such in the chronology of English landscape painting. Michel, who had not been admitted until then, took part in the 1791 Salon and in subsequent Salons until 1814, but the critics were either openly

Girodet-Trioson *The Deluge*. 1806

hostile to his work, or ignored him. He finally became disenchanted with 'official' events. Lebrun gave him commissions to paint copies of Dutch artists: Ruysdael, Hobbema, Rembrandt. From 1821 until his death, he lived an isolated existence in Montmartre, where he devoted himself entirely to painting, and taking notes in the course of walks on the outskirts of Paris. The sale of his studio in 1841 comprised more than a thousand paintings and over two thousand drawings. He died two years later, a forgotten man. Whereas Boilly was no more than a faithful observer, depicting the mores of his time with much humour, François-Marius Granet by contrast, although his work was influenced by Neo-Classicism, can be regarded as a Romantic painter 'par excellence'. His chiaroscuro technique and his choice of subjects are evidence of this, in, for instance *Stella painting a Virgin on the Wall of his Prison*.

But the Napoleonic myth was not celebrated only by David, Peyron, Vincent, Drouais and Girodet. Many other painters depicted it in their work – Gros, for instance, Meynier, Géricault, Delacroix, and Goya, on the far side of the Pyrenées.

Gros, who had entered David's studio when he was only fifteen years of age, had rapidly shown a strong predilection for romantic subjects: he illustrated the work of Young and Ossian, and exhibited his *Sappho at Leucadia* (Musée de Bayeux) at the Salon of 1801, while at the same time making his mark as a portrait painter and revealing himself to be one of the most faithful interpreters of the main military exploits of the time of the Consulate and the

Antoine-Jean Gros *The Battle of Aboukir*. Detail

Empire. After he had won a competition organised for *The Battle of Nazareth*, the sketch for which is at the museum of Nantes, he received the commission to paint the *Plague Victims of Jaffa*, one of his major works. These two paintings reflect a definitive shift away from the Classical tradition. They are profoundly Romantic and espouse that cult of heroism and the intensity of inner life that was to be expressed by the French philosopher Maine de Biran.

Maine de Biran, as Rene Huyghe tells us, 'revises Cartesian teaching, seeking through the *cogito* knowledge of the soul, of its substance, which is as completely unknown to us as any other substance in the universe'. Is Man then incapable of understanding anything about himself? On the contrary: 'Each *individual* person knows, *certissima scientia* at least, what he is in terms of the *power to act* and operates by means of the *will*.' Man does perceive himself, but as an 'individuality', as an effort or endeavour: 'the power-self ... the strength self ... The immediate sensation of power ... is none other than that of our very existence, from which that of activity is inseparable'; it brings about the 'knowledge which is immediate and self-evident' which neither the senses, the basis of Realism, nor the mind, basis of Classicism, can give.

In a single sentence, three foundation stones of the Romantic movement and of the 19th century are laid and lucidly perceived: '*individualism*, nurtured by the intuition of *subjective life* perceived as a *living intensity*'. Furthermore, this intensity implies a 'continual tendency to change'. There is perhaps no clearer way to express the fact that the fixed and definitive rules were about to lose their sway and that art was on the threshold of a great creative adventure, a perpetual state of revolutionary development. 'From the definition of *Being*, on which the old, particularly Cartesian, philosophy was based, art moved into the realms of *Becoming* and German thinkers especially were intoxicated with its headiness.' This discovery of Man and of his moral nature prefigured the attitudes of Stendhal and Vigny as well as those of Delacroix and Géricault, while still safeguarding the Latin humanism which was held so dear.

Stendhal said that Géricault belonged to the generation which bore the mark of the glory and the downfall of 'the greatest man to have appeared in the world since Caesar'. Born in 1791, at the height of revolutionary ferment, Géricault attended Guérin's studio where the formation of the whole Romantic generation took place. A passionate admirer of the horse, and inspired by the emotional and Romantic links which bind it to man, he devoted a whole section of his work to it: officers charging and fighting on horseback, studies of horses in their stables, horse races, carthorses and plough-horses, horse training. In each case he depicted the struggle between the man and the animal, or their mutual understanding and common drive to win.

In 1812, Géricault submitted to the Salon his equestrian portrait of *The Light Cavalry Officer* which won a medal and was admired for the fiery spirit and the power of the rearing horse and of the officer charging with sabre drawn. But at the Salon of 1814, his *Wounded Cuirassier*, whom he depicted dismounted and struggling to control his horse, was not well received by the critics. Perhaps they saw it as a symbol of the fall of the Empire. To escape from a particularly turbulent love affair, Géricault spent a long time travelling around Italy and went to Rome where he spent time in the company of Ingres, Delacroix and other French artists and drew a great deal of benefit from their friendship.

It was on his return from Italy to Paris that he set to work on his most famous painting, *The Raft of Medusa* (Musée du Louvre). Over the course of the next sixteen months, he made sketch after sketch and carried out alterations to the canvas right up to the last moment. Haunted by Michaelangelo, remembering Caravaggio, inspired by Gros and also perhaps by Schnetz whom he had met in Rome, he created a work that stands as one of the pinnacles of Romantic painting. Everything is there: the emotional content of the scene, the moving pathos

Jean-Auguste-Dominique Ingres *The Turkish Bath*. 1859–1863

of the incident, the distress of men abandoned in the middle of the ocean, their bodies distorted with suffering and destitution. In his method of treating the human body, his rather macabre taste for portraying the agonies of men, his practice of studying the physiognomies of madmen and his understanding of their obsessions, and his sober and realistic technique with its vigorous impastos, he bears a ressemblance to Goya. But not everything was as black as this in Romantic painting. If *The Raft of Medusa* remains Géricault's most famous work, he also painted less dramatic and happier subjects. Indeed, he was no stranger to love, as is shown by that admirable pair of lovers clasped in each other's arms in a passionate embrace. The same was true of Baron Gérard who did not consider it beneath him to depict love scenes such as his *Psyche and Eros* (Musée du Louvre) which brought him fame when he exhibited it at the Salon of 1798, while he devoted himself elsewhere to military scenes (*The Battle of Austerlitz*, Musée de Versailles), to historical compositions (*The Coronation of Charles X*, Musée de Versailles) or to allegorical subjects (*Ossian summoning the Ghosts*, Hamburg Museum). But during this period it was still Prud'hon who was painting's high priest of love. When he was not painting portraits, he was illustrating *l'Art d'aimer*, *Paul et Virginie*, *la Nouvelle Héloïse* and painting *Venus and Adonis*, *Hymen and Eros*, *Zephyr swinging above the Water*, *Innocence putting Love before Riches*. Although he

43

could also be violent and dramatic, as in *Justice and divine Vengeance pursuing Crime*, his style on the whole was light and graceful.

The great flowering of the Romantic movement came with the Restoration. It was a time of quarrels and disputes between protagonists of the old and the new, Classicists and Romantics. But the movement was not confined to a single school: it was above all a new way of thinking, of understanding life and Man, which was to influence both the defenders of Classicism like Ingres and champions of Romanticism like Delacroix. As René Huyghe so rightly says: 'With Ingres, the stringent ideal of Antiquity slipped definitively towards an affectation and a *manièrisme* which betrayed it utterly. His art, driven by an authentically bourgeois and meticulous passion for what was real, was consumed by a sensuality that, in the Orient, saw only harems and dreamed of the soft damp flesh of *The Turkish Bath*.' If this *manièrisme* could on the one hand engender Baudry, Cabanel, and Bouguerau, exponents of a hard, official art, it also repudiated the ideal of Beauty propounded by David in favour of the harmony of an extensive study of nature. Ingres recommended to his pupils the truth, the 'naivety' of drawing from life, and reminded them of the diversity in nature which emphasised individual character. Only after a first stage of preparatory studies did he allow elaboration, simplification or stylisation to intervene. He himself did not hesitate, for harmony of composition, to elongate or to deform the human body with no account taken of anatomy. He simplified relief: 'beautiful forms', he said, are those which have firmness and fullness and where the detail does not compromise the appearance of the large masses' and further 'the modelling should be round and with no inner details apparent'. This smooth relief, with some delicate use of half-tones, is particularly noticeable in *The Bather of Valpinçon*. It is especially in his nudes, in *The Spring*, *The Turkish Bath* that one can fully appreciate the care he took to stretch proportions and orchestrate the undulation of forms. 'A single superfluous half-figure is enough to spoil the composition of a painting' he wrote. Similarly, he used light to bring out important figures in his works. He worked slowly, piling drawing on drawing, sketch on sketch. For the arm of a sick man in *Stratonice*, he made two hundred sketches, and painted it fifty times. It made no difference if the odalisk had three vertebrae too many: it was no mistake on the part of the artist, but quite intentional art.

But Ingres was first and foremost a portrait painter. If his great historical compositions were constantly criticised, the truth and the faithfulness of his portraits were always done justice. When a portrait was commissioned, he always attempted to achieve a finish and a perfection of detail that portraits painted in a spirit of friendship and in more spontaneous vein, did not always achieve. Like Delacroix, he drew inspiration from the British tradition of the aristocratic portrait, notably from the style of Thomas Lawrence. In any event, it was in his work that Romanticism reached its height.

Delacroix was twenty-four years old when he exhibited for the first time at the 1822 Salon with *Dante and Virgil in Hell* (Musée du Louvre) which gained him instant notoriety. Some disputed his talent, but Thiers and Gros greatly admired his work. In 1824 he exhibited *The Massacre at Chios* (Musée du Louvre) and, as Géricault had just died, this work established him as the leader of the new school, despite the fact that Ingres proclaimed it a massacre of painting. Delacroix treated this episode of the Greek War of Independence, which was to arouse the passions of artists as well as intellectuals, with a fervour and a richness of colour that surpassed any similar composition by Gros and Géricault. Whereas Ingres referred constantly to nature, Delacroix maintained that it was 'only a dictionary', 'a store of images and signs to which the imagination will give a place and a relative value', added Baudelaire.

For Delacroix, even more so than for the Romantics who preceded him, imagination was the motive force that inspired his themes of dreams and visions, and transformed reality into fantasy, according to the artist's own aspirations and passions.

It was at this time that the English Romantic artists were exhibiting at the Salon in Paris and that Delacroix went to London where he admired Turner, Constable, Reynolds and Gainsborough, and became a friend of Bonington. On his return from London he painted *The Death of Sardanapalus* (Musée du Louvre) and exhibited it at the Salon of 1828. He surrendered himself completely to imagination, and gave his fantasy free rein with a verve, passion, and explosion of colour that delight today's public, but at the time were considered scandalous.

In his *Journal* of 9 May 1824, he wrote: 'I do not like sensible painting; I can see that my muddled brain has to get agitated, has to erase, has to make a hundred attempts to arrive at the goal that I need and that obsesses me in everything I do.' Like Ingres, he drew any number of sketches and drafts before he decided upon a construction that had been thought out at great length. He produced masterpieces like *Liberty guiding the People* (Musée du Louvre), inspired by the Three Glorious Days of 1830, which he exhibited at the 1831 Salon *The Women of Algiers* (Musée du Louvre) and *Christ on the Mount of Olives* (Eglise Saint-Paul-Saint-Louis, Paris).

Always an object of admiration and contention, he varied his theme with true virtuosity: from a religious composition to an exotic scene, from a historical canvas to an allegorical work. 'Those who view me with favour' he wrote to his friend Soulier, 'agree in their opinion that I am an interesting madman, but one whose flights of fancy and eccentricities it would be dangerous to encourage.' Although the return of the Bourbons had encouraged a certain Classicism, Romanticism continued nonetheless to attract its followers. One of these was Ary Scheffer who, after attending Prud'hon's studio and passing through a 'Davidian' period, was inspired by the Hellenic cause. It was the inspiration for several of his paintings, for instance *The Suliote Women* (Musée du Louvre) which was exhibited at the Salon of 1827. Some saw in him one of the leaders of the Romantic school but, although his education and his talent as a writer led him to illustrate Shakespeare and Goethe and to paint Marguerite and Faust, his works are very far from having the breadth of Delacroix.

Beside them was Paul Delaroche, an influential Romantic painter, though more reserved than Delacroix. For this very reason, he was more acceptable to his contemporaries. His work bore no evidence of political commitment, but it was imbued with an overweaning and Romantic love of history: paintings on subjects from French and English history proliferated and he became one of the leaders of the 'juste milieu'. He won great acclaim for his 1834 *Jane Grey* (National Gallery) and his *Assassination of the Duc de Guise* of 1835 (Musée Condé, Chantilly). Eugène Devéria, a confirmed Romantic as was his brother Achille, also had a predilection for historical subjects: at the Salon of 1827, he exhibited a gigantic *Birth of Henri IV*, which at the time was considered as a Romantic manifesto to rank with *The Death of Sardanapalus* by Delacroix and *The Death of Elizabeth, Queen of England* by Delaroche.

Two artists, Paul Huet and Théodore Chassériau, occupied an important, but rather special place in Romantic painting.

Paul Huet, a friend and fellow-student of Delacroix and Bonington, was, together with them, to influence the evolution of landscape painting in France, not only in Romantic art but also in what was later to become Impressionism. He had settled on the Ile Seguin, 'a corner of Paradise on earth, forgotten especially by Romantic painters, at the gates of Paris' wrote Philippe Burty. The young Paul Huet found there a quite unspoiled nature which inspired him, as early as 1820, to paint studies comparable to those of English parks that Constable and Bonington were to exhibit at the Salon of 1824. His style, in canvases like *Flood at Saint-*

Eugène Delacroix *Liberty guiding the People*. 1830

Cloud (1855, Musée du Louvre), was realistic, but he later surrendered to his passion and lyricism when he painted landscapes inspired by the Auvergne and the forest of Fontainebleau.

Chassériau, who died at the height of his success when he was thirty-seven years old, was one of the most influential personalities of his time. The portraits that he painted when he was only sixteen were already impeccably drawn, and vibrant and warm in colour. When he entered Ingres' studio at the age of about twelve, Ingres said of him: 'This child will be the Napoleon of painting!'

He acquired from Ingres a skill in drawing that would combine with a genius as a colourist to rival Delacroix. His decoration of the Cour des Comptes, which was unfortunately destroyed during the fire of 1871, showed that he deserved to be ranked among the greats and that he had a very personal way of achieving classical perfection.

The *Sleeping Bather* in the Musée Calvet in Avignon, The *Marine Venus* of 1838 (Musée du Louvre) which so enchanted Théophile Gautier, *Suzanne au bain* (1838, Musée du Louvre), *Esther adorning herself to receive Ahasuerus*, and the *Tepidarium* (1853, Musée du Louvre) are among the most poetic depictions of women in painting.

His portraits are admirable as much for their intensity of expression, for instance the portrait of *Père Lacordaire*, as for the grace and charm of some of his models, such as *Alice Ozy* or *Madame Cabarrus*.

In complete contrast to the gentle and aristocratic Romanticism of Chassériau is the Romantic realism of Daumier. He was a witness of his time – to the misery of the people, injustice, the cruelty and stupidity of the ruling classes – and it roused all his indignation. He rebelled, using his talents as an engraver and a painter in the service of all victims of oppression. His caricatures, political lithographs and paintings railed against established power, the judiciary and arbitrary repression, while still bearing all the characteristics of Romanticism. His *Rue Transnonain* represented a cry of rage and indignation, as the *Raft of Medusa* did for Géricault. His freedom of expression, enthusiasm of style and dynamism are Romantic. But his work represented the end of Romanticism: concern for the truth made its appearance, suddenly altering the direction of painting, be it that of Daumier, Courbet, Daubigny, or Théodore Rousseau. Gone were the battle scenes, of more or less fictitious inspiration; gone were the poetic evocations and the heroes of Antiquity. Henceforth, art was to seek its inspiration in everyday life.

As far as England was concerned, the foundations of Romantic painting, from 1780 onwards, were expounded in the writings of the philosophers Hume and Locke, as they had been in France in those of Jean-Jacques Rousseau. But in England, the birth of the Romantic movement in painting was not hampered by the imposition of the peremptory rules that governed every discipline in France, from the theatre to painting. In England, since the time of Shakespeare and the Elizabethan theatre, the dramatic rule of unity of time and place had not been applied. Ossian and Young had shown that, in the field of poetry, imagination

Honoré Daumier *Rue Transnonain*

Théodore Chassériau *The Tepidarium*. 1853

and fantasy could reign unhindered by the shackles of convention. Fuseli and Blake, the two precursors of the movement, brought about the evolution of English painting into the realms of hallucination, prophetic vision and the world of the supernatural.

Fuseli was born in Switzerland, the son of a painter. Destined for the Church, he became a pastor, which explains the breadth of his education and later, when he abandoned the cloth to devote himself to painting, his love of literary themes, scenes from Shakespeare and Milton, for example, whose works he had translated into German. He depicted Lady Macbeth as haggard, holding a flaming torch or surrounded by witches – nightmarish scenes full of disturbing monstrous apparitions and skeletons. The world that he created was a deeply alarming one, always macabre and often erotic. This in itself means that Fuseli can be regarded not only as a precursor of Romanticism, but also as an early exponent of what would later be termed Symbolism and even Surrealism.

The same can be said of Blake who was both poet, painter and engraver. He spent his whole life in London, indifferent to nature and reality, taking pleasure in the imaginary and in a 'Platonic paradise' which represented the transposition of his celestial visions. He saw himself as a prophet and assigned to himself the role of privileged intermediary between the Eternal and the temporal worlds. He had experienced hallucinations since childhood, when he saw God through a window, and this unprecedented experience marked the entirety of his work. He was visited by angels, by the spirits of famous men long dead, even by 'the horrible ghost of a flea'. Owing to his talent for drawing and also to his extensive study of Antiquity and the Gothic, he achieved vivid and striking transcriptions of his visions and his conversations with the powers of the Supernatural. He was also attracted to the Ideals of revolution, of which *The French Revolution* (1791) and *The Marriage of Heaven and Hell* (1793) are the finest expression.

In his illustrations for Young's *Nights* and the *Bible*, for the *Divine Comedy* by Dante or Thornton's *Pastorals*, Blake transports us into a fantastic and supernatural world, a world where the spirit becomes incarnate in sublime or frightening forms, forms born of the unconscious which creates an imaginary and irrational universe. He joined Goya in the world of which Goya said that 'the sleep of reason begets monsters'. But although both Fuseli and Blake played an essential and fundamental role in Romanticism, they remained nonetheless isolated from the mainstream of English Romantic painting. On the whole, it was characterised more by its attachment to reality, the absence of any reference to the ideal form, and by its constant recourse to the emotions: 'Painting and emotion are one and the same word to me' said Constable. But it was marked above all by the triumph of light, colour and, most importantly, Nature. Even in portraits, Nature plays an essential part: the little *Count of Dalkeith* by Reynolds appears by moonlight flanked on either side by a dog and an owl; *Sir John and Lady Clark* by Raeburn stand against an enchanting landscape lit by the setting sun; *William Beckford the Younger* by Romney is portrayed leaning nonchalantly on an ancient corbel at the edge of a wood, through which deer can be seen in the distance. His slightly disdainful and blasé look, the unselfconsciousness of the pose, and the setting, make it the archetypal Romantic portrait that was to be imitated so often, notably by Lawrence, and later by Delacroix in his *Portrait of Baron Schwiter*. After 1815 that Lawrence was to perfect this type of aristocratic

William Turner *The Shipwreck*. 1805

portrait. It inspired French taste and was to remain the model for nearly a century, until the time of Boldini and van Dongen. The freedom of treatment and sensitivity of stroke are equally evident in the portrait of *Pope Pius VII* painted in Rome in 1819, *Charles, Archduke of Austria* painted in Vienna in 1818, and *Charles X, King of France*, painted in Paris in 1825 (all three are part of the collection of Her Majesty Queen Elizabeth II). 'He dazzles', Delacroix said of Lawrence, 'not at the expense of delicacy and of the truth of his drawing, which, of heads, is incomparable'. But although the portrait was one of the most perfect genres of English Romantic painting, nevertheless it was the English landscape that was to open up the newest perspectives in its field.

The two masters, who ruled between 1790 and 1810, were Constable and Turner. Although fundamentally different, they had the same sensitivity and love of Nature which also inspired the poetry of Wordsworth and Byron.

The emotion and exaltation that animated Constable is evident both in his large compositions and in his small studies in oils. The loving care with which he treated all the nuances and variations of light already heralded the Impressionist movement. His work, which was favourably received in Paris as early as 1820, particularly at the Salon of 1824, was to have a profound influence on French landscape painters, notably on Huet and Delacroix. Parisian art dealers bought more than twenty of his canvases, including *The Hay Wain* (National Gallery), which is considered his masterpiece. French artists of the time extolled his naturalism, the freedom of his technique, the freshness of his colours, his ability to capture fleeting phenomena such as the vibration of air and light, the breeze, the clouds or the foam on the waves (*Weymouth Bay*, 1816, Musée du Louvre; *Stonehenge*, Victoria and Albert Museum).

If Constable remained more or less within the limits of poetic naturalism, Turner on the other hand set out along a new path, which would lead to Impressionism. Every year he travelled to Europe and wandered around Switzerland and Italy, returning with a wealth of watercolours and sketches. He would then use them as the basis for large or smaller paintings, in the execution of which composition gradually became secondary to the general effect, and the actual subject of the painting was incidental to what might be called the atmosphere and 'feeling' of the work.

Whatever the subject, be it an avalanche, a snowstorm in the Alps, a beach at low tide or a raging sea with storm-tossed flotsam, the first impression is not of the theme itself, but of light, colour, mistiness and humidity.

He introduced yet another novelty, the inclusion of machinery in a picture, with his painting *Rain, Steam and Speed* (National Gallery) in which we see the Great Western locomotive plunging through the misty countryside. Théophile Gautier wrote in his *Histoire du Romantisme*; 'It was a real cataclysm. Quivering flashes of lightning, wings like great fiery birds, immense clouds toppling under the claps of thunder, swirling windswept rain: it could have been the setting for the end of the world. Through all this, like the beast of the Apocalypse, writhed the locomotive, its eyes of red glass shining through the gloom, dragging its vertebrae of carriages like a huge tail. It was probably a rapid sketch of wild fury, jumbling the sky and the earth with the stroke of a brush, an act of pure extravagance, but the act of a madman of genius'. Turner's approach was totally original, but it opened the door to such a wealth of possibilities that both the Impressionists and the Symbolists claimed him as one of themselves. Huysmans and Gustave Moreau found their vindication in his work. Turner was a friend of Bonington and they worked together around 1820. Bonington exhibited in England as well as in France, where he was also a friend of Huet and of Delacroix, whose studio in Paris he shared.

Bonington painted genre scenes or scenes from history in the Romantic style, but he was esteemed primarily for his landscapes. His associations in Paris brought to his work a subtlety and delicacy that was entirely French, but the influence of Turner and Constable is evident in the breadth of his skies and in his spatial awareness. Thomas Girtin who, like Bonington, died young, met with great success with his contemporaries and was admired by Turner as well as Constable. The watercolours that he painted during the many journeys he undertook in England and in France considerably influenced both English and French artists. The group of landscape painters that included John Martin, John Crome, David Cox and Richard Wilson was more traditional. Some drew their inspiration from Ruysdael and Hobbema, others from Cuyp and Claude Gelée.

John Martin was very popular in Europe. He loved battle pieces and dramatic scenes (*The Deluge, The Fall of Babylon*), precipitous landscapes and crushing perspectives peopled with miniscule figures and bathed in an apocalyptic light.

John Crome animated his landscapes with scenes that were both more realistic and more familiar, such as market scenes or water galas. Wilson depicted peaceful landscapes in the Italian style such as a lake surrounded by mountains, a castle beside a river or an Italian villa. David Cox, for his part, devoted himself primarily to representing the fleeting and ephemeral qualities of light.

Finally Stubbs, a Classicist by temperament and a Romantic in his choice of subjects, stands in a class somewhat apart. His love of the horse made him probably the greatest exponent of animal art in England. He also painted landscapes and hunting scenes, but his art was most successful in his paintings of monkeys, lions, panthers and especially horses. He exerted a marked influence on Gros and Géricault.

By 1840, the great school of English Romantic painting had entered a decline and towards 1850, a new group of artists appeared. They were to be christened the Pre-Raphaelites and they drew their inspiration from the Nazarene group formed in Germany a short time previously. Like them, and like their Romantic predecessors, they turned to poetry for their themes. Yet, while there was an essentially decorative aspect to their painting, they remained more faithfully attached to nature than their German counterparts. This emerging force and new inspiration definitively marked the end of the Romantic era in England and opened the way towards Symbolism.

The fact that Germany of that time was fragmented into a multitude of self-governing principalities and independent states and that, unlike France and England, it did not have a capital city in which art could crystallise new doctrines, meant that the Romantic movement in Germany was even less homogeneous there than elsewhere. This was true not only of literature, but also of the arts. A new spirit was manifesting itself simultaneously in various different personalities, and a new way of thinking was being born.

German painting was fed by the new ideology which inspired the bourgeoisie in its battle for emancipation and the right to assume its place in the power structure and, during the period between the two Revolutions of 1789 and 1848, art was to reflect this new state of mind. As was the case in France, the German Neo-Classicists were gradually to become imbued by the Romantic way of thinking, accentuated by the upheavals which, from 1780 to 1850, were to undermine the very foundations of the social structures of the old regime.

Between 1780 and 1810, this Neo-Classical influence is perceptible in the work of artists like Philipp Friedrich von Hetsch, from 1780 artist to the court of Wurtemberg, whose historical paintings are full of the sentiment and pathos associated with the Davidian school. It is also in evidence in his pupil, Gottlieb Schick who worked with Ingres in David's studio and whose *Eve* is reminiscent of Prud'hon and Gérard; and in the work of Eberhard Wächter who was influenced first by David and then by Carstens and the Nazarenes. Jakob Carstens

Philipp Otto Runge *The Rest of the Flight into Egypt.* 1805–1806.

was in fact the most original of the Neo-Classicists. He was a remarkable drawer, similar to Philipp Otto Runge in his sense of the monumental and the spirituality of his compositions. Like Runge, he died young, before he had time to consolidate his work. But it is to his credit that while he remained under the sway of Antiquity, he succeeded in detaching himself from it sufficiently to find his own personal and original form. He was to have a determining influence on Koch, Cornelius and the Nazarene school.

Philipp Otto Runge, like Carstens, studied at the Academy in Copenhagen and although his early work, influenced by Tieck and Jacob Böhme, was still in Neo-Classical style, he soon broke away from it. He declared: 'We are no longer Greeks; faced with the perfection of their works we no longer experience the same emotions as they did, still less can we produce similar works.' By means of landscape, he attempted to produce a kind of synthesis of Nature filled with symbolic and metaphysical significance, and in a return to a form of innocent primitivism, he conceived a whole series of paintings depicting the cycle of human life, *The Hours of the Day.* His dream of achieving this complete work was cut short by his untimely death.

Runge's theories about landscape and nature were adopted by Caspar David Friedrich, without doubt the most significant exponent of Romantic painting in Germany. Friedrich shared with Runge that 'Weltgefühl', the cosmic impression of the universe and, like him, refused to regard Italy as the only home of the arts. 'The painter must not paint only what he sees in front of him, but also what he sees within himself...' he said.

Caspar David Friedrich *The First Snow*. 1828

Born in Pomerania, he identified himself most strongly with northern Germany, as well as with the scenery of his childhood which was to impregnate his Romanticism: the shores of the Baltic, the Harz mountains, the banks of the Elba. He was fond of sunsets, monuments, figures in *contre jour*, moonlit landscapes and skeletal trees. He was interested in the phenomena of Nature, atmospheric variations and the succession of the seasons, to which his thousands of studies are witness. He based his art on an extensive knowledge of Nature, at the same time sharing Runge's idealised spirituality. He 'transforms Nature as perceived by the eye into a symbolic landscape of his soul. In the tangible phenomenon, he sees a manifestation of the invisible, which corresponds to the spirit of Schelling and to Romantic philosophy. Friedrich's paintings are monologues about the elementary questions of the life and death of man, and in particular about the relationship between man, God and Nature.' (H.J. Neidhart). His work represents a 'supernaturalisation' of the landscape, which becomes a timeless setting with an almost metaphysical and sometimes tragic dimension. In *The Monk at the Edge of the Sea* he expressed the infinite solitude of man in the face of the elements and the distress that solitude brings. It is embodied in the very composition of the painting: the monk, a tiny silhouette, stands at the edge of a narrow strip of land beyond which there is nothing but the immensity of the sea and the sky. The monk is only there to remind us of the presence of humanity at the heart of the elements and of its insignificance, to give us the physical scale of the landscape and to suggest its spiritual scale.

But this cult of Nature followed by Friedrich was not pagan in any way. He was himself a devout Christian and, by virtue of his Protestant education, he regarded all art as religious and every aspect of Nature as sacred. He considered that saintliness could be just as well, if not better, expressed in a mountain, a tree or a meadow as in the face of a saint. His most intensely mystical paintings are those in which he associates in a single vision forest, mountains and the Cross – the sublime symbols of the earth alongside the Christian Redeemer, who is represented entire by the Cross or by a Gothic church, often included in Friedrich's compositions, as its architecture moved him deeply.

Coming as it did in the wake of 18th century landscape art which was either mere entertainment or pure melancholy, Friedrich's approach was an innovation which aroused the enthusiasm as well as the criticism of his contemporaries, but which is considered today as one of the most significant elements of German Romantic painting.

Friedrich had many pupils: Karl Gustav Carus who also devoted himself of landscape painting, but was, in addition, a philosopher and a writer (*Nine Letters on the Painting of Landscape*, 1815–1824); Oehme who joined the Nazarene group in Rome and excelled in atmospheric landscapes; Heinrich; Dahl, born in Norway, who had a deep feeling for nature and expressed so well all the poetry of his native land; Georg Friedrich Kersting, one of Friedrich's youngest disciples, whose work in his interior as well as in his genre scenes, contained Romantic accents that were typically German.

Karl Friedrich Schinkel stands slightly apart from this group. Both painter and architect, he was torn between allegiance to the Greek ideal and the Gothic spirit: he succeeded in resolving the dilemma with a very Romantic compromise. Feeling that the Gothic could never be more beautiful or more mysterious than as he saw it in his dreams, he abandoned it in his architectural work, constructing his buildings in a solid and squat Doric style, and reserved the Gothic for imaginary scenes painted on canvas (*Mediaeval Town on the Bank of a River*). While, in northern Germany, Romantic painting was gradually influencing the work of all the artists who followed Runge and Friedrich, a group of young men from the Academy in Vienna abandoned it as a sign of protest against its formalism. Even before their exodus to Italy, they had formed what became known as the Lukasbund, or Brotherhood of Saint Luke. This

Friedrich Overbeck *Germania and Italia*. c. 1828

brotherhood was to be the nucleus of the Nazarene group and installed itself in the deconsecrated Roman convent of Sant' Isidoro in 1810. Their purpose was the renewal of German art on Christian foundations and according to the principles of the artists of the Middle Ages.

They found support for their doctrine in the writings of Schlegel, Tieck and Wackenroder, and their leaders were the painters Franz Pforr and Overbeck. The former preached the art of Dürer and of the German Primitives, the latter the pure Primitivism of the Italian Quattrocento. When Peter Cornelius, followed in 1817 by Julius Schnorr von Carolsfeld, joined the group, their strong personalities gave it new impetus and in consequence even greater influence. They were invited by Bartholdy, the Consul General of Prussia, to decorate the Zuccaro Palace in Rome with frescoes relating the life of Jesus, and then the Casino of the Villa Massimo, for which they drew their subjects from Dante, Tasso and Ariosto. They were inspired by frescoes by Raphael and Pinturicchio that they had seen at the Vatican and at the Farnese. Their smooth technique, rather impersonal stroke, a degree of restraint in the use of colour, and idyllic landscapes peopled with conventional characters, derive both from Romanticism and from Neo-Classicism. Theirs were, in any event, the first collective works of the German Romantic movement, and their cycles of frescoes were to instigate a blossoming of grand historical compositions in all the public buildings in Germany.

When the Villa Massimo frescoes were completed, the Nazarene group disbanded and, with the exception of Overbeck, they all left Rome and scattered to teach in the German university centres, while Cornelius and Schnorr were commissioned by Ludwig I of Bavaria to decorate the Glypothek in Munich, the Residenz and the Ludwigskirche.

The Nazarenes did not confine themselves only to grand compositions with figures, but were also fairly active as landscape painters. Joseph Anton Koch, who maintained friendly relations with Rome and with the Nazarenes, started out in this field in rather Neo-Classical vein, after the style of Carstens. Then, from 1803, he was very obviously inspired by Poussin and Claude Lorrain, depicting with great simplicity and meticulous regard for truth. In Vienna, a whole school of Romantic painters, which centred around the Schlegels, Philipp Velt and the Rheinhold brothers, in the course of their excursions, discovered in their turn the scenery around Salzburg and in the Berchtesgaden.

The end of the Romantic period in Germany is marked by two talented artists, Ludwig Richter and Moritz von Schwind, who succeeded in marrying the aesthetic ideal of the Nazarenes to themes of a folkloric nature. Richter, who had been a pupil of Koch, returned, after a period of infatuation with Italian subjects, to a deeply Romantic style of painting dedicated to the landscape of his native land (*The Crossing of the Elbe*). Koch drew his inspiration from popular tales and legends and from the exploits of the knights of the Middle Ages.

Mention must also be made of Lessing, regarded as the leader of the Düsseldorf school, who painted in the 'heroic' style and also produced realist landscapes; Alfred Rethel, whose wood engravings are reminiscent of Dürer; and finally Wilhelm Schirmer, who excelled in his nordic landscapes, seascapes and coastal scenes.

There were to be no more than a few final flurries of Romanticism in German painting. Traditional academic teaching which idealised the truth and rejected the faithful representation of reality was progressively abandoned more or less everywhere, in Düsseldorf, Munich, Dresden and Berlin, in favour of figurative realism. In the wake of Adolph Menzel, whose first major works date from around 1840, a new generation of artists was to throw off the chains of theories inherited from its predecessors and to lead German painting along new paths.

From then on, in every country, the artist knew that he could, in Baudelaire's words, 'create an evocative magic which contains both the subject and the object, the world outside the artist and the artist himself'. And, as Delacroix said 'he achieves it by such an arrangement of colours, lights and shadows ... with everything that the soul has added to the colours and to the lines, to reach the soul'.

Rene Huyghe concluded: 'Romanticism marks the culmination of a slow evolution of minds; their conception of themselves is different, their conception of the Universe and their relationship with it is different. The civilisation that had firmly established itself from the Renaissance to the 18th century was convulsed by an earthquake which disrupted the order of the stratifications on which it rested. The deepest, the most hidden layers rose up and dislocated the organisation of the surface.

'Europe revealed herself more complex and richer, more tumultuous than she had ever thought herself to be. She still had surprises to come: the whole world was to be transformed, precipitating a crisis, the effects of which our 20th century is still far from having measured.'

Romanticism opened the door to all the coming movements in art: Symbolism and Impressionism, as well as Cubism or Abstract art. There were to be no more rules, no more precepts, no barriers; everything was possible.

ABILDGAARD Nicolas Abraham (Copenhagen 11.9.1743 – Copenhagen 4.6.1809). Studied in Copenhagen, then Rome from 1772–1777, where the influence of the Italian painters led him to paint Neo-Classical works on subjects from Greek and Roman mythology. (*Wounded Philoctetes, Jupiter weighing the Destiny of Men*). His best work was inspired by the theatre, poetry and history. He illustrated Ossian, Shakespeare, and Milton (*Fingal's Ancestors Appear to him by Moonlight*). In this drawing (wash tint and Indian ink) the structure of the figures, man and domestic animals, is lost in whirlwinds over a dark sea and crushed by huge sinister rocks, in a powerful expression of the poet's vision. Abildgaard is considered one of the major Danish artists of the late 18th century.

ALLSTON Washington (Waccamaw, South Carolina 5.11.1779 – Cambridge 9.7.1843). Italy and its landscapes, through the works of Poussin, inspired this American Romantic painter. After a stay in Europe where he began his painting studies under Benjamin West in London and spent time in Rome absorbing the Italian landscape, he was attracted by the Middle Ages, so dear to the Pre-Raphaelites. He returned to Boston where he devoted himself to historical works depicting the heroes of chivalry. In the vast expanses of the American countryside, he found fulfilment for his love of wide open spaces and the past (*The Flight of Florimell*).

Nicolas Abraham Abildgaard *The Spirit of Culmin appears to his Mother*

AUGUSTE Jules Robert Auguste (Paris 1789 – Paris 15.4.1850). 'Monsieur Auguste' might have been a picturesque figure at most, a model of the nonchalant art-lover spending his life in search of Beauty. But he was more than that. After winning a Prix de Rome for sculpture, he was one of the first travellers to the Near East and brought back sketches, studies and a host of colourful things. He preached a love of exoticism which, given the time, could not fail to find favour. His was a prestigious salon, where everyone who had anything to do with the Romantic movement gathered to find everything from Egyptian art to the subtle charm of a Watteau canvas.

He was also a painter, a good colourist and voluptuous in his portrayal of the female form, bringing to it all his talent as a sculptor. Though probably one of the least known artists of his generation, he was not without influence.

Monsieur Auguste *Two Odalisques in a Landscape*

BINGHAM George Caleb (Augusta County 20.3.1811 – Kansas City, Missouri 7.7.1879). Born in Virginia, spent his childhood on the shores of the Missouri, where he studied portrait painting. In 1837 he went to the Pennsylvania Academy of Fine Arts in Philadelphia and decided to take up genre painting (*The Fur Traders descending the Missouri*, 1845, Metropolitan Museum, New York). Between 1856 and 1859, he spent three years in Europe, mainly in Germany, which added a touch of sentimentality to his style. Back in America, he was elected as a Deputy and devoted himself to many political activities, which were reflected in some of his paintings (*The County Elections*, 1852).

William Blake *The Great Red Dragon and the Woman enveloped in the Light of the Sun*

BLAKE William (London 28.11.1757 – London 12.8.1827). A Revolutionary in technique, visionary, isolated creative genius, who was both painter, engraver and poet, Blake is the most remarkable and most typically Romantic figure in English art. From early childhood, he experienced hallucinations that were to have a profound effect on the whole of his work. As an apprentice to the engraver Basire, he was set to work copying details of old churches which gave him his taste for Gothic and mediaeval art. He then attended the Royal Academy where he worked with Reynolds. He met the sculptor and drawer Flaxman, and Fuseli, who influenced, and was influenced by, him. In 1784, he opened his own studio with his brother, published a first collection of poems and became his own illustrator. He invented *illuminated painting*, apparently revealed to him in a dream by his dead brother: this process enabled him to print the text and the engraving, to which he later added watercolour, on the same plate. As a general rule, he used watercolour often because he liked its transparent quality. Under the influence of Michaelangelo's drawings, he made his composition secondary to his own inner vision. Attracted by the French revolutionary ideal, inspired by the writings of Dante, Milton and Swedenborg and by the Bible, impelled by a mystical and libertarian vision, he wrote his *Songs of Innocence* in 1789, the *Book of Thal*, *The French Revolution* (1791), *The Marriage of Heaven and Hell* (1793) and the *Songs of Experience* (1794), while in Ras he printed *Newton*, *Nebuchadnezzar* and published *Urizen* and the *Song of Los*. Besides illustrating his own poems, he also illustrated Young's *Night Thoughts*, passages from the Bible, the *Divine Comedy* and Thornton's *Pastorals*. He was a Romantic not only in the way he blended literature, dreams and the graphic arts, but particularly in his nocturnal vision of the world and creation of an oppressive and disturbing dream-like atmosphere (*The Struggle of the Good and the Evil Angels for the Possession of a Child*, 1795; *Adam and Eve and the Archangel Raphael*, 1808; *Dante and Beatrice meeting in Paradise*, 1824). Although he had few disciples, his influence was manifold and he is regarded today as one of the forerunners of Symbolism.

BRÜLLOW or **BRJULOV Karl** (St Petersburg 12.12.1799 – Marciano, near Rome 23.6.1852). Russian painter of French origin (Bruleau), born in St Petersburg where he won a scholarship from the Society for the Encouragement of the Arts to study in Italy. He is known chiefly for his vast work *The Last Days of Pompeii*, which he exhibited in 1833. In general, he drew his themes from Antiquity or from the Bible and although his work had a certain Romantic spirit, it left no lasting impression. Turgenev said that Brüllow had the gift of expressing everything that he wanted to say, but had nothing to say.

Karl Brüllow *The Last Days of Pompeii*. 1828

CARSTENS Asmus Jakob (St Jürgen, Schleswig 10.5.1754 – Rome 25.5.1798). The son of a poor family, Carstens was not able to devote himself to painting as early as he would have liked. Obliged to earn his living very young, he entered the Copenhagen Academy only in 1776 and studied under Abildgaard. He travelled through Italy, then went back to Germany, where he settled in Lübeck and became a teacher. He finally returned to Rome where he spent the rest of his life. His work, which was typically Neo-Classical and was greatly to influence the Nazarene school, consisted mainly of drawings, some set off in watercolour, on themes from mythology, Dante and Ossian.

Asmus Jacob Carstens *Night with her Children*. 1795

Gustav Carus *Monument to the Memory of Goethe*. 1832

CARUS Karl Gustav (Leipzig 3.1.1789 – Dresden 28.7.1869). A painter and philosopher and one of the first Germans to study and teach comparative anatomy, Carus published many works on the nervous system and the circulation of the blood. But it was as a painter, philosopher and aesthetic writer that his effect on the first generation of German Romantics was decisive. He was a disciple of Caspar David Friedrich, whose theories he published in his *Nine Letters on the Painting of Landscapes* (1815–1824). He also wrote *Paris and the Banks of the Rhine* (1836), and *England and Scotland* (1846), in which he developed a Romantic vision and a perception of God's infinite greatness contrasted with the smallness of his creatures as revealed in Nature. In his drawings (such as *Gothic Cathedral seen through Ruins*), the vision is illustrated by a technique of blurred light and shadow.

CHASSÉRIAU Théodore (Santo Domingo 20.9.1819 – Paris 8.10.1856). Born of a Creole mother in Santo Domingo, where his father was French Consul, the family returned to France soon after his birth. At the age of

Théodore Chassériau *Self Portrait*. 1858

Théodore Chassériau *Macbeth and the Three Witches*. 1855

eleven, he became apprenticed to Ingres in Paris and worked with him until 1834. In 1838, he exhibited at the Salon *Marine Venus* (Musée du Louvre) and *Suzanne au bain* (Louvre). In 1840, he spent a year in Italy where he joined Ingres. On his return, he painted some portraits that were admirable for the balance struck between the use of colour and the overall structure of the work (Lacordaire, The Two Sisters). From 1841 to 1856, Chassériau painted many murals: at Saint-Merri in 1844, Saint-Roch in 1854, *Descent from the Cross* at Saint-Philippe du Roule in 1856, as well as frescoes for the Cour des Comptes, which were unfortunately destroyed during a fire in 1871. In these large works, he managed to combine the Classicism of Ingres, which had marked his youth, with his own personal sensuality. He used still warmer colours after a visit to Algeria to paint the portrait of *Ali-Hamed, Caliph of Constantine*, exhibited at the 1845 Salon. His taste for the exotic was given full rein in genre scenes and Moorish interiors (*Arab Riders, Harem Interior*). He paved the way for Gustave Moreau and the French Symbolists.

COLE Thomas (Bolton-le-Moor, Lancashire 1.2.1801 – Catskill, New York 11.2.1848). Cole's education was a combination of the European and the American. He emigrated to Ohio with his family in 1819 and from portrait painting went on to devote himself to landscapes. He enrolled at the Pennsylvania Academy of Fine Arts in Philadelphia in 1824 and later went to New York where his work met with great success. But it was in the wild areas of the Catskill Mountains that he chose, with the exception of a few trips to Europe, to spend the rest of his life. His presence there attracted other painters who were later known as the Hudson River School. While in Europe, he was much influenced by the work of Claude Lorrain and also by Turner and Friedrich, but he found his inspiration in the scenery of the New World (*In the Catskills*, 1837, Metropolitan Museum, New York). His minutely detailed landscapes were bathed in a golden light and often embellished with allegorical or imaginary figures

Thomas Cole *In the Catskills.* 1837

(*The Course of the Empire*, 1835–1836, Historical Society, New York; *The Journey of Life*, 1839–1840, Munson-William-Proctor Institute, Utica).

CONSTABLE John (East Bergholt, Suffolk 11.6.1776–London 1.4.1837). Opposed at first by his father who did not wish him to fulfil his artistic vocation, Constable began his career painting picturesque scenes in the area around his native town. He came to London to pursue his studies in 1795, but returned to Suffolk where he found solace in contact with Nature through landscape art. Back in London in 1799, he was admitted to the Royal Academy and studied under Joseph Farrington and Benjamin West. He started some portraits in the style of Gainsborough, Lawrence and Reynolds, experimented with historical and religious subjects, but very soon returned to landscape painting, a predilection reinforced during this period by his study of masters such

John Constable *Weymouth Bay.* 1818

as Rubens, Ruysdael and, particularly, Claude Lorrain. Their influence was considerable, but interpreted in such a personal way by Constable that he succeeded in setting new rules for this field of art, in his ability to capture fleeting phenomena: the vibration of air and light, the breeze, the foam on the waves (*Weymouth Bay*, 1816, Musée du Louvre; *Brighton Beach*, 1824–1827, Victoria and Albert Museum; *Flatford Mill*, 1817, Tate Gallery). The apotheosis of his art was probably his series of views

John Constable *Brighton Beach with Sailing Ships*. 1824

of Salisbury (*Salisbury Cathedral from the Bishop's Grounds*, 1823, is the most famous). Although elected to the Royal Academy in 1819, he was less popular in England than in France where his *Hay Wain* was exhibited with great success at the 1824 Salon. He played a leading role in English landscape art and was to have a decisive influence on the Barbizon School and the Impressionists.

CORNELIUS Peter von (Düsseldorf 23.9.1783 – Berlin 6.3.1867).

Influenced by archaeology and the discoveries of Winckelmann, drawn to Neo-Classicism and an admirer of Titian and Tintoretto, Cornelius dreamed of being a great Renaissance artist. After studying at the Academy in Düsseldorf, he went to Rome in 1811 and joined the Nazarene group installed at the Sant'Isidoro convent. Their aims coincided with his own: this 'Brotherhood of Saint Luke' was attempting to recapture the spirit of the Italian and German Primitives. Cornelius took part with the group in the decoration of the Zuccaro Palace, commissioned by Bartholdy, the Prussian Consul General, with two major compositions: *The Interpretation of Pharaoh's Dreams* and *Joseph recognised by his Brothers* (c.1816, Staatliche Museen, Berlin). He settled in Munich in 1819, where he painted frescoes for the Gly-

Peter von Cornelius *Faust and Marguerite in Martha's Garden*. After 1809

pothek and a *Last Judgment* for the Ludwigskirche (1830–1838). It is mainly on account of his theories and the texts that he illustrated (*Faust, die Niebelungen*) that Cornelius belongs to the Romantic movement.

COROT Jean-Baptiste-Camille (Paris 16.1.1796 – Ville d'Avray 22.2.1876).

Born of a well-to-do merchant family, Corot did not have to worry about earning a living, but he did have to fight the opposition of his parents to his following an artistic career. Not until he was 26 years old was he able to fulfil his ambition. He enrolled at the Ecole des Beaux-Arts where he studied with the painters Bertin and Michallon. He completed his training by painting and sketching in and around Paris and with a first visit to Italy (125–1828). He fell in love with the scenery and the light and immediately expressed that love in famous paintings: *The Coliseum, The Ruins of the Forum, The Bridge of Narni*, all three in 1826 (Musée du Louvre). The demands of his vision and the rigour of his composition were the result of a great number of preparatory studies. Back in France, he submitted some works to the Salon and made some attempts at historical painting, but he would always stand apart from the movements of the time, as well as from the quarrels between Classicists and Romanticists, and from the doctrines of the Barbizon School. Although the painters of the School were his friends, especially Daubigny, he did not espouse their ideas. He lived at Ville-d'Avray but spent much time travelling around France. The balance and

Jean-Baptiste-Camille Corot *Self-Portrait*

the severity of his compositions mellowed into a more original vision, albeit of subjects that tended to lack imagination (The *Collégiale of Mantes, Chartres Cathedral*). He often used a dominant shade which he modulated with a subtle use of transparency, losing himself sometimes in an introspective vision of an ideal world (*Memory of Mortefontaine*, 1864, Musée du Louvre).

His introspectiveness and natural sensitivity led him to paint portraits as well, which he did throughout his life, but he never considered them as important as his landscapes. (*Marietta, The Roman Odalisk*, 1843, Musée du Petit-Palais; *Claire Sennegon*, c.1845; *The Woman with the Pearl*, 1868–1870, Musée du Louvre; *The Gypsy Woman with the Mandolin*, 1874, Museu de Arte, Sao Paulo). One can sense his leaning towards harmony in the use of colour, which, in a way, augurs the work of Degas.

Jean-Baptiste-Camille Corot *Florence: View from the Boboli Gardens.* 1835–1840

Jean-Baptiste-Camille Corot *Woman with the Mandolin.*
1826–1828

COURBET Gustave (Ornans 10.6.1819 – La Tour de
Peitz Switzerland 31.12.1877). Son of a rich landowner,
Courbet studied at the Petit Séminaire in Ornans and
then at the Collège Royal at Besançon, where he also
attended the Beaux-Arts school and the classes of the
painter Flajoulot, a pupil of David. In 1839 he litho-
graphed illustrations for a volume of poems by his friend,
the writer Max Buchon. In 1840, he left for Paris and,
giving up his law studies, attended painting academies
and the copy sessions at the Louvre. He modelled himself
above all on Giorgione, Correggio, Rembrandt and the
Spanish painters, but he was interested in Caravaggio
and admired Gros, Géricault, Ingres and Delacroix. He
began to earn a living by painting nudes and portraits.
His many self-portraits reveal the extent of his fascina-
tion with his own image: *Man with Pipe*, Musée Fabre,
Montpellier; *Self-Portrait with Black Dog*, Musée du Petit-
Palais. He lived a Bohemian life, joined many political
movements and met Baudelaire, of whom he painted a
famous portrait (Musée Fabre, Montpellier). His first
submissions to the Salon were rejected but his *Après-diner
à Ornans* exhibited in 1849 was a success: it attracted
attention, notably that of Ingres and Delacroix. This was

followed by the *Stonebreakers* and *Burial at Ornans* which
caused a scandal and became in a sense the manifesto of
Realism. But his realism met with a mixed reception: his
Baigneuses exhibited at the 1853 Salon provoked the scorn
of Napoleon III. As for the *Artist's Studio* (1855, Musée
du Louvre), it was rejected for the Universal Exhibition
and Courbet, as a protest, exhibited it with thirty-nine
other canvases in a pavilion at the Exhibition entrance,
which he called the 'Pavilion of Realism'. It was a success in spite of criticism which had no effect whatsoever
on Courbet's confidence in his own genius: his *Self-
portraits*, the *Studio* and *The Meeting* (or *Bonjour, Monsieur
Courbet*) are clear indications of his narcissism. He
painted some landscapes (*The Big Oak at Ornans*, 1864,
Philadelphia Museum of Art; *Cliff at Etretat after the
Storm*, 1870, Musée du Louvre) to which he sometimes
added a dramatic dimension, as in *Stag at the Waterside*
(1861, Musée des Beaux-Arts, Marseille). But he always
returned to the theme of the nude, which he now suffused
with warm and sensual light (*Baigneuses à la Source*, 1862,
Metropolitan Museum New York; *Les Dormeuses*, 1866,
Petit-Palais; *Woman with Parrot*, 1866, Metropolitan
Museum, New York). His political leanings had dis-
astrous consequences at the end of his life. After the
Commune, he was accused of being the prime mover of
the demolition of the Vendôme Column. He was court-
marshalled, imprisoned and heavily fined. He took
refuge in Switzerland where he died shortly afterwards.

Gustave Courbet *The Woman in the Waves.* 1868

CROME John (Norwich 22.12.1768 – Norwich 22.4.1821). Called Old Crome to distinguish him from his son John Berna Crome. After being in service, Crome became apprenticed to a sign painter. It was probably by studying and copying the works of the Dutch and English Masters in a private collection that he formed his style. In 1803, this self-taught painter became a teacher of drawing in Norwich and later founded the school there where he was to spend most of his life.

John Crome *Boulevard des Italiens.* 1815

Gustave Courbet *Self-Portrait with Black Dog.* 1840–1844

Johann Christian Clausen Dahl *Eruption of Vesuvius*. 1826

With the exception of *Forge Interior* (1809) and *Boulevard des Italiens* which resulted from a visit to Paris in 1814, Crome's work was devoted almost entirely to landscapes and Nature (such as *Landscape with Cottage and Trees*, Victoria and Albert Museum). He could recreate the atmosphere of the Dutch Masters to perfection and added old buildings, contrasts of light and shade, groups of trees reflected on water (*Moonrise on the Marshes of the Yare*, 1808–1810, National Gallery) and occasionally figures (*The Shepherd and his Sheep*, Tate Gallery).

visited the Tyrol, Naples and Rome and brought back studies and landscapes (*View of Vietri*, *In the Island of Capri*, *Eruption of Vesuvius*). In 1818 he settled in Dresden where he was the pupil and friend of Caspar David Friedrich, taught at the Academy of Fine Arts and remained the rest of his life.

A large part of his work was devoted to northern landscapes (*The Shipwreck*, *Saxon Switzerland*, *Winter Landscape in Zeeland*). He was also interested in archaeological research and in the restoration of mediaeval wooden buildings, which prompted him to illustrate a history of Norwegian wooden architecture, published in Dresden in 1837.

DAHL Johann Christian Clausen (Bergen 24.2.1788 – Dresden 14.10.1857). The son of a fisherman, Dahl had to earn his living when he was young as a house painter. Only when he was 23 years old was he able to enrol at the Academy of Fine Arts in Copenhagen, where his teacher was the painter Eckersberg. Summoned to follow King Christian VIII of Denmark on his travels, Dahl

DAUBIGNY Charles-François (Paris 15.1.1817 – Paris 1878). Learnt the rudiments of his craft from his father who was a landscape painter, then, after a year's stay in Rome which had little effect on his work, he attended Delaroche's studio at the Beaux-Arts. He also worked

Charles-François Daubigny *Portrait by Bracquemond*

where he not only learned about books but probably acquired his taste for lithography. In 1822, he met Alexandre Lenoir who taught him sculpture while he was attending the Swiss Academy. From 1825, he worked as a lithographer with Belliard, was an artistic collaborator on *La Silhouette* and on the new satirical paper *La Caricature*, founded in 1830 by Philippon. It was then that he drew his famous caricature of Louis-Philippe with a pear-shaped head entitled *Gargantua*, which earned him six months in prison (1832–33). It was probably on his release from prison that he started working in coloured clay, moulding the series of busts of members of Parliament after the lithographs published in *La Caricature*. These original, very fragile, clays were cast in bronze in about 1930 (the Musée des Beaux-Arts of Lyon and of

Honoré Daumier *Portrait by Eugene Monnier*

with Grasset, was friendly with Corot and, to earn a living, sold historical paintings and illustrations (notably for *The Mysteries of Paris* by Eugène Sue). He had links with the Barbizon painters, but did not belong to their group. He was a member of the Salon jury where he defended Monet and introduced him to Durand Ruel. With him, and with Courbet and Boudin, he spent the summer in Trouville and was enchanted by the marine light. He finally settled in Auvers-sur-Oise where he launched a school of painting that prefigured Impressionism. His landscapes are full of the subtle interplay of light and colour (*Barges, Setting Sun on the Oise, The Watergates at Optevoz*).

Marseille house the only two complete series).
Daumier then moved into a kind of community of artists with Diaz, Huet, Jeanron, Corot and Daubigny and tried to make his mark as a painter and sculptor. He avenged himself on permanently hostile juries with a series of political lithographs, the most famous of which is the *Rue Transnonain*. It tells the tragic story of the residents of a building who were murdered in the middle of the night by troops sent to put down the Republican insurrection of April 1834. Though an isolated incident, it had unprecedented political repercussions. Daumier denounced the excesses of police repression and the misery and helplessness of its victims. *La Rue Transnonain* was seized, *La Caricature* was banned, but Daumier continued his crusade from the pages of *Le Charivari*, against the bourgeoisie this time, who supported the power structure (*The Hundred and One, Robert Macaire, les Gens de Justice*). He followed current events and working class life closely (*The Refugees, The Third-class Carriage*). In 1851, he created the character of *Ratapoil*, half-starved ex-officer and Bonapartist agent provocateur.
Daumier gave up journalism in 1860 to devote himself to

Charles-François Daubigny *Setting Sun on the Oise*

DAUMIER Honoré (Marseille 26.2.1808 – Valmondois 10.2.1879). Born of a poor family, Daumier followed his father to Paris in 1816. He had to start work very young, first as a bailiff's clerk, then as a bookshop assistant,

painting. His canvases have a lithographer's sureness of line and in their expressive simplification and powerful monochrome colours, they are akin to the work of Goya (*The Print Lover*, *Crispin and Scapin*, *The Laundress*, Musée du Louvre; *Don Quixote*, Neue Pinakothek, Munich).

In 1865, thanks to Corot's generosity, Daumier, now almost blind, settled at Valmondois, where he ended his days.

Honoré Daumier *Don Quixote and the Dead Mule*. 1867

Honoré Daumier *Ratapoil*

DAVID Jacques-Louis (Paris 30.8.1748 – Brussels 29.12.1825). Pupil of the Neo-Classical painter Vien, David won the Prix de Rome in 1774 with *Antiochus and Stratonice* (Ecole des Beaux-Arts, Paris). The following year, Vien was appointed Director of the Académie de France in Rome and took David with him around Italy, visiting museums, collections and the excavations at Pompeii and Herculaneum. David absorbed this classical atmosphere and drew a great many studies.

Back in Paris in 1780, he imposed the concept of Neo-Classicism in painting, the school of which he was to be the master. For him, the ancient Greeks and Romans immortalised absolute Beauty, especially in sculpture: a beauty synonymous with balance, calm, rhythm and harmony between the bodies of the heroes and their environment. He was admitted to the Académie in 1783 with *Andromache Mourning the Death of Hector* (Ecole des Beaux-Arts, Paris), then he left again for Italy and in 1785 exhibited *The Oath of the Horatii* (Musée du Louvre) in Rome. It received a triumphant reception in Paris and was considered to be the manifesto of Neo-Classical art. In similar vein he then painted *The Death of Socrates* (1787, Metropolitan Museum of Art, New York), *The Loves of Paris and Helen*, 1789, and *Brutus and his Dead Sons* (1789, Musée du Louvre).

He threw himself with passion into the 1789 Revolution (*Oath of the Jeu de Paume*, Versailles Museum). A member of the *Montagne*, political comrade of Marat, Robespierre and Saint-Just, he voted for the death of Louis XVI and staged great popular festivals. The martyrs of the Rev-

Jacques-Louis David *The Rape of the Sabines*. 1796–1799

olution aroused in him emotions that had nothing to do with theory, and affected him as a man, artist and bereaved friend (*The Assassination of Marat, 1793*, Brussels; *The Death of Bara*, 1794, Avignon). His political stance cost him imprisonment under Thermidor, but he was soon released under the 1795 amnesty. He returned to Antiquity with *The Rape of the Sabines* (1796–1799, Louvre), and painted some admirable portraits (*Madame Recamier*, 1800, *Portrait of Pius VII*, 1805, Louvre). With the new century, he found inspiration in the new Imperial era, which he immortalised in *The Coronation of the Emperor* (1806, Louvre) and *Napoleon distributing the Eagles* (1810, Versailles). David was then at the height of his fame. But, come the Restoration, he was exiled as a regicide and took refuge in Belgium where he died, cherished by his pupils and esteemed by all.

Jacques-Louis David *Self-Portrait*

DELACROIX Eugène (Saint-Maurice 26.4.1798 – Paris 13.8.1863). Born into a family of artists, and related to the famous cabinet-maker Riesener. Delacroix was believed to be the illegitimate son of Talleyrand. He spent his childhood between Marseille and Bordeaux and after his father's death in 1805, his mother returned to Paris where Delacroix was a boarder at the Lycée Impérial, where he received a good classical education. Then his uncle Riesener sent him to the studio of the painter

Eugène Delacroix *The Death of Ophelia*. 1844

Guérin, a disciple of David. He met Géricault and in his company discovered the works of the great northern painters in the Louvre, particularly those of Rubens and Rembrandt. He made his first step along the road to fame at the Salon of 1822 where he exhibited *Dante and Virgil in Hell* (Musée du Louvre). The followers of David were shocked but the rest of the critics, with the young journalist Adolphe Thiers as their spokesman, regarded it as a masterpiece.

It was also in 1822 that Delacroix started his *Journal* (Diary) which affords us a better understanding of the painter and his contemporaries. He met Bonington and discovered the style of the English landscape artists, which was considerably to influence his view of things. It is said that this was the reason why he modified the background of his *Massacre at Chios* (1824, Musée du Louvre) on the very eve of the day when the painting was to be hung at the Salon. This work, which depicts the tragic episode in 1822 when twenty thousand Greeks were massacred by the Turks, was not only a political declaration of faith but also a real manifesto of Romanticism and a hommage to Byron who died that same year.

Eugène Delacroix *Self-Portrait as Hamlet*. c. 1824

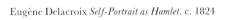

Eugène Delacroix *Jacob's Struggle with the Angel.* 1856–1861

Eugène Delacroix *Algerian Women in their Apartments.* 1834

The following year, he travelled to England where he discovered not only colourist painting but also the whole stream of English literature from Shakespeare to Byron. On his return, he started work on *The Death of Sardanapalus*, the sensuality of which was to scandalise the critics at the 1828 Salon. Politically committed and attracted by the proliferation of liberation movements, his inspiration became allegorical (*Greece expiring on the Ruins of Missolonghi, Liberty guiding the People*). He did not ignore historical fact, but his *Assassination of the Bishop of Liège*, with its sombre lyricism of composition, is closer to the world of opera than that of anecdote.

In 1831, the Count of Mornay, a diplomat, suggested that Delacroix accompany him to Morocco and Algeria. Delacroix was transfixed by the Mediterranean light and brought back innumerable books of sketches and new sources of inspiration (*Algerian Women in their Apartments*, 1834; *The Jewish Wedding*, 1839, Musée du Louvre).

He produced major works like *The Battle of Taillebourg* (1837, Versailles) and *The Capture of Constantinople by the Crusaders* (1841, Musée du Louvre), while at the same time fulfilling official commissions: frescoes and murals for the salon of the King and the Palais Bourbon library; a *Pieta* for the Saint-Denis du Saint-Sacrement church in Paris; a ceiling for the Galerie d'Apollon in the Louvre (*Apollo vanquishing the serpent Python*, 1849–1851); the

Salon de la Paix at the Hotel de Ville, destroyed by fire under the Commune, and finally, *Jacob's Struggle with the Angel* for the Saints-Anges chapel of the church of Saint-Sulpice. At the Universal Exhibition of 1855, his work was officially honoured with the Grande Medaille d'Honneur. Géricault's successor, he gradually achieved a lyricism based on his use of colour and an essentially expressive stroke. He spent the remainder of his life between his studio on Place Furstenberg and his country house on the outskirts of Paris.

DELAROCHE Hippolyte, known as Paul (Paris 17.7.1797 – Paris 4.11.1856). A pupil of Gros, the son-in-law of Horace Vernet, whose work was much appreciated by his contemporaries. His Romanticism was more tempered than that of Delacroix, which made it more acceptable. He devoted himself mainly to French and English history which he treated with somewhat mawkish sentimentality (*The Assassination of the Duc de Guise*, 1835, Musée Conde, Chantilly); *Edward's Children*, Musée du Louvre; *The Execution of Jane Grey at the Tower of London*, 1834, National Gallery).

Eugène Devéria *Birth of Henri IV.* 1827

Eugène Devéria *Heloíse and Abelard*

Paul Delaroche *Edward's Children*

DEVÉRIA Achille (Paris 6.2.1800 – Paris 23.12.1857) and **Eugène** (Paris 22.4.1805 – Pau 3.2.1865). Achille, who had been a pupil of Girodet, was an excellent drawer and engraver. He is known mainly for his countless illustrations, for his fashion plates and for his many portraits of personalities of the Romantic era.

His brother Eugène, also a pupil of Girodet, was a good colourist and devoted himself essentially to historical subjects. His major work, exhibited at the Salon of 1827, was a gigantic *Birth of Henri IV* (Musée du Louvre) which was considered at the time to be a manifesto of young Romantic painting.

Narcisse Diaz de la Pena *Landscape with Pond*

DIAZ DE LA PENA Narcisse (Bordeaux 20.8.1808 – Menton 18.11.1878). Orphaned very young, and obliged to become an apprentice in a porcelain factory. It was not until 1830 that he went to Paris and devoted himself to painting. His early work was inspired by the Middle Ages and the Orient, but his friendship with Théodore Rousseau soon persuaded him to join the Barbizon group. It was in the open air of the Fontainebleau forest that he really found himself: his early landscapes were peopled with allegorical and mythological figures (*The*

Sleeping Nymph, c.1850–55, Musée du Louvre), but he later concentrated on the pure evocation of Nature. He depicted it with strong contrasts of light and shade, rendered in vehement, sometimes very visible, strokes (*Jean de Paris in the Forest of Fontainebleau*, 1867, Musée du Louvre; *The Approaching Storm*, 1871, Pushkin Museum, Moscow).

Gustave Doré *Gargantua's Entry into Paris*

DORÉ Gustave (Strasbourg 6.1.1832 – Paris 23.1.1883). Doré's artistic gifts were evident when he was still very young, and he took up drawing and lithography very early. At the age of fifteen, in Paris, he was lucky enough to meet Philippon, the director of the journals *Le Charivari*, *La Caricature* and the *Journal pour Rire*, who gave him a three-year exclusive contract for two engravings a week. His success was such that he was able to support his needy family.

Doré's style evolved from caricature and parody to the illustration of literary works. His *Rabelais* appeared in

Gustave Doré *Self-Portrait*

1853, Balzac's *Contes Drolatiques* in 1855 and *The Wandering Jew* by Eugène Sue in 1856. In 1861, he produced an edition of Dante's *Inferno*, then illustrated Perrault's *Tales* for Hétzel, the *Bible* in 1866 and La Fontaine's *Fables* in 1867. His talent was as great as his verve and imagination. His fantastic vision of characters is unnerving in the extent to which likeness is distorted at will to be reconstructed in his own world: in his *Witches' Sabbath in Macbeth*, the dance of the witches round the fire is in rhythm with the dancing flames that light up eerie ruins, and his *Ship among the Icebergs* (1876) is reduced to a dreamlike juxtaposition of whitish patches out of which the icebergs loom like great white ghosts.

DURAND Asher Brown (Jefferson Village, New Jersey 21.8.1796 – South Orange 17.9.1886). Durand practised engraving until he was thirty-five years old. Then he devoted himself to landscape painting, with which he had become familiar while executing a series of engravings, *The American Landscape*, after the works of his friends in the Hudson River School. His work entitled *Kindred Spirits* (1849, New York Public Library) is a homage to the School's leader, Thomas Cole. Durand's ambition was to be an essentially American painter with a mission to represent the unspoilt wildness of a Nature that owed nothing to Europe. But after his encounter, during a study trip, with the Barbizon painters and their open air theories, he could not help transposing those Catskill scenes with their rocks, waterfalls and broken trees, and their blue-tinged distances, into a picturesque vision that was closer than he might have wished to Old World Romanticism.

Karl-Philipp Fohr *Self-Portrait*. 1816

FOHR Karl-Philipp (Heidelberg 26.11.1795 – Rome 29.6.1818). Worked in Heidelberg and Darmstadt before going to Munich and discovering the German Primitives there. In 1816, he went to Rome where he was enchanted by the Italian landscape and the colour of Venetian painting. His art became a synthesis of German Romanticism, the classic structure and light of the Roman landscape, and the Nazarene teachings of Koch. Even his death was Romantic in its manner: he drowned in the Tiber shortly after drawing *Hagen listening to the Rhine Maidens*. His landscapes show a remarkable sense of the

Karl-Philipp Fohr *Landscape in the Sabine Mountains.* 1818

value of colour in creating a natural setting. The structure of the trees against the light and the blue shading of the mountains are evidence of how well he fitted into the line of artists who were inspired by the Roman countryside (*Waterfalls at Tivoli*, Städelsches Kunstinstitut, Frankfurt).

FRIEDRICH Caspar David (Greifswald 5.9.1774 – Dresden 7.5.1840). Friedrich's Romanticism was indelibly stamped by the scenery of his childhood: the shores of the Baltic, the Harz mountains, the banks of the Elba where his young brother drowned after falling through the ice, and the town where he was born and lived until he was twenty. He spent four years at the Academy of Fine Arts in Copenhagen before settling permanently in Dresden. There he was in contact with the great German Romantics: Kleist, Tieck Novalis and Runge, as well as Goethe whom he met in 1810.

His ideal was more one of 'supernaturalisation of landscape' than of deep analysis. In this, he was closer to the thinker Gustav Carus and the Norwegian painter Dahl, with whom he was close friends, than he was to the philosophy of Geothe. The emotions that ruled over his creative work were so deep and intense that he was eventually to fall prey to mental illness and meet a tragic end. On the technical front, his art has an objectivity of design, a highly individual use of colour and a meticulousness of composition that might leave the casual spectator unmoved. An immediate feeling of anxiety emanates from this perfection of form which evokes a sadly empty and quasi 'surreal' world. In this world of landscapes and timeless scenes, real *leitmotives*, like those of a Romantic opera, appear: their repetition corresponds to the mental state of the painter.

The idea of death is permanently dominant. It is seen in a tragic vision among pine trees (*Cross and Cathedral in the Mountains*), though tempered by the divine and redeeming presence of a Cross or a church.

Curiously enough, he saw Nature as a hostile force (*The Sea of Ice*, c.1823–1824, Kunsthalle, Hamburg), and above all as an austere setting in which Man is an uneasy presence (*Two Men contemplating the Moon*, 1819, Gemäldegalerie, Dresden; *Moonrise over the Sea*, 1820–1826, Staatliche Museen, Berlin). Man appears to be artificially placed into the painting; he is lost in reverie and his back is turned. Warmth of colour fortunately tempers the perhaps overly dramatic nature of composition and subject.

One of his most significant works is *The Monk at the Edge of the Sea*, 1808–9, which was purchased at its first exhibition by the Crown Prince of Prussia. Never before had Friedrich taken the spectator so far into what might be termed the 'hereafter' of painting. The canvas is divided into three unequal registers: the whitish earth in the foreground, the almost black sea with a few white patches of foam, and a gigantic sky. The tiny brown silhouette of the monk stands to the left, so small that it is there not so much to bring life to the painting as show the insignificance of humanity in the face of the immensity of Nature. The light cannot shine through; it merely gives presence to the elements of earth, water and air. For the first two, the artist's stroke is precise, but air, ranging in colour from white to a shade of green, is no more than a vast empty stain. That great emptiness reveals a rather destructive desire for abstraction.

Friedrich's influence was considerable. The world he de-

Caspar David Friedrich *Self-Portrait*. c. 1810

Caspar David Friedrich *The Sea of Ice*. c. 1823–1824

Caspar David Friedrich *The Swans*. 1820

picted, his projection of the intimate into a quasi-mineral universe powerfully embodied all the currents of German 19th century art.

made several trips to Algeria, which was to be a source of inspiration (*The Falcon Hunt*, 1863, Musée du Louvre). On the other hand, he was a colourist deeply influenced by the work of the northern painters, so much so that he

Eugène Fromentin. *The Falcon Hunt*.

FROMENTIN Eugène (La Rochelle 24.10.1820 – Saint-Maurice – 27.8.1876). Fromentin was a man of letters, art critic and painter at the same time. Although he is mainly known today as a writer for his novel *Dominique* and his travelogues, there were two sides to his work as a painter. On the one hand, he was a landscape artist, a keen traveller, attracted by North African exoticism (he

Henry Fuseli *Lady Macbeth*. 1784

made a pilgrimage to the great Belgian and Dutch museums which resulted in a remarkable literary analysis, *Les Maitres d'autrefois* (1876).

FUSELI Henry (Zurich 6.2.1741 – Putney Heath 16.4.1825). Fuseli learnt the rudiments of his craft from his father who was a painter. Then, intending to enter the Church, he received a sound classical education, particularly in Latin and Greek, but also in English, which enabled him to translate Shakespeare into German. In 1763, he renounced his clerical ambitions and went to London, where he decided to take up painting again. On Reynolds' advice he left for Italy and spent several years there. He was impressed by the ruins and monuments of the past, and by the work of Michaelangelo (*The Artist in Front of the Ruins*, 1778, Kunsthaus, Zurich). On his return to London, his style remained strongly influenced by Neo-Classicism, but took on a melancholy aura which soon developed into a dreamlike and imaginative style. His *The Nightmare* (1781, Kunsthaus, Zurich), of which he made several versions, assured his popular success.

He illustrated Milton, drew inspiration from Shakespeare (*Titania, Bottom and the Fairies*, *Lady Macbeth*) and created a disturbing world haunted by the erotic and the macabre.

In 1790 he was elected to the Royal Academy and taught aesthetics there from 1799. His fruitful career was a successful synthesis of the wildest of the German Fantastic and the English Romantic.

GAINSBOROUGH Thomas (Sudbury, Suffolk 14.5.1727 – London 2.8.1788). Having served a solitary apprenticeship as a landscape painter in the Suffolk countryside, Gainsborough worked with the French en-

Thomas Gainsborough *Mrs Richard Brinsley Sheridan*. 1783

Thomas Gainsborough *Self-Portrait*. 1787

graver Gravelot in London until 1745. Then he entered the St Martin's Lane Academy and the studio of the historical painter, Francis Hayman. While apprenticed for four years to this relatively mediocre artist he was first noticed as a portrait and landscape painter. His first major works date from this period, notably *Charterhouse* (1748, Foundling Hospital, London) which established him as a landscape artist, and portraits (*Mr and Mrs Andrew*, 1748, National Gallery) in which landscape occupied most of the canvas. In 1759, he moved from Ipswich where he had been living, to Bath, then an elegant spa, and soon became *the* fashionable portrait painter. His wealthy clientele appreciated the talent he had of adding a touch of kindness to the precision with which he portrayed the personality of the sitter. Around 1770, he painted the freest of his works, the famous *Blue Boy*, often considered as being in defiance of Reynolds who thought that blue was a cold colour, though it may perhaps have been an imitation of Watteau's *Gilles*. Gainsborough returned to London in 1774, where he continued to paint portraits (*Mrs Sheridan*, 1783, National Gallery) and 'fantasy' paintings. He used colour to capture the essence of

Thomas Gainsborough *The Blue Boy*. 1770

people and objects and to give them a poetic dimension. His art is an exquisite synthesis of the artistic currents of the late 18th century.

François Gérard *Madame Récamier*. 1802

GÉRARD François (Rome 4.5.1770 – Paris 11.1.1837). Gérard's father was attached to the French embassy in Rome and his mother was Italian. He returned to Paris very young and in 1784 entered the studio of David who encouraged his career. Attracted at first by historical and mythological painting in pure Neo-Classical style, he later concentrated on portraiture with outstanding success, tempering realism with graceful poses and an ease of style: his *Portrait of Madame Récamier* (1802, Musée Carnavalet, Paris) is probably the most famous, together with the later portrait of the painter *Isabey and his Daughter* (1795, Musée du Louvre). He was Napoleon's favourite painter (*The Battle of Austerlitz*, 1810, Musée de Versailles), but also official painter to Louis XVIII; his

portrait of the latter was exhibited at the 1814 Salon and earned him the title of Baron. He also painted *The Coronation of Charles X* (1829, Musée de Versailles). To-day, however, his grand historical pieces are appreciated far less than his more modest graceful, and genuinely Romantic, compositions.

GÉRICAULT Théodore (Rouen 26.9.1791 – Paris 26.1.1824) The son of a bourgeois family, left his native town to study under Carle Vernet, Guérin and Gros; meanwhile, he admired and copied the works of Rubens, Caravaggio and Velasquez at the Louvre. He learnt from them the art of painting strongly lit sculptural forms. He also loved horses and drew many sketches at riding schools and stud farms. These would result in his first major work, *The Light Cavalry Officer* (1812, Musée du Louvre).

He enlisted enthusiastically in Louis XVIII's Guards but resigned, disillusioned, after the Hundred Days. As a result of a love affair, he had to leave France and go to

Théodore Géricault *The Light Cavalry Officer*. 1812

Théodore Géricault *The Raft of the Medusa*. Sketch

Italy in 1816. There he re-discovered the classic works that he had admired in the Louvre — Michaelangelo's frescoes in the Sistine Chapel, the paintings of Raphael and the works of Caravaggio, of which he made innumerable sketches. He was also interested in horse-racing (*The Barbary Horse Race on the Corso in Rome*, 1817, Musée du Louvre). Back in France, he used painting as a political weapon by illustrating an event that scandalised public opinion at the time: the terrible wreck of a French ship, 'La Meduse', which, because of the captain's incompetence, ran aground on a reef. Géricault made many sketches and studies before he chose to depict on canvas the pathetic moment when the exhausted survivors, on the brink of madness, glimpse a sail on the horizon (*The Raft of the Medusa*, 1818, Louvre). The pyramidal movement, the effects of the light, the horror and madness of the scene, together with the political and philosophical

import of the work make it one of the most significant examples of Romanticism in painting, despite its realism of detail. It met with a mixed reception and Géricault left for England in disappointment. There he discovered a different light, a more 'liquid' atmosphere, a new way of approaching landscape art and making colour the dominant element of the painting. He also indulged his love of horses (*The Epsom Derby*, 1821, Musée du Louvre), but that love was to prove fatal since, on his return to France, he would have a fall from which he never recovered. He insisted on continuing to ride and work despite two further accidents. The morbid side of his character became dominant, manifesting itself in a questioning of life and Man, which he illustrated in a series of portraits of madmen and madwomen at the Salpetrière asylum. He finally died in 1824, a true Romantic hero, after enduring appalling physical and mental pain.

Théodore Géricault *The Madwoman*

Girodet-Trioson *The Two Dohler Brothers*

GIRODET Anne-Louis, called GIRODET-TRIO-SON (Montargis 29.1.1767 – Paris 8.12.1824). Studies under David and Prud'hon and then a visit to Italy placed the beginnings of his career under the aegis of Neo-Classicism. His first subjects were mythological (*The Sleep of Endymion*, 1792, Musée du Louvre; *Danaé receiving the Golden Rain*, 1799, Museum der Bildenden Künste, Leipzig). When Fontaine commissioned work for the château de Malmaison, Girodet-Trioson executed an epic work based on a Macpherson poem, *The Shades of Heroes who died for their Country, received by Ossian into Odin's Paradise*. But he abandoned epic painting and turned towards the Romanticism of Chateaubriand, from whom he drew new sources of inspiration (*The Funeral of Atala*, 1808, Louvre) and whose portrait he painted (1809, St-Malo). He also painted *The Cairo Revolt*, (1810, Versailles) and ended his career by illustrating Bernardin de Saint-Pierre's *Paul et Virginie* and revealing himself as a precursor of the Romantic movement.

GIRTIN Thomas (London 18.2.1775 – London 9.11.1802). A pupil of the topographer Edward Dayes, he was a friend of Turner, who would always have great admiration for him. His first works (monastery ruins and old churches of England and Wales) were examples of that picturesque topography that engraving and a kind of escapism were to make popular throughout most of

Thomas Girtin *Rue Saint-Denis*. c. 1802

Europe. After travelling in Scotland and Wales, he went to Paris where he painted a series of watercolours, published after his death in a collection of etchings entitled *A Selection of the most picturesque Views in Paris and its environs* (1803).

It was essentially through etching and above all water colour that he evoked a Romantic vision of landscape; the transparency and lightness of his colours completely transform the light (*Bolton Abbey*). His work had considerable influence on the generation that followed him.

Francisco Goya *The Charge of the Mamelukes*. 1814

GOYA Y LUCIENTES Francisco (Aragon 30.3.1746–Bordeaux 16.4.1828). Goya was very young when he began to study painting in Saragossa with the artist José Luxan. But his dissipated youth and some rather dubious episodes forced him to leave Saragossa for Madrid. He then went to Rome where he devoted himself to the study of Italian styles, until another love affair sent him back to Madrid. There he worked with Mengs and Bayeu and drew sketches for tapestries and frescoes for various churches. He became well-known enough to receive royal favour: he was appointed Academician of Merit at the San Fernando Academy in 1780 and painter to the King in 1789. His life was then divided between

Francisco Goya *Self-Portrait*. 1816

the Court, where his liaison with the Duchess of Alba caused gossip, and the common people, whose daily life he portrayed. His art involved him totally in life, and later in the Franco-Spanish war. He was able, in painting and lithography, to be at one and the same time a documenter of terrible episodes, a pitiless analyst of social unrest and a visionary who saw all the nightmare and horror of war.

In 1814, he went into exile to Bordeaux where he continued to work until the end of his life, despite the ravages of illness and the deafness that had partly cut him off from the world (*The Deaf Man's House*). All of Goya's work is in Romantic vein: the audacious characterisation and monstrous expressionism of his portraits (*The Family of King Charles IV*), the intimate lasciviousness of the *Portrait of the Duchess of Alba* and the *Majas*, the social analysis rendered in visionary choreography (*Burial of the Sardine*), the terrible indictment of war (*Second and Third of May*), the nightmare upheavals of history (*The Giant Saturn devouring his Children*). His pictorial technique, with its emphasis on light and colour, delves into the unconscious mind, which becomes the determining feature of the composition. Detail disappears in the sheer mass of the picture, faces are no more than grimacing masks, caricatures or death-heads. It was perhaps in his etchings and lithographs (*The Caprices, The Proverbs, The Bull Races, The Disasters of War*) that he plumbed more deeply still that inner dimension which gives the drawing its meaning, and transforms the image into a vehicle for a fantastic and monstrous expressionism (*Man walking among the Ghosts, The Carnivorous Vulture, The Sleep of Reason, Scenes of Cannibalism*).

It would perhaps be going too far to assume that his

Francisco Goya *The Burial of the Sardine*. 1793

work had a conscious political motive. But as his personal isolation gradually increased, his art, with its procession of monsters, outcasts, and dead gods, became all-enveloping and acquired a universal dimension.

GRANDVILLE (Jean-Ignace-Isidore GÉRARD) (Nancy 15.9.1803 – Vanves 1847). This drawer and etcher met a truly Romantic end, dying insane in Paris, where he first settled in 1825. His first series of lithographs, *Metamorphoses of the Day*, brought him to public attention. He published etchings in *Caricature*, *Charivari*, and *Magasin Pittoresque*, inventing the famous caricature of Louis-Philippe in the shape of a pear, which was much copied. His great speciality was the systematic transformation of

Jean-Auguste-Dominique Ingres *Portrait of Granet*. 1807

Grandville *Balzac, Frederic Lemaitre and Theophile Gautier*

all his contemporaries into animal shapes. He had solid technique but sometimes his ideas were rather forced. He also illustrated Swift, Defoe, Florian and la Fontaine. His perverse vision sought the monster in everyone and took delight in the strangest and most pernicious transfiguration of the human shape ever produced by the Romantic imagination.

GRANET **François-Marius** (Aix-en-Provence 17.12.1775 – Aix-en-Provence 22.11.1849). Granet was indisputably influenced by Neo-Classicism: he was a pupil of David from 1797 and from 1802 to 1819 lived in Rome, where he was to return again and again. However, the originality of his work distinguished him from other Neo-Classicists. He had a very personal and Romantic way of expressing the effects of light – the rays of the sun filtering into a cavern or a church steeped in shadow (*The Choir of the Capuchin Church*, Musée des Beaux-Arts, Lyon). He was the curator of the Palace of Versailles from 1820 and a member of the Institut from 1830. He made a few experiments in pseudo-historical genre (*Montaigne visiting Tasso*, 1820, Musée Fabre, Montpellier), but he is known above all for his wonderful Roman landscapes, with their sober architecture bathed in golden light (*Church of Ognissanti*, Musée Granet, Aix-en-Provence).

Antoine-Jean Gros *Self-Portrait*

Antoine-Jean Gros *Bonaparte at the Bridge of Arcola*. 1796

GROS Antoine-Jean, Baron (Paris 16.3.1771 – Meudon 26.6.1835). First initiated in painting by his father who was a miniaturist, Gros was very young when he entered David's studio in 1785. He would remain a fervent admirer of David all his life and was deeply influenced by his teaching. Thanks to the patronage of Josephine de Beauharnais, he met Bonaparte, then First Consul, in Italy. This meeting was of enormous significance for Gros. He followed the evolution of the future Emperor's career and later became his official painter: from *Bonaparte at the Bridge of Arcola* (1796, Musée de Versailles) to *Napoleon at the Battle of Eylau* (1808, Musée du Louvre), by way of *Bonaparte visiting the Plague Victims in Jaffa* (1804, Louvre). It is very curious that, in these works dedicated to the glorification of the Emperor in the public eye, one can sense that Gros was torn between his professed respect for classical theory and his own passionate temperament: it is as though he could not prevent himself from amassing the hideous dead and wounded bodies on the grey snow of Eylau bathed in apocalyptic light, while in the Jaffa scene, man appears, saint-like, amid misery and suffering, in an oriental setting that reveals typically Romantic escapism.

He became a member of the Institut in 1815, ran David's studio after the latter's exile and continued his career as

Antoine-Jean Gros *Sappho at Leucadia*. 1801

a historical and portrait painter. But he was criticised from all sides, abandoned by his pupils, who preferred Ingres, and suffered more and more from neurasthenia. He finally committed suicide by throwing himself into the Seine.

HOPPNER John (London 4.4.1758 – London 23.1.1810). Hoppner wavered at first between a career in music and one in painting. He decided on the latter and an allowance from King George III enabled him to enter the Royal Academy in 1775. In 1782, his *King Lear*, of pre-Romantic inspiration, met with a measure of success, but he soon turned to portraits: in 1785, he painted the King's three youngest daughters and in 1793 he became the Prince of Wales's official painter. After Reynolds' death, Hoppner was, together with Lawrence, one of the most popular portrait painters of his time (*Portraits of Young Girls*, published in 1803; *Mrs Jordan as Viola*).

Like his contemporaries, he was fond of using chiaroscuro, rapid strokes that contrast light and shade. The decors in which he set his subjects tended to have a dramatising effect and the poses often reflected a slightly exaggerated sensitivity.

Paul Huet *The Ruins of the Château de Pierrefonds*. c. 1868

HUET Paul (Paris 3.10.1803 – Paris 9.1.1869). Pupil of Guérin and Gros, he was influenced first by the work of Géricault and was a friend of Delacroix. His career, nonetheless, took a very personal course. Attracted mainly by nature, he painted, as early as 1817, subjects along the Seine, on the Ile Seguin, then at Honfleur, Trouville and Le Tréport. He loved painting the sea (*Breakers at the Granville Point*, 1853, Musée du Louvre) or the unbridled elements (*Flood at Saint-Cloud*, 1855, Musée du Louvre). His friendship with Bonington introduced him to English painting and its influence is perceptible in his style. He also painted in the Fontainebleau forest but did not adhere to the Barbizon school. He made a very significant contribution to the evolution of landscape art in France, not only towards Romanticism but also the later development of Impressionism.

John Hoppner *Portrait of a Young Woman and a Young Boy*

INGRES Jean-Auguste-Dominique (Montauban 29.8.1780 – Paris 14.1.1867). The son of an ornamenter, Ingres wavered between music and painting before starting his training in the studio of the painter Roques in Toulouse. He went to Paris in 1797, worked in David's studio, entered the Beaux-Arts in 1799 and two years later won the Grand Prix de Rome for his *Envoys of Agamemnon* (1801, Ecole des Beaux-Arts, Paris). He did not leave immediately for Rome due to a delay in payment of his scholarship by the State. During this period, he produced some very fine portraits including those of the Rivière family which are in the Louvre. In 1806 he finally went to Italy where he discovered the work of Raphael to whom he remained passionately devoted all his life. He painted landscapes (*The Casino of Raphael*, Musée des Arts Decoratifs, Paris), portraits (*François-Marius Granet*, 1807, Musée Granet, Aix-en-Provence), nudes (*The Bather of Valpinçon*, 1808, and *La Grande Odalisque*, 1814, Musée du Louvre), mythological subjects

(*Oedipus and the Sphinx*, 1808, Louvre; *Jupiter and Thetis*, 1811, Musée Granet), and literary subjects (*Ossian* for the ceiling of the Quirinale Palace commissioned by Napoleon). Until this time, the works he sent back to Paris had not met with the success he hoped for and the resentment he felt kept him in Rome, and then Florence, until 1824. In that year he returned to Paris with an official commission from the Restoration government, *The Vow of Louis XIII*, which was widely acclaimed at the Salon and critically compared with the work of Delacroix. From then on, Ingres was held to be the absolute master of beauty and Classicism, in contrast to the colour and Romanticism of Delacroix. Ingres became a member of the Institut in 1825, was appointed Professor at the Beaux-Arts in 1829 and became its Director in 1833.

Jean-Auguste-Dominique Ingres *The Spring*. 1856

Jacques-Louis David *Portrait of Ingres*

After the critical failure of his *Martyrdom of Saint Symphorian*, he went back to Rome where he was Director of the Villa Medicis until 1841. On his return to Paris and until his death, he was finally and definitively recognised for his perfection of technique, his beautiful use of colour, his individual way of assimilating and adapting classical art, and the wealth and variety of his subjects. He was showered with official as well as private commissions, executed portraits such as those of the *Vicomtesse d'Haussonville* (1845) and *Madame Moitessier* (1856), and also the sumptuous nudes in which, setting all Classicism aside, he gave rein to the sensuality of his drawing (*The Spring*, 1856; *The Turkish Bath*, 1859–1863, Musée du Louvre).

IVANOV Alexander Andreyevich (St. Petersburg 16.7.1806 – St. Petersburg 3.7.1858). This painter's career is reminiscent of Man's pursuit of an impossible ideal. The main body of his work consisted of two vast compositions, *The Temple of Humanity* and *Christ's First Appearance to the People* (Tretyakov Gallery, Moscow) for which he made countless studies and in which one can sense the strong influence of Overbeck and of the Nazarenes whom he had met in Rome in about 1830.

Joseph Anton Koch *The Waterfall*. 1796

However, this ideal of purity was counter-balanced by his need for a kind of objective truth, in search of which he dreamed of travelling to Palestine. His work drifted eventually into a cold impotence.

JOHANNOT Tony (Offenbach 9.11.1803 – Paris 4.8.1852). Worked with his brothers Charles and Albert, and was one of the major exponents of Romantic book illustration. His mastery of woodcutting enabled him to introduce an element of fantasy to the mediaeval atmosphere he evoked so well, thus creating the so-called 'troubadour' style. He illustrated Walter Scott, Balzac, Vigny, as well as *The Story of the King of Bohemia and his*

Tony Johannot Illustration for *Cromwell* by Victor Hugo

Seven Castles by his friend Charles Nodier (1830). He collaborated on the magazines *l'Artiste, le Magasin Pittoresque, le Musée des familles,* and made engravings for *Paul et Virginie* (1838), *Manon Lescaut* and *Werther,* as well as for older texts brought back into fashion by the great bibliophilia of the early 19th century (*Don Quixote,* 1836).

KOCH Joseph Anton (Obergibeln, Austria 27.7.1768 – Rome 12.1.1839). Born in the Tyrol, studied at the Beaux-Arts Academy in Stuttgart, then travelled on foot through the Swiss mountains and along the Rhine before settling for good in Rome in 1795. He worked with the Nazarenes but escaped the full force of their doctrinaire influence. He enjoyed painting 'emotional landscapes' (*Waterfalls near Subiaco*) in which he presented a Romantic view of Nature.

He was impregnated with the teachings of the classical Roman landscape painters, but unhappily he lacked their qualities and their solid training: his concern was all too often merely for composition. Despite some of his technical weaknesses, he made his name with his landspaces (such as *Heroic Landscape with Rainbow,* Staatliche Kunsthalle, Karlsruhe).

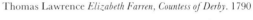

Thomas Lawrence *Elizabeth Farren, Countess of Derby.* 1790

LAWRENCE Thomas (Bristol 13.4.1769 – London 7.1.1830) The young Lawrence followed his father who worked in turn as a lawyer, customs official and finally as an innkeeper, to the towns of Bristol, Devizes, Oxford, Weymouth and Bath. His artistic talent was obvious from an early age and in Bath he received advice from the painter William Hoare. Lawrence practised portrait painting, first in pastels, then in oils. In 1787, he settled in London where he attended classes at the Royal Academy. He came to the notice of Sir Joshua Reynolds and found success at Court.

In 1790, he exhibited thirteen portraits, including those of the Queen, the Duke of York and Princess Amelia, and in 1792 he succeeded Reynolds as painter to the King.

Elected to the Royal Academy in 1794, his career as a fashionable portrait painter was one long success story. In 1814, he went to Paris to study the works in the Louvre but was soon recalled to England to paint a series of portraits which were to hang in Windsor Castle.

In 1818, he returned to Paris where he painted portraits of Charles X and the duc de Berry. While he was there, he met Delacroix who was a great admirer of his work. He died in London in 1830 of heart disease.

Although he occasionally tried his hand at narrative painting (*Coriolanus*, *Hamlet*, *Satan*), his career was first and foremost as a portrait painter: *Sir William Curtis*, *Lady Dover*, *Mary Palmer* and the official portraits: *King George IV*, *Pope Pius VII*, the *Duc de Richelieu*. His sensitive portrayal of women, picturesque settings and flowing, luminous brushwork mark him as a Romantic.

MARTIN John (Haydon Bridge, Northumberland 19.7.1789 – London 17.2.1854). Began his career painting porcelain and coats of arms on carriage doors. Settled in London in 1806 and exhibited at the Royal Academy Exhibition of 1812. Martin had the visionary inspiration, if not the breadth, of Blake (*Sadak in Search of the Waters of Oblivion*, 1812, Southampton Art Gallery). His audacity caused him some problems but his *Joshua commanding the Sun to Stand Still* (1816) brought success. He proceeded to produce large, haunting canvases of vast architectural perspectives, milling with minute figures bathed in light (*The Deluge*, *The Death of Moses*, *The Last Man*, *The Fall of Babylon*, *The Calming of the Waters*, *The Celestial City and Pandemonium*, *Belshazzar's*

John Martin *The Great Day of His Wrath*. 1852

Feast). His three great canvases, *The Great Day of His Wrath* (1852), *The Last Judgment* (1853) and *The Pastures of Heaven* (1853) are even stranger and more apocalyptic.

MERYON Charles (Paris 23.11.1821 – Charenton 13.2.1868) Meryon started his career as a naval officer before, in 1849, devoting himself to drawing and particularly to engraving. From a technical viewpoint, his etchings had incomparable precision and definition. His style was fantastic and visionary. His work was almost entirely devoted to Paris, but to a mysterious Paris, ingeniously evoked: a Paris of eerie winding alleys, fleeting shadows, and gargoyles in the shapes of monstrous animals. Between 1850 and 1855, he painted *The Apse of Notre-Dame* and the *Petit-Pont* (1850), the *Pont-Neuf* (1853), and *The Morgue* (1854). In 1862, he painted the *Grand Châtelet* and in 1865, the *Ministère de la Marine*, in

Charles Meryon *The Notre-Dame Gallery*. 1853

which strange flying machines and fantastic birds cross the sky above the Place de la Concorde. The dream is surreal, the seemingly peaceful city is taken over by a terrifying science-fiction nightmare. Meryon was, in fact, prone to attacks of dementia and was interned at Charenton in 1866, where he died two years later.

Jean-François Millet *Self-Portrait*

MILLET Jean-François (Gréville 4.10.1814 – Barbizon 20.1.1875). Born near Cherbourg, into a family of poor but relatively educated peasants. He initially taught himself to paint, then became apprenticed in Cherbourg to Mouchel, a pupil of David, and continued his training under a pupil of Gros before leaving for Paris in 1837. There he worked with Delaroche and haunted the Louvre where he studied the Italians, particularly Michaelangelo, as well as the French Classicists, notably Poussin.

In 1840, he submitted his first canvas to the Salon but it was rejected. He returned to Normandy and married, but was soon left a widower. He was already painting admirable portraits (*Portrait of Madame Millet, Louis Courtois,* and *Portrait of a Naval Officer*). Meanwhile, in order to earn a living, he painted genre scenes inspired by Boucher.

He spent a year in Cherbourg, married again and painted popular themes and genre scenes, such as *The Child Birdnesting* and *The Sleeping Seamstress*. In 1845, he

Jean-François Millet *Spring*

returned to Paris and to the start of the golden period of his career (*Saint John tormented by the Women, The Winnower, Haymakers resting by a Haystack*). The problems caused by the 1848 Revolution and then the cholera epidemic that raged in Paris prompted Millet to take his family and settle in Barbizon, where he was to spend the rest of his life, leaving only for a journey to central France in 1860 and two visits to Normandy. The main body of his work depicting peasant life dates from this period: *The Quarriers, The Pitsawyers, The Sower, The Sheepshearer, The Man with the Hoe, The Gleaners* (1857), *The Angelus* (1859). These last two, his most famous works, are also known for the very beautiful sketches he did for them. His work, with its thick and often sombre strokes set off with patches of light, had a mixed reception. Some were shocked by the 'triviality' of his rustic subjects and his sociological vision of man was only belatedly accepted. His 1867 exhibition finally brought success: he was named Chevalier de la Légion d'Honneur. He returned to Cherbourg during the war of 1870 (*The Little Church in Gréville*). Shortly afterwards, he was asked to partici-

pate in the decoration of the Pantheon, but he died before he was able to fulfil the commission.

Jean-François Millet *The Gleaners*. 1857

OVERBECK Johann Friedrich (Lubeck 3.7.1789 – Rome 12.11.1869). Studied in Vienna, then, after having founded the Lukasbund (Brotherhood of Saint Luke) with Franz Pforr in 1809, settled in Rome at the convent of Sant'Isidoro. There he founded the Nazarene movement which, with its aesthetic return to a solid and moral art worthy of the Middle Ages, reflected his own spiritual mood (he converted to Catholicism in 1813). Very soon, what had been a personal standpoint became an aesthetic doctrine: a return to the 'pure' Primitivism of the quattrocento. He took part in the decoration of the Casino of the Villa Massimi and in the painting of the Zuccaro Palace frescoes, commissioned by Bartholdy, Consul General of Prussia. His art as a drawer, however, (*Joseph telling his Dreams*, *The Foolish and Wise Virgins*) was no more than a pale pastiche of Raphael. That influence is even more evident in his painting *The Triumph of Religion in the Fine Arts* (1840, Städelsches Kunstinstitut, Frankfurt): he saw a kind of religious mission in art. But it was for his doctrine and his aesthetic position that he dominated the German Romantic era: despite an insipidity of execution, his ideas provided a clear underlying structure for artists of the time. This attempt at doctrinal novelty, allied with a reassuring conservatism, undoubtedly brought him much contemporary admiration.

Samuel Palmer *On the Hill*. c. 1826

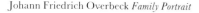

Johann Friedrich Overbeck *Family Portrait*

PALMER Samuel (London 27.1.1805 – Reigate 24.5.1881) Palmer took up watercolour when still very young and also assiduously studied the work of German and Dutch engravers such as Dürer, Lucas de Leyden and Elsheimer. He had deep admiration for Cox and Turner, but the influence of William Blake was to be decisive. Between 1826 and 1832, he gathered around him a group of like-minded painters in Shoreham. Drawn to literature, he plunged into mystical writings and occult works of German origin, though he retained a predilection for his compatriots, Wordsworth and Coleridge. He painted in oils (*Corn-Field by Moonlight with the Evening Star*, *The Valley of Vision*), but it was in his sumptuous watercolours that he produced his finest work (*In a Shoreham Garden*, c. 1829, Victoria and Albert Museum).

The strange link that he succeeded in forging between Nature, man and objects made him an extremely individual artist, outwardly calmer than Fuseli or Blake and more drawn towards a poetic vision.

within: the dramatic use of light, interplay of lines and planes, and adaptation of perspective, result in a striking suggestion of new worlds, of unsuspected interconnecting expanses. The eerie quality of his vision and the obsessive atmosphere of his accumulations of tangled ruins foreshadow the Romantic movement.

PIRANESI Giovanni Battista (Venice 4.10.1720 – Rome 9.11.1778). Piranesi followed a dual career as an architect and an etcher, and in both fields displayed visionary talents. He was first taught in Venice by his uncle Lucchesi, then went to Rome to study architecture, painting and engraving, and painted theatre scenery to earn a living. He returned to Venice to work as an architect but continued to travel around Italy drawing Roman remains, views of Rome, and the ruins of Herculaneum and Pompeii, all of which he was to use in his magnificent engravings.

In 1748, he published *Le Antichite romane de tempi della Republica*, his first collection of etchings, followed by over 2000 plates. Their apotheosis was the famous series of the *Carceri*, where the actual drawing suggests the space

PRUD'HON Pierre-Paul (Cluny 4.4.1758 – Paris 16.2.1823). Began his apprenticeship in Dijon with the founder of the museum there, François Devorge. Lived in Paris from 1780 until 1783 and then went to Rome where he stayed until 1788. He became friendly with Canova and discovered Antiquity by way of the Renaissance, particularly in the work of Leonardo and Correggio. Their influence is evident in his 'sfumato' technique.

He returned to Paris in 1789, became involved in politics

Giovanni Battista Piranesi *View of Pompeii*

Pierre-Paul Prud'hon *The Rape of Psyche*. 1808

Pierre-Paul Prud'hon *Josephine at Malmaison*

RAFFET Denis (Paris 2.3.1804 – Genoa 11.2.1860). Although mainly known as a lithographer, Raffet had a very successful aritistic career following his training with Gros and Charlet.

He was the Romantic painter who chronicled the great Napoleonic saga. His work is an exaltation of War, of the Year II and of the soldiers of Napoleon's Old Guard. He travelled throughout Europe and as far as Algeria in search of an inspiration which is more akin to that of the able reporter with an eye for the picturesque than that of a great painter (*Reveille, La Grande Revue*).

Denis Raffet *Episode during the Retreat from Russia.* 1812

and began a career as a portrait painter (*Portrait of Saint-Just*, Musée des Beaux-Arts, Lyon), but left the capital again during Thermidor. Back in Paris in 1796, he illustrated books for Didot, undertook a commission to decorate the Hôtel de Lanois and successfully exhibited his *Virtue and Truth descending on Earth* (Musée du Louvre) in 1799. He obtained the favour of Josephine and painted a highly Romantic portrait of her, a composition in which the mistiness of the setting captured the melancholy of the sitter, engraved in an exquisite 'sfumato'. He later succeeded in retaining the favour of both Napoleon and Marie-Louis. He then painted large works (*Justice and Divine Vengeance pursuing Crime*, 1808; *The Rape of Psyche*, 1808, both in the Louvre; *Venus and Adonis*, 1812, Wallace Collection, London). After the events of 1815 and the fall of the Empire, Prud'hon devoted himself entirely to portrait painting.

RAMBOUX Johann Anton Alban (Trier 5.10.1790 – Cologne 2.10.1866). Ramboux was quickly drawn to the doctrines prevailing in the early years of the 19th century. While he lived in Rome, he was a member of the Lukasbund, or Brotherhood of Saint Luke, founded by Overbeck. He made numerous copies of 15th and 16th century works, and these periods were to have a strong influence on his own art. He then went to Paris, where he attended David's classes, and on to Munich, where he was to spend most of his career.

Despite his Classical technique, Ramboux's art is that of reverie and the picturesque (*The Choir of Cologne Cathedral seen from the South-west*). He worked mainly with water colour because it was his preferred medium for copying Renaissance works. But, in a medium which usually entails greater precision, he sometimes worked in unexpected ways. In *Cologne Cathedral*, for example, the eye is first drawn to the solid architectural structure, underlined by scaffolding, but is gradually struck by the almost total absence of people. The gigantic mediaeval building stands out, unfinished, against a disturbing sky some

Johann Anton Alban Ramboux *The Choir of Cologne Cathedral seen from the South-west*. 1844

what reminiscent of Blake. The painting is in Neo-Gothic style, which transforms an architectural study into dreamlike fantasy.

REGNAULT Jean-Baptiste (Paris 19.10.1757 – Paris 12.11.1829). Worked in Vien's studio in Paris and in 1776 won the Prix de Rome for his painting *Alexander the Great and Diogenes* (Ecole des Beaux-Arts, Paris). In Rome, he studied Antiquity and the Renaissance, which were to influence his own art. His Neo-Classicism was much more attractive and mannered than that of David, with whom he was often compared. His inspiration raised from the religious (*Descent from the Cross*, Musée du

Jean-Baptiste Regnault *The Three Graces*

Adrian Ludwig Richter *Saint Genevieve*. 1841

Louvre), the historical (*The Death of Desaix at Marengo*, Versailles), the allegorical (*The Spirit of France between Liberty and Death*, Kunsthalle, Hamburg) to the mythological (*Io*, Musée de Brest; *The Education of Achilles*, Musée du Louvre). His delicate use of colour is proof of the ability of an artist who has been rather unfairly neglected, despite the fact that he succeeded in creating a happy marriage between Neo-Classicism and Romanticism.

RICHTER Adrian Ludwig (Dresden 28.9.1803 – Dresden 19.6.1884). Career began in Dresden when he came

to the attention of Prince Narichkine and was invited to accompany the Prince on his travels and paint. In 1823, the copyist Arnold sponsored him for a three-year stay in Italy. There he became deeply involved with the Nazarenes and particularly with Schnorr von Carolsfeld. He then returned to teach in Dresden. He was a landscape painter but, as for other German artists, mountains and lakes (*Mountain Lake in the Riesengebirge*) were for him the reflection of an inner vision. His treatment was rather dry with almost geometric use of cold colours. His drawings were superior and revitalised a Romantic vision of the urban landscape of mediaeval Germany.

ROBERT Hubert (Paris 22.5.1733 – Paris 16.4.1808). Robert's formative years were spent in Italy where his father, valet to the Duc de Choiseul, accompanied his master when the latter was appointed Ambassador to Rome. Robert was a friend of Fragonard and the Abbot of Saint-Non. He travelled widely within Italy making a great many sketches of monuments, ruins and landscapes. Influenced by the treatment of ruins of Pannini and Piranesi, he was to launch this style in France and become its master. His work thus consisted chiefly of more or less imaginary landscapes: even when his intention was merely narrative (*The Burning of the Opéra*, 1781, *The Demolition of the Bastille*, 1789, Musée Carnavalet, Paris), the anecdotal took second place to the imaginary. Some of his finest paintings resulted from a journey to Provence in 1783: *The Maison Carrée at Nîmes*, *The Pont du Gard*, *The Triumphal Arch* and *The Amphitheatre at Orange* (Musée du Louvre). His technique was based on rapid and precise strokes with expressive, often warm, colours

George Romney *Lady Hamilton as Cassandra*. c. 1785–1786

Hubert Robert *Ancient Temple*

ROMNEY George (Dalton-in-Furness 15.12.1734 – Kendal 15.11.1802). The son of a cabinet-maker, Romney first studied painting with a portrait painter, Edward Staele, in his native town. He began his career as a travelling portrait painter, then went to London in 1762 and produced compositions of a historical nature (*The Death of General Wolfe*). He went to France in 1764 and to Italy in 1773. In Rome he met Fuseli who was to influence him considerably. Back in London in 1775, he became one of the aristocracy's favourite portrait painters. His own favourite model for allegorical compositions was the future Lady Hamilton with whom he was very much in love and whom he painted as *Ariadne* (1785, National Maritime Museum, Greenwich). Towards the end of his life, he was commissioned by the engraver Boydell to paint *The Tempest* for his 'Shakespeare Gallery'. Romney was then practising the wash-tint technique and his style was resolutely Romantic. Drawn also to Milton, his final works became increasingly dramatic (*Nature unveiling herself to Shakespeare*, pen and wash, 1786). He lapsed into insanity some years before his death.

(*The Fire of Rome*), but, despite an apparent ease of execution, he took great care with his juxtaposition of architecture and elements of landscape (*The Wharf, Monk preaching among the Ruins*). The result was an art of fantasy where poetry and melancholy are constant reminders of the passing of time.

ROUSSEAU Théodore (Paris 15.4.1812 – Barbizon 22.12.1867). Started painting in the studio of the Neo-Classical painter Lethière and with the landscape artist Rémond. To get a better feeling for Nature, he set out on a 'tour de France' in 1830, starting in the Auvergne and going on to Normandy. At the same time, he studied the Dutch landscapes of Goyen, Hobbema and Ruysdael in museums. In 1833 he went to work with Huet in Saint-

Théodore Rousseau *Road in Fontainebleau Forest. Storm Effect*

Cloud and submitted *The Environs of Granville* to the Salon, followed in 1824 by *The Avenue of Chestnut Trees*. His work was rejected for several years in succession. He then settled in the Fontainebleau forest where he was joined by Millet, Diaz, Daubigny, Dupré and Barye to form a new school of landscape painting that became known as the Barbizon School. The 1848 Revolution marked his triumphal return to Paris with an official commission, *The Edge of the Forest of Fontainebleau at Sunset* (Musée du Louvre), but he remained a wanderer, ceaselessly studying the many landscapes he loved to visit. He liked harmonies of brown and green, pink and blue clouds, *contre-jour* effects, the structure of trees and the play of vegetation. His use of coloured strokes augurs the Impressionists.

Thomas Rowlandson *The Port of Knaresborough*, 1807

ROWLANDSON Thomas (London 14.7.1756 – London 22.4.1827). After his initial training at the Royal Academy, Rowlandson left London to travel around Europe. His stay in Paris was to have a decisive influence on his career. When he returned to London in about 1780, he abandoned portrait painting in favour of satire and caricature, becoming a ruthless analyst of society. He left a great many works, though many of then lack real depth. He illustrated Goldsmith, Fielding, Sterne and Combe, always looking for the picturesque element in the text. His best work was probably the rapidly drawn sketches for *English Story* and *The Humorist*.

RUNGE Philipp Otto (Wolgast 23.7.1777 – Hamburg 2.12.1810). Runge's work is important despite the brevity of his career. Having dabbled in commerce until he was in his twenties, he was able to devote himself to art with the help of a family allowance. He worked in Hamburg, Copenhagen and Dresden, where he became a friend of Friedrich.

He was above all a portrait painter who sought to portray the character of his subjects rather than their social rank (*Self-Portraits, We Three, The Hülsenbeck Children*). Like all true Romantics, he searched passionately for a link between Nature, landscape and passing time, life and Man's destiny. In a kind of return to primitivism, he conceived a series of paintings which evoked the cycle of human life, *The Hours of the Day*, which he dreamed of showing to the accompaniment of appropriate music in order to bring the spectator into communion with the universe. His technique, his sense of composition, his use of colour (*The Rest on the Flight into Egypt*, 1805, Kunsthalle, Hamburg), all stem from a single fundamental idea. His knowledge of literature and philosophy made him a central figure of that ambiguous art form in which the ideal is portrayed in a basically Classical structure. The essence of his intellectual development stemmed from his meeting with Ludwig Tieck, for whom art becomes plastic reality by means of the soul (*Seele*) and the emotions (*Empfindung*). Tieck disdained the mere copying of Nature, but saw in Nature's elements a means of translating his own feelings into signs that could be transmitted to others. Such a doctrine became a rule for Runge, and was reinforced by his contact with Schelling, and the Baroque painter and theoretician Jakob Böhm. Finally, Novalis had an even greater influence in that he brought Runge to perceive a mystical message in the slightest of Nature's elements. Thence Runge came to conceive his paintings as a sort of realisation of a cosmic rhythm, the canvas becoming a 'symbol for the eternal rhythm of the Universe'.

Philipp Otto Runge *We Three*. 1805

SCHEFFER Ary (Dordrecht 10.2.1795 – Argenteuil 15.5.1858). Born in Holland, Scheffer went to Paris in 1812, attended Prud'hon's studio and became a Court painter in 1830. He painted numerous portraits and many historical scenes (*Charlemagne subduing the Saxons*, 1837, Versailles); was a champion of the Hellenist cause (*The Suliote Women*, 1827, Musée du Louvre); and a chronicler of his time (*The Death of Géricault*, 1824, Louvre). Some of his contemporaries saw him as the leader of the Romantic school, but although his education and writing talent led him to illustrate Dante, Shakespeare, Goethe and Byron, his work was more Romanesque than Romantic.

Ary Scheffer *The Death of Géricault.* 1824

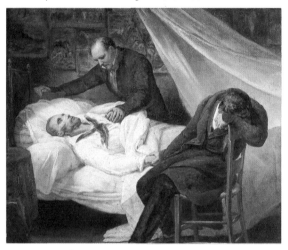

Julius Schnorr von Carolsfeld *Young Boy with a Reed Pipe.* 1822

SCHNORR VON CAROLSFELD Julius (Leipzig 26.3.1794 – Dresden 24.5.1872). Initially a member of the Nazarene group in Rome, where he re-discovered the ideals of the Italian quattrocento, but he was soon influenced by the far more expressionist German art of Albrecht Dürer. He then pursued his career in Munich, where he painted frescoes for King Ludwig I of Bavaria. If his drawings (*Portrait of Johann Schaffer von Leonhartshoff*) reveal a desire to adhere to Classical doctrine, the vigorous colour of his paintings (*The Family of Saint John visiting the Family of the Infant Jesus*) underlines the conflict between Italian and German influences. The *Portrait of the Painter Victor Emil Janssen* demonstrates the ambiguity of Schnorr's art: he was an avowed doctrinarian, but his temperament urged him to far more individualistic ends. The subject here is portrayed in three-quarter view, underlining the structure of the face, the parted lips, and the eyes gazing towards some unseen object. The dual ambition here is to preserve Classical structure while also seeking a new form of expression.

SCHWIND Moritz von (Vienna 21.1.1804 – Munich 8.2.1871). In his youth, Schwind moved in a circle of artists which included Franz Schubert. He studied under Nazarene painters such as Cornelius and Schnorr von Carolsfeld and began his career by illustrating the work of contemporary poets. He then turned to painting frescoes. He decorated the Royal Palace in Munich (1828), the Kunsthalle in Karlsruhe (1840–2), Hohenschwangau, Wartburg Castle (1855), and the Vienna Opera House (1869). He also made sketches for the stained glass windows of Glasgow Cathedral.

Although his style is related to the Nazarenes, his subjects came from German mediaeval legends: his colours are rather cold and his draughtsmanship perhaps a little too classical for his subject matter.

Moritz von Schwind *The Symphony*

Carl Spitzweg *The Poor Poet*

SPITZWEG Carl (Munich 5.2.1808 – Munich 23.9.1885). Spitzweg's earliest ambition was to become a pharmacist, but after a journey to Italy in 1832 and a long convalescence, he decided to take up painting. He loved the Dutch masters, worked with Hansonn and Edward Schleich the Elder, and began his career as an illustrator of genre scenes for the magazine *Fliegende Blätter*. He was a post-Romantic artist, but revealed a strongly poetic vision in his painting of cities, and was an exquisite painter of popular and genre scenes (*The Country Outing*). If his art occasionally ressembles theatrical scenery, in the main he was a fine colourist whose sensitivity came close to the most advanced trends of the late 19th century. He transposed his critique of the times into an antiquated setting, a sort of old fairy-tale Germany: his *Poor Poet*, curled up in bed and sheltering under a big umbrella from the rain dripping into his squalid room, is a fine illustration of this.

George Stubbs *Lion attacking a Horse*

STUBBS George (Liverpool 24.8.1724 – London 10.7.1806). Stubbs was without doubt England's foremost painter of animals. While earning his living as a portrait painter, he studied medicine and anatomy, and even taught anatomy at York Hospital. He travelled to Rome and, on his return, wrote and illustrated his *Anatomy of the Horse*, published in 1766. Horses were his passion: he studied and painted them not only as flesh and blood creatures, but as true objects of worship. Géricault much admired one of his set of three famous paintings of the *White Horse frightened by a Lion*. He also painted landscapes and hunting scenes but the horse was a constant and permanent presence in his work.

TURNER William (London 23.4.1775 – Chelsea 19.12.1851). Friendship with the watercolour painter Thomas Girtin and the opportunity to copy the Old Masters owned by a rich private collector initiated Turner in the rudiments of art. He also met Cozens whose researches into the quality of the air were to have a considerable influence on him. Turner entered the Royal Academy School in 1789 and the following year exhibited a view of Lambeth Palace. As a result, he was commissioned to provide views of towns for fashionable 'picturesque' publications and set out on tours of central England, Wales and Yorkshire.

In 1793, he exhibited his first painting in oils, *The Squall*; in 1796, *Fishermen at Sea*; and in 1797, *Sunrise*. In 1802, he travelled to the Continent for the first time, to France, along the Rhine, and to Switzerland. In 1807 he began to teach perspective at the Academy, having learnt the technique from Thomas Malton and the architect Thomas Hardwick. In the same year, emulating the 'Liber Veritatis' by Claude Lorrain, he began to publish his 'Liber Studiorum', a collection of engraved studies, which established a classification of types of landscape. In 1804, as a result of his success, he opened his own gallery. In 1819 he went to Italy which he was to visit

William Turner *The Burning of the House of Lords and the House of Commons*. 1834

William Turner *The Great Falls at Reichenbach*

William Turner *Self-Portrait*

VERNET Horace (Paris 30.6.1789 – Paris 17.1.1863). Painter of seascapes and battle-pieces, he celebrated all the events of the different regimes he lived under: Napoleonic history (*Napoleon I at the Battle of Friedland, The Massacre of the Mamelukes*); the reign of Louis-Philippe, from whom he obtained commissions for the Louvre and for the 'Battle Gallery' at Versailles; and finally the Second Empire, of which he became the official painter. He was very popular with his contemporaries, but despite his enthusiastic depiction of the military epic, his art is rather cold and superficial.

Horace Vernet *The Ballad of Lenore*. 1839

again in 1829 and 1840. He was a very reserved and misanthropic character. He became virtually a recluse and died in 1851 in lodgings on the banks of the Thames, where he was living under an assumed name.

His work can be divided into distinct periods. Initially influenced by Dutch painting, he was then inspired by Claude Lorrain until 1819 (*The Founding of Carthage, Sun rising through Vapour, Dido and Aeneas, The Ruin of Carthage*). After 1819, following a visit to Italy, it was luminosity that he sought. He began to use pure tones and above all, he gradually destroyed the image itself in favour of suggestions of light and colour. He played with weather, and its changing states – air, clouds, water and fog. Movement was evoked with a streak of colour. He later turned towards lyrical abstraction, which went beyond his impressionistic vision (*Fire at Sea, Steamer in a Snowstorm* (1842), *Sunrise with Sea Monster* (1840), *Rain, Vapour and Speed* (1844).

But he was not only an atmospheric painter: his interiors reveal him as an extraordinary intimist (*Interior at Petworth, The Concert, The Bedroom*). An avid reader, he was inevitably drawn to illustrate Milton, Byron and Walter Scott.

Obsessed by a desire to capture and render light, and bold in his disregard for all conventional principles of drawing, Turner is one of the great painters of all time.

VERNET Joseph (Avignon 14.8.1714 – Paris 3.12.1789) Initially a decorative painter, fascinated by the meridional light, he soon left France for Italy where he remained from 1734 until 1753.

On his return, he was commissioned by the Marquis de Marigny to paint twenty-four pictures depicting the great sea ports of France and was to spend the next nine

Joseph Vernet *Evening Landscape*

years travelling. He completed only sixteen, of which two – *The Port of Marseille* and *The Town and the Roads of Toulon* – are in the Louvre; the others are in the Musée de la Marine. In spite of the topographical and artificial requirements of the commission and some overprecision and rigour of execution, Joseph Vernet achieved a perfect balance between architecture and the elements that presages the art of Corot.

WILSON Richard (Penegoes 1.8.1714 – Llamberis 15.4.1782). The son of a clergyman, Wilson received a sound classical education which was to influence him deeply. He worked first in London with the portrait painter Thomas Wright for six years and then took up his own career in portraiture until he left for Italy in 1749. He spent a year in Venice where he became a friend of the landscape painter Zuccarelli. Then he went to Rome where he discovered the Classical landscape, and met Joseph Vernet who encouraged him to persevere in that field. Attracted by the sky and the light of Italy, he aspired to emulate the work of Lorrain and Poussin (*The Villa of Maecaenas at Tivoli*, 1765, Tate Gallery). All his landscapes thereafter were marked by this influence,

even those that he painted in Britain, notably his series of views of Mount Snowdon of which he made many copies.

Richard Wilson *On Hounslow Heath*. c. 1770

Sculpture

Few aspects in the history of art have been as misunderstood and neglected as that of sculpture in the Romantic era. For decades, it was regarded as falling somewhere between a rigid decorative approach, at best interesting from a technical point of view, and vulgar sentimentality. Countless of those marble and bronze groups, grand historical works, and plaster figures that caused such a stir at the international exhibitions in London, Paris and Vienna or at the Salons and spectacular exhibitions of the different aesthetic movements, ended up in the vaults of museums. Art historians and collectors only rarely considered them as objects that might one day be worthy of critical and scientific study.

We know that it is difficult to arrive at a definition of Romantic architecture and that we should really talk of the architecture 'of the Romantic period'. But is it possible to talk about 'Romantic sculpture'? Did Romantic sculpture exist in the same way as Romantic music and painting existed? Sculpture during the Romantic era developed in a completely different way from music, which was totally autonomous, or painting, still confined to a strictly limited surface. Sculpture throughout the Classical period had no autonomy. To understand the situation, a number of factors must be considered.

There were various problems. There was, for example, the concept of 'progress'. Belief in progress, which was characteristic of the 19th century, was quite naturally transposed into the field of architecture, as witness the use of metallic frameworks, and into that of sculpture. The art historian, Hans Gerhard Evers, drew the following conclusion which sheds some light on why our verdict on Romantic sculpture is so ambiguous:
'If, in the West, it was evident that in modern times, from 1500 to 1900, art was born of the need to observe Nature and to reproduce it in the work of art, then the absolute limits of what could be perceived or seen in the optical sense, and technically reproduced by means of colour or of stone, were achieved in the 17th century: for example, in the interiors of Dutch painting, as faithful as photographs, or in the marbles of Bernini and his pupils. In the 19th century, no artist possessed the technical competence to compare with that of the artists of that earlier era and art, from then on, could be perpetually different, perpetually new and creative, but it could no longer progress.'

Progress was thus not to be found in the realm of art, but in fields related to it, such as the natural sciences, the search for historical accuracy, social conditions of manufacture and technology. Inventions such as galvanoplasty, which brought with it the possibility of mass production, were of great importance to sculpture but had little effect upon it. It was only the advent of plastic materials in the 20th century which altered this situation. Contemporary sculpture would be unthinkable without these new materials. So on the one hand, there was a belief in progress which could not be fulfilled and which was attacked by the 20th century. On the other hand, there was, and is, a continual temptation to define Romantic sculpture between Classicism and Historicism in terms of the aesthetic principles of the 20th century, that is to say in terms of criteria and classifications which are totally inappropriate to the task. All too rarely have we tried to understand the specific forces which moved it and the fundamental questions that it was posing itself.

The focus of sculpture in that period was the human body. The image of man was inherited in all its inimitable beauty and clarity from Antiquity became the ideal. The theory of art in the 20th century committed a fundamental error of judgement when it referred to the 'imitation' of these Ancient models, instead of understanding the forces and the phenomena that were actually involved. In fact, the deepest of Romantic aspirations never took the form of mere imitation of Antiquity. On the contrary, at the very most, it had a nostalgic quality. Thus Goethe wrote in *Iphigenie auf Tauris* of 'the land of the Greeks that my soul seeks'; Hölderlin in *Hyperion* formulated a new Greek ideal; and the sculpture of the time did not in fact, copy Greek statues, which were actually only to be found in a few European cities and a number of royal collections, for example the sculptures of the facade of the Parthenon and of the temple of Aegina.

The sculptors, and their audience, reacted in a typically Romantic way: they created a new ideal Greek spirit, not a copy or imitation, but which expressed in a modern context their aspirations towards this idealised, almost sacred, Greek culture. The same forces which shaped the attitude of Karl Friedrich von Schinkel towards the sacred and the 'saintly' in architecture, also conditioned the development of Romantic sculpture.

Romantic Sculpture and Classicism

In an address to celebrate the birthday of the King of Bavaria in 1807, Schelling spoke of the relationship between Nature and the plastic arts. His theory that art aspires by preference towards that which is both most developed and most exalted – that is to say, the human body – was of crucial significance.

'Since you are not granted the power to seize the immeasurable Whole and that all the other creatures can be no more than isolated representations of it, it is only in man that the total being appears in its plenitude: so it is not only your right but also your duty to perceive Nature in its totality through man.'

But it was a knowledge of Classical sculpture that gave rise to this new image of man. German art terminology created the term *plastik* to define this Romantic sculpture, which took Greek Antiquity as its model. The concept was defined by Johann Gottfried Herder in his work *Plastik: Wahrnehmungen über Form und Gestalt aus Pygmalions bildendem Traum*, written between 1768 and 1770 and published in Leipzig in 1778. In it, he contrasted the 'optical' creation of painting with the 'tactile' creation of sculpture. It was this 'plastic' element which gave Greek art its domination over contemporary art.

In Schelling's philosophy of art, the term *plastik* was continually used. The *plastik*, which materialised their ideas in the form of realistic bodies, creating at one and the same time the real and the ideal, was sculpture: it realised their ideas through objects that were organic and totally independent. Goethe, in 1817, summarised this view once again: 'The chief aim of all *plastik'* (a word which would thenceforth be used in honour of the Greeks), 'is to materialise the dignity of man through the representation of his body'.

It was at this time that 'modern man', released from the religious and social fetters that had bound him for centuries, made his appearance and sought to recognise himself in art. His goal was not to recreate Classical form in and for itself, but the idea that lay behind it. Seen in this light, Romanticism is also a historicising style, like Classicism, concomitant with it and at the same time superimposed upon it; in other words, it is not, in the final analysis, to be seen as a fundamental contradiction, but as a different attempt to postulate new ideas.

It is necessary to use this knowledge to understand the predominance of architectural sculpture, the dependence of sculpture on architecture at the beginning of the Classicist period and its ulterior development. It was only when the bourgeois of the time had acquired an increased awareness of himself as an individual and had finally rejected any portrayal of an exclusively generalised and formal character in sculpture – gods, heroes, symbolic figures, metaphors, etc. – that he created a form which embodied this new attitude. Man's incipient isolation corresponded with the fact that sculpture was beginning to free itself of the rigorous bonds it had had with architecture, and that it still had with the other arts. Historicism did indeed try to integrate sculpture once more within its architectural concepts in order to realise its concept of the total work of art. But there is no question of the fact that this integration of sculpture was only successful on the surface. The irruption of political motivation into the idealised world of gods and heroes, the use of sculpture as a means of political representation, created a rift that was to prove impossible to mend.

When Schelling recommended bringing Antiquity back to life, he wanted to capture the idea of a Beauty that was external to the senses, to arrive, in and through the Greek ideal, at a conception of Beauty and Truth. It is, therefore, extremely difficult to make a satisfactory appraisal of Classicism purely on stylistic grounds: this would be to judge by a purely formal aesthetic to the detriment of the great expressive power of the art itself. 'The radicalism and the revolutionary element contained in many of the political and cultural declarations of the time are, paradoxical as it may seem, embodied, in as far as sculpture is concerned, in its absolute and exclusive orientation towards the Ideal in itself.'

One has only to look at the castles, palaces, villas, churches, chapels, tombs, monuments and monumental sculpture, to realise how this period must have swarmed with minor masters, while a few figureheads of the art assumed all but god-like status. When we talk of Classical sculpture, we think of the busts sculpted by Houdon, Schadow, Tieck, Canova, Zauner, Grassi, Schaller, and Fischer; these are in the main rather severe works, erected on pedestals or plinths and often installed in niches. Busts of the Emperor Napoleon, portrayed as Caesar, became an all but ubiquitous element of decoration. Vertical folds falling from the shoulder and across the chest invariably connected the head with the tectonic shape of the plinth. Bust portraits were to be found in every town, in princely mansions and in the houses of the aristocracy or the affluent bourgeoisie. The vast majority of them were the work of minor masters, very sound from a technical point of view, but owing more to meticulous craftmanship than to real artistry.

However, this is not without significance so far as the Classical period is concerned, because the scale of values was not supplied only by artists like Canova, Thorwaldsen and Sergel; the influence of the ideals of ancient Greek art was still perceptible. This influence raised the level of artistic quality in the minor masters' works. It is evident in religious and funeral sculpture, portrait and genre sculpture, animal sculpture, low and high relief, and in the tendency towards caricature that appears in artists as interesting as Jean-Pierre Dantan, in Pierre-Jean David d'Angers' famous *galerie des contemporains*, or in the thirty-six famous sculptures by Honoré Daumier, that is to say artists who exemplified a conscious opposition to bourgeois concepts.

The beginnings of Classicising sculpture can be traced back a long way. The excavations of Herculaneum and Pompeii gave rise, as they did in the field of architecture, to a wave of enthusiasm in the minds of sculptors for Antique proportions. The Marquis de Vandières, brother of Madame de Pompadour and Director of Buildings to the King of France, undertook the journey to the temple of Paestum, together with Soufflot and Leblanc, to see what it was that had captured the imagination of so many radical intellectuals. Johann Joachim von Winckelmann, in his very first essays, condemned the decadence of French taste as it had ruled since Louis XIV. In France, intellectuals such as the Comte de Caylus, Cochin and Diderot drew up the death certificate of the Rococo style, while artists like Edmée Bouchardon had adopted the Classicist approach as early as 1723. In Rome, Bouchardon copied the Barberini faun and portrayed a famous numismatist, Baron Stosch, bare-breasted and wearing only a drapery. He created for the Académie Française a *Christ carrying his Cross* which was characterised by its coldness of expression, its moderation of movement and its inner calm. From then on, the road was open to artists as sensitive as Pigalle, Falconet and Houdon, who were very close to the philosophers and encyclopaedists Voltaire, Diderot, d'Alembert, Helvetins and Rousseau.

Furthermore, it should not be overlooked that the theoretical foundations, as well as the teachings and the genesis of 'archaeological Classicism', issued not from Paris, but from Rome. In the cosmopolitan atmosphere of the papal city, the tone of the time was being set by the Germans, English and Scandinavians. Artists there all shared the same passionate ambition to bring back to life the ideals of Antiquity, and Antiquity which, with innumerable finds being uncovered by archaeological excavations, was almost being rebuilt before their eyes.

Canova, Sergel and Thorwaldsen

The Italian creative force – in as far as sculpture is concerned – seems to have increasingly atrophied over the second half of the 18th century. The French artists, who spent their Prix de Rome years in Italy, were fortunate because they could take advantage of a very strong plastic tradition which had never been tempted by the excesses of the Baroque, as it had in Italy, but had, on the contrary, always remained close to a Classical conception of proportions. In fact, in the Italian propensity for a Classical ideal they found an inspiration that corresponded with their own artistic temperament, way of thinking and Romantic aspirations.

For sculptors like Houdon, in particular, who worked in Rome from about 1764 to 1769, the discovery of Italian 'archaeological Classicism' acted as a decisive shock. The models of Antiquity provided Houdon, who had been a pupil of Slodtz, with an inexhaustible source of inspiration. But he also made anatomical studies in hospital dissecting rooms, which enabled him to vary and enrich his means of expression. Thus in some of his purely Classical works he is akin to Canova, while his more Romantic works place him closer to artists like Falconet.

Like Houdon, the majority of the artists then resident in Rome adapted themselves to Classical taste. Chaudet, who was to become the archetypal exponent of Imperial sculpture, Clodion and his pupil Marin, as well as a whole generation of French provincial sculptors, copied the models of Antiquity with something approaching frenzy while they were in Rome.

But in this group of interesting but rather mediocre sculptors, there was no artist of

Canova *Cupid and Psyche*. 1787–1793

genius who could have surpassed them all by synthesising and rising above the theory of Classical art in which late 18th century Rome was becoming increasingly bogged down.

Antonio Canova (1757–1822), a young Venetian who had previously worked in sculpture of Baroque tradition with Bernardi Toretti II, arrived in Rome in October 1779, at the age of twenty-two. He was immediately fascinated by the works of Bernini, Algardi and Rusconi. He undertook, as the result of a commission from Zuliano, the Venetian ambassador to Rome, a *Theseus and the Minotaur* in which the influence of the Scottish painter Gavin Hamilton, who worked in the Classical tradition, should not be underestimated. Hamilton was to advise him in the execution of his later works. Canova, who was able to capture and assimilate the most diverse of influences with astonishing speed, met with triumphant success with his works in a 'new Classical taste', in which he moderated his realist figurative style. His monument in honour of Pope Clement XIV ensured him an international career. Sculptures like *Cupid and Psyche*, *Hebe* and *Venus and Adonis* carved in perfectly polished white marble, in which barely disguised prudishness contends with insipid coquetry, made him the favourite sculptor of the princely courts.

In 1805, he arrived in Vienna where the Emperor Franz Josef II hailed him as the first artist of the Empire. The list of purchases of Canova's work for Habsburg, Napoleonic, Prussian and Vatican collections, as well as those of the aristocratic salons, is staggering. There was almost more work than his studio could handle. He sculpted gods, heroes, nymphs, naiads and busts, as well as some impressive funeral monuments, such as that of the Archduchess Maria-Christina in the Augustinian church of Vienna, which represents a funeral procession in marble inside a tomb shaped like a pyramid.

In 1783–1784, Canova met the Swede Johan Tobias Sergel (1740-1814) in Rome. Sergel had come there to accompany his king, Gustav III of Sweden, and to advise him with a view to forming a collection of Ancient works of art. He may have been unmoved by Canova's Classicism. Sergel had worked in Paris from 1758, where he was a pupil of Larchevêque, then, from 1767 to 1778, in Rome, where he had been strongly influenced by Antiquity. With his circle of Roman friends as intermediaries, he met the Nazarenes and, above all, Henry Fuseli. Fuseli's Romantic and fantastic imagination, which produced hallucinatory visions, had an overwhelming influence on Sergel. Evidence of this is to be found in works such as his *The Faun*, *Diomedes*, *Minerva* and *Cupid and Psyche*. Sergel's vigorous Classicism, which is corroborated by his fondness for Clodion and Bouchardon, had very little in common with Canova's style.

When, in 1779, Sergel returned to Sweden at the invitation of the King to take up the post of official sculptor to the royal court, he travelled via Paris. It was then that he produced the statue of *Otryade wounded*, which he hoped would open the doors of the Académie des Beaux-Arts to him. Dyveke Helsted suggested that 'the expressive Classicism of this work could have had a determining influence on David and, through him, on the development of the whole of French Classicism.'

Another Scandinavian considered 1797 the year of his 'Roman birth'. It was the year that Bertel Thorwaldsen arrived in Rome, where he moved in a circle that included young radicals like Carstens, and became a friend of the archaeologist Zoëga. Sergel already admired the earlier work of this former pupil of Abildgaard's and he had, albeit indirectly, served as a model for Thorwaldsen. For the young Dane, Sergel represented his exact opposite: Sergel's sensuality contrasted strongly with his own strict and harmonious, often linear style, which was very close to the theories and concepts of Winckelmann. Thorwaldsen never deviated from this peaceful and interiorised style.

In 1801, he created his *Jason and the Golden Fleece* in Rome. Canova, his senior by more than twenty years, was so taken with it that he helped young Thorwaldsen, who was then in precarious financial straits, to produce a larger version of the work. The success of *Jason* resulted in a flood of commissions. Thorwaldsen, in his studio in the Barberini Palace, soon became a local attraction that no foreigner visiting Rome would have missed at any price. He returned to Denmark in 1838 and his country greeted him with unanimous respect and admiration. His marble statues accorded so well with the ideas of art prevalent at the time that thousands of moulds were immediately cast of his work. His famous *Christ blessing the*

Throng was perhaps one of the most popular and it was certainly one of the 19th century's most frequently copied religious statues.

The formal canons of Classicism and the Romantic sensitivity expressed in Thorwaldsen's work were perpetuated in the work of his pupils. Ludwig von Schwantaler (1802–1848), a Bavarian sculptor who had studied under Thorwaldsen in Rome, was probably the one of his pupils who took furthest the synthesis of Ancient aesthetic principles and the modern ideal that Thorwaldsen held so dear. His statue of *Bavaria* which stands in front of the pantheon of Leo von Klenze in Munich, his statues at the northern portal of Cologne Cathedral, the ornamental facade of propylaea in Munich, and fountains such as that of the Emperor Ferdinand I in Vienna, are all works in which this harmony of concepts is expressed. It was, according to Oswald Hederer, 'the national historic consciousness of Bavaria caught between nostalgia for Antiquity and German mythology'. It was a sculpture that lay equidistant between the *Odyssey* and the song of the *Niebelungen*. In the work of Schwantaler, a precocious historicism was, rather unexpectedly, born of Thorwaldsen's Classicism.

Dualism and Monism

It is not altogether surprising that the enthusiasm for the sacred that was perceptible in the Classicism of Schinkel as well as in the work of Canova and Thorwaldsen, did not survive for the whole of the century. Very soon, a levelling and secularising force intervened. As the bourgeoisie gained ground in the political arena, as the power of the princes was gradually eroded in the wake of the French Revolution, as concepts like 'king or prince by the grace of God' tottered, and as what had been seen as the mission of the Germanic Holy Roman Empire lost its significance, so the images of idealised gods were deprived of their meaning and relevance. The bourgeoisie demanded a representation of itself – of its own history and political and social evolution. This necessarily entailed a rejection of apotheoses and classical metaphors. Simultaneously, historical personalities moved to centre stage: great leaders, monarchs and artists. But depiction of them had long since ceased to show an idealised image. They were shown in contemporary dress, and represented as individuals, warts and all.

With the growth of large cities and vigorous economic expansion came the need to erect more monuments, and it was at this time that historical monuments began to be secularised. The least evident aspects of these new works were the sacred element, and the subject's personality; for monuments to the glory of a nation's heroes, the uniform itself was enough. All kinds of soldiers bearing different arms surrounded those monstrous marble tombs that were erected in the dying years of the 18th century for the exhortation of the people.

How did this irruption of realism into the world of ideal forms come about – the rupture in French sculpture, for example, between ageing masters who, like Rude, were creating 'dualist' work and the younger ones, like Jean-Baptiste Carpeaux, whose work was 'monistic'? The rift was already tangible in the field of architecture, if only in the perception architects had of the materials to hand.

Too few studies have been made to enable any conclusive statement to be formulated about the tension which arose between Classicism and Realism, and which should be seen chiefly as a clash between a 'dualist' aesthetic principle on the one hand and a 'monist' principle on the other. However, a look at some examples will go some way towards providing an understanding of the forces which caused this tension.

Jacques-Louis David's painting *The Oath of the Horatii* is a typically dualist work: the

Bertel Thorwaldsen *Mercury about to kill Argus*. 1812–1822

figures are clearly drawn and of the utmost plasticity, shadows and light are clearly defined. The oath is clearly perceptible, the weight of its consequences is evident in the women's lamentations. A strict architectural framework, pictorially represented, holds the scene together. The contrast between a person and his surroundings is a characteristic feature of the structure of a dualist work. This conception of structure can also be seen in the work of painters like Philipp Otto Runge and Caspar David Friedrich when, in their paintings, they 'use the light to express something which is in contrast to the clearly defined contours of the forms they paint' (Rudolf Zeitler).

This dualism also appeared in sculpture, as, for example, in the *Christ blessing the Throng* at the Notre-Dame church in Copenhagen. Christ is represented like an ancient god in the cellar of a temple, but his gesture symbolises the very opposite: He is reaching out towards the onlookers. Such a gesture would have been inconceivable in an Ancient statue or any statue that had hitherto stood at a Christian altar. With this gesture, Christ, the fisherman of souls, comes closer to the worshipper in prayer. Thorwaldsen was in the tradition of Canova when he made his Christ a deeply introverted figure, waiting, kind, and withdrawn into Himself. Here too the dualist principle is evident: the Almighty is personified as helpful, almost friendly, a person 'of great physical power, but at the same time of great psychological reserve'. This dualist conception was to be very widely found from 1780 on, that is to say from the time of Canova's major works, in the architecture of Chalgrin in Paris and of Valdier in Rome.

But there were many artists who were opposed to this dualism: Sergel, for example, Schadow, and the English Classicists from 1800 on. The principle of monism evolved in a different way. Its exponents rejected the world of ideas, the concept of an after-life and the whole conception of art held by the heirs of Classicism, and set themselves up as the champions of a more or less radical Realism. The French Revolution had set in motion a series of political and social changes so vast that the new desire for rationality and emphasis on the character of the individual also brought about a new 'monist' train of thought. The latter paved the way for a new monist art, and for the launch of the new Realism which can be seen, for instance, in the works of Jean-Baptiste Carpeaux.

The question here, however, is not to establish precise divisions between dualist and monist standpoints, or to say that one particular artist conceived his work in a way that was exclusively monist and that another worked in a way that was still dualist. The aim is to find a means of explaining particular developments in European sculpture: in France, for example, the position of François Rude, who was typically 'dualist' and who caused a sensation with his figures for the *Marseillaise* at the Arc de Triomphe (1836), which were both dynamic and contained, and with the unbridled dynamism of his statue of *Maréchal Ney* (1853). With his Realism, he threw overboard all the aesthetic principles of Classicism – its harmony, its taste for balance, its polish and its discreet beauty. In his late masterpiece *The Awakening of Napoleon* (1845–1847), he created the perfect example of the historical work of plastic art.

Historicism

Classicism, Romanticism, Historicism, Dualism, Monism… How are the boundaries of these different phenomena and criteria of style to be defined? How do we place artists in one or other of these artistic categories? The borderlines are blurred. The links that tie the different trends within European sculpture one to another are many and varied. The events and experiences of the time, prevailing tastes, the evolution of political thought, all had a part to play, although much depended on the placing of commissions with certain artists for specific works.

To take the Albert Memorial in London as an example: the apparition of the Prince Consort is obviously an allegory and his ascension is staged with all the theatricality available to architecture and sculpture. But a Classical 'hieratic' approach would not have been appropriate for a work such as this, because it would have lacked sufficient individuality.

This is where Historicism comes in. A whole panoply of civilisation – leaning towards the didactic as do most of the 'cultural programmes' which generally figure on Historicist monuments – animates the frieze of the Albert Memorial. Continents, groupings of professions, industry, agriculture, and the crafts, surmount the figure of Prince Albert. One might say that it was 'the Historicism of a whole millennium depicted'. This phrase succinctly captures the positivist and eclectic attitude that made the creation of such monuments possible: for the most deeply rooted motivation that underlies the building of this type of monument is the desire to dominate and to summarise history itself.

The Albert Memorial in London can be contrasted with a Viennese work of much stricter design: the monument erected in honour of the Empress Maria-Theresa on the imperial forum created by Semper and Hasenauer between the Hof museums. Zumbusch, with this monument, showed himself a 'modern', that is a supporter of the historical Baroque movement of the 1870s. Areas of relief were still dominant in Rauch's work, but in the monument to Maria-Theresa the immense full-length statues stand completely detached, on perfectly polished pedestals and *trompe-l'oeil* staircases, between columns of worked bronze and niches: generals on horseback, men of state, scholars, artists of the time of Maria-Theresa. Ruling over them all, on a raised throne, is the Empress herself.

The 19th century created another style in the equestrian statue (or, strictly speaking, rediscovered and recreated it). An early example is the very imposing equestrian statue of the Emperor Josef II by Franz Anton von Zauner in Vienna (1795–1806). A conception of Empire and of Roman traditions, and a strict vision of Classicism all played a decisive role in Zauner's work; he had lived in Rome after winning a scholarship. He created for the city of Vienna a work of such importance that a whole generation of sculptors were to refer to and draw upon its inspiration (Kassmann, Kissling, Schaller, Schmelzer, etc).

In Munich in 1836, Thorwaldsen completed his exemplary monument to the Prince Elector Maximilian. In the years that followed, a whole series of significant equestrian statues appeared. These included the rather theatrical Duke *Emmanuel Philibert of Savoy* by Carlo Morechetti in Turin; *The Maid of Orleans* by Denis Foyetiers in Orleans; and *Godefroy de Bouillon* by Louis Eugéne Simoni in Brussels. Finally, between 1853 and 1859, Dominik Anton von Fernkorn created one of the most dynamic works of the genre: *The Archduke Charles as the Conqueror of Napoleon at the Battle of Aspern*. This statue became famous solely by virtue of its technical perfection, at a time when there was still widespread opposition to Historicism.

Goethe, Schiller, Dante, Molière, and Luther were among the many figures that the educated bourgeoisie of the 19th century endeavoured to glorify by erecting commemorative statues to them, and by this means to enhance themselves as upholders of their cultural traditions. Unlike the absolutist 18th century, when such statues were almost invariably placed inside buildings (for example, the magnificent bust of Voltaire by Houdon at the Comédie Francaise), now they were erected on the outside. No longer were squares and streets and vistas of grand avenues the sole preserve of stone prince and kings. Now the public wanted to see individuals, for their own sake, no longer dressed in idealised costumes, redolent of Antiquity and completely timeless. Their clothing was carved with great care for the minutiae of historical accuracy, thus reinstating the subject of the statue within his historical context. All the great political figures, from Garibaldi to Bismarck, were portrayed in this way.

The end of the 19th century was a period symbolised by the co-existence of extremes, particularly in sculpture. Almost at the same time as *Chaste Pandora* by John Gibson, appeared *The Tarentine Girl* by a pupil of Thorwaldsen, Pierre Alexandre Schoenewerk; the full-bodied sculpture of Reinhold Begas, *Venus and Cupid stung by a Bee*; and *Young Woman with Child* by Auguste Rodin; *The Woman reading* by Pietro Magni; *The Passionate Sleep and the Happy Dream* by Rafaello Monti; and the *Peasant feeding Child* by Jules Dalou, with its marvellous simplicity and sobriety. Also dating from the same period are the biblical figures by Johannes Benk for the

François Rude *The Awakening of Napoleon*. 1845

Ernst Rietschel *Bust of Rauch.* 1857   Jean-Baptiste Carpeaux *Bust of Garnier.* 1869

Votivkirche in Vienna; *Music* by Eugène Guillaume and *Dance* by Jean-Baptiste Carpeaux on the facade of the Paris Opera House; the procession of the bacchantes by Rudolf Weyer, in triumphant Baroque tradition, on the facade of the Burgtheater; and Viktor Tilgner's sculpted portraits, which brought about an increasing use of an impressionistic treatment of surface.

Everywhere there were contrasts; everywhere there was a mingling and blending of traditions and schools, and of attempts at aesthetic theorising. The use of perfectly polished materials in architecture, according to the fashion prevailing at the time, coexisted with vigorously modelled surfaces. A coquettish, almost lascivious, elegance reigned alongside contours that were clearly and sharply accentuated. A seemingly directionless *fin de siècle* ornamentation was juxtaposed with a modern, almost frenetic, passion for allegory. An unwieldy heaviness vied with the most ethereal and subtle sensuality.

In fact, there has been all too little research into the significance that this mass of contradictions might have had for the 19th century. But two portraits that were sculpted at the same time during this period may serve as an illustration of the depth of the chasm that had opened up: the bust of Christian Daniel Rauch, the great sculptor of Goethe's time, by Ernst Rietschel; and the bust of the architect and decorator Charles Garnier, by Jean-Baptiste Carpeaux. These two busts are proof of the fundamental differences that could exist between two works of the same period. Carpeaux's work is mundane and monist to the core, whereas Rietschel's looks speculatively to the past, in search of the ancient tradition of the classical portrait. It is as if there were a century between them.

ABART Franz (Schlinig, Switzerland 1768 – 1863). Served his apprenticeship with the sculptor Mathias Punt, then worked in Strasbourg and in Lucerne where his crucifixes met with much success. In 1804, took part in the Berne salon with *Nikolaus von der Flühe*, which won him a prize. In 1812, the State commissioned his *Three Graces*, and in 1828 he created one of his most famous works, the *Bears of Berne*, a group of sculptures which stands by the entrance to the town's Historical Museum.

ADÁN Juan (Saragossa 1741 – Madrid 1816). A pupil of José Ramirez in Saragossa, Adán went to Rome in 1765, where he was strongly influenced by Classicism. In 1768, the Academy of San Fernando granted him an allowance which enabled him to remain in Rome until 1776. On his return to Spain, he created sculptures for the cathedrals of Malaga, Lerida, Grenada and Jaén. He also created the *Hercules and Antaeus* fountain for the park of Aranjuez. In 1814, Ferdinand VII, who particularly admired his busts (*Charles IV*, 1797; *Marie-Louise of Parma*, 1797), appointed him Director of the San Fernando Academy.

BACON John (London 1777 – London 1859). Trained in his father's studio, then at the Royal Academy of Arts. Created busts, statues, Neo-Classical allegories and tombs, some of which are in Saint Paul's Cathedral and in Westminster Abbey: an example is his large marble tomb for General Sir John Moore, who died in 1809 near Corunna during the battle against Napoleon.

BANKS Thomas (London 1735 – London 1805). The son of one of the Duke of Beaufort's stewards, Banks was first influenced by Kent and the ornamental sculptor Barlow. As early as the 1760s, he was one of the first English Neo-Classicists and devoted himself almost exclusively to subjects from Antiquity. In 1770 he received a prize from the Royal Academy, and in 1772 a seven-year scholarship to Rome. Sergel and Fuseli were his closest friends. In 1781–1782 he worked in Saint Petersburg where the Czarina Catherine the Great acquired his *Cupidon*, executed in Rome. It was to become famous, but, like so many of Bank's other works, was later destroyed. Among his contemporaries, Reynolds remarked that his subjects were worthy of the ancient Greeks and Cummings wrote in 1830 that he was the first Englishman whose 'objectives were uniformly sublime and heroic' and who 'attempted to bring poetry to each of his compositions'. In 1805 Flaxman delivered *An Address on the Death of Thomas Banks* to the Royal Academy.

BARTOLINI Lorenzo (Savignano, near Prato 1777 – Florence 1850). Apprenticed initially to the marble-masons Pisani in Florence, from 1795 onwards Bartolini worked in alabaster. He discovered Flaxman's illustrations for Homer and Aeschylus. A great admirer of Napoleon, he enlisted as a drummer in 1796. From 1799 he lived in Paris. David accepted him into his studio; he was a friend of Ingres and Granet, and studied sculpture with Lemot. In 1802, Canova invited him to Rome, but Bartolini did not want to leave Paris. In 1808, he became director of the sculpture class at the Academy of Carrara. He created his major busts: *Madame de Staël, Ingres, Lord Byron*, and *Rossini*, as well as statues of Napoleon and allegorical works. His studies of the Florentine Quattrocento had a strong influence on his work, and his aspiration to revitalise Classicism with studies from nature make him appear as the direct antithesis to the rigorous Classical style of Canova. The most characteristic of his works are the *Carità Educatrice* (1824, Pitti Palace) and the tomb of Princess Czartoryski-Zamoyski (1837–1844) in the Salviati Chapel at Santa Croce in Florence. In 1839, he became a professor at the Academy in Florence. His *Nymph with Scorpion* greatly impressed Baudelaire at the 1845 Salon.

Lorenzo Bartolini
Faith in God.
1835

BARYE Antoine (Paris 24.9.1796 – Paris 25.6.1875). French sculptor who, from 1818, was Bossio's pupil at the Ecole des Beaux-Arts. He had long been a frequent visitor to the Jardin des Plantes when he first met with success as a sculptor, notably at the 1831 Salon, with his *Tiger attacking a Crocodile*; this success came in spite of the fact that the Romanticism of his subject was not in line with the standards of the academic jury. Animal artist *par excellence*, influenced by Géricault and Delacroix (he was also a painter), Barye was one of the greatest masters of French sculpture of the 19th century and the Romantic school. His taste for Antiquity, perceptible in his group representing *Theseus fighting the Minotaur*, is complemented by a perfect knowledge of anatomy, an acute feeling for life, and great powers of expression. He was, nevertheless, excluded from the 1837 Salon, and it was only in 1847 that his famous *Lion* was finally accepted.

BEAUVALLET Pierre-Nicolas (Le Havre 1750 – Paris 1818). A pupil of Pajou, Beauvallet soon excelled as a decorator, and in 1784 created the reliefs of the Salle des Gardes at Compiègne. A revolutionary, he exhibited his *Belisarius* at the Salon of 1791, sculpted busts of Marat and Chalier and, while in prison, drew political allegories. To decorate the *Fountain of the Egyptian*, he copied the Antinous on the Capitol in Rome. From a stylistic point of view, he is particularly close to Canova. In 1804, his *Fragments of Architecture, Sculpture, Painting in the Ancient Style* appeared.

Antoine-Louis Barye
Lapitha and Centaur

BEGAS Reinhold (Berlin 15.7.1831 – Berlin 3.8.1911). Pupil of Wichmann, Schadow and Rauch. During his journey to Rome in 1856, he met Böcklin, Lenbach and Beuerbach. He was deeply influenced by Renaissance and Baroque art and increasingly turned away from the Classicism of his teacher Rauch. In 1861, he became a professor at the new School of Fine Arts in Weimar. After spending time in both Paris and Rome, he settled in Berlin in 1865, where he was overwhelmed with commissions. He created monuments in the realist Neo-Baroque style (*Fountain of Neptune*; a national monument to the Emperor Wilhelm I; monuments to Bismarck and Schiller), statues, reliefs, and bust portraits (notably that of his teacher Ludwig Wichmann, modelled before 1860 and executed in marble in 1876).

BENK Johannes (Vienna 1844 – Vienna 1914). Studied in Vienna and in Dresden with Haehnel. His stay in Rome in 1870–1871 on the one hand confirmed his grounding in the academic and Historicist tradition, without which Viennese sculpture of the time of the Ringstrasse would be inconceivable; and on the other hand, opened him up to the influence of the naturalism that was evident in his work in Vienna from the mid-1870s onwards. He executed numerous sculptures for the great official buildings of the Ringstrasse (*Victories* in the Museum of Art and the Museum of Natural History, *Allegories* in the Parliament, the Burgtheater and the Votivkirche, tombs for the painter Friedrich von Amerling and for Johann Strauss, statue of the Emperor Franz-Josef). His masterpiece is the monument to the great leaders of the Teutonic order, completed in 1907, which must be ranked among the great architectural monuments of German Historicism. Benk's late work, especially his reliefs, is of a quality that 'recalls the haut-reliefs of the historical monuments of Northern Italy at the end of the 19th century' (Maria Pötzl-Malikova) and this is particularly of Balzico's equestrian statue for Duke Ferdinand of Genoa.

BEYER Wilhelm (Gotha 27.12.1725 – Vienna 23.3.1806). Studied architecture in Paris and then painting in Rome where he also trained as a sculptor. After his return to Germany, joined the Ludwigsburg porcelain works where he worked as a designer. In 1768 he was already working in Vienna where, in 1770, he became 'painter of the Court and sculptor' and where he entered the Academy. Beyer is known above all for his Neo-Classical garden sculptures in the park of Schönbrunn castle (1773–1781), where he contrived to combine Baroque allegory with Historicism, in tune with bourgeois taste. Beyer's collaborators at Schönbrunn were Johann Martin Fischer, Anton Grassi, Johann Baptist Hagenauer and Franz Anton Zauner.

BOSIO François-Joseph (Monaco 19.3.1768 – Paris 29.7.1845). First studied under Pajou but was above all influenced by the latter's teacher, Canova. Bosio received a commission from Denon for the reliefs on the Place Vendôme column in Paris. Following a bust of the Empress Josephine, there were more commissions: statues of Cupid, Aristides, Hercules and Achelous. During the period of the Restoration, he taught at the Ecole des Beaux-Arts, was ennobled and became First Sculptor to the King. Among his finest works are the sculptures of *Henri IV as a child*, the *Quadrige du Carrousel* and *Louis XIV on horseback* in the Place des Victoires, Paris.

CANOVA Antonio (Possagno, near Treviso 11.11. 1757 – Venice 13.10.1822). Worked initially with his father, a stone-cutter, then went to Venice in 1768

Antonio Canova *Tomb of the Stuarts*. Detail

Antonio Canova *Pauline Borghese*. 1804–1808

where he was a pupil of Toretti II and opened his own studio in about 1775. In 1779, he left for Rome and joined the international circle of artists which surrounded Gavin Hamilton. As a result of the artistic discussions there, he turned away from the late Baroque school and attempted to develop an uncompromisingly idealistic style. The group *Theseus and the Minotaur* (Victoria and Albert Museum) was perhaps the most important response to the incitement contained in the theoretical writings of Winckelmann, which upheld the classical values of proportion, noble simplicity and calm grandeur. Canova was commissioned to create the tombs of Popes *Clement XIV* (completed in 1787) and *Clement XII*, works which made him famous throughout Europe. The Roman sculptors felt victimised by his success and reacted energetically by preventing his election to the Accademia di San Luca until 1800. He was nonetheless elected as its President in 1810 and as President for Life in 1814. Showered with honours and prizes, Canova used a considerable part of his income to help gifted students. Finally, the Pope elevated him to the rank of *Cavaliere* in 1801 and in 1816 made him Marchese d'Ischia, after Canova had played a decisive role

in bringing home to Italy the art treasures carried off by Napoleon. The Emperor Franz II, who was a great admirer of his, tried, as from 1805, to persuade him to settle in Vienna and gave him the rank of an Austrian knight. But Canova refused. He also rejected an offer from Catherine the Great of Russia, just as he had refused Napoleon on the occasions of visits to Paris in 1802 and 1810. Even though, during the Empire, he had worked for nearly every member of the Bonaparte family, he always retained the favour of the Habsburgs and the Czars.

Canova had adopted Winckelmann's dictum: 'The Muses do not care for terrifying spectres', which he applied even when he was working on tombs or representing death. Thus the *Spirit of Death* on the tomb of *Clement XIII* (1787–1792) at Saint Peter's in Rome is a handsome youth adopting an elegaic pose, obviously copied from the *Apollo* of the Belvedere. For Canova ancient models were a vital source, even if he did not always copy them and even if there is sometimes a hint of the Rococo in the turn of a head or the carving of curls. He completed about 168 works, including monumental groups like *Theseus and Chiron*, for which the Emperor Franz had the *Temple of Theseus* built in Vienna; the gigantic tomb of Archduchess Maria-Christina in the Augustinerkirche in Vienna; exquisite sculptures like *Venus and Hercules*; terracotta models as fine and delicate as *Cupid and Psyche* (1787, Museo Correr, Venice); and his *Polyhymnia* in marble (1816, Hofburg, Vienna).

CARPEAUX Jean-Baptiste (Valenciennes 11.5.1827 – Château Bécon, near Asnières 11.10.1875). From 1842, was a pupil at the Royal School of Drawing and Mathematics in Paris, where he was for a time taught by François Rude. From 1846, he was a pupil of Duret at the Académie des Beaux-Arts. In 1850, he won the Académie's medal of honour and, in 1854, the Prix de Rome. During his five-year stay in Rome, he acquired his char-

acteristic style. He created the group *Ugolino and his children*, exhibited at the Villa Medicis in 1862, in which all his sensualist and anti-academic tendencies were already apparent. The years between 1866 and 1869 saw the creation of his famous *Dance* for the facade of the Paris Opera House. Originally the sculptors Cavelier, Jouffroy, Guillaume and Perraud had been commissioned to execute the four groups (*Dance*, *Harmony*, *Music* and *Opera*) which were to decorate the building, but Cavelier withdrew due to pressure of work. Carpeaux first chose *Opera*, but in 1865 the architect Charles Garnier commissioned him to do *Dance*. In 1871 Carpeaux left for London and did not return until after the revolutionary disturbances were over.

Critical opinion has seen Carpeaux's work as the only sculpture of significance of the whole Opera building, and he himself has been considered the most interesting sculptor of the period of the Second Empire because of his sensual, erotic approach and his rejection of the academic eclecticism of the time. He was alone in defying Garnier, who demanded that artists adhere strictly to his typically Historicist and pedagogic sculptural programme. Carpeaux's work is free, dynamic, and almost

Jean-Baptiste Carpeaux *Dance*

Jean-Baptiste Carpeaux *The Three Graces*

impressionistic: this can be seen in those of his works that remain – at the Opera in Paris, in the Louvre and at the Glypothek in Copenhagen. It reached the point where he quarrelled with Garnier and a public scandal ensured. The basis of this conflict is evidence of the tensions between architecture and decorative Neo-Baroque sculpture, inspired by Rubens and Bernini, which became increasingly difficult to overcome in the 19th century.

CERACCHI (or CIRACHI) Giuseppe (Rome 1751 – Paris 1801). Won the Accademia di San Luca prize in 1771. Having executed a bust of *Baron Firmians*, Governor of Lombardy in Venice, he left on the latter's recommendation for London, where he fulfilled decorative commissions for Carlini, Robert Adam (*Somerset House*) and William Chambers. Between 1776 and 1779, twelve of his best works were exhibited at the Royal Academy in London. In 1780, he went to Vienna on the recommendation of the Austrian ambassador, Belgiojoso, whose bust he had made in 1779. In 1782, the Emperor Josef II awarded him 50 ducats a month; in 1784, he married in Vienna. After stays in Rome and Berlin, Ceracchi went to America where he created many busts, notably those of *Jefferson* and *Washington*. He returned to Paris where, as a revolutionary, he became implicated in a plot against Napoleon and was guillotined in 1801. Ceracchi drew his inspiration mainly from Antiquity and cultivated a very smooth, cold style (busts of *Sir Joshua Reynolds*, 1778; *Prince Kaunitz*, 1780; *Emperor Josef II*, 1783).

CHAUDET Antoine-Denis (Paris 31.3.1763 – Paris 19.4.1810). Pupil of Stouf and Gois, won a prize at the age of twenty-one for his bas-relief *Joseph sold by his brothers*. From 1784 to 1788, worked in Rome where he joined Canova and his circle and was initiated in the rigours of Neo-Classical aesthetics. In 1789, he was a candidate for the Académie Royale, but was eventually rejected. During the Revolution he collaborated in the decorative sculptures for the Panthéon, illustrated books, and designed medallions. *Cyparisse, Oedipus and Phorbas* and *Cupid with butterfly* were his greatest successes. Chaudet's bust of *Napoleon, First Consul* was accepted as an official portrait. In its wake came some major commissions: statues in ancient style, bronzes for the Place Vendôme, a statue of *Napoleon* for the facade of the Palais Bourbon, reliefs at the Louvre, etc. Four weeks before his

death he was appointed Professor at the Ecole des Beaux-Arts. Chaudet's success rested on the elegance of his hellenistically inspired forms. His official works often seem massive and powerful, while his private works often possess a subtle and gentle grace. According to Gérard Hubert, he was France's leading exponent of Neo-Classical idealism, in the style of Canova.

CHINARD Joseph (Lyon 1756 – Lyon 1813). In 1784 in Rome won the prize of the Accademia di San Luca for his sculpture *Perseus freeing Andromeda*, a work which revealed his love of Antiquity, but also his reserved attitude towards Canova. Imprisoned in Rome for his anti-religious and pro-Revolutionary ideas, he then returned to Lyon where he was put in prison as a reactionary. In 1795, he became a member of the Institute. He lived in turn in Italy, Marseille, Paris and Lyon. After executing his bust of *Madame Récamier*, he was in great demand as a portraitist (*Empress Josephine*, *Prince Eugène* etc). He also took part in the decoration of the Arc de Triomphe du Carrousel and other projects.

CLODION (Claude MICHEL) (Nancy 20.12.1738 – Paris 28.3.1814). Clodion's father was First Sculptor to the King of Prussia, his mother was one of the Adam family of sculptors. In 1754, he worked in the studio of his uncle Lambert-Sigisbert Adam, and then with Pigalle. He competed three times for the Prix de Rome and won it in 1759; and in 1762 he went to Rome where he worked for nine years. Catherine II tried in vain to bring him to Saint Petersburg. In 1773, he was a member of the Académie Royale and exhibited at the Salon until 1810. He made designs for the Sèvres and Niderviller porcelain factories. From 1806 to 1809, he worked on the decoration of the Grande Armée column (Vendôme column) and on a relief, *Napoleon's entry into Munich*. Clodion is best known for his reliefs and terracotta figures of nymphs, bacchantes, satyrs and groups of children and animals. His terracotta figures in Egyptian style, inspired by an account of Napoleon's travels in Egypt caused a sensation.

DALOU Aimé Jules (Paris 31.12.1838 – Paris 15.4.1902). After training with Duret at the Ecole des Arts Décoratifs, was admitted to the Ecole des Beaux-

Aimé Jules Dalou *Peasant feeding Child*. 1873

Canova, who influenced his work and who called him 'il beato'. He became an honorary member of the academies of Milan and Bologna. From 1790 to 1794, he taught at the Karlsschule and in 1794 executed a portrait of Schiller. In 1808, his house became the intellectual centre of Stuttgart ("Danneckerei"). Canova came there in 1815 and Thorwaldsen in 1819. Ever since his stay in Rome, Dannecker had been entranced with the balanced beauty of the sculptors of Antiquity, which he constantly attempted to 'translate'. Canova's idealism dominated his youth, while later he tended more towards the realistic. Among his most impressive works, apart from the 1794 bust of *Schiller*, are the bust of *Johann Caspar Lavater* (1802–1805), *Ariadne on the Panther* (1803–1814), *Ceres in mourning* (1818–21) and the versions of *Christ* (1817–1832). The first of these had been commissioned by Elizabeth of Russia and was executed in marble in 1823, while the second (1827–1832), for the Thurn and Taxis chapel of the Saint Emmeram church in Regensburg, was partly the work of Dannecker's favourite pupil, T. Wagner.

DANTAN Jean-Pierre (Paris 8.12.1800 – Baden-Baden 12.3.1869). Studied at the Ecole des Beaux-Arts and in Rome. Dantan devoted himself almost exclusively to the sculpting of portraits and to caricature. Works and miniatures such as *Franz Liszt at the Piano*, where the expressiveness seems almost exaggerated, are characteristic. The majority of his work is in the Musée Carnavalet in Paris.

Arts through Carpeaux's offices. 1861 saw his first Salon success and in 1871 he went to London as a political exile. In 1899, the monument *Triumph of the Republic* which he had worked on since 1880, was inveiled in the Place de la Nation. Dalou created many statuettes, of which the most convincing are his works of a domestic nature, rather than those with a political motive. One of his finest works is *Peasant feeding Child* (Victoria and Albert Museum).

DANNECKER Johann Heinrich von (Stuttgart 15.10.1758 – Stuttgart 8.10.1841). Pupil at the Karlsschule in Stuttgart, and a friend of Schiller. in 1780, he was made Court sculptor, and in 1783 went to Paris where he worked in Pajou's studio. While in Rome, from 1785 to 1789, he joined the circle of artists around

DAVID D'ANGERS Pierre-Jean (Angers 12.3.1788 – Paris 5.1.1856). Studied in his father's studio, then in drawing classes with Marchand and Delusse at the Ecole Centrale, and completed his studies in 1808. Worked on the decoration of the Louvre under Philippe-Laurent Roland and Jacques-Louis David. In 1811, David won the Prix de Rome and lived in Italy until 1815, where he was decisively influenced by Canova. Fame arrived in 1816 with his statue of *Prince Condé*, made for the Pont de la Concorde. He began to teach in 1816. David d'Angers also had literary interests and felt drawn to Romanticism: he began to write some very interesting notes for a theory of art during his second visit to England in 1828, and while on a trip to Germany in 1829 was influenced by his discussions with Goethe and Tieck. A particular characteristic of his work is the care he took to ensure that his subjects wore clothes that befitted their time: this certainly accounted for the success of his countless busts (close to 150, and including *Goethe, Tieck, Rauch, Thomas Jefferson, Gutenberg*), of his statues, reliefs and

David d'Angers *Tympanum of the Panthéon*. Paris

medallions of well-known personalities. But he also created many figures in antique style, including nudes wearing Neo-Classical draperies, like his *Young Greek, Bonchamp* and *Racine*. In 1848, he was a *député* for a district of Paris and also a member of numerous Academies, in Rome, Berlin, London and New York. Among his major works are the reliefs on the pediment of the Panthéon and for the Arc de Triomphe in Marseille.

DRAKE Johann Friedrich (Pyrmont 23.6.1805 – Berlin 6.4.1882). In 1827, entered Rauch's studio as a pupil and later became the master's assistant. He received his first important commissions thanks to Rauch's good offices. His stay in Italy (1836–1837) and a visit to Thorwaldsen helped to establish his style as a bourgeois variation of monumental sculpture in the Neo-Classical tradition. King Friedrich-Wilhelm was his patron in Berlin: among his major works are the monument for Friedrich-Wilhelm III of Prussia in the Tiergarten in Berlin (1849) and the colossal *Victory* on the Victory Column in Berlin.

ESTE Antonio d' (Venice 1754–1837). D'Este first studied under Toretti, then in 1787 followed Canova to Rome to become his assistant. He soon attracted attention to himself for his very sensitive bust portraits: he made five for the Secretary of State, Cardinal Consalvi and his Protomoteca Capitolina in Rome, and then a monument for Cardinal Rezzonico at the Lateran. In 1810, he became a member of the Accademia di San Luca, and finally Director of the Vatican Museum. His work *Memorie della vita di Antonio Canova* (published in 1864) was an important contribution to the theory of art.

FALGUIÈRE Alexandre (Toulouse 1831 – Paris 1900). From his teacher Carpeaux, learnt the sensitive qualities of sculpture and an anti-academic attitude to material and form. Like his co-disciple, Jules Dalou, he sought, by means of a powerful and individualistic style, to re-animate the study of reality, which the academic style had made sterile. His best work is the monument to *Balzac* in Paris.

FERNKORN Anton Dominik (Erfurt 17.3.1813 – Vienna 16.11.1878). Studied sculpture and bronze casting at the Stiglmaier foundry and at the Munich Academy. In 1840, he settled in Vienna. He obtained his first major commission in 1853: the equestrian statue of *Archduke Charles* who had conquered Napoleon (cast in 1859). In order to fulfil his artistic ambitions, he opened an ore foundry on the Gusshausstrasse in 1856, financed by the State and with himself as Director. It was here that almost all of the great sculptures of the Ringstrasse were to be cast. Fernkorn was the technical instigator of the new wave of Austrain monumental sculpture, in Neo-

Baroque and realist style. His important works also include the monument to Prince Eugène, the fountain *Saint George and the Dragon* (cast in 1853) for the Viennese palace of Prince Montenuovo, and the monumental fountain under the glass dome of the Bank of Austria-Hungary in Vienna, built by Ferstel. Fernkorn died insane in 1878.

Dominik Anton Fernkorn *Archduke Charles*. 1853–1859

FISCHER Johann Martin (Bebele, near Füssen in the Allgäu 1740 – Vienna 1820). He worked in Vienna from 1760 and studied at the Academy with Schletterer from 1762 to 1766. In 1780 he solicited the post of Professor of Sculpture and in 1785 the post of sculptor to the town planning department of the Court. In 1785, he entered the Academy; in 1786 he became Professor of Anatomy, in 1806 Professor of Sculpture and in 1815 Director of the Academy. Fischer first collaborated with Beyer on the sculptural programme for the park at Schönbrunn. In the very complex spatial design of his sculptures, there is

no mistaking the very strong influence of Georg Raphael Donner. It was only gradually that he strove to attain a classical harmony, a softening of the very sharp edges of his folds and an exaggerated lengthening of his faces. Among his most impressive works are the reliefs in lead (*Orestes and Pylades*, c.1786), *Hygeia* (1786) in front of the Josephinum Canevales in Vienna, the fountain statues of *Saint Joseph* and of *Leopold* in Vienna and the allegorical monumental sculptures *The Loyalty of the Austrian Nation towards the Emperor and the Fatherland* and *Agriculture* (1812), in which he combined the ideals of ancient sculpture and feeling – which had been totally lost in Vienna – for Baroque volume. He thus maintained the tradition that was to gain the ascendant once more at the end of the 19th century.

FRÉMIET Emmanuel (Paris 6.12.1824 – Paris 10.9.1910). A nephew of François Rude, Frémiet was also his pupil from 1840. Through his work modelling anatomical preparations for the Ecole de Médecine Museum, he developed particular precision in the representation of anatomy, which won him great success, especially with his animal sculptures, which were realistic and expressive. In 1887 his *Woman carried off by a Gorilla* was the great attraction of the Salon. In 1875, he became a professor at the Natural History Museum in Paris and in 1892 a member of the Académie des Beaux-Arts.

Emmanuel Frémiet *Orang-utan strangling a Native of Borneo*. 1893–1895

GIBSON John (Gyffin, Conway, Caernarvonshire 19.6.1790 – Rome 27.1.1866). Having worked as a wood sculptor in Liverpool, Gibson went to Rome on John

133

Flaxman's advice and studied for three years with Canova at the Accademia di San Luca. Canova introduced him to Thorwaldsen, whose work increasingly attracted him. In 1826, he became an honorary member of the Bologna Academy, in 1829 of the Accademia di San Luca and in 1839 of the Royal Academy in London. He caused a sensation with his experiments with the colouring of his classical statues in the ancient style. In 1851–1855, he produced his famous *Tinted Venus*, between 1844 and 1861, a series of statues of Queen Victoria, and in 1855–1856, the sumptuous *Pandora* for the Duke of Wellington, who rejected it. Gibson was regarded as the greatest English sculptor of the 19th century.

GUILLAUME Jean-Baptiste-Claude-Eugène (Montbard 1822 – Rome 1905). A pupil of Pradier at the Ecole des Beaux-Arts, where he studied the academic style. In 1845, he won the Prix de Rome and studied Baroque and Neo-Classical sculpture there for three years. From 1852 onwards, he exhibited every year at the Paris Salon. He received some major commissions, became a member of the Institut de France and in 1864 director of the Ecole des Beaux-Arts. In 1869, he was made an honorary member of the Berlin Academy of Fine Arts, as his work *Music* on the facade of the Paris Opera House (1867) was seen as an important influence on the Berlin school of sculpture, with its Neo-Baroque tendencies. In 1878, he was made director general of the Beaux-Arts and in 1891, director of the Ecole in Rome. In 1896, he wrote his *Essai sur la théorie du dessin et de quelques parties des arts*.

HAGEMANN Karl Friedrich (Berlin 1773 – Berlin 1806). Caused a sensation at the Berlin Academy from 1795 to 1797 with his very successful copies of Ancient works. Between 1797 and 1804, influenced by his stay in Rome and by Thorwaldsen's studio, he executed several mythological groups. On his return to Berlin, he became Gottfried Schadow's collaborator and worked notably with Rauch and Ridolfo Schadow on the stucco reliefs of Schadow's house. There he met some of the most important artists of the next generation of sculptors, including Friedrich Tieck, Karl Wichmann, Christian Daniel Rauch, Ludwig Wichmann, Emil Wolff and Heinrich Kaehler.

HILDEBRAND Adolf von (Marburg 6.10.1847 – Munich 18.1.1921). Served his apprenticeship in Zumbusch's studio, worked with Siemering in Berlin from

1869, then started his own studio and settled in Italy in 1872. Hildebrand's work was influenced mainly by the Classical tradition of Schadow, the picturesque style of Siemering and Rauch's last school. Like Reinhold Begas, who had shortly beforehand discovered Neo-Baroque style in Rome, Hildebrand, thanks to Hans von Marées, arrived at a tectonic and plastic Neo-Classical style which drew mainly on archaism. The aim was to purify sculpture of all pictorial influences by using the laws of Antiquity and of the first Italian Renaissance; to overcome naturalism with a reduction of form and content, and to replace the momentary and the impressionistic, with universal ideals. Hildebrand wrote: 'Every natural phenomenon as a singular instance must be transposed into a universal instance.' So he attempted to conquer the realist element in Neo-Baroque art. Hildebrand's masterpiece is the *Wittelsbach Fountain* in Munich.

HOUDON Jean-Antoine (Versailles 20.3.1741 – Paris 15.7.1828). Trained at the Académie Royale, and in

Jean-Antoine Houdon *Voltaire*. 1781

1761, while studying with Slodtz, won the Prix de Rome. He left for Rome in 1764 and stayed there until 1768. In 1771, he was the guest of the Duke of Saxe-Coburg-Gotha; and in 1785, travelled to America to study his model for the monument of *Washington* in Richmond, Virginia, which was executed in marble between 1790 and 1796. He became a member of the Académie in 1777 on the strength of his marble statue of *Morpheus*. His funeral monuments and commemorative statues became famous, especially those of *Voltaire* and *Rousseau*. These monuments have a vivid realism: Voltaire, for example, is sitting in his chair, clearly in a bad temper: the mood of a moment captured and preserved. Houdon had started work on the statue in 1778, shortly before Voltaire's death; the author's niece wanted to present it to the Académie Française, but it was eventually placed in the foyer of the Comédie Française. In 1783, the Czarina Catherine II commissioned a replica of it for Tsarskoe Selo (now at the Hermitage).

Houdon's fame rests mainly on his brilliant bust portraits: these included Rousseau, Diderot, Washington, Molière, Lavoisier, Franklin, d'Alembert, Jefferson, Lafayette, Mirabeau, La Fontaine, Cagliostro, Gluck, members of the Court of Louis XV and Louis XVI, the families of the Duke of Gotha and Prince Henry of Prussia, and also Napoleon. While in his Court portraits (with the exception of Napoleon) the mannered Rococo style is still perceptible, the thinkers and artists are marked with an enlightened pathos befitting Realism. Houdon depicted his subjects with courageous truth in order to convey their individuality. Schadow inherited this approach directly from him.

KAESSMANN Josef (Vienna 1784 – Fischau 1856). Studied with his father who was working as a sculptor on the Michaelerkirche in Vienna. In 1818, he became substitute teacher in Johann Martin Fischer's sculpture class, then was provisionally appointed to the post. A grant allowed him to live in Rome from 1823 to 1829, and this had a decisive influence on his strict Viennese Classicism. Thorwaldsen inspired his group *Jason and Medea* (1829). In 1829, he visited Rauch in Munich. In 1830, he was appointed as a professor in Vienna. After 1835, he planned a monument to the Emperor Franz I.

KALIDE Theodor (Königshütte 1801 – Gleiwitz 1864). After an apprenticeship at the Gleiwitz foundry, went to work with Rauch in 1821, after briefly attending Schadow's studio. In 1831, Kalide became a member of the Berlin Academy and devoted himself to genre sculpture with great success: his *Boy with Swan* (1834) and his *Young*

Girl with a Lyre (1838) were recast time and time again and erected in many provincial towns. But these successes were followed by setbacks, culminating in the scandal that broke out over his *Bacchante on a Panther*. This was regarded as showing revolutionary tendencies and as a crime against good taste, even as a rejection of Classical man, a 'proclamation of anti-Classical barbarity', which prefigures Begas. Deprived of commissions from then on, Kalide confined himself to little bronze groups of Hellenistic grace.

KISS August Karl Eduard (Paprotzen, Upper Silesia 11.10.1802 – Berlin 24.3.1865). Like Kalide, was apprenticed at the Gleiwitz foundry, and then in Berlin. Rauch admitted him to his studio in 1825 and he remained there until 1840. He caused a sensation with his *Wounded Amazon* (1834) on a pedestal decorated with reliefs. He also undertook the sculpture of an 'anti-monument' which radically transformed Classical statuary and dignity. His first monumental work was another *Amazon* (1837–1841) for the Altes Museum in Berlin: Schadow found its dramatic emphasis 'very audacious and bold in execution'. This work brought Kiss fame as a sculptor of horses. Replicas of it were seen at the Great Exhibition in London in 1851.

It is characteristic that Kiss, whenever he executed commissions for public monuments, was shackled by the rigours of Rauch's stylistic doctrine, whereas in his 'free' works, like the *Saint Michael* for Babelsberg castle (1849) and the very dramatic *Saint George* (1855), formerly in the Schlosshof in Berlin, he abandoned sober realism and menia for detail.

KISSLING Leopold (Schöneben, Austria 1770 – Vienna 1827). Worked with Straub and Schroth as from 1791. Count Cobenzl encouraged him and, in 1801, sent him to Rome for nine years. In 1810, he became Court sculptor and also worked for Prince Metternich, for Esterhazy, Palffy and Sinzendorf. Kissling was strongly influenced by Canova, who gave him much support, giving him subjects, visiting him, and correcting his work. Kissling's most beautiful work is a group in Carrara marble, *Mars, Venus and Cupid* (1810), an allegory of the marriage of Napoleon and Marie-Louise of Austria, for which a special temple was planned in the grounds of Laxenburg castle near Vienna.

KUNDMANN Carl (Vienna 1838 – Vienna 1919). Studied at the Vienna Academy, with Bauer, as early as 1853, then with Hähnel in Dresden from 1860 to 1865. In 1872, he became a professor at the Vienna Academy; he had been a member of the Künstlerhaus since 1868. Kundmann was one of the main artists to work on the sculptures of the Ringstrasse in Vienna and of the Viennese 19th century in general: he executed sculptures for the Vienna Arsenal, for the Rathaus, the Neue Hofburg and the Court museums. His largest work was the *Pallas Athene* fountain in front of the Parliament. In 1872, he created the Schubert monument, in 1866, the monument to Admiral Tegetthoff and in 1889, with Rudolf Weyr, the Grillparzer monument. His sculpture conforms strictly with the demands of Historicism and has a Classical calm and elegance.

MAINDRON Etienne-Hippolyte (Champtoceaux 1801 – Paris 1884). Originally a disciple of David d'Angers, in his whole life Maindron only created one work which has become famous, the sculpture of the priestess *Velléda* (1843–1844) from *Les Martyrs* by Chateaubriand (1809), which is at the Tuileries. He lived on a very modest income from public commissions. In 1871, he created a group in marble *La France resignée* for the peristyle of the Panthéon.

MAROCHETTI Carlo, Baron (Turin 14.1.1805 – Paris 28.12.1867 or – according to Oettinger – London 1868). A pupil of François-Joseph de Bosio in Paris, Marochetti made his Salon debut in 1829. In 1848, in the wake of Louis-Philippe, he fled to London where, from then on, he took part in Royal Academy exhibitions. In 1833, he created his masterpiece, the equestrain statue of *Emmanuel Philibert of Savoy*, which earned him the title of Baron. The statue was shown in the courtyard of the Louvre and erected in 1838 on the Piazza San Carlo in Turin. In England, his works include an equestrian statue of *Queen Victoria* in Glasgow, and the monument to Richard the Lionheart at Westminster.

MENNESSIER Louis-Charles-Justin (Metz 1815 – Novara 1859). During his officer's training, Susse, then Daubrée, encouraged him as a sculptor. His first works were the *Porte Saint-Pancrace* and the *Tireur de Vincennes*. He was fatally wounded at the battle of Magenta in July 1859 and died at the age of 44. His bronze statuette of the Duc d'Aumale, Henri Eugène Philippe Louis d'Orléans, son of Louis-Philippe, is a characteristic work of French Historicism. (The Duc d'Aumale built the Château de Chantilly, which was of particular significance for His-

toricism; he later bequeathed his art collections, and the château itself, to the Institute de France.)

MERVILLE Karl Georg (Württemberg 1751 – Pressburg 1798). In 1779, married in Vienna, and probably worked there until 1788, before settling in Pressburg. His major works date from the 1780s: the high altar of the Michaelerkirche in Vienna (1780–1782), the monument to Catherine II of Russia (1788), probably made at the request of Josef II, and a lead bust of *Emperor Leopold II* (1792). His sculptures of horses were probably inspired by Leonardo da Vinci's studies of the horse.

MESSERSCHMIDT Franz Saver (Wisensteig, Swabia 6.2.1736 – Pressburg 21.8.1783). After training with his uncle Straub in Munich and with the latter's brother in Graz, Messerschmidt went to Vienna in 1752 and attended the Academy there. He worked mainly with Matthäus Donner and Schletterer and was engaged at the Arsenal as a 'stucco cutter'. While on a journey to Paris and London, he was offered a place at the Académie in Paris, but refused. In 1769, he became a teacher in Vienna, but was discharged in 1774 when the first symptoms of mental illness appeared. He died in utter isolation in Pressburg. Messerschmidt, probably the most fascinating Viennese sculptor of the second half of the 18th century, caused a sensation with his so-called 'character' heads. These were grimacing self-portrait busts which were all the more successful after 1770, as the study of physiognomy had just begun. Posterity christened these masterpieces with names like *The Grumbler, Gloomy Man, Dark and Sinister Man.*

MONTI Rafaello (Iseo, Ticino 1818 – London 1881). Trained at the Brera Academy in Milan, Monti went to Vienna in 1841, and made sculptures for the facade of the Budapest National Museum. In 1846, he went to London and in 1847 back to Milan. After the uprising of March 1848, in which he took part, he returned to London where he created political allegories in historicist didactic style. The marble group entitled *Painful Sleep and Happy Dream* (1861) represents Italy, exhausted by her resistance to Austrian domination, asleep among thorns, while in a dream a veiled woman promises her a happy future.

PISANI Giuseppe (Carrara 1758 – Modena 1839). In the service of the house of Este, Pisani led an important sculptor's studio in Vienna and made bust portraits of members of the Imperial household (*Francis II*; *Archduke Charles*). He took part in the decoration of the Empress Maria Ludovica d'Este's apartments. In 1811, he created the monument to Marshal-Lieutenant Schmidt. In 1814, he was made Primo Scultore of the Modena Academy and was appointed its Director in 1821. His style was vigorously Classical, without resorting to copying Antiquity.

PRÉAULT Antoine-Auguste (Paris 1809–1879). A pupil of David d'Angers and Moine. His early work was especially successful with young Romantic sculptors who found in *The Dying Poet* and the *Ophelia* in the Musée des Beaux-Arts in Marseille, an echo of their own thoughts. His Romanticism was also deeply imbued with his socialist and pacifist ideas, as works such as *The Famine*, *The Pariahs*, and *The Slaughter* bear witness. However, in his historical subjects, his expressive power and his plastic qualities sometimes erred towards pomposity, while in his religious subjects he was prone to fussiness. This is probably why his *Christ on the Cross* of 1840 – which is today in the Saint-Gervais church in Paris – was rejected by the Salon jury. Not until 1848 was he allowed to exhibit there.

RAUCH Christian Daniel (Arolsen 2.1.1777 – Dresden 3.12.1857). Having begun his training in Kassel, Rauch became Schadow's pupil in Berlin. At the same time, he was a valet to Queen Louise of Prussia and made a bust portrait of her in 1804. From 1805 to 1811, he worked in Italy where his style developed in the studios of Canova and Thorwaldsen. Thanks to his friendship with Wilhelm von Humboldt, he obtained the commission for a ceremonial sarcophagus for Queen Louise, who died in 1810; it was executed in marble between 1812 and 1815, in Italy. In 1817, thanks to the offices of Baron de Stein, he was commissioned to create the Blücher monument in Breslau. From 1819, Rauch shared a studio in Berlin with Tieck and the architect von Schinkel. For the city of Berlin he created monuments to Blücher, Scharnhorst and Bülow, as decoration for Schinkel's *Hauptwache* (main guard-house); from 1822 to 1834, the monument to the memory of Maximilian I in Munich, the Dürer monument in Nuremberg, and from 1842 to 1851 the colossal equestrian statue of *Frederick the Great*, erected in Berlin, and transferred to Sans-Souci after 1945. Rauch is an important figure in German 19th century sculpture, not only because he was one of its most original personalities, but also because it was he who brought Canova and Thorwaldsen's Roman influence to Berlin and passed it on to his pupils. Notable among them were Ernst Rietschel, Albert Wolff, August Kiss and Friedrich Drake. His *Victories* of the Valhalla near Regensburg and his portraits of Goethe, one of which represents the poet as Zeus on his throne, show how close he was to Thorwaldsen. Elsewhere, he adopted an increasingly realist approach: thus he eventually depicted Frederick the Great in the costume of his time, after numerous experimental sketches which showed the monarch with chariots on a sort of Trajan column. Rauch, whose style was initially purely classical, became unconsciously an early exponent of realist Historicism.

RIETSCHEL Ernst Friedrich August (Pulsnitz 15.12.1804 – Dresden 21.2.1861). Rauch's pupil from

Antoine-Auguste Préault *Ophelia*

1826, Rietschel's early work was in Classicist style reinforced by a stay in Rome from 1830 to 1831, financed by
the State of Saxony. In 1832 he taught at the Dresden
Academy where Johannes Schilling (sculptor of the
Schiller monument in Vienna) and Julius Hähnel were
among his pupils. Rietschel obtained many important
commissions: he contributed to the monument in honour
of Goethe and Schiller in Weimar (until 1856), the Lessing monument in Brunswick, and the Luther monument
in Worms. The latter shows he had freed himself almost
entirely of Rauch's Classicism and had adopted a Realist
style characteristic of bourgeois Historicism.

ROLAND Philippe-Laurent (Lille 1746–1816).
Studied at the Ecole de Dessin in Lille. His first works
were under Pajou in Paris: he collaborated on the decoration of the Versailles Opera House. From 1771 to 1776
he lived in Rome, at his own expense, to complete his
training. He married the daughter of Potain, the chief
architect of Fontainebleau and, through his father-in-
law, obtained some important commissions; he was recognised by the Academy and became sculptor to the
King. Among his many statues, his *Condé* is a masterpiece of movement and balance. Even during the Revolution and the Empire, his work was much in demand: his
works included statues and reliefs for the Luxembourg
Palace and the Louvre, a *Minerva* for the Palais-Bourbon,
and a *Napoleon* for the Institut de France. In 1809, he
became a professor at the Ecole des Beaux-Arts, where
David d'Angers was among his pupils. In all his works,
he remained a proponent of 18th century Classicism, and
a lover of Antiquity and the study of Nature.

RUDE François (Dijon 4.1.1784 – Paris 3.11.1855). In
1807, left Dijon for Paris and commended himself to
Vivant Denon, director of the Musée Napoléon, with two
small and vigorously Classicist works. He worked
under Edmé Gaulle on the Place Vendôme column and
became a pupil of Cartellier at the Ecole des Beaux-Arts.
In 1812, with the statue of *Aristaeus*, he won the first Prix
de Rome, but because of the Academy's financial straits
and political circumstances, he was not able to leave. A
supporter of Napoleon, he had to flee France in 1814,
and went to his brother-in-law, Louis Frémiet in Brussels. He made a bust of *Jacques-Louis David*, a fellow-exile,
and some reliefs which earned him commissions and
then the post of Sculptor to the Court of the Netherlands.
In 1828, he returned to Paris.

François Rude *Young Fisherman with Tortoise.* 1833

In 1833, Rude had his first great success with the *Young
Fisherman*. At the same time, he was making sketches for
reliefs, the *Departure of the Volunteers* (known as *La Marseillaise*) for the Arc de Triomphe in Paris, a masterpiece of
French Romantic sculpture, with its expressive realism
and power of movement. This work brought him fame
throughout Europe. Other major works followed: *Jeanne
d'Orléans*, the *Maréchal de Saxe*, *Maréchal Ney*, *Godefroy
Cavaignac*, and particularly his late work *The Awakening
of Napoleon*. In Rude's sculptures, almost all of which are
in the great traditions of French sculpture, the conflict
between Neo-Classicism and Romanticism is resolved.
Although he was clearly influenced by Academism, his
realistic and eclectic approach augurs the magisterial
works of Historicism.

SCHADOW Johann Gottfried (Berlin 20.5.1764 – Berlin 27.1.1850). After early studies with Giovanni Battista
Selvino, in 1780 Schadow went to study under the Belgian Jean Pierre Antoine Tassaert, and in 1788 succeeded him. From 1785 to 1787, he was in Italy: he studied the masterpieces of the sculptors of the Renaissance
and Baroque periods in Florence, then went to Rome,

where he was strongly influenced by Canova who drew his attention to the works of Antiquity. Schadow competed in the Concorso di Balestra of the Accademia di San Luca and won it with his group *Perseus freeing Andromeda*. In 1786, Frederick the Great died and Schadow made the first sketches for a monument and a mausoleum. Minister von Heinitz convinced Friedrich Wilhelm II to bring Schadow home. After a stay in Vienna, he returned to Berlin, made models for porcelain manufacture, became a member of the Academy and in 1815, 'Director of All Sculptures'. In 1788, he succeeded Tassaert at the Royal Sculpture Studios where he soon had seventeen assistants and where he trained a series of notable pupils: Karl Friedrich Hagemann, Karl Friedrich Wichmann, Ludwig Wilhelm Wichmann, his own son Ridolfo Schadow, a nephew, Emil Wolff, Heinrich Kaehler, and his most important pupil Christian Daniel Rauch, as well as the young Reinhold Begas. Schadow was already regarded as the leading sculptor in Neo-Classical Germany.

During the reign of Friedrich Wilhelm II (1786–1797) Schadow produced his major works, the tomb of Graf Alexander von der Mark (1790), the chariot of the Brandenburg Gate (1793), the statue of *Frederick the Great* for Stettin (1793), and the statue of *Zieten* (1794) and the royal princesses (1795–1797). After Friedrich Wilhelm's

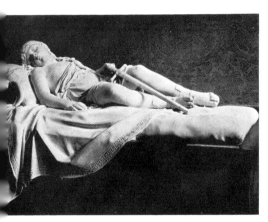

Johann Gottfried Schadow *Tomb of Graf Alexander von der Mark*. 1790

death, he produced fewer works: the statues of the *Old Man of Dessau* at the Lustgarten in Berlin (1800), *Blücher* in Rostock (1819), *Martin Luther* in Wittemberg (1821) and the *Young Girl Resting* (1826). Finally, Friedrich Wilhelm III commissioned an equestrian statue of *Frederick the Great* for which, after travels in Sweden, Russia and Denmark, Schadow made seven different rough models. In the event, the King decided not to use Schadow, who was still very attached to the Rococo style, and commissioned a younger Neo-Classicist, the more 'mod-

ern' Rauch. Schadow was, basically, a transitional artist, treading a path between the spontaneity and realism of, say, Houdon and the ideal forms of Canova. It was this that provoked vehement criticism from Goethe in Weimar: 'In Berlin ... poetry is replaced by history, character and the ideal by the portrait, symbolic treatment by allegory, landscape by perspective, and human eternity by the patriotic ...' Schadow finally devoted himself entirely to his theoretical writings: *Polyclete or Measures of Man* was published in 1834, *National Physiognomies* in 1835, *Artistic Works and Opinions* in 1848.

SCHALLER Johann Nepomuk (Vienna 1777 – Vienna 1842). A pupil of Herbert Maurer at the Academy's School of Artisans of Art, then of Anton Grassi and Franz Anton Zauner. In 1791, he was engaged as a designer at the Vienna porcelain works. From 1812 to 1823, a grant enabled him to live in Rome working with Canova and Thorwaldsen, who became his friend. In 1823, he became a professor at the Vienna Academy of Sculpture. His major works include a statue of *Andreas Hofer* in Innsbruck; portraits of the *Emperor Franz I*, *Empress Maria Ludovica* and *Emperor Ferdinand I*; and very delicate ancient scenes (*Venus shows Mars her hand wounded by Diomedes*, 1810; *Adolescent Cupid*, 1815–1816; *Venus leaving her Bath*, 1816; *Concordia*, 1816). In 1835, he executed the plan for a monument to the Emperor and in 1836, the Romantic Marguerite fountain in Vienna. He owed his success mainly to his lead sculpture, *Philoctetes* (1808–1809, Schloss Belvedere), created (in plaster) by order of Graf Stadion, curator of the Vienna Academy. The work was cast in Zauner's studio and its masterly execution brought a wave of public acclaim for Schaller. When he worked with marble, his work showed that to some extent he had been influenced by the Viennese Biedermeier style. Schaller, together with Kissling, is among the best sculptors of the post-Napoleonic era in Austria.

SCHOENEWERK Pierre-Alexandre (Paris 1820 – Paris 1885). Pupil of David d'Angers, Jollivet and Triqueti. His best-known work is the marble sculpture *The Tarentine Girl* (1872), inspired by André Chénier's poem, which was purchased for the Château de Compiègne. Schoenewerk's smooth style was very much in tune with the tastes of the Second Empire.

SCHWANTHALER Ludwig von (Munich 26.8.1802 – Munich 14.11.1848). From 1818, studied at the Munich

Academy and, after the death of his father, resumed work at the sculpture studio, making decorations for tombs and buildings. For Maximilian I of Bavaria, he made a wax model inspired by mythology for a table centrepiece, and this won him the favour of King Ludwig I. He was sent to Rome on a scholarship and Thorwaldsen welcomed him there. He stayed in Rome again from 1832 to 1834; then worked in Munich, and also in Salzburg, Vienna, Prague, Budapest and Frankfurt. Between 1837 and 1848, he created the colossal bronze monument *Bavaria*, although this was only erected, on the Theresienwiese, Munich, in front of Leo von Klenze's Ruhmeshalle, in 1850 after Schwanthaler's death. From 1844, he created the Romantic fountain in honour of Emperor Ferdinand I for the city of Vienna: this fountain, with its statue of *Austria* surrounded by heroic personifications of the four great rivers of the Habsburg Empire, the Danube, Po, Vistula and Elbe, was to inspire a whole series of monumental fountains. Schwanthaler left a varied body of work, which includes the relief in the Göttersaal of the Glypothek in Munich, his own castle in the Isar valley, the figures on the south portal of Cologne Cathedral, and the Propylaea facade in Munich. Few sculptors were as successful as Schwanthaler in achieving a synthesis between the rigorous Classicism of Thorwaldsen's school and the new Romantic Historicism.

SERGEL Johan Tobias (Stockholm 28.8.1740 – Stockholm 26.2.1814). The son of a German saddler living in Stockholm, for ten years Sergel was the pupil and assistant of Larchevêques who was working on the Royal Palace in Stockholm; in 1758, he accompanied the latter to Paris. In 1760, he won an Academy of Stockholm prize and in 1767, on a State scholarship, went to Rome, where he stayed until 1778. He was much preoccupied by the desire to eliminate 'French style' from his work, particularly after meeting Thorwaldsen and Canova. In 1778–1779, he returned to Paris to study modelling at the Académie. He met Houdon and Clodion, but considered his friends to be the best teachers. Later, he also met Fuseli, whose works and whose Romantic and eccentric artistic views were closely related to his own. In 1779, he returned to Stockholm to succeed his teacher Masreliez as Court sculptor. The main body of his work consisted of portraits.

Sergel is the most important and vivid sculptor of 18th century Sweden. His Classicism, laced with strong realist tendencies, was mainly formed in Rome: it was there that all his major works were conceived, that he studied the works of Antiquity, concentrated on Nature and the nude, and took as his models the works of Raphael, Michelangelo, the Caracci and Domenchino. The

wealth of drawings and sketches he left show the intensity with which he studied everyday life, genre scenes and caricature. Dyveke Helsted stressed the extent to which these reflect his own psychological problems, his profound melancholy and recurring depressions.

Johann Tobias Sergel *Mars and Venus*. 1770

THORWALDSEN Bertel (Copenhagen 13.11.1768 – Copenhagen 24.3.1844). Received his first artistic training when he was only eleven. Abildgaard's pupil at the Royal Academy, in 1796 he won a prize from the Academy of Copenhagen and left on a scholarship for Rome. With the exception of a brief return to Denmark in 1819–1820, he remained there until 1838. His Classicism was influenced by his study of Antiquity, but also by contact with the works of Asmus Jakob Carstens. From 1803 onwards, he obtained numerous commissions from Germany, Austria, England, Denmark, Poland and Russia. In 1808, he was elected as a member of the Accademia di San Luca in Rome. In 1811, Napoleon commissioned the frieze of *The Campaign of Alexander* for the Quirinale Palace; in 1819 he executed the *Amor Triumphans* and the busts of *Prince Metternich* for Vienna,

Bertel Thorwaldsen *Ganymede*. 1817

with him for Berlin, where they shared a studio together with the architect Schinkel. The masterpiece of this collaboration was the Kreuzberg Monument (1818–1821). The decorative sculptures of the Gendarmenmarket Theatre occupied him for almost thirty years, but he had many minor commissions as well. In 1830, Tieck became Director of the Sculpture department of the Berlin Museum and compiled the first catalogue of Ancient sculptures (1834) and of the works of Della Robbia (1835).

and was invited to decorate the Church of Our Lady in Copenhagen. He sculpted statues of Christ and the Apostles which were to have a decisive influence on the whole of religious decorative art in the 19th century and were to be copied endlessly in plaster, even in the smallest villages. In 1823, he created the tomb of Pope Pius VII, one of his masterpieces (dedicated in 1831 in the Clementine chapel of Saint Peter's). Among his most impressive statues are his *Jason* for Thomas Hope, the *Poniatowski Monument* in Warsaw and his statue of *Byron* in Cambridge. In 1838, he returned to Copenhagen, but kept on his Rome studio to which he returned in 1841. He bequeathed his personal collection to the city of Copenhagen. When he died in 1844, the Thorwaldsen Museum was only partly built; it was inaugurated in 1848.

TIECK Christian Friedrich (Berlin 14.8.1766 – Berlin 12.5.1851). Brother of the Romantic poet, Ludwig Tieck, Tieck worked from 1794 to 1797 in Schadow's studio and from 1798 to 1801 with Jacques-Louis David in Paris. On his return journey through Weimar, he met Goethe, to whom Wilhelm von Humboldt had recommended him for the decoration of the new castle. As a sample of his work, he created his first bust of *Goethe* (Weimar), followed by a second in 1820. Until 1805, Tieck was making reliefs and sculptures for the staircase and the salons of Weimar Castle. In 1805, he left for Rome and in 1809, in Munich, he created bust portraits for the Valhalla near Regensburg (executed in marble 1812–1819 in Carrara). In 1811, he met Rauch for the first time, and, in 1819, left

TILGNER Viktor (Pressburg 25.10.1844 – Vienna 16.4.1896). A pupil of Gasser and Bauer at the Academy in Vienna (1859–1871), his early works were influenced by French sculptors, particularly Déloyes. In 1874, he travelled in Italy. He became sculpture's chief exponent of the Neo-Baroque in southern Germany during the Habsburg monarchy. Among his major works are the decorative sculptures of the Vienna Court Museums, of the Burgtheater, the Neue Hofburg, the fountains at Empress Elisabeth's hunting lodge, the 'Hermes Villa', the *Mozart* monument in the Volksgarten and a great many bust portraits (*Empress Elisabeth* and *Emperor Franz-Josef*, and the architect *Hasenauer Charlotte Wolter*).

Viktor Tilgner *Monument to Mozart*

TRIQUETI Henri-Joseph-François de (Conflans 1804 – Paris 1874). After training as a painter, came to public attention in 1831 with his bas-relief *The Death of Charles the Bold*. Reliefs were to remain his favourite medium and he obtained many commissions to decorate churches and public buildings. Pierre Alexandre Schoenewerk was one of his pupils.

WANGER Anton Paul (Koniginhof, Bohemia 1834 – Vienna 1895). Studied in Prague and Vienna and became a member of the Künstlerhaus in Vienna in 1869. His work showed a delicate naturalism, his fountain of the *Goose Girl* (1866) being a good example. He received important commissions for the Rathaus in Vienna, built by Friedrich von Schmidt, for Hansen's Parliament building and the Museum of the Army, decorative sculptures for Semper's Burgtheater and Ferstel's main University building. He also produced various works in Prague (National Theatre and National Museum).

WESTMACOTT Sir Richard (London 15.7.1775 – London 1.9.1856). From 1793, trained with Canova in Rome, and in 1795 became a member of the Accademia del Disegno in Florence. On his return to London, he was represented every year at the Royal Academy Exhibition, became a member in 1811 and Professor of Sculpture from 1827 to 1854. His best-known works include the tomb of Charles James Fox in Westminster Abbey, the statue of *Achilles* in Hyde Park and that of the *Duke of Bedford* in Russell Square.

WYATT Matthew Cotes (London 1777 – London 1862). Son of the architect James Wyatt, trained at the Royal Academy in London. He exhibited several times between 1804 and 1814 and was encouraged by King George III, for whose equestrian statue in London he was responsible. He created many monuments, such as that to the Duke of Wellington and the cenotaph for Princess Charlotte Augusta (1820) in Saint George's Chapel at Windsor Castle. Here Wyatt created a pictorial allegory in marble: the work can be better understood in the knowledge that Wyatt was also a painter.

ZAUNER Franz Anton von (Kaunsertal, Tyrol 5.7.1746 – Vienna 3.3.1822). A pupil of Horer and Deutschmann in Passau, who went to Vienna in 1766. There he joined Schletterer's studio and worked on Beyer's sculptural programme for Schönbrunn. From 1776 to 1781, he was in Rome on a scholarship, where he was influenced by Canova and studied the works of Antiquity (the statue of Marcus Aurelius became the model for his colossal equestrian statue of *Emperor Josef II*, already among his favourite subjects). On his return, he became a professor at the Vienna Academy in 1784 and its Direc-

tor in 1806. From 1795 to 1806, he worked on his statue of the Emperor and in 1807 this work earned him a title. His tomb for Emperor Leopold II, who died in 1792, is another masterpiece. Zauner fulfilled a great number of commissions: among the finest are the tympanum of the old Fries, now known as Pallavicini, Palace (1783), the bust of the *Emperor Franz II* (1796) and the *Genius Bornii*, an allegory of the Freemason and naturalist Ignaz von Born, inspired by Praxiteles' *Eros*, and one of the finest statues of Viennese Classicism.

ZUMBUSCH Kaspar Clemens von (Herzebrock, Westphalia 23.11.1830 – Rimsting Prien, Chiemsee 27.9.1915). Trained in the modelling class of the Munich Polytechnic School with Johann von Halbig, with whom he went to Milan in 1849. In 1857–1858, he studied Ancient sculpture in Rome. On his return, he executed many commissions, including a bust of *Richard Wagner*. In 1867, he returned to Italy. His monument to Maximilian II in Munich, created between 1866 and 1872, brought him fame throughout Central Europe. From 1873 until 1901, he was professor at the Vienna Academy of Plastic Arts. He was also a member of the Künstlerhaus in Vienna. It was in Vienna that he created his masterpieces: the *Beethoven* monument (1873–1880, in collaboration with the architect Karl von Hasenauer), one of Europe's most colossal sovereign monuments; the equestrian statues of *Count Radetzky* and *Archduke Albrecht*; and many bust portraits and tombs. Zumbusch's gigantic monuments have to be seen in the context of the architecture which surrounds them, which they were designed to complement. Zumbusch is the most important monument sculptor of the Neo-Baroque at the time of the Ringstrasse; he translated into gigantic proportions what Tilgner and Weyr had represented on a smaller scale. Zumbusch is typical of the late 19th century in his use of materials, with his sharp-edged smooth marble surfaces and his bronze figures, clay green and often richly decorated.

Architecture

Architecture of the Romantic era is often seen as a mere repository of older stylistic patterns. But to see it in this way is to ignore the fact that throughout the history of architecture there has always been imitation, from the moment a 'style' first appears. Thus chinoiseries was evident as early as the Middle Ages. A retrospective Gothic appeared in different countries and in different guises, from the end of the actual Gothic period: one has only to measure the stylistic gap between Saint Paul's Cathedral in London built from 1675 to 1710, and Tom Tower at Christ Church College in Oxford, built in 1681–1682. Even more prevalent was the influence of 'Classicism' in European architecture. The Greeks and Romans, both in their theories about the proportions of the human body and architecture, and in matters of mere technique, provided solutions, and a teachable system, that have had a determining influence down the centuries on European artists. It is not surprising that there was recourse to Classical criteria each time an empire was formed.

The Classical tendencies of the Carolingian Renaissance can be explained in this way, as can the Empire style of Napoleon or the megalomaniacal Classicism of Hitler. Similarly, in Gottfried Semper's vast plan for an Imperial forum in Vienna, the dominant idea was that of the Imperial palace as the centre and focus of an Empire.

What was different each time was the extent to which different periods derived their own artistic methods from the model of Antiquity. During the Renaissance, and in the Palladio and Baroque styles, the Ancient model was virtually unrecognisable. During the Classicist period, on the other hand, everything hinged, temporarily at least, on a radical return to the Ancient laws of proportion, only to become all the more emancipated in Historicism.

In any event, it seems that the combination of style and history and the 'delight of transporting oneself into the spirit of an era' by faithfully reproducing its style, could not help but find favour with educated audiences and princes.

The same phenomenon can be observed in other art forms, but it is architecture which provides some of the most striking examples, of which only a few can be mentioned here. In 1788, Johann Ferdinand Hetzendorf von Hohenberg created at the gates of Vienna, in the park of the palace of Schönbrunn, an impressive Roman ruin and an Egyptian obelisk; between 1793 and 1801, Heinrich Christoph Jussow built the Löwenburg at Kassel-Wilhelmshohe, which seemed to have sprung from different mediaeval periods and then fallen into ruins; while from 1747 to 1797, Horace Walpole's Strawberry Hill was being built. In 1795, and eccentric English gentleman, William Beckford, author of *Vathek*, a fashionable oriental novel of suspense, engaged James Wyatt to build Fonthill Abbey in Wiltshire.

Wyatt's brief was to create a 'genuine' artificial ruin, which would include a few habitable rooms where the poet could seek inspiration. By 1800, it had already grown into a gigantic edifice in which everything was Gothic except the shape, which took the form of an almost regular Greek cross with four arms radiating from an octagonal central structure.

In 1798, Ludwig de Traux of Amsterdam, at the order of the Emperor Franz II, designed a highly Romantic 'manor' in the landscaped grounds of Laxenburg Castle near Vienna, surrounded by a lake, waterfalls and canals: Franzensburg was a kind of fortified castle built in supposedly Gothic style, with mediaeval lists and a seigniorial vault, a throne room, great halls, an observatory, *oubliettes* and a torture chamber. As late as 1870–1880, Dollmann, Julius Hofmann, Peter Herwegen and Christian Jank were building for Ludwig II of Bavaria, the eccentric Wittelsbach who was obsessed with building, castles whose fantastic architecture now draws throngs of tourists: Herrenchiemsee, inspired by Versailles; Linderhof, a small castle in Louis XV style; and Neuschwanstein, a highly Romantic fairytale castle in Romanesque style. When the King died, drowned in Lake Starnberg, near Berg Castle, many buildings were still at the planning stage: a Chinese palace, a Byzantine palace, a castle of the 'Holy Grail', Moorish summerhouses, and many more, conceived by Ludwig's fantastic imagination.

Throughout Europe, work was being carried out to restore and refurbish historic castles; while the old aristocracy, as well as the 'nouveaux riches', were building themselves castles in which they tried to evoke the appearance of a secular past. It was a type of architecture intended to evoke an atmosphere of times gone by, and it was all but ubiquitous, from Anif near Salzburg to Kreuzenstein and Hernstein near Vienna, or Grafenegg on the Danube; from James and Jeffrey Wyatt's Ashridge Castle in Hertfordshire to the maritime Miramare castle of Archduke Maximilian in Trieste; from the great castles of the Rhine to the monstrous Guelph castle in Hannover; from the château de Chantilly, extended by the Duc d'Aumale, to the 'Neo-Hellenic' palace built for Empress Elisabeth of Austria on Corfu in 1891 by Rafaele Carito. Castles that are of interest from a history-of-art point of view, built between the middle of the 18th and the last third of the 19th century, can be counted in hundreds. As for town halls, schools and barracks built according to different variations of Classical or Romantic style, the number is higher still.

These stylistic decisions were not necessarily dictated by aesthetic norms alone, but also by philosophical ideas, ideological principles and the intellectual context of the period. It is easier to understand the evolution of Romantic architecture if it is seen in the context of the 'world order' in which it developed, first in relation to the idea of the State, and secondly in relation to a bourgeoisie that was seeking its own intellectual identity. It should thus be seen in a clearly defined ideological context: 'An architecture designed to promote moral development'.

The rejection of Baroque and Rococo

Politically, the move towards strict Classical ideals resulted from a change in the balance of power. Rome of the Baroque period had lost its political hegemony, and Paris under Louis XIV succeeded it. Even Bernini, who had been summoned to the presence of the Sun King, no longer met with any success at all with his Baroque ideas. A national Classicism, imposed by a centralist policy, reigned throughout France and extended over frontiers even into the Holy Empire, influencing the taste of the German courts and eventually even the court in Vienna, which had long been dominated, for political reasons, by the Baroque and by Italy. The exuberance of the Baroque and the sensual charm of the Rococo were finally sacrificed to the cult of Reason.

Adapted to suit monarchy by divine right and the all-powerful church, as represented by the Habsburg Emperor Charles VI, Baroque individualism was soon to give way to the norms of logic. The dream of replacing reality with illusion was coming to an end. Walls built with concave and convex broken joints were rejected, as were the bulging columns with their bold lines; the graceful curving of cornices; artistically cut passages between buildings; and domes with heightened vaulting, symbolising the apotheosis of monarchs, and 'glimpses of heaven'. There was a new desire to focus on the human being, to be free of the absolutism of Louis XIV or Charles VI, which, where it still existed, was now no more than a facade. The intellectual context had evolved too far and had left feudal absolutism far behind it.

From the philosophy of Enlightenment to the Greek ideal

The expression 'Enlightenment' had, since the 1760s, become the magic word that placed the keys of power into the waiting hands of a bourgeoisie thirsty for knowledge. This was very soon reflected in the art of building. Recourse to the 'typical' rather than the individual was to last until towards the end of the 19th century. Science became the pattern upon which architecture modelled itself. The single most important influence was that of archaeology, because of the finds brought to light at this time. At Naples, Pompeii, and Herculaneum, archaeologists were continually unearthing new treasures; architects made pilgrimages there, as they did to Paestum and to Greece. The Marquis de Vandières, brother of Madame de Pompadour, eulogised in 1750, with his travelling companion Jacques-Germain Soufflot, about the temples at Paestum. Joseph II visited the archaeological excavations in Naples; Winckelmann advocated that it was the duty of every architect to visit the high places of Antiquity in Italy and Greece. The science of history, and in particular the discovery of the Middle Ages, which were to become a major preoccupation, shared pride of place with philology. New literary and philosophical sources were popularised and put to use for the education of bourgeois taste. It was chiefly by means of Ancient plays and legends that the mythical figures of Antiquity lived again on opera and theatre stages. Gods and heroes were installed, in the form of paintings or sculptures, in palaces and in bourgeois homes, occupying wall niches, staircases, mantelpieces and bookcases. Meanwhile architecture laid claim to the tympanums of temples and to the Classical column. The favourable reception met with by the forms and proportions of Antiquity can be explained by the need felt by this 'enlightened' era for a return to the roots of the Western world.

Even in politics, in the great Empires of Europe Greece was not forgotten. Lord Byron exiled hiself to liberate ancient Greece from Hispanic tyranny, Hölderlin composed his hymn *Patmos*; Goethe wrote *Iphigenie auf Tauris*; a Wittelsbach became the first sovereign of Greece; and the English brought home from Greece their first archaeological finds. A Bavarian prince bought the Aegina frieze and gave Thorwaldsen, one of the most prestigious sculptors of the time, the task of completing it. European architects loved the idea of reliving the birth of Western civilisation. But few of them were as farsighted as Karl Friedrich von Schinkel, who defined the utopian goal of architecture in these words: 'Not to build like the Greeks, but to build as they would have done if they had been alive today!'

Architecture in France during the reign of Louis XVI already showed strong Classical tendencies. The use to which Inigo Jones (1575–1652) and John Webb had put Classical forms in England, still intellectually 'Palladian', was mirrored in France by the work of Jean-François Blondel, the most respected theoretician of the 18th century, and above all by Jacques-Ange Gabriel (1698–1782) who, in the Petit Trianon at Versailles, the ministerial buildings on the Place de la Concorde, and the Ecole Militaire in Paris, gave new life to these Classical structures. In fact, Gabriel had done no more than adapt to his own era the colonnade of the Louvre by Claude Perrault.

Architects like Peyre, Chalgrin, Gondoin, Paris and Brongniart, joined by decorators such as Clérisseau, Dugour and Lhullier, committed themselves further in favour of rigorous Classicism. In 1765, Peyre published his *Oeuvre d'architecture* which, for the first time, made a comparison between the austerity of ancient building – the Roman Pantheon, for instance, or Diocletian's Thermae – and French geometric order. Its consequences quickly because apparent. The last vestiges of 'vine-stem' decor were suddenly replaced by severely formed lines; surfaces were divided by lines drawn with almost pedantic precision; ornamental mouldings became increasingly rigid; niches, where busts of the Emperor were enthroned, were framed with stereotyped laurel wreaths; the winding staircases of old became straight-lined blocks; Doric and Ionic columns replaced the Corinthian; the strong colours of the Baroque and the iridescent shades of the Rococo faded in favour of white offset with gold. The Etruscan style gained importance under the influence of Piranesi who held that the Etruscans above all, and not the Greeks, were the artistic precursors of the Romans, and that they, in consequence, were the inventors of the primitive monumental forms of Roman architecture.

Gondoin's design, which was never realised, for the Ecole de Chirurgie (School of Surgery) in Paris (1771–1776) caused the definitive breach: with its smooth walls, endless colonnades, an anatomy room with a transparent dome, it made Blondel's school look old-fashioned at a stroke. Buildings such as Peyre's Odéon (1778–1782) Brongniart's Convent of the Capuchins (1789), and the Doric gallery of the *Salle des Menus Plaisirs* (1787), had the monumental architecture of the temples at Paestum as their inspiration.

Revolutionary architecture

Towards 1780, a number of French architects established this taste for massive and grandiose proportions as a new architectural idiom. Reason alone, based on Classical constructions, was to rule. Museums, libraries, mausoleums, town halls, customs houses, new industrial towns, even the layouts of cities: everything suddenly became geometric in form and towns began to look like graphs. The pyramid and the prism, the cone and the sphere, were seen as archetypes of the art of construction to which architecture had to return. People quoted Rousseau and demanded an autonomous architecture which would not need any decoration and which would create severe and monumental proportions based on pure form. Typical of the end of the 18th century was a tendency to give an intellectual 'label' to each new building: the building itself was thus to take on a symbolic form in keeping with its function.

Claude-Nicolas Ledoux (1736–1806) was the most successful of the 'revolutionary architects'. In spite of the whimsical patterns which adorn his works, he was neither fantasist nor utopian. At the age of 40, he was already in great demand. He worked for Madame du Barry, decorated palaces (the salon of the Hotel d'Uzès in Paris, 1768), and built the fashionable Château Bénouville in the Calvados (1768). He eventually came to the attention of the King who gave him large commissions such as the building of 120 toll-houses in Paris and, in 1774, the drafting of plans for the model Salines at Arc-et-Senans. Yet this temperamental

Claude-Nicolas Ledoux *The Salines, Arc-et-Senans: The Director's Building*

theoretician's nature is clear from his designs. His imagination led him to reflect on the architectonic integration of 'primitive elements': the waterways authority building, shaped like a cylinder, had a river running through it; the house of the country policeman was a windowless sphere; in the 'maison de la moralité', stark and completely devoid of eroticism, young lovers were to be able to learn to master life's problems. Ledoux's design for a metallurgical plant is an astonishing attempt to give an industrial enterprise an aesthetically pleasing appearance.

Finally, Ledoux's conception of his ideal city (which was, in some ways, similar to Robert Owen's New Lanark), was on the grand scale. For Ledoux, building was the representation of an idea; architecture was the embodiment of a 'philosophical construction'.

What, for him, was a thoroughly real possibility, was transformed by Etienne-Louis Boullée (1728–1799) into romantico-mystic and eccentric speculation. All his projects – his unfulfilled plans for cathedrals, museums, stadiums, his libraries with their monstrous proportions, or his designs for extending Versailles – were designed to accommodate vast throngs of people and reflect, above all, the disturbing idea that emerged in the 18th century: that 'the universe is immeasurable and unforeseeable'.

Adolf Max Vogt said of him: 'It is true that when Boullée set himself the task of expressing the immensity of the cosmos in his vast sacred monuments, he was undertaking the impossible. But that very utopia stems from tradition, for it is nothing else but the idea, handed down from the mists of time, of imitating the structure of the world in the construction of sacred buildings. A requirement that was already defended by Palladio (the spiritual ancestor of Classicism) as well as by Plato, and which was very probably even one of the principles of the great primitive civilisations (ziggurats of Mesopotamia or pyramids of Egypt) ...'

This desire for grandeur, which Boullée pursued to extremes in his Romanticism (in this respect he is close to poets like Novalis), had close links with cosmology, astronomy and science. It was not coincidental that he imagined a gigantic cenotaph for Newton in the shape of a sphere. The interior was to represent the vault of the heavens with openings cut out to represent the stars. An altar the size of the one in the Panthéon was to stand in the centre of the room and be lit, at night, by the rays of a 'starry sphere'. The new ideas which Ledoux actually applied, but which for Boullée remained no more than utopian fantasy, degenerated in the work of other Revolutionary architects into eccentric and extravagant Romanticism. Jean-Jacques Lequeu (1757–1825), to all intents and purposes, designed monuments which are a startling reminder of the stylistic mish-mash of Historicism. His Indian Pavilion can be compared, for example, with the famous designs of John Nash for the Pavilion in Brighton; the manor house Rendez-vous de Bellevue is a pot-pourri of different styles; he built public baths in the shape of a boat ... Lequeu certainly demonstrated a mastery of the theatrical, as did all the other Revolutionary architects. However, one might well ask whether the expression 'Revolutionary architecture' is, under the circumstances, apposite. These works were still close to the architecture of the Ancien Régime, and the only claim that they had in common with the French Revolution was to the social utopia, a claim that was widespread at the time even among princes and monarchs: even Emperor Josef II was described as 'revolutionary by the grace of God'.

The heritage of the Revolutionary architects

The Revolutionary architects left behind them, above all, an inspired 'rough draft', and fragments of Romanticism. They were instrumental, however, in establishing a clear line of thought which was to influence the architectural conceptions of the following era. Many of the best artists adopted their ideas and method of structural thinking: Verly, Tardieu, Vien, Barbier, Gay, Vaudoyer, Sobre and Bélanger, as well as Soane in England, Latrobe in the United States, with his hydraulic factory in Philadelphia, Thomas de Thomon with the Saint Petersburg Stock Exchange, Peter Speeth with his women's prison in Würzburg, and Isidor Canevale with the Augarten door in Vienna. Traces of the influence of Ledoux and Boullée can also be found in the work of Friedrich von Schinkel in Berlin; at the turn of the 20th century, in Joseph Maria Olbrich's Sezession building in Vienna; and, also in Vienna, in many of the designs of Otto Wagner, whose *City without limits* carried over Romantic and utopian ideals into 20th century architecture.

A new Roman Empire: the Napoleonic Empire

Napoleon set out to bring an end to Revolutionary architecture. Seeing himself as the successor of the Roman Emperors, to him politics and architecture were closely intertwined; so he strove to create a new Classical Imperial style, on a grand scale. It was difficult to reproduce the style of the Roman Republic; all that could be borrowed were the richly decorative forms of Roman Imperial architecture. In 1807, Napoleon declared: 'The realisation of great architectural projects is as necessary for the interests of my peoples as it is for my own satisfaction.' France, the occupied countries and, above all, the conquered countries had to be strewn with monuments to the glory of the new Empire. However, Napoleon placed his trust less in architects than in military engineers, who had the pick of favourite sites for these

Thomas de Thomon *The Stock Exchange*, Saint Petersburg (Leningrad)

monuments: roads and bridges, fortifications, administrative buildings. In Paris, Charles Percier (1764–1838) and Pierre-François-Léonard Fontaine (1762–1853) were commissioned
first of all to erect the Arc de Triomphe du Carrousel (1806) to commemorate the battle of
Austerlitz. Subsequently, the two architects were charged with one of the most interesting
projects in the field of urban architecture: to line the Rue de Rivoli (1811) with a series of
uniform arcades. Jean François Chalgrin (1739–1811), the most brilliant of the French Classical architects, built Saint-Philippe-du-Roule and, above all, the Arc de Triomphe de
L'Etoile, which was begun in 1806 and built along completely new lines in a style without
columns. These achievements of urban architecture were to be highly influential throughout
the the 19th century. The Arc de Triomphe, the most important of the monuments com-
memorating the Grande Armée, was erected at the exact point of intersection of new roads,
which radiated out like the rays of a star. It was situated precisely along the central axis of the
Louvre, and connected to it by the prestigious Avenue des Champs-Elysées.

Other great buildings of the Empire period include the temple of the Grande Armée, known today as the church of La Madeleine, designed by Vignon; the column on the Place Vendôme, designed by Gondoin and also dedicated to the Grande Armée, modelled on the Trajan column in Rome (itself restored by order of Napoleon); and finally, the reconstruction by Bélanger, in 1811, of the Halle au Blé (now the Bourse du travail).

From Josephism to Biedermeier

Classicism left numerous monuments in almost every state and principality in Europe, from England to Russia, from Sweden to Italy. They were all related stylistically, even though in some countries, in Saint Petersburg for example, particular phases of Classicism lasted longer than they did in others where new styles and new criteria overtook them. This can be explained by the fact that political, social and economic evolution progressed in different ways in different countries. In the Habsburg capital of Vienna, for example, we find a French-inspired Rococo. Jean-Nicolas Jadot de Villiers d'Issy, in the hall of the old university, built a palace of graceful proportions, its facade decorated with columns, which, at the very height of the Rococo period during the reign of Maria-Theresa, heralded the emergence of Classicism. Isidor Canevale built the Josephinum for Maria-Theresa's son Josef II, as well as the Augarten gate of Vienna which has links with Parisian revolutionary architecture, the Lusthaus in the Prater, and numerous palaces. But there is an air of coldness in the austere and functional architecture of 'Josephist' Vienna, in line with the Emperor's conceptions. The reforming work that he imposed strictly on the Empire, on the aristocracy or on himself, is in many ways reminiscent of the utopian attitude that accompanied the birth of Classicism and Romanticism. As a centralist, he had to organise his positivist Classicism around a central axis. Similarly, the severity of the Classical architecture of this period – which is perhaps most clearly expressed in the gigantic general hospital in Vienna – proclaimed its quest for a modern humanitarian ideal, a desire to concentrate on the essential. The social structures of Vienna were transformed, permitting the development of a specifically bourgeois culture recognisable in its way of life and its buildings. Thus the foundations were laid for the rise of the bourgeoisie, which accompanied the expansion of Vienna during the Historicist period.

The links between political thought and Classical architecture are even more evident in the anti-nationalistic and masonic centralism of Josef II. His dearest wish would have been to wipe out all traditions, and all the privileges of the different nationalities that made up the Empire, at a stroke. He dreamed of a strongly united nation which he, as the leading civil servant, would lead to happiness. The spiritual link with Classicism and its 'international' tendencies becomes evident here. The cold and imposing structures of this period can still be seen in almost any country today: residences of heads of state, commemorative monuments, city dwellings, museums, schools, banks, churches, and administrative buildings with colonnaded porticos. A list of some of the most famous gives some idea of how international was this type of building: in Paris, the Panthéon by Soufflot, Saint-Philippe-du-Roule by Chalgrin, the church of the Madeleine by Vignon; in Saint Petersburg, the Stock Exchange in the Strelka, by Thomas de Thomon, the State Bank and the Hermitage theatre by Quarenghi, Starow's Alexander Nevski Cathedral, the Kasan Cathedral by Woronichin, the Isaak Cathedral by Montferrand (1817–1857), and the Hermitage by Leo von Klenze (1839–1852). Quarenghi admitted to an Englishman that so many examples of 'that incongruous architectural accumulation of Greek columns' disgusted him. In Vienna Peter von Nobile built the *Temple of Theseus* and the *Ausseres Burgtheater*; Theophil von Hansen, at the height of

Thomas Jefferson *The Capitol*, Washington

Historicism (towards 1850–1880), built the Parliament, inspired by the Greek temples; Louis de Montoyer, the Rasumovsky palace with its heavy colonnaded portico; Josef Kornhäusel, the Vienna *Schottenstift* library (1826); Karl Schleps, the Coburg Palace (1842), with its great facade in two storeys of eight columns each. In Naples, Pietro Bianchi built the San Francisco di Paola (1816–1824), taking the Roman Pantheon as his model; Antonio Niccolini built the San Carlo theatre; Peter von Nobile, in Austrian Trieste, the church of San Antonio di Padua (1826–1849); in Milan, Giuseppe Piermarini, at the order of the Austrian Court, built the theatre of La Scala (1776–1778) and the residence of the Austrian envoy Belgiojoso. In Athens, there was the Academy, the Zappeion and the library by Theophil von Hansen, and the Royal Residence by Friedrich von Gärtner. In Munich, the Nationaltheater (1812–1818) by Karl von Fischer, and the Glypothek (1816–1831), the Propylaea on the Königsplatz and the Monopteros by Leo von Klenze, who also built the Valhalla near Regensburg. In Berlin, the Neue Wache (1816), the Schauspielhaus (1818–1821), the Altes Museum (1823) and in Potsdam, the Nicolai church, all by Karl Friedrich von Schinkel. In Madrid, the Prado Museum (1785) by Juan de Villanueva. In Washington, the Capitol (begun in 1792) by Jefferson and Hallet. In Philadelphia, the Pennsylvania Bank (1807–1808) by Latrobe; in Boston, the Customs House by Young (1804).

Classical architecture was not only an 'aesthetic monoculture'; in the end it degenerated into a universal style, which served as a cover for every conceivable type of representation. Classicism symbolised centralised power as well as democratic parliamentarianism; it could be applied to the bourgeois institutions of education and learning, and to the Church as well as banking institutions, stations, and exhibition halls. This influence lasted well into the present century, until the 1920s and 1930s, particularly in the United States and in the Soviet Union (witness the colonnade at the entrance to the Smolny Palace in Leningrad, dating from 1922). The Biedermeier in Germany and in Austria was expressed above all in the manufacture of remarkable pieces of furniture of strict geometric inspiration. The importance of this transposition of style to artefacts was to transform the craft industry, wiping the slate clean of Historicism and its exaggerated tastes. The movement was begun in England by John Ruskin and William Morris and ended about 1920, with the Wiener Werkstätte.

The 'political Gothic'

The artists of the Romantic century, very much a time of paradox, dreamed of bringing about a fusion of the Ancient and the Gothic through architecture. In fact, it was in the context of the German Gothic and of the Renaissance that the idea of nationalism was born, and where the roots of German Romanticism and Classicism are to be found. Karl Friedrich von Schinkel, fervent champion of the Greek ideal, spoke of the 'purification of the Gothic by Antiquity', of a fusion of styles after the manner of Goethe who, in a metaphor, brought Faust and Helen together in the theatre. 'We have a mission', proclaimed Novalis, 'we are called upon to shape the earth!'. Gothic now appeared side by side with Classicism: the primitive formal doctrine and the supranationality of Classicism, were contrasted with the dynamic, transcendant form of the Gothic, striving ever upwards – a form which, to the Romantic, symbolised nobility, purity and truth. Gothic was seen as the 'romantic' aspect of Romanticism, as opposed to its 'classical' aspect. (Similarly, many theoreticians regarded Romanticism as no more than a variant of Classicism, referring to 'romantic' Classicism and 'classical' Classicism). There were thus two parallel phenomena: on the one hand, the memory of the West's ancient and glorious past, and on the other, the historical consciousness of the greatness of mediaeval Germany. The most direct consequence of this growing awareness of the more recent past was, without question, the completion of the great German cathedrals; in France, the same movement was evident in the scientific and technical work of Eugène-Emmanuel Viollet-le-Duc (1814–1879), who applied his theories of engineering to the construction and restoration of cathedrals and castles.

In Germany, work started in about 1804 on the restoration of Cologne Cathedral, which was in a state of severe disrepair. The plans were drawn up to complete it were based on mediaeval sketches. During this time, the work on the cathedral unquestionably came to symbolise the German spirit and German art. The decision to complete it not only aroused the enthusiasm of the German people, but also contributed towards reinforcing their awareness of nationality. The movement born around this project gave the bourgeoisie the impetus necessary to consolidate its role as a builder. Romantic Gothic, which took inspiration from its setting, as had already been seen in the mid 18th century in England, in Wörlitz's *Gothic House*, and in the Franzensburg in Vienna, thus gave way to a true Gothic. Neo-Gothic, moreover, was very different from primitive Romantic Gothic. The Gothic Revival in England was created by writers like Horace Walpole; it was an intellectual game, devoid of political significance. There were also great differences in its technology. To build his refuge, Walpole did not call upon workers who specialised in Gothic, but on the modern craftsmen of London, trained by Robert Adam. As early as 1753, an English critic remarked that the intellectual side of the Gothic fashion was altogether too much attuned to 'English' 18th century trends; in consequence, it was not true Gothic, but more of a fashion, comparable to that of chinoiserie.

The Neo-Gothic of Historicism rather disapproved of this tendency. It even boasted that it was, with its rigorously precise copies, 'more Gothic than the Gothic'. When, in memory of the failed assassination attempt on Emperor Franz-Josef, Heinrich von Ferstel conceived his Votivkirche in Vienna (1856–1879), it was with such strict conformity to his models, the French cathedrals, that he felt he should correct all asymmetry, although asymmetry was a feature of the real Gothic, in order to achieve an idealised Gothic. This led the censors of Historicism to reproach him, with justification, for his academic eclecticism.

The apotheosis of patriotism: Nationalist Historicism

Architects had bridged the gap between the sober purity of Antiquity, regarded as the essence of architectural form, and the Gothic. It was at this time that the German passion for its own history, which had engendered the restoration of Cologne Cathedral, because evident: the influence of French culture, imposed on Germany for centuries, was increasingly resented, as was that of Italian culture in Austria. Although the Germans were still building in Classical style, particularly in Berlin and in Munich, patriotic themes were gradually replacing the themes of mythology. The Holy Roman Empire had not taken the place of the homeland, and now, in the century of national states, the notion of 'homeland' mobilised the middle classes. Architecture, sculpture and painting took on the task of expounding and interpreting that notion. One of the first great testimonies to this trend was the project to create what was called the 'building of the union' in the Franzensburg castle, at Laxenburg near Vienna. It was built between 1822 and 1836 (well before Klenze's Valhalla) and, in the Habsburg-Lorraine Hall, featured a patriotic spectacle in which the bourgeois Gothic glorified the reigning dynasty. In one respect, however, Germany differed from other countries: although the idea of the 'nation' was asserting itself more and more there, it could be no more than the idea of 'homeland', since it would be impossible to apply the concept of nationhood to such a multiplicity of different peoples.

This tendency gained ground and proliferated. The Nazarene Kupelwieser decorated the hall of the seat of government of Lower Austria with frescoes depicting the history of the Empire. When Theophil von Hansen built the temple to the glory of the Austrian army – the Byzantine wing of the Arsenal in Vienna – Emperor Franz-Josef demanded that this marble mausoleum should have a strongly didactic effect. There, as in so many other great buildings of the period – sacred monuments or state palaces – the same tendencies are apparent. Rich colouration suddenly succeeds cold Classical monotony; and an illusion of space, banished for decades, is characteristic of the new movement. Painting became the intermediary, bridging the gap between mural decoration and the illusion of space. 'Intersection' and 'overlapping' characterise the position it held in relation to the architectonics of interior volume. On the one

Heinrich von Ferstel *Votivkirche*, Vienna

hand, painting submitted totally to architecture, but on the other, architecture often deliberately allowed painting to dominate structural space.

As painting, which had been relegated by Classicism to the role of a mere tool, flowered once again, so sculpture and the art of stucco found themselves invested with new tasks. The plastic element was either an integral part of the decoration, or contributed to the creation of space itself. There was little common ground between Classicism and this new concept which emphasised the total work of art, where appearance, structure and atmosphere created a homogeneous whole, as, for example, in the architecture of the Ringstrasse. Creativity, whether architectural, sculptural, pictorial or decorative, had, almost unwittingly, thrown off its bonds. It was the dawn of Historicism, the Romantic phase of which began towards 1830. One of the best examples of the work of this period is the Alt Lerchenfeld church in Vienna, which Johann Georg Müller had built between 1848 and 1865. Its incredible pictorial richness is the work of Josef Führich, under the direction of the architect Eduard van der Nüll (who also built the Hofoper in Vienna). This basilica, which has three naves and a transversal nave with an octagonal dome above the crossing, is a typical example of the new Romantic Historicism, which is subtly reminiscent of the Lombard and Tuscan 14th century and has echoes of the Venetian San Salvatore.

It was in 1857 that the most important Viennese work of Romantic Historicism was born: the Vienna Hofoper. Its style recalls that of the early Florentine Renaissance, with a Romantic fresco, unique of its kind, by Moritz von Schwind. From then on, it seemed quite natural that almost all the buildings lining the immense Ringstrasse of Vienna should present such a wealth of architectural, pictorial, plastic and decorative effects. To gauge the extent of the break that occurred between Classicism and Historicism in Europe, one has only to compare the work of Karl Friedrich von Schinkel with that of Gottfried Semper, both of whom were among the leading architects of the 19th century.

The consistency with which these distinguished theoreticians justified their stylistic choices lends credibility to both of their arguments. However, a comparison shows that for Schinkel, the Gothic and Antiquity represented 'exalted missions and aims'. The Altes Museum in Berlin owes its dignity, as a sacred monument dedicated to Humanist thought, to the architecture of the Greek temples. In the grounds of Glienicke Castle, transformed by Schinkel in 1826–1827, he placed fragments of Ancient works here and there, which give the impression of having been discovered where they stand: the aim was to confer a more noble appearance on the castle and on the park. All of this symbolised the idea of humanity taught by history, the idea of a superior culture. The wild Romanticism of the park designed by Peter Lenne is representative of an attachment to the mystique of Nature. Wherever one looks, one is aware of this fusion of the Classical temple with Nature, of Classicism with Romanticism: in the temples of Concord which, since the time of Louis XVI, have proliferated in Europe, in Klenze's Valhalla, in the Gothic 'world' of Laxenburg. This idea was to reach its culmination in Schinkel's dream of building a royal palace on the Acropolis in Athens (1834), a dream which mercifully remained unfulfilled. The sacred element was also still a determining influence in Schinkel's Gothic buildings: in the funeral monument conceived for Queen Louise in 1810 there were typically Gothic effects of contrasting light and shadow, which expressed the Romantic notion of transcendency. Schinkel did not, however, draw upon this Romantic and humanistic conception of the world when working on his 'common buildings', that is to say utilitarian constructions such as department stores and houses.

By contrast, for the democratic Semper – a revolutionary unpopular in Germany and who worked in England on the Great Exhibition of 1851 – town halls, schools and stations

Johann George Muller *Altlerchenfelder Kirche*, Vienna

represented what Schinkel saw in palaces. In 1842, in Hamburg, Semper's Gothic style assimilated German and Dutch bourgeois tradition. In Zurich, he borrowed elements characteristic of the proud southern German bourgeoisie of the Renaissance period; the town hall of Winterthur, a raised temple in Roman style, ranks with Hansen's Academy of Athens, his Zappeion and his Parliament in Vienna, as one of the major works of this movement.

In analysing the distance that separated Semper from Schinkel, we can arrive at a better understanding of Historicist concepts. The turning point of 1830 did more than bring about a profusion of styles or weigh the scales in favour of the Renaissance. It was the very principles of style that had been radically transformed, in England as in France, Germany, Austria and Italy. Art no longer sought to represent the sacred or the human: the requisite now was that the style should 'marry' with its function, a concept which provided scope for the most varied of stylistic effects. The problem of the era was that of choosing a style, and of man's self-questioning as he endeavoured to reach an understanding of himself. Like his great contemporaries, such as Viollet-le-Duc, Semper attempted to conceive the principles of style by process of reason. The neo-Humanist ideals of early Romanticism seemed to have been assimilated, and the way seemed open to create new forms based on technique, as so fervently advocated by Semper, Viollet-le-Duc and Paxton.

Following the period of 'international' Classicism, the need for a national architecture arose, which had political inspiration. John Ruskin in England and Viollet-le-Duc in France supported national Gothic. It was epitomised by the French Renaissance (seen in the enlargement of the Hôtel de Ville in Paris and of the Louvre); the English Tudor style in the reign of Queen Victoria (Barry's Houses of Parliament, Highclere Castle); the brick-built Gothic adopted in Germany for innumerable churches, town halls and administrative buildings; and, concurrently, the exotic forms which abounded during this period until the end of the great era of the Ecole des Beaux-Arts in Paris. In addition, the International Exhibitions in London, Paris and Vienna gave the art of each country its own individual stamp.

The evolution of forms followed the same pattern. Although, in the Classical ideal of the first decades, many compositions can be found which combine elementary geometric forms with carefully planned volumes, a supremacy of symmetry and axes, enclosed and barely decorated surfaces, and priority of form over material, new forms and newly acquired notions were now becoming increasingly integrated with them. New trends emerged clearly towards 1850: forms were amalgamated, and skilfully erased former geometric clarity; designs became more and more complex, asymmetry reigned (particularly in England), sculptural and plastic effects became popular, and eventually real architectural luxuriance predominated. There was a passionate enthusiasm for colours, so muct so that Theophil von Hansen wanted to paint the Vienna Parliament in many colours, and Semper and Hasenauer, in their decoration of the

Gottfried Semper *Town Hall*, Winterthur

Imperial Museums in Vienna, produced a veritable riot of marbles of different colours and sorts, ornamented with burnished bronzes, pictures, reliefs and sculptures placed in wall niches.

Conclusion

It is too easy to regard the architectural heritage of the 19th century as no more than a motley collection of styles and forms. The temptation to do so is strong, but only partly justified. The architecture of this period did not confine itself merely to borrowing certain forms or typical motifs in order to use them as a starting point, as was the case in the relationship between the Renaissance and Antiquity. For the first time, motifs were regrouped into thematic categories. Also typical of this stylistic positivism was the attempt to arrive at a synthesis of styles. Anders Aman stressed that each of these groups of styles reflected a distinct development. To trace schematically the relations between these developments seems impossible, which is why it is so difficult to describe this period of architecture. It is only necessary to take one example, the Gothic, to see how wide the gap was between the Gothic Revival, which gave rise to strict geometric masses and fortress-like buildings, and the Neo-Gothic, with its skeletal lines, based on a precise study of ancient architectural forms. It is equally difficult to place these stylistic movements accurately in time: there was almost constant overlapping, which can be explained in terms of regional tradition, or national thought, or political and social trends, or even the predominant influence at a given time of one or other great architect.

ADAM Robert (Kirkcaldy, Fife 1728 – London 3.3.1792). Son of the eminent Scottish architect William Adam (1689–1748), Robert Adam travelled in Europe from 1754 to 1758 and spent two years in Rome studying architecture. There he became friendly with Piranesi. He travelled around Italy with Clérisseau visiting ancient sites. He went to Spalato (Split) to study Diocletian's Palace, and in 1764, published *Ruins of the Palace of the Emperor Diocletian at Spalato* in London. He received important commissions, such as Hatchlands Park, Surrey (1758–1759), Osterley House, Middlesex (1761), Home House, London, Syon House (1763–1764), and Kenwood House, Hampstead (1767–1769).

With his brothers, Adam developed a characteristic style of decoration: ceiling motifs borrowed from Roman tombs, mural decorations from Pompeii and Herculaneum, architectural forms from Palmyra and Baalbek, motifs from Raphael and the works of Clérisseau, from the painting of Greek vases and the English Palladian style.

In his later work, Adam also turned towards Gothic art and used it in a most imaginative way at Culzean Castle in Ayrshire, for example (1777–1790). Adam was the leading British architect of the 18th century.

Eglise de la Trinité, Paris

ALTHANS Ludwig Karl (Bückeburg 1788 – Sayn 1864). Initially a craftsman (musical instrument maker), then studied in Göttingen before being appointed clerk of works to Prince Lippe. In 1817, was appointed to the department of mine administration in Bonn to develop existing mines and forges. It was in this function that he built the metallurgical works at Sayn, Lohe and Hamm. The Sayn foundry was built according to an entirely new principle: for the first time, Althans replaced the external pinion with a metal construction. From a formal point of view, the building, which can be compared to a three-naved basilica, still represented a conservative solution. The iron pillars are shaped like columns. Even the ornamental effects are all derived from the functions of support and pillar. The factory was operational until 1926, and is now classed as a historical monument.

BALLU Theodore (Paris 1817 – Paris 1885). Pupil of Lebas at the Ecole des Beaux-Arts in Paris (1835–1840). After winning the Prix de Rome in 1840, Ballu went to Italy and Greece. He then worked in Paris with Franz Christian Gau on the construction of the Neo-Gothic Sainte-Clothilde Church. He restored the Saint-Jacques tower of the Saint-Germain-l'Auxerrois Church. Together with Deperthes, he worked on the reconstruction of the Hôtel de Ville, destroyed during the 1871 Commune. It was completed in 1882 and is one of his most important works, alongside the churches of La Trinité and Saint-Ambroise (1863–1869). Ballu mainly used the forms of the Renaissance, which he tried to adapt to modern requirements.

Ballu was accused of having brought a 'profane' element into his churches; but as works of architecture they are comparable to the Paris Opéra or the Palais Longchamp in Marseille.

BALTARD Victor (Paris 10.6.1805 – Paris 13.1.1874). An architect's son, studied at the Ecole des Beaux-Arts in Paris and lived in Rome from 1834 to 1839, after winning the Grand Prix for architecture. Appointed Inspector of the Beaux-Arts and Civil Buildings, he directed the restoration of several churches. In 1845, he was commissioned to build the new Halles, the Halle au Blé having been built in 1809–1811 by Bélanger and Brunet. He wanted to use stone, but his first building was violently criticised and he was obliged to draw up new plans in

Les Halles, Paris

collaboration with Félix Emmanuel Callet. The Halles, demolished in the 1970s, was the most important iron construction, outside England, of the mid 18th century. From 1853, Baltard was the architect of the Hôtel de Ville in Paris; with Hippolyte Flandrin, he decorated the interior of the church of Saint-Germain des Prés (1854–1863). In 1860, he became Chief Architect of the City of Paris. Beside the Halles, his other masterpiece is the church of Saint-Augustin (1860–1867); the roof and dome are built of iron, but this infrastructure is invisible behind the 'neo-Byzantine' or 'neo-Romanesque' style. Baltard ranks with Viollet-le-Duc, Labrouste and Garnier among the most brilliant and most important architects of the Second Empire. Although in style they were eclectic, they made some fundamental technical innovations.

BARRY Sir Charles (London 23.5.1795 – London 12.5.1860). After working in drawing, Barry then studied architecture. He was decisively influenced by a three-year journey in Europe and the East, and this was reflected in his work. His buildings are characteristic of English architecture after 1820: in church building, the Romantic Gothic tradition was emerging, while for public building, Greek forms were preferred. Barry attempted to invest Classical elements with a solemn intensity: the Traveller's Club (1830–1832) and the Reform Club (1838–1840) in Pall Mall have an air of the Italian

'palazzo' which might suggest that his work evolved along similar lines to that of Klenze (Leuchtenberg Palace in Munich; Fries-Pallavicini Palace in Vienna). Between 1834 and 1837, he worked with Augustus Welby Northmore Pugin for the first time, on King Edward's Grammar School in Birmingham. From 1840 until his death, he and Pugin directed the construction of the Houses of Parliament.

In 1834, the old Palace of Westminster was destroyed by fire. The rules of the competition for its reconstruction demanded either Gothic or Elizabethan style, to conform with Westminster Abbey and Westminster Hall, which were undamaged. In 1837, Barry's design was chosen in preference to ninety-six other designs that had been submitted. This gave rise to much dispute about the 'secularisation' of Gothic style and how to use it in a contemporary way. Construction began in 1840. The House of Lords was completed in 1848, and the House of Commons in 1852. With the exception of some asymmetrical elements (Big Ben, Victoria Tower), the building was conceived in strictly symmetrical fashion, which is not in fact compatible with Gothic style, but more in keeping with English tradition. During the construction of the Houses of Parliament, Barry also built Pentonville Prison, transformed Highclere Castle in Hampshire and built Bridgewater House.

Houses of Parliament, London

BOGARDUS James (Catskill, New York 1800 – New York 1874). A clockmaker and engraver, Bogardus invented chronometers, printing presses and a machine to produce compressed glass. But his most brilliant invention was that of building structures made entirely of iron. His first experiment was the construction of his own factory in New York, where he assembled his clocks. This factory, where everything – props, external walls, doors, window frames – was made of iron, was built in 1848–1849 on the corner of Centre Street and Duane Street.

It was practically the first building to be constructed from prefabricated elements that were bolted together. There was very little decoration on the facades, and costs were considerably lower than those for a normal building. As was the case later with Paxton's Crystal Palace in London, the construction was easy to dismantle. Bogardus built other edifices of prefabricated materials in New York and Baltimore. In 1856, he published *Cast Iron Buildings: Their Construction and Advantages*.

BOULLÉE Etienne-Louis (Paris 1728 – Paris 1799). Boullée's father, Louis-Claude Boullée, was a brilliant architect and his mother was related to François Boucher. Etienne Louis was a gifted painter who studied with Lancret. Until about 1778, he designed private houses and their decorations: the Tourolle house (1762), the Alexandre house (1763), the hôtel de Monville (1764), the Château de Chaville (1764), plans for the reconstruction of the Palais-Bourbon (1764), the hôtel d'Evreux (1768–1805), the Beaujon house, the hôtel de Brunoy, and designs for the palace of the Count of Artois (c. 1780). After legal wranglings with the financier Nicolas Beaujon, he devoted himself mainly to projects in the public sectors, such as his design for a Neo-Classical transformation of Versailles (c. 1780), plans for the church of the *Madeleine* in the form of a temple with a central dome, a plan for the new Opera House (1781) as a circular temple decorated with columns, sketches for museums – in short, his architecture assumed larger and larger dimensions, and aspired to a Classical yet utopian ideal.

However, Boullée gradually drew away from the forms of Vignola and Palladio and tried to return to more ancient times: the Babylonian and Assyrian mastaba, the Tower of Babel, and the Egyptian pyramids, the simple symmetry of which he found so convincing. Finally, like Claude-Nicolas Ledoux, he adopted the spherical shape: his cenotaph of Newton, conceived in 1784, was to have been a spherical construction that reproduced the vault of the heavens. In the centre, an altar the size of the Panthéon in Paris would stand.

BURTON Decimus (London 1800 – St Leonards on Sea 1881). Burton's interest in architectural matters was influenced by his father, also an architect. At the age of 23, he erected the Colosseum in Regent's Park in London, a domed exhibition hall which was later pulled down. He sought inspiration from Greece and there developed his architectural ideas. In 1825, he designed the monumental arch at Hyde Park Corner with its colonnades and then, in 1829–1830, his masterpiece, the Athenaeum Club, built in pure Neo-Classical style and decorated with a copy of the Parthenon frieze. Burton built the Athenaeum directly opposite the United Services Club by John Nash (1827) on the other side of Waterloo Place. A comparison of the two buildings shows how much more 'modern', or more 'Greek', Burton's was. In fact, in 1858 Burton transformed Nash's club and decorated it with a frieze. His other work includes Charing Cross Hospital (1831) and three other constructions which also helped to establish him as a

Athenaeum Club, London

pioneer of modern architecture: the greenhouses at Chatsworth, which he erected from 1837 in collaboration with John Paxton, the architect of Crystal Palace; the Botanical Garden at Regent's Park (from 1840), and the Palm House in Kew Gardens (from 1845), built entirely in iron and glass.

CAGNOLA Luigi Marchese (Milan 9.6.1762 – Inverigo, near Milan 14.8.1833). The son of an aristocratic family, Cagnola was destined for a diplomatic career. His interest in archaeology and his studies of architecture at the Collegio Pio Clementino in Rome while he was also studying Law, made him a civil servant of wide-ranging education and culture.

In Venice, he studied the building of Palladio and Sansovino, and, under the influence of their work, developed some of the characteristics of his own style. On his return to Milan, he was a member of the Municipal Council and responsible for many aspects of town planning. In 1795, he was summoned to Vienna where he designed the tomb of the Empress Maria Ludovica d'Este. He returned to Vienna in 1820 to present the Emperor with his plans for the transformation and development of the Hofburg and for the construction of the Neue Burgtor. At the same time, he designed a funeral chapel for Prince Metternich in Königswarth and drew up plans for the conversion of Milan Cathedral. His most important work was the Arco della Pace in Milan, a triumphal arch erected on the occasion of the marriage of Eugène de Beauharnais and Augusta Amalia of Bavaria in 1806. Initially made of wood and canvas, it was built in stone in the context of the Foro Buonaparte, a project of Cagnola's commissioned by Napoleon. Only two-thirds of it was built when, after Waterloo, construction work was halted. After 1827, Franz I of Austria had work resumed and the triumphal arch served to glorify the Peace of Vienna (1815). In 1859, following the peace between Napoleon III and Victor Emmanuel, this masterpiece of Italian Classicism was officially re-named Arco del Sempione.

CAMERON Charles (Scotland c. 1740 – Saint Petersburg 1812). At the time when Cameron arrived in Russia in 1774, the undisputed leader of the architectural community in Saint Petersburg, Bartolomeo Francesco Rastrelli, had just fallen from favour because of his extravagant Rococo style. The Czarina Catherine the Great (1762–1796), who was attempting to impose Classical architecture with the help of Vallin de la Mothe and his Academy of Fine Arts (1765–1772) and Rinaldi with his Marble Palace (1768–1772), saw Cameron as the ideal architect to realise her goal. With Cameron, the purity of Anglo-Scottish Classicism became the height of fashion. He drew on all the impressions and experiences he had gathered in Rome in 1768 while preparing his folio *The Baths of Rome*, the work that had brought him to Catherine's attention. Many of his constructions in Russia resemble the work of Robert Adam, because, like Adam, Cameron was friendly with Clérisseau and had been influenced by him. Thus, at the Palace of Tsarskoe Selo (known today as Pushkin), there are baths built in the Romano-Classical style of his drawings. In 1781–1796, he built the Summer Palace of Pavlovsk for Catherine's son, the Grand Duke Paul. After a brief period of disfavour on Paul's accession to the throne, during which he worked for private clients, later, at the time of the construction of the Admiralty in Saint Petersburg, he was appointed architect-in-chief by Alexander I.

CANEVALE Isidor Marcellus Amandus (Vincennes 1730 – Vienna 1786). Came to Vienna in 1760 with his teacher Giovanni Niccolo Servandoni. His first works were influenced by the Rococo (Palace of Count Paar, 1769). He worked for the Austrian and Hungarian nobility, for Cardinal Migazzi, from 1762 to 1772, on the cathedral in Waitzen, and, from 1775 on, together with Ferdinand Hetzendorf von Hohenberg, he was one of the architects of the Court of Empress Maria-Theresa and Emperor Josef II. Hohenberg built in Neo-Classical and Romantic style in which Baroque pomp was still much in evidence, but Canevale soon emerged as the ideal architect to satisfy Josef II's spartan tastes. Severity of form prevailed in all his buildings. Constructions like the gates of the Augarten, of the Kaiser-Josef-Stöckl or the Lusthaus in the Prater, are related to those of the French revolutionary architects, particularly Ledoux. What characterises the gateway to the *Augarten*, for example, is the cubist effect of the gatekeepers' lodges, with the three-arched triumphal arch, reduced in size, and a completely flat Attic style crown. A typical example of Canevale's summerhouses is the stark *Lusthaus* in the Prater, with its three galleries of columns, one on top of the other, and devoid of ornamentation. Canevale's major works include the surgico-medical academy of the *Josephinum*, built in 1783–1785; here, although he used a main courtyard typical of a French palace, he employed a modern and functional division of interior space (the ceilings of the library rooms are supported by very slender modern columns, which are metal-covered and topped with Egyptian capitals). He also built the huge hospital, the Wiener Allgemeines Krankenhaus, with seven courtyards and a 'madmen's tower' built like a fortress and clearly derived from the architecture of the Revolution.

Pont des Arts, Paris

CESSART Louis Alexandre de (Paris 1719 – Rouen 1806) Cessart's bridges and harbour installations at Cherbourg, Dieppe and Le Tréport are among the oldest and most important examples of engineering architecture in France. His major works include a swing bridge at Le Havre and the Pont des Arts in Paris which he built with de Lacroix Dillon in 1801–1803, the first iron bridge ever built in France (the first German iron bridge was built in 1796).

CHALGRIN Jean-François (Paris 1739 – Paris 20.1.1811). A pupil of Loriot, colleague of Canevale under Giovanni Niccolo Servandoni and a colleague of Moreau-Desproux. In 1758, he won the Grand Prix for architecture and left for Rome in 1759. On his return, he was appointed Inspector of Buildings in Paris. In 1769, with his Neo-Classical church of Saint-Philippe-du-

Palais du Luxembourg: grand staircase, Paris

Roule, he created the model basilica of the last third of the 18th century.

He rebuilt the north tower of Saint-Sulpice in Paris after the church had been partly destroyed by lightning, and also the baptistry and Saint-Viatique chapel. Between 1780 and 1784, he worked on the conversion of the Collège de France and from 1795, at the Palais du Luxembourg, where he built the grand staircase and the right wing and designed the colonnades of the courtyard and the Senate chamber. He also worked on the interior of the Odéon theatre.

From the point of view of style, Chalgrin belonged to the old generation of architects which had little in common with the modern Classicism of revolutionary and Napoleonic architecture. However his masterpiece, the Arc de Triomphe on the Place de l'Etoile in Paris, conceived from 1806 at the request of Napoleon, was one of the most controversial monuments of the 19th century and had a strong influence on urban development until the time of Napoleon III.

Chalgrin did not live to see the completion of his Arc de Triomphe. After his death, his pupil Goust, then Jean Nicolas Huyot and later Guillaume Abel Blouet, supervised the building work. The Arc de Triomphe was finally completed in 1836–1837. It was 49 metres high, 46 metres wide and 22 metres in depth. The decorative sculptures are by Rude, Cortot and Etex. At the same time as the Arc de Triomphe, Napoleon had commissioned Percier and Fontaine to make a smaller version of it for the Place du Carrousel (1806–1808), to complete the perspective between the Tuileries and the Etoile.

CHAMBERS Sir William (Göteborg, Sweden 1723 – London 8.3.1796). Born in Sweden of Scottish parents. In the service of the Swedish East India Company, Chambers spent ten years travelling around India, mainly in Bengal, and then in the Far East. In 1749 he decided to become an architect. After studying with Jean-François Blondel in Paris and five years' studying in Italy, he returned to London.

Thanks to the influence of Princess Augusta, he created the various exotic buildings in Kew Gardens – a ten-storey pagoda, a mosque, a temple, and a Roman arch (1752–1762) – which reveal stylistic influences from many lands. During this period he also published his *Designs of Chinese Buildings* (1757) and *Civil Architecture* (1759).

During the years that followed, Chambers was heaped with honours and, in 1782, became chief architect to the King. In 1768, he played a decisive part in the foundation of the Royal Academy in London. In 1770, he was awarded a Swedish knighthood by King Gustav III.

William Chambers, together with his principal rival

Robert Adam, was the most important English architect of the late 18th century. His most characteristic building is the administrative block of *Somerset House* in London, on which he worked from 1776 until his death. Chamber's composite style, which had affinities with Roman Antiquity and the Renaissance, showed the influence both of French style (of Le Roy, for example) and of Palladian Classicism. However, he totally rejected the Gothic Revival and Neo-Gothic style.

CLÉRISSEAU Charles-Louis (Paris 1721 – Auteuil 1820) Studied at Blondel's school in Paris, won the Prix de Rome in 1746, and studied in Rome from 1749 under Pannini. He developed Pannini's art of designing ruins with extraordinary skill. He loved ancient architecture and drawing and was on good terms with Piranesi, Winckelmann and Gavin Hamilton's circle. In 1753 he left the Académie Française in Rome as a result of disagreements with its Director. In Florence, he met Robert Adam who engaged him as a guide and draughtsman (Hadrian's Villa, Tivoli, The Thermae, Diocletian's Palace). Before finally leaving Italy in 1766, he created the sumptuous 'decoration of ruins' for the convent of the Roman Trinita dei Monti church. In 1778, he spent time in the French Midi studying the Roman monuments there for his work Les Antiquités de la France.
In 1779, he was summoned by Catherine of Russia who commissioned many projects; and in 1780 Jefferson consulted him about the construction of the Virginia State Capitol, one of the first administrative 'temples' in Classical style. Clérisseau left a vast collection of architectural drawings.

CORAZZI Antonio (Livorno 1792 – Florence 1877). Pupil of Giuseppe del Rosso in Florence. In 1818, Stanislaw Stazsic summoned him to Warsaw, where he became chief architect to the Polish government. He built the Stazsic Palace in 1820–1823, the Committee of the Interior Building in 1823, the Committee of State Finance Building in 1824–1825, the Minister of Finance's Palace in 1824–1830, and, in 1825–1828, the Polish State Bank. He also built the Grand Theatre in 1825–1833 and, in 1841, the Saxony Square obelisk. Like Rossi in Saint Petersburg and Engels in Helsinki, he was the figurehead of construction in Warsaw and one of the foremost representatives of Classicism in Eastern Europe.

CUYPERS Petrus Josephus Hubertus (Roermond 16.5.1827 – Roermond 3.3.1921). Took part in the restoration of Roermond Cathedral, assisted by Viollet-le-Duc and Vinzenz Statz of Cologne. From 1863, he worked in Amsterdam where he built the Rijksmuseum (1877–1885) and the central railway station (1881–1889, with Adolf Leonard van Gendt). Cuypers attempted to create a neo-Renaissance Dutch national architecture. He also built several churches, including the Saint Dominic and Magdalen churches in Amsterdam. Cuypers was particularly fond of early French Gothic style, which he adapted to suit the brick-built style of his country. His finest church constructions are similar to the works of William Butterfield.

DANCE George the Younger (London 1741 – London 1825) Like most of his colleagues, Dance's education came from a stay in Italy (1758–1767). In 1768, he succeeded his father as architect to the City of London. Between 1770 and 1780, he built the London municipal prison, Newgate Prison, which was a synthesis of stylistic elements borrowed from Serlio, Palladio and Giulio Romano from the Italian cinquecento as well as from his friend Piranesi. He also experimented with a Gothic style devoid of all picturesque elements : Coleorton Hall (1804–1808) and Ashburnham Place (1813–1817) are examples. Dance, a founder member of the Royal Academy in London, became one of the most interesting pioneers of English Classicism: his pendentive domes for All Hallows Church and the Guildhall Council Chamber influenced his famous pupil John Soane to adopt these elements in his construction of the Bank of England.

DURAND Jean-Nicolas-Louis (Paris 1760 – Paris 1834) A pupil of Boullée, Durand was an architect, an archaeologist and a theoretician. In 1788, he created the *Maison Lathuile* which already embodied all the characteristics of his style: ancient elements – especially massive doric columns and caryatids – combined with fashionable elements, similar to those used by Bélanger. Vaulted rooms were joined into long wings and grouped around square courtyards. During the Revolution, he and Thibault took part in various competitions. After the success of his Temple Décadaire in 1795, he finally became Professor of Architecture at the Ecole Polytechnique. He published his *Accounts of Architecture Lessons Given at the Ecole Polytechnique*, followed in 1810 by his reference work on *Ancient and Modern Edifices remarkable for their Beauty and Size*, known under the title *Grand Durand* and influential throughout the 19th century, in Germany and America as well as in France.

pieces were the pilgrimage church of Notre-Dame de la Garde with its elements of Byzantine style, and the Palais Longchamp, a vast arc, built around a group of monumental figures sculpted by Bartholdi, and representing an allegory of the Durance river which, via an aquaduct, had provided Marseille with water since 1847. The Palais Longchamp is the largest and most grandiose structure of the Second Empire outside Paris.

DU RY Simon Louis (Kassel 13.1.1726 – Kassel 23.8.1799). The last architect of the old Huguenot dynasty that left its mark on the Baroque town of Kassel. He studied from 1746 to 1748 in Stockholm with Harleman, then until 1752 at Blondel's Academy of Architecture in Paris, and after that in Italy. After the end of the Seven Years' War, it was decided in 1756 to undertake a major rebuilding programme on the Oberneustadt in Kassel and to demolish the ramparts. Du Ry built the Town Hall, the French Hospital, palaces for the nobility and houses for the bourgeoisie. The influence of English Classicism was increasingly evident in his work after 1770. From 1767 to 1770, he created the Königsplatz, and the Museum Fridericianum, with its massive colonnaded facade reminiscent of Ledoux, was completed in 1779.

ESPÉRANDIEU Henri (Nimes 1829 – Marseille 1874). A pupil of Léon Vaudoyers at the Ecole des Beaux-Arts in Paris, and of Charles Auguste Questel. From 1855, he supervised the building of Marseille Cathedral, the architect of which was his teacher Vaudoyers. In 1872, he became architect to the City of Marseille where he built the Ecole des Beaux-Arts and the Bibliothèque municipale in a pompous, composite style. His master-

Palais Longchamp, Marseille

FERSTEL Heinrich von Freiherr (Vienna 1828 – Vienna 1883). Studied from 1847 to 1850 at the Kunstakademie in Vienna. At the age of 27, he won first prize in an international competition organised to build a commemorative church after Emperor Franz-Joseph had survived an assassination attempt, and became famous throughout Central Europe. The Votivkirche (1856–1879) was built of squared limestone in the style of the 14th century cathedrals. It is one of the most important monuments of Neo-Gothic style. Afterwards, Ferstel designed some of the most beautiful buildings of the Vienna Ringstrasse. The first, which corresponded to the beginning of his return to the Italian high Renaissance, was the Osterreichisch Ungarische Nationalbank in Vienna (1855–1860): it was characterised by galleries with stained glass windows and an octagonal courtyard with a glass dome, monumental fountains and sculptures and highly Romantic interior decoration. Later buildings were designed in Italian Renaissance style: the palace of the Archduke Ludwig Viktor (1864–1869); the main buildings of the University of Vienna (1873–1883); the so-called Belvedere Wing of the Liechtenstein Palace in the Rossau (1873–1875); and the Museum of Applied Arts, constructed in richly decorated unpointed brickwork.
Like almost all the great architects of the Ringstrasse, Ferstel refined the decorative arts to an extreme degree in the decoration of his buildings (which, in the final analysis, explains the influence of the craftsmanship of Viennese Historicism until the time of the Wiener Workstätte).

FISCHER Karl von (Mannheim 19.9.1782 – Munich 12.2.1820). On student journeys to Paris and Italy, Fischer embraced rigorous Classicism with enthusiasm and made the Palladian positioning of columns the criterion of his architecture. From 1803 to 1806, he built the Prince Karl Palace in Munich. Before he was twenty, Fischer won the competition to build the national theatre in Munich and proceeded to do so, from 1812 to 1818, in strictly Classical style, decorated with ten monumental columns. At the same time, he built eight palaces, including the Max-Vorstadt, the Glypothek, the Valhalla and the Residenz for Crown Prince Ludwig. Gravely ill and overburdened with work, he died in 1820. In 1816, the Crown Prince gave him Leo von Klenze, a pupil of Gilly, as an assistant.

Fischer's achievement was that, in the face of the Rococo style of Schedel von Greifenstein, Cuvillié the Younger and Lorenzo Quaglio, and the Pre-Classicism of the Administrator of the Court for building works, Andreas Gärtner, he imposed stately forms and opened the way for the Classicism of Palladio and Ledoux.

FONTAINE Pierre-Francois-Léonard (Pontoise 20.9.1762 – Paris 10.10.1853) and **PERCIER Charles** (Paris 22.8.1764 – Paris 5.9.1838). During a visit to Italy together, Fontaine and his friend Charles Percier studied the buildings of the Renaissance and ancient ruins. On their return to Paris, they became scenographers at the Opéra. At the time of the Revolution, Fontaine left for London where he developed his characteristically pleasing decorative style. Percier, who had stayed in France, was favoured by the Directoire: he called Fontaine back to Paris and worked with him on several decorative commissions. Percier and Fontaine, together with Clérisseau, Gondoin and Bélanger, attempted to popularise English Classicism in France. Jacques-Louis David introduced Percier and Fontaine to Napoleon, who gave them various commissions during the Empire period. In 1814, Percier retired from public life, but Fontaine continued to work. At the Louvre, he completed the colonnaded staircase and decorated the sculpture galleries between the Cour Carrée and the Seine. He built the commemorative chapel to Louis XVI and Marie-Antoinette

Arc de Triomphe du Carrousel, Paris

in the Madeleine. After 1820, he worked on the interiors of the Palais-Royal and finally became artistic adviser to Louis-Philippe.

The best-known works by Fontaine and Percier are the *Arc de Triomphe du Carrousel*, at one end of the Tuileries-Etoile axis, built in 1806–1808 and modelled on the Arch of Septimus Severus in Rome; and the arcades of the Rue de Rivoli (1811). One of their most charming, but never realised, projects was a palace for Napoleon's sons on the Chaillot hill.

FÖRSTER Ludwig Christian Friedrich von (Bayreuth 8.10.1797 – Bad Gleichenberg in Styria 16.6.1863). Trained at the Munich Academy, then in Vienna where he was appointed to the Academy by Peter von Nobile, the director of the department of architecture of the Vienna Academy. In 1836, Förster founded the 'Allgemeine Bauzeitung', through which he exerted decisive influence, particularly as a theoretician, on the architecture of Austria-Hungary. From 1839, he worked on plans for enlarging the city of Vienna. From 1843 to 1846, he was Professor of Architecture at the Vienna Academy. He worked with Theophil von Hansen on the Museum of Army History in the Vienna Arsenal (1849–1856), built the Elisabeth Bridge (1854), the Leopoldstadt Synagogue in Moorish style (1853–1858), and various palaces and dwelling houses.

For almost twenty years, Förster worked on the plans for the Ringstrasse, the magnificent avenue begun in 1857. It was built to a width of 57 metres and stretches 5.3 kilometres in length. It is one of the rare thoroughfares in Europe that perfectly embodies Historicism and all its ideas in a didactic programme, and provides a synthesis of historical references and modern techniques which embodies the Romantic conception of the total work of art.

GABRIEL Jacques-Ange (Paris 1698 – Paris 1782). Initiated from childhood to the tasks of a royal architect, as he was the son of the famous Jacques Gabriel, architect to the Court of Louis XV. Jacques-Ange collaborated on his father's designs and completed them after the latter's death (1742). He was the king's Controller of Buildings and a member of the Academy of Architecture. In 1742, he was First Architect to the King. He remodelled sever-

Opera House, Versailles

Arts in Paris and worked as a draughtsman with Viollet-le-Duc. A six-year scholarship to Rome familiarised him with Antiquity and with the architectural forms of the Renaissance and Roman Baroque.

On his return to Paris in 1852, he worked with Théodore Ballu on the restoration of the Tour Saint-Jacques. In 1860, he took part in the competition for a new Opera House in Paris and was chosen out of 170 other contenders. Thus, although hardly known and barely noticed as an architect until then, he was entrusted with the largest construction to be commissioned in Paris in the 19th century. With his Neo-Baroque overladen with detail, Garnier, supremely confident, wanted to create, as he said himself, 'a Napoleon III style'. His Paris Opéra (1862–1874) gave rise to a wave of Neo-Baroque architecture in France (Espérandieu, for instance), which spread to Germany, Italy and even to North and South America. Garnier left a relatively small number of large buildings: the most fascinating of them is the Casino in Monte-Carlo (1878–1879) which is based on the Opéra in Paris. Garnier's importance, success and influence resulted not necessarily from an extraordinarily bold and modern formal solution, but rather from the synthesis and accumulation of detail seen in his work. Each element of the structure is accentuated, almost to a theatrical extent: the vestibule, the staircase, the foyer, the stage, the cloakrooms, the iron dome visible for miles around, the reflection of the interior decoration on the facades, and the sculptures (very conventional, with the exception of

Paris Opera House: grand staircase

al royal residences (Fontainebleau, 1749; Compiègne, 1751; Choisy, 1752; Blois, 1752) and did not retire until after Louis XV's death in 1774.

Among his masterpieces are the embellishment of the Place Louis XV, now Place de la Concorde, by the addition of the two palaces which form the north side of the square (from 1756). He borrowed from the Louvre the idea of an isolated colonnade on a massive plinth, but without using the principle of double columns. He built the Ecole Militaire in Paris (1769), the Opéra (1768–1770), and the Petit Trianon (1762–1764) at Versailles. From 1755, he worked on the restoration of the Louvre. For the interiors, he collaborated for the most part with Verberckt and Guibert. His Neo-Classical stance gave rise to criticism, but Ledoux and Viollet-le-Duc ranked among his great admirers and heirs. Louis XV particularly appreciated the balance and clarity of Gabriel's compositions, the sobriety of his ornamentation and his sense of urbanism.

GARNIER Charles (Paris 6.11.1825 – Paris 3.8.1898). Studied with Hipollyte Lebas at the Ecole des Beaux-

Paris Opera House: detail of main facade

In 1814, Gärtner went to Paris and studied with Percier and Fontaine, whose Ruc de Rivoli greatly impressed him. During study trips to Italy (1815–1817) and to London (1819–1820), he familiarised himself with all aspects of town planning and modern architectural aesthetics. In 1820, he became a professor at the Munich Academy. But it was not until 1827 that he gained favour with King Ludwig I of Bavaria who was to promote him to a rank equal to that of Leo von Klenze, then Director of Architectural Administration to the Court. In 1835–1836, he travelled to Greece with the King and, in competition with Klenze, conceived a design for the royal castle in Athens to be built for Ludwig's son, King Othon of Greece (built 1837–1841). According to the King's wishes, he started, in 1837, to design the Befreiungshalle at Kelheim, but after his death in 1847, Leo von Klenze carried out the construction of it according to his own designs.

Gärtner's principal works are the Odeonplatz in Munich and the facade of the Ludwigstrasse into which he integrated the Feldherrnhalle; he modified its Florentine design in such a way that it acts as a balancing element between the Baroque Theaterkirche, the Renaissance style facade of the Residenz, the Hofgartentor and the Odeonplatz.

GENTZ Heinrich (Breslau 5.2.1766 – Berlin 3.10.1811) Brought up in a family of artists, Gentz trained in drawing and architecture and studied with Karl von Gontard.

Neue Münze, Berlin

La Danse by Carpeaux and *La Musique* by Guillaume), each of which, unusually, had a life of its own. The spatial vision seems daring, precisely because of this extraordinary accumulation of detail, which Garnier consciously borrowed from a great number of illustrious sources (Sansovino, Palladio, Perrault, Levau, Piranesi...)

Other characteristics of Garnier's architecture are the variety of the materials he used, his original combinations of colours and the exuberance of his designs.

GÄRTNER Friedrich von (Koblenz 10.12.1792 – Munich 21.4.1847). Sent by his father, the architect Andreas Gärtner, to the Munich Academy, Gärtner was introduced into the Karlsruhe studio of Friedrich Weinbrenner who, as early as 1806, was radically transforming German town planning.

After study trips to Paestum and to Sicily, he stayed in Rome where he was welcomed into the circle of artists around Carstens and Weinbrenner. In 1795, he became Inspector of Building to the Court and in 1796 a professor at the Academy. He created a sensation with his Neue Münze (New Mint), built in Berlin in 1798, which, in its unconventional use of Classical elements, paved the way for modern architecture. The *Münze* is one of the few buildings of the first Classicist period to demonstrate a purely spatial conception and to have an enduring influence (as in Vienna with the work of Canevale, von Nobile, Fischer and Sprenger).

His contribution to the great competition organised in Berlin for a monument to Frederick the Great was an immense construction with Egyptian-style funeral chambers, vast staircases, obelisks and a triumphal arch. From 1801 to 1803, Gentz worked for Duke Karl August on the conversion and interior decoration of Weimar Castle. His major works include the mausoleum in the grounds of Charlottenburg Castle (in collaboration with Schinkel) and the design for the princesses' palace, which was never built. Gentz had a strong influence on Schinkel who learnt from him to develop the character of a building from its interior and its intended purpose.

Gentz's architecture is characterised by massive cubes, heaviness and original proportions, which both reflect the architecture of the French Revolution and herald modernity.

GILLY Friedrich (Berlin 16.2.1772 – Berlin 3.8.1800) Trained with his father, a Prussian architect and Director of works in Pomerania. Fascinated by the national monuments of Germany, he made drawings for the inventory of the Marienburg. In 1788, he studied in Berlin under Langhans, Becherer and Erdmannsdorff. He became Inspector of Buildings to the Court and at the same time studied Ancient literature and art, which awakened an interest in Greek style. At the age of nineteen, he was teaching at the Bauakademie in Berlin, taking the line that German architecture had to work towards a 'rebirth of Antiquity'.

In 1796–97, he conceived extraordinary designs for the monument to Frederick the Great in Berlin, in which the influence of French Revolutionary architecture was palpable: Egyptian funeral chambers, exterior staircases in Oriental style, obelisks, Greek temples and huge triumphal arches. In 1798, he made a design for a theatre in Berlin, a construction of great sobriety, built of rustic blocks.

Gilly's classes were as important as his few buildings. He was at the centre of a circle of architects that included, notably, Haller von Hallerstein, Klenze and Schinkel. Schinkel later acknowledged his indebtedness to Gilly, just as Klenze's Valhalla would have been inconceivable without Gilly's design for the monument to Frederick the Great.

GONDOIN Jacques (St. Ouen-sur-Seine 1757 – Paris 1818). This rigorously Classicist French architect drew on the examples of Greek and Roman Antiquity. He created the column on the Place Vendôme, inspired by the Trajan column in Rome. In 1780, he drew the plans for the School of Surgery in Paris, which was considered 'the most Classical building of the 18th century'. His inspiration for the amphitheatre of anatomy was the Roman Pantheon of Agrippa, while the facade may well have been influenced by Robert Adam's Admiralty in Whitehall, which Gondoin saw during a journey to England.

HALLER VON HALLERSTEIN Carl Freiherr (Hillpolstein near Nuremberg 10.6.1774 – Ampelakia, Thessaly 5.11.1817). Having served briefly as a page at the court of Nassau-Sarrebruck, started his architectural studies at the Academy of Fine Arts in Stuttgart, then went to Berlin where he joined the circle around Friedrich Gilly, who influenced his work decisively.

Haller became Inspector of Buildings of the town of Nuremberg; in 1808 he went to Italy, and in 1810 to Greece where he made friends with Charles Cockerell who had made an album of all Wren's London churches. Until his death in 1817, Hallerstein devoted himself, in Greece, to archaeological research and to the study of the Aeginetan frieze, which he found in the remains of the temple of Heracles and which was taken to Munich. Hallerstein's major works include his plans for the Valhalla near Regensburg, strongly influenced by Gilly's monument to Frederick the Great in Berlin and his plans for the Munich Glypothek. Both of these monuments were eventually built by Klenze, his co-disciple of Gilly.

HANSEN Christian Fredrik (Copenhagen 29.2.1756 – Copenhagen10.7.1845). After studying at the Copenhagen Academy of Fine Arts, from 1784 to 1804 Hansen was regional architect in Holstein. In 1804, he built the Town Hall in Copenhagen' and, after the fire of 1794, Christiansborg Castle. The Baroque forms of the past were replaced by a strict Classicism. The only one of Hansen's many works that survives today is the church of the castle, which escaped another fire in 1884. From 1811 to 1829, he built Vor Frue Kirke (destroyed during an English bombardment), Copenhagen Cathedral and the Metropolitan School, in strict Classical style.

HANSEN Theophil Freiherr von (Copenhagen 1813 – Vienna 1891). Studied architecture in Copenhagen from 1834 to 1837, then travelled on a scholarship to Berlin, Munich, Northern Italy and Athens, where he taught and practised architecture. From 1846, he was in Vienna at the studio of Ludwig von Forster, whose daughter he married. He worked with von Förster on the plans for the gigantic Arsenal in Vienna and decorated the Museum of the Army, built in Romantico-Byzantine style, with precious marble sculptures and frescoes by Blaas. It was an overwhelming success. Hansen received important commissions for the Ringstrasse: in 1861–1863, the Heinrichshof (with frescoes on gold by Carl Rahl and Eisenmenger and richly sculpted decoration); the Musikverein building (1867–1869); the Börse (Stock Exchange) (1874–1877); the Academy of Fine Arts (with the ceilings of the grand hall by Anselm Feuerbach) (1872–1876); and the Parliament (1873–1883), as well as many private mansions and villas. In Athens, he built the Academy of Sciences (1859–1887) and the Library (1885–1892), which are among the greatest Neo-Classical buildings of Europe. Hansen's buildings, which were always developed from Greek or 'Renaissance' style, are evidence of his great ability to marry the most precious materials. Hansen also contributed to the decorative arts with his designs of furniture, fabric and porcelain.

HASENAUER Karl Freiherr von (Vienna 20.7.1833 – Vienna 4.1.1894). From 1850 to 1855, studied under Eduard van der Nüll and August Siccard von Siccardsburg. Like most architects, he took part in 1860 in the competition for the Vienna *Hofoper*, which was won by his teachers. In 1869, Gottfried Semper, charged with the construction of the Court Museums in Vienna, took Hasenauer on as a collaborator. During the years that followed, the project of a Kaiserforum, which was to be the largest square of the 19th century, was studied, but was never quite completed (see entry on Gottfried Semper). When Semper left Vienna in 1876, Hasenauer directed this colossal project alone. The Hofmuseen, destined to house the history of art and natural history collections, were built between 1871 and 1891 and decorated by Semper and Hasenauer in a sumptuous style typical of Historicism. Hasenauer's works were typified

Burgtheater: the staircase, Vienna

Heinrichshof, Vienna

by vast domed halls and gigantic staircases of precious marbles, decorated with imposing sculptures, either in marble (Benk, Hellmer, Tilgner, Kundmann, Weyr) or in bronze, painted ceilings and medallions (von Munkacsy, Hans Makart, Hans Canon, Gustav Klimt).

Hasenauer, who ranks among the major architects of the generation of the 1870s, was also Architect-in-chief of the Universal Exhibition of 1873 in Vienna, and took part in the construction of the Rotunda (built of iron by the naval engineer, Scott-Russell), which, until the fire of 1937, was unequalled in height and size.

Hasenauer did not live to see even the partial completion of the Kaiserforum. When he died in 1894, only the Hofmuseen, the monument to Maria-Theresa, the fountains and Fernkorn's equestrian statues for the Heldenplatz were completed; the left wing of the Neue Hofburg was only started in 1881. After Hasenauer, Emil Ritter von Forster, Friedrich Ohmann and Luwig Baumann directed the work.

'Since Trajan's forum, there had been no achievement down the centuries to compare with the Kaiserforum. It was to have been the crowning glory not only of Vienna, but also of Historicist architecture, a combination of princely residences and museums, the artistic incarnation of the Habsburg monarchy ...' (Klaus Eggert).

HOHENBERG Johann Ferdinand Hetzendorf von (Vienna 1733 – Vienna 1816). Studied at the Vienna Academy and travelled in Germany and Italy. After the departure for Brussels, in 1755, of Jadot de Ville d'Issey, architect to the Empress Maria-Theresa, Hohenberg was charged with the architectural design of the park of Schönbrunn Castle and, from 1773 on, with a series of monumental works such as the open arcades of the Gloriette, the water tower of the Roman Ruin, and the waterfall and Egyptian obelisk. He probably worked from Fischer von Erlach's earlier designs, and produced a synthesis of Baroque tradition and contemporary Neo-Classical ideas, coloured with French and Italian Romanticism. From 1772 to 1816, Hohenberg was Director of the School of Architecture in Vienna, and from 1775 Court Architect. He started a great many designs for the transformation of the Hofburg. In the 1780s, he turned to the Gothic style that had developed in Romantic opposition to the strict Viennese Classicism of Josef II. The Gothic transformation of the Augustiner and Michaeler churches in Vienna and the Gothic designs for the Franzensburg at Laxenburg were Hohenberg's masterpieces of this period. One of his most interesting Neo-Classical constructions is the Fries Palace (now known as the Pallavicini Palace) in Vienna.

HAUSSMANN Georges Eugène, Baron (Paris 27.3.1809 – Paris 12.1.1891). An administrator and man of politics, Haussmann was Prefect in turn of the regions of the Var, the Yonne, the Gironde, then of the Seine in 1853. During his seventeen-year tenure of this post Haussmann, granted full powers by Napoleon III, undertook the reshaping of Paris. He surrounded himself with engineers to execute a vast plan to improve sanitation and embellish the city: it involved demolishing insanitary areas are replacing them with whole districts of new buildings, the creation of wide avenues (Avenue de l'Opéra, Place de l'Etoile), the installation of canals to supply the city with water, and a major drainage system. A man of keen artistic taste and judgement, Haussmann played a decisive role in the aesthetic development of the city of Paris, and parts of his design survive to this day. He was forced to resign in January 1870 by the Ollivier government, before Napoleon III's fall.

JEFFERSON Thomas (Shadwell, Virginia 13.4.1743 – Monticello, Virginia 4.7.1826). Jefferson, one of the most remarkable of American statesmen (President from 1801 to 1809), was also a great, if unrecognised, architect: throughout his life, he was involved in architecture and town planning. From 1772, the Governor's mansion in Williamsburg was transformed according to his designs and from 1776, he drew up plans for the town of Richmond, the capital of Virginia, as well as for the Capitol, which was inspired by the Maison Carrée in Nîmes.

He modelled his works on those of Vitruvius and Palladio, of which he had new editions sent from France and England. Etienne Hallet, a French architect who had emigrated to America before the French Revolution and founded a school of architecture in 1779, and George Hadfield, collaborated with him on buildings such as the Capitol in Washington. The University of Virginia (1817–1826), where Jefferson created a school of architecture, is one of his masterpieces.

KLENZE Leo von (Bockenem, near Hildesheim 29.2.1784 – Munich 27.1.1864). Trained in Berlin with Friedrich Gilly, then in Paris with Percier and Fontaine, von Klenze visited Italy and Greece and was impressed by what he saw there. His meeting with Crown Prince

New Hermitage, St Petersburg (Leningrad)

Befreiungshalle, Kelheim

on the one hand and Greece on the other opened two possible stylistic avenues: the Renaissance palaces of Northern Italy or the temples of Greece. His Glypothek (1816–1831) and the Alte Pinakothek (1826–1836) in Munich earned him his reputation as a specialist in museum building. This was probably the reason why Nicholas I commissioned him to build the New Hermitage, an annexe to the Winter Palace in Saint Petersburg (1839–1852), to house the art collections of the Czars. The decoration was not ornate, but the exquisite quality of the materials used and the sumptuous granite telamones in the vestibule made it a model of its kind. Klenze produced other masterpieces, such as the Befreiungshalle in Kelheim, which was essentially completed according to his designs after Gärtner's death; the Leuchtenbergpalais in Munich (1817–1819), the Ministry of War (1824–1830) the Königsbau (1826–1835), the Allerheiligen Hofkirche (1826–1837), inspired by the Cappella Palatina in Palermo, the Grand Hall of the Residenz in Munich (1832–1842) and the Ruhmeshalle (1843–1854). His most impressive works in Greek style are the Glypothek, the Propyleae (1846–1860) and the Valhalla near Regensburg (1830–1842), a monument to the glory of the heroes of Germany, inspired by the work of Gilly as well as that of von Hallerstein.

Klenze's goal was to recreate the purity of Greek architecture in the 19th century. To him, the temple represented the union of spiritual values and technical perfection.

Thus, he conceived the Königsplatz in Munich as a temple enclosure, to invest it with a sacred solemnity. But when King Ludwig wanted to apply the temple style to other buildings, Klenze refused: 'The ancient heroes did not live in layers, one on top of the other.' He succeeded in convincing the King that Italian Neo-Renaissance style would be more appropriate and, for the Königsbau for example, he copied the characteristics of the Palazzo Pitti in Florence. Klenze did not only work as an architect but also as an archaeologist and town planner: he undertook a scientific study of the Acropolis in Athens which he saved from destruction; ensured the protection of Greece's principal ancient sites; and drew up for Athens, as he had for Munich, urban designs that made the city more functional while preserving its aesthetic qualities.

Ludwig of Bavaria was to be the turning-point of his career. Ludwig put him to the test with the construction of the Glypothek, engaged him as the architect for Munich and appointed him Director of Buildings to the Court. His only, temporary, rival was Friedrich von Gärtner, eight years his junior. Klenze's passion for Italy

KORNHÄUSEL Josef (Vienna 1782 – Vienna 1860). After training with his father, Kornhäusel began his career as an architect in 1802. A member of the Vienna Academy in 1808, he replaced Hardtmut in the service of the Prince of Liechtenstein and worked for him in Vienna and elsewhere. He then made study journeys to Italy and Western Europe. Kornhäusel's major works were in

Vienna: the triumphal entrance to the park of the Liechtenstein Palace (1814); work on the Albertina Palace for Archduke Charles where, in 1822–1824, he built the Minervahalle, a peristyle, and the Sphinxstiege; the theatre in Josefstadt (1822), the monumental facade of the Schottenstift in Vienna, the library (1828–1832), and the Synagogue (1825–1826). His vast Weilburg Palace for the Archduke, one of the masterpieces of Romantic Neo-Classicism in Vienna, was demolished after it had been badly damaged during the Second World War. Kornhäusel's success was due to his vivid decorative style, in which the traditional grandeur of the Baroque, which had only just been outmoded, was allied with the bourgeois sobriety of the Biedermeier period, and which found its best expression in his great halls, courtyards and peristyles decorated with sculptures.

LABROUSTE Henri (Paris 1801 – Fontainebleau 1875). A solid training with Léon Vaudoyer and Hippolyte Lebas, then at the Academy in Rome, enabled Labrouste to make a critical and analytical assessment of Neo-Classicism. He was in conflict with the Ecole des Beaux-Arts in Paris, whose academism he firmly rejected. His rationalist architectural thinking soon brought the young generation of students to his studio, including Jean-Baptiste Lassus, Emile Boeswillwald, Julien Guadet and Anatole de Baudot, who was to be the most important pioneer of concrete construction. Labrouste's most famous works are the Bibliothèque Sainte-Geneviève in Paris, built from 1843 to 1850, for which he used a visible metallic structure, and the Reading Room of the Bibliothèque Nationale, the ceiling of which is composed of nine square domed bays, supported by slender iron columns. It was above all with the Bibliothèque Sainte-Geneviève, combining an exterior envelope of stone and a metallic interior structure, that Labrouste paved the way for modern architecture. As a theoretician, he was particularly opposed to the Classical pattern of severe colonnaded facades, devoid of meaning, and often of anything in common with the building behind them.

Bibliothèque Nationale: the reading room, Paris

LATROBE Benjamin Henry (Yorkshire 1.5.1764 – New Orleans 3.9.1820). After training as an architect with Cockerell and a brief study of mechanical construction with Smeaton, Latrobe built two important houses in Greek Revival style. In 1796, he went to America where, over the next twenty years, his major works were built (in Richmond, Philadelphia, Baltimore and Washington). Thanks to him, American Neo-Classicism took on its truly original character. The prison he built in Richmond (1797), for example, shows that he was particularly close to the metaphorical ideas of Ledoux; while the Bank of Pennsylvania (1798–1800) was the first 'Greek' building in America, with a structure corresponding to an Ancient facade. Both buildings have since been demolished. In 1799, in Philadelphia, Latrobe built a water supply works with an added rotunda, typical of American Neo-Classicism. From 1804, he worked on Baltimore Cathedral, where the arcatures and apertures owe much to Piranesi. Like so many other architects, he also participated in the Washington Capitol. Latrobe's pure Greek Neo-Classicism devoid of all Roman traces, was influential in America until the 1930s (in, for instance, the Jefferson Memorial, Washington, 1934–1943).

LEDOUX Claude-Nicolas (Dormans, Marne 1736 – Paris 19.11.1806). Studied in the studios of Blondel and Trouard. Ledoux built churches and bridges in Burgundy and designed many town houses in Paris, such as the Hallwyl (1766), Uzès (1767), and Montmorency (1770), and the Château de Bénouville (1768). From about 1774, he concentrated on industrial architecture: he made plans for an ideal city and built the Salines of Arc-et-Senans as well as the theatre in Besançon. At the King's request, he undertook, in 1775, the building of the gates of Paris, designed for collecting tolls, in which he made extensive use of rotunda and massive blocks of Greek simplicity. They were partly demolished during the Revolution, and Ledoux was arrested and imprisoned. In 1793, he wrote his major work: *De l'architecture considerée sous le rapport de l'art, des moeurs et de la legislation* (volume I, 1804). The most important of the 'architects of the Revolution', Ledoux preached, through his buildings but especially through his visionary designs, a return to

'Cowshed on a south-facing meadow' Design

Rotunda of La Villette, Paris

primitive forms: cylinder, pyramid, prism, cone or sphere, which related to the function of the building. Unlike Boullée, Ledoux confined himself to feasible and workable conceptions. In his industrial constructions (above all the Salines of Arc-et-Senans), there are clear signs that the theatrical effects of his Neo-Classicism are borrowed from artists such as Piranesi.

LEQUEU Jean-Jacques (Rouen 1757 – Paris 1825). In the early 1780s worked with Soufflot, then in 1783 went to Italy and built two country houses in the form of ancient temples. Unfortunately, the Revolution put an end to his short career in the service of a wealthy aris-

tocracy. He was employed by the land registry and, from 1801 to 1815, worked as a cartographer. He ended his days in poverty and neglect. In 1825, unable to sell his

designs, he donated them to the Bibliothèque Nationale (then the Bibliothèque Royale). These very original drawings are strange visions, a mixture of the mediaeval and the exotic, Greek and Oriental, artificial ruins and curiosities, with no one dominant style. Elements of the irrational and emotional lend them a touch of the surreal, even though they were absolutely in tune with late 18th century taste. In one of his most remarkable Romantic designs, 'Cowshed on a south-facing meadow', the shed itself is in the form of a colossal stone cow.

MONTOYER Louis de (Marimont, Hennegau 1749 – Vienna 1811). Architect to the court of Duke Albert of Saxe-Teschen, for whom he constructed many buildings in Belgium. From 1782 to 1784, he built Laeken Castle near Brussels for the Duke, then Governor General of the Austrian Netherlands, and husband of the Archduchess Marie-Christine. He was in Vienna from 1795 and became court architect in 1802. In 1795, he transformed the Silva-Tarouca Palace for Duke Albert, who used it to house his collection of drawings and engravings, soon famous throughout the world, and his abundant art collections (the basis of the Albertina collection). Montoyer's success in Vienna was such that he was soon charged with important Court commissions: in 1804–1807, he created the sumptuous ceremonial hall of the Hofburg, one of the most harmonious achievements of

Viennese Neo-Classicism. Here, as in his palace for the Russian ambassador to Vienna, Prince Rasoumovski (1803–1807), Montoyer used his favourite effect, which was to accentuate the character of his great halls with a 'veil of coloumns' – huge columns several storeys high – surrounding the state room with promenades. One of Montoyer's most impressive spatial creations was the domed rotunda built for the Rasoumovski Palace in Vienna. The combination of white marble and gilded artificial marble, of gigantic Corinthian capitals and rich coffered ceilings is characteristic of his talent.

MOREAU Charles de (Marimont near Neufchâteau, Haute Marne 1758 – Vienna 1840). In 1794, Prince Esterhazy sent for Moreau to come to Hungary to draw up plans for the transformation of his castle at Eisenstadt, in the Neo-Classical utopian style of the Revolution. The garden facade of the Palace, with its very marked French character, was to influence Josef Kornhäusel in his Weilburg for Archduke Charles. In 1807 Moreau built the Apollosaal in Vienna, in 1809–1813 the Palffy Palace (Wallnerstrasse 6), and in 1819–1823 the old Nationalbank.

Unlike Montoyer, with his sumptuous and dynamic Neo-Classicism and his Baroque spirit, Moreau systematically used the cube construction in late Viennese Biedermeier style. Moreau was responsible for much of the building to house the festivities of the Congress of Vienna in 1815.

NASH John (London 1752 – East Cowes Castle, Isle of Wight 1835). After training with Robert Taylor and having tried to establish himself in London, Nash went to Wales where his 'villas' met with great success. These very original, sometimes fantastic, constructions were christened the Picturesques, because of their mediaeval or oriental decorative elements. On returning to London, he collaborated with the landscape architect Humphrey Repton, with whom he designed Neo-Classical villas like Cronkhill and Sandridge Park. For the future King George IV, then Prince of Wales, he built the Royal Pavilion in Brighton (1815–1818), an exotic residence in what can be defined as Indian Gothic style. As a town planner, Nash was commissioned to transform the northeast side of Regent's Park in London, in strict Neo-Classical style: this resulted in his Chester and Cumberland Terraces with a facade several hundred metres long.

His most important project was the transformation of Regent Street. Stylistically, his Terraces are somewhere between Neo-Classicism and the Picturesque: some details are Greek, the composition is derived from Palladian style, and the overall effect is theatrical, spontaneous and varied.

Cumberland Terrace, Regent's Park, London

NOBILE Peter von (Tesserete, Lugano, Switzerland 1774 – Vienna 1854). After studying in Rome, Nobile built the Saint Anthony of Padua church in Trieste, at the end of the main canal, a massive construction on which he worked until 1849. Summoned to Vienna by the Emperor Franz I, he was appointed Director of the Academy's School of Architecture in 1816, and in 1820 put forward a very modern new programme of studies. From 1817, he worked on the Ausseres Burgtor of the Hofburg in Vienna. While work continued on the Burgtor, Nobile built one of the strictest of Neo-Classical structures, the Doric Theseustemple (1819–1823) in the Vienna Volksgarten. It was copied from the Theseion in Athens and was intended to house Canova's monumental marble sculpture of Theseus and Chiron (which, for climatic reasons, was eventually placed on the staircase of Semper and Hasenauer's Kunsthistorisches Museum). In 1820–1822, also in the Volksgarten, he created the Zweite Cortische Kaffeehaus, a semi-circular, rigorously Classical, colonnaded building, with two temples, reduced scale ancient baths and elements borrowed from the villas of Palladio. Nobile, whose buildings were successful, despite their Doric severity, worked for Prince Metternich, restored Mirabell castle in Salzburg, contributed to the Schauspielhaus in Graz and the Redoubt for Archduke John, vicar of the Holy Roman Empire. His architecture is characterised by a strict, very massive, yet finely proportioned Neo-Classicism.

NÜLL Eduard van der (Vienna 9.1.1812 – Vienna 3.4.1868) and **SICCARD VON SICCARDSBURG August** (Pest 1813 – Vienna 1868). The work of the two men is inseparable. In 1828, van der Nüll came to the Polytechnic School in Vienna, where he and Siccardsburg met; from 1835, he was at the Academy under Peter von Nobile, Paul Sprenger and Carl Roesner. In 1838 both took part in an Academy competition and won identical prizes. Nobile allowed them a scholarship to Rome and to travel in Northern Italy, France and England. In 1843, they were both appointed to the Academy: Siccardsburg eventually became Ludwig von Förster's successor, while van der Nüll was appointed to the newly created post of Professor of Ornamentation. Independently of their architectural work, they became Vienna's most important teachers: their classes produced the most eminent artists of the Ringstrasse, Ferstel, Hasenauer, and Otto Wagner. At the Academy, they developed the theoretical foundations of a new style, which was that it should correspond to the function of the building, which in turn conditioned the choice of type of construction. But it was their theoretical clarity, pragmatism and practical sense that raised the architecture of the two men above the 'consumer' Historicism of the second half of the 19th century.

After their first major commissions, the Carl-Theater in Vienna (1847), the Alterchenfeld Church, parts of the Vienna Arsenal (which was to become one of the major masterpieces of Viennese Historicism), and projects for the Vienna Military Academy, van der Nüll and Siccardsburg won first prize for their Hofoper design, followed by the commission to build it The Hofoper – in the style of the first Florentine Renaissance, an allusion to the time of the birth of opera – was the first construction of the early Romantic period on the Ringstrasse, and, artistically, the most important one. Moritz von Schwind carried out the artistic decoration: his Magic Flute frescoes in the Ringstrasse loggia and in the foyer are among the masterpieces of German Romantic painting. The auditorium and the halls of the Emperor, Empress and Archdukes were destroyed during the Second World War, but the loggia decorated by Schwind, the foyer, and the grand staircase are still intact. Van der Nüll and Siccardsburg also built the Haas store in Vienna and the Larisch-Moennich Palace, with very original adaptation of motifs from the Hôtel de Vogue in Dijon and the Town Hall of Arras. If the Hofoper is the finest representation of Viennese Romanticism in its maturity, the Larisch-Moennich Palace is perhaps the most original palace of the Viennese Historicist movement at its height.

PAXTON Sir Joseph (Milton Bryant, near Woburn 3.8.1803 – Sydenham 8.6.1865). Head gardener to the Duke of Devonshire, then travelled throughout Europe with his friend George Stephenson. In 1838–1842, he created the model village of Edensor and, in 1843–1847, the first public park in England, the landscape garden in Birkenhead. In 1860, he created Queen's Park in Glasgow. He had always been interested in conservatories, which he built first in wood and then in metallic materials. In 1850, he was commissioned to design the main building for the Great Exhibition in Hyde Park (1851), where he made definitive use of cast-iron in the construction. In 1852–1854, this building, christened the Crystal Palace and already hailed at the time as the miracle of the 19th century, was dismantled, and reassembled at Sydenham. It was destroyed by fire in 1936.

Crystal Palace, London

Paxton's genius was to conceive of the almost total prefabrication of building elements and a simple assembly procedure. The decorative paintings had been designed by Owen Jones, whose Islamic ornaments contributed to creating the Oriental fashion in England. After the success of the Crystal Palace, this building method was used for the Universal Exhibitions of Dublin in 1852, New York in 1853, Munich in 1854, and in Vienna, in 1873, for the Rotunda, the largest of the glass domes.

PERCIER Charles (Paris 22.8.1764 – Paris 5.9.1838) see **FONTAINE**.

PIERMARINI Giuseppe (Foligno 18.7.1734 – Foligno 5.2.1808). Piermarini added to the Baroque style, inherited from his teachers Posi and Vanvitelli, a Classical severity. In the reign of Maria-Theresa of Austria, he was summoned to Milan by the Austrian court, where he eventually opted for pure Neo-Classicism. His works, like the Teatro della Scala, commissioned by Maria-Theresa, the Palazzo Belgiojoso (1779) in Milan and the royal villa at Monza (1780) are among his principal Neo-Classical creations between 1770 and 1780 in Northern Italy. Piermarini's style is distinguished by great clarity of composition, elegant use of Palladian forms and a taste for the spectacular. He was Professor of Architecture at the Brera Academy in Milan, architect to the Emperor of Austria and Inspector of Buildings in Lombardy. For twenty-five years he worked on the twon planning of Milan. The French invasion put an end to his career: in 1798, he retired to Foligno where he died, all but forgotten.

POELAERT Joseph (Brussels 1817 – Brussels 1879). From 1850 to 1859, Poelaert's works included the Congress Column in Brussels, schools, and the royal church in Laeken. In 1860, he won first prize in the competition for the Law Courts in Brussels, which he started building in 1866, but did not live to see completed (1883). This particularly original work, Poelaert's main achievement, was the largest single building of the 19th century. Although he used Neo-Classical motifs, his treatment of elements of Historicist architecture was unconventional. He invented Gothic and Renaissance styles with greater dimensions, and a striking dissonance of detail. One of the great admirers of the building, which caused violent controversy, was Charles Garnier, architect of the Paris Opera.

skoe Selo (Pushkin) the Palace of Alexander, and many private palaces. In 1810, he returned to Bergamo to build a triumphal arch for Napoleon, and in 1811 worked in Vienna on the transformation and interior decoration of the palace of the Archduchess von Modena-Este. Quarenghi's style is marked by the influence of Palladio and by a love of Antiquity; it contains allusions to the works of Giulio Romano and Sangallo de Bramante, but also to the ideas of the time (particularly to Gabriel and Adam).

Academy of Sciences, Saint Petersburg (Leningrad)

QUARENGHI Giacomo (Bergamo 20.9.1744 – Saint Petersburg 18.2.1817). In Rome from 1763, where he was influenced by the painter Anton Raphael Mengs and initially devoted himself exclusively to painting, drawing and the study of Antiquity. The discovery of the Quattro Libri by Palladio and his meeting with the French draughtsman Derizet decided him on a career as an architect. In 1771, he built the Benedictine church of *Santa Scholastica* in Subiaco, his only Italian building, in strictly Ancient style. Through the offices of Winckelmann's friend, Reiffenstein, Quarenghi was introduced to the court of Catherine the Great in Saint Petersburg. She, until her death in 1796, preferred him to his rivals, the architects Vallin de la Mothe and Clérisseau. In Saint Petersburg, Quarenghi built the State Bank, the Academy of Sciences, and the Hermitage theatre; at the Summer Palace of Peterhof, the English Castle; at Tsar-

REMY Ludwig von (Reichshofen, Alsace 1776 – Vienna 1851 or 1856). Official architect to the court of Franz II in Vienna, Remy was famous for his 130 metre long house of glass, with its pineapple-shaped column capitals. Built before 1822 during the installation of the Hofburg Kaisergarten, this iron construction was to remain as one of the most remarkable examples of this type of architecture (it was demolished in 1901 and replaced by a winter garden). Remy's designs for the Hofburg combine the finest elements of both French and Italian influences, and bring an element of solemnity to the rigour of Viennese Biedermeier.

RICHARDSON Henry Hobson (New Orleans 1838 – Brooklin, Mass. 1886). After studying at Harvard, went to Paris where he attended the Ecole des Beaux-Arts from 1859 to 1865. He then worked in New York and Brooklyn. Much influenced by the style of the Second Empire, he nevertheless developed his own original style which was dubbed 'Richardsonian Romanesque'. This highly Romantic style, which combined elements of Romanesque cathedrals with almost archaic forms, had a decisive influence on the work of Sullivan in the United States and even on European architecture during the 1890s. Among his most characteristic buildings are the Marshal Field Wholesale Store in Chicago (1885–1887), the Glessner private house in Chicago, and Sherman House in Newport.

Trinity Church, Boston, Mass.

ROSSI Carlo Ivanovich (Naples 18.12.1775 – Saint Petersburg 1.4.1849). This Italian architect worked in Moscow from 1808 and from 1814 undertook work for the Summer Residence at Pavlovsk. In 1816, he became Imperial Architect at Saint Petersburg. After the death of his main rivals, among them Quarenghi and Thomas de Thomon, he was responsible for the major buildings of Saint Petersburg. He rebuilt four squares: the Mikhail Square with the new Mikhailov Palace (1819–1825) and that surrounding the Alexandra Theatre. He completed the square in front of the Winter Palace, and the then Senate Square; on the former, he built the huge General Staff headquarters (1819–1825) with the Alexander Column, while on the latter, the houses of the Senate and the Synod (1829–1833). Rossi's buildings generally have long facades pebble-dashed in yellow, with white-painted decorative highlights.

SCHINKEL Karl Friedrich von (Neuruppin 1781 – Berlin 1837). Schinkel's interest in architecture was fostered by Friedrich Gilly, with whose father, David Gilly, he started his training. On a journey to Italy from 1803 to 1805, he studied the ancient monuments, then visited Paris. Returning to Berlin, he concentrated above all on painting, since the political situation precluded major building commissions: he painted Romantic panoramas and came to fame with his many theatre decors, of which those of The Magic Flute are the best known. He then became chief architect to the town planning department and, in 1816, obtained his first major commission: the Neue Wache in Berlin. This was followed, in 1818, by the Schauspielhaus, the Alte Museum (1823), the Hauptwache in Dresden (1831), the Nikolaikirche in Potsdam (1830–1837) and, above all, buildings in which Schinkel put to spectacular effect the technique, characteristic of his work, of unpargeted brick facades (Werdersche Kirche, 1824–1830; Bauakademie).

In his theoretic principles and in some unrealised designs, Schinkel had shown himself to be a champion of a German national Gothic style, but eventually, to comply with the demands of the royal house of Prussia, he executed most of his commissions in strict Neo-Classical style. However, he did, in his series of princely castles, build the Neo-Gothic Babelsberg (1834) and Kamenz Castle in Lower Silesia. His architectural ideas during the 1830s were influenced by a journey to the industrial towans of France and England in 1826. The unpargeted brick facades that Schinkel favoured represented a means for him to achieve a synthesis between a national Gothic style and the principles of Classical order. His later designs, most of them unrealised, showed the consequence of his architectural thinking: the large store for Berlin (1829), and the castle on the Acropolis for King Othon of Wittelsbach (1834), which he was prevented from building by his rival Leo von Klenze. He executed innumerable other commissions: small villas, monumental castles, furniture designs, and work on the upkeep of monuments in Berlin.

Bauakademie, Berlin

At the end of the 19th century, Schinkel, who had been greatly esteemed during his lifetime and had represented Neo-Classicism and the national Gothic in Prussia, fell from popularity. It was only during the Bauhaus period that his standing as the inspiring force and pioneer of a functional yet humane architecture was rediscovered.

SEMPER Gottfried (Hamburg 29.11.1803 – Rome 15.5.1879). After studying law and mathematics, Semper turned to architecture and worked with Gärtner in Munich in 1825, with Gau and Hittorff in Paris from 1826 to 1830, and from 1830 in Italy. During this period, he elaborated theories on the use of ancient elements in modern European architecture, notably a principle according to which ancient forms could only be actual and meaningful if transposed into the forms of the Renaissance. His visit to Schinkel in Berlin in 1833 confirmed him in this belief.

Schinkel had recommended him to Dresden where he became Director of the School of Architecture. Semper worked in Dresden from 1834 to 1849, and while there wrote his *Provisional remarks on coloured architecture and sculpture of the ancients* (1834), which still bore the influence of Italian Antiquity. He built the Dresden Synagogue in pseudo-Romanesque style (1838–1840); then the Hoftheater (1838–1841), which burned down in 1869. In parallel, he made plans for the reconstruction of the town centre of Hamburg, destroyed by fire, and for the Nikolaikirche in Hamburg (1844).

In 1849, Semper had to leave Dresden after taking part in the revolutionary disturbances in May. He took refuge in London and played and important part in the plans and construction for the Great Exhibtion of 1851. From his experiences of the practical requirements of the Exhibi-

tion, and also of the decorative arts and industrial production, he wrote one of the most important theoretic works of the 19th century, *Wissenschaft, Industrie und Kunst, Vorschläge zur Anregung nationalen Kunstgefühls* (1852, 'Science, industry and art: suggestions for the creation of a national feeling for art'). Semper's ideas were decisive in European thinking about industry and art. His predominantly pedagogic conception of museums was adopted by the Victoria and Albert Museum, which had just been founded. In Vienna, Eitelberger drew on Semper's ideas and Emperor Franz-Josef founded the Austrian Museum of Art and Industry (today the Museum of Applied Arts), with a school of Decorative Arts. From this time on, Semper's influence in Vienna was so pervasive that, in 1869, Franz-Josef commissioned him to design the largest construction project of the 19th century: the Kaiserforum in Vienna with the new Imperial Palace, the Hofmuseen, Burgtheater etc.

In 1855 he was appointed to the Polytechnikum in Zurich which he had built, as he had the Town Hall in Winterthur, in Roman style. His years in Zurich (1855–1871) also produced designs for the reconstruction of the Dresden Hoftheater (1871–1878), which was carried out under his son Manfred Semper. In Zurich, as a result of his famous work *Der Stil in den technischen und tektonischen Kunsten* ('Style in the technical and architectural arts'; Parts I and II, 1861–1863; Part III, on architecture, unfinished).

In 1869, Prince Constantin von Hohelohe-Schillingsfürst summoned Semper to Vienna to consult him on the subject of new wings for the Hofburg and the museums. Semper's proposals were accepted and in 1870, he presented designs for the whole palace up to the Michaeler Wing of the Hofburg. He chose the young Carl von Hasenauer to collaborate on the work but after serious differences of opinion, Semper retired in 1876, leaving Hasenauer to complete it. Semper's works, characterised above all by his use of Roman and Renaissance elements, adapted to the formal requirements of the day, are among the most significant achievements of the 19th century, and his theoretical writings had considerable influence until well after the Historicist period.

SICCARD VON SICCARDSBURG August (Pest 1813 – Vienna 1868) see **NÜLL**.

SOANE Sir John (Goring-on-Thames 10.9.1753 – London 20.1.1837). Interested in architecture from the age of fifteen, Soane was apprenticed to George Dance, then from 1772 to Henry Holland. In 1778, William Chambers presented him to the King and procured a grant for him to travel to Italy (1778–1780). There he met Piranesi and, like most of his contemporaries, fell under his influence. In 1806, he became Professor of Architecture at the Royal Academy in London. Officially, as a theoretician, Soane was expected to condemn Piranesi's picturesque and fantastic visions, but as an architect he drew on Piranesi's conception of space, to a remarkable extent. At the age of twenty-three, Soane received a gold medal for his triumphal bridge, inspired by Piranesi's Ponte Magnifico. In 1788, he was appointed architect of the Bank of England, on which he worked for many years. But between 1924 and 1930, this vast complex was transformed, so that little of the original character of the building now survives. A very unusual feature was the vast windowless outer wall with recesses ornamented with Corinthian columns, in 'Tivoli' style.

Whitehall, London

Most of Soane's buildings have now been demolished, even though he was one of the most important English architects of the 19th century. He had, in fact, been commissioned for the buildings in Whitehall, in St James (1791), Chelsea Hospital (1807), and, together with Nash and Smirke, was appointed Royal Architect for Richmond Park, Kew Gardens and Hampton Court Palace (1814–1832). Soane's style, symbolised in its maturity by the Bank of England, is of a mannered Classicism in which the heritage of Vitruvius and Palladio, and thus the classical column and entablature, are transformed into linear and two-dimensional decorative elements. After 1800, Soane also used some features of Gothic and Pompeian style, in keeping with picturesque Regency fashion.

SOUFFLOT Jacques Germain (Irancy, near Auxerre 22.7.1713 – Paris 29.8.1780). After studying in Lyon, Soufflot left for Rome in 1731, where, from 1734, he received a grant from the Académie de France. After drawing up designs for Lyon (the facade of the Hôtel-Dieu, and the Change Lodge), he travelled in Italy in 1750 with the Marquis de Vandières, Director of Buildings to the King. In 1753–1756, he built the theatre in Lyon.

It was thanks to Vandières, who later became Marquis de Marigny, that he was appointed as architect of the new Sainte-Geneviève Church and the Ecole de Droit in 1755. Other important works include: the Fontaine de l'Arbre Sec in Paris (1776); the Orangerie and the Nympheum of the Château de Ménars near Blois; the grotto in the park of the Château de Chatou, etc. In 1773, Soufflot became Controller of Buildings in Lyon, and in 1776 Administrator of Buildings to the King. In his buildings he attempted to emulate the pure Greek style of the Paestum temples. He was one of the first admirers of Gothic architecture.

VIOLLET-LE-DUC Eugène-Emmanuel (Paris 27.1. 1814 – Lausanne 17.9.1879). With his uncle, the historical painter Delécluze, set out in 1831 on his first study journey to the Midi of France, then travelled to Normandy, to the Loire and the Pyrenées. He had been drawing since the age of sixteen, but refused to consider going to the Ecole des Beaux-Arts, rejecting both its ideas and its teachers. It was chiefly the influence of Victor Hugo that turned him to the study of mediaeval architecture. In 1840, he was 'Inspector' of the restoration of the Sainte-Chapelle in Paris and the west facade

Château de Pierrefonds: tribune of the salle des Preux

of Versailles, worked with Gabriel on the construction of the Opéra and built a great number of private palaces. In 1771, he was a member of the Académie de Peinture. His grreatest success was the building of the Odéon in Paris, in collaboration with Peyre. He was charged with the transformation of the Place Louis XV and with linking the Ile Saint-Louis and the Ile Louviers. Among his most grandiose designs was one for a Théâtre des Arts (1798), which was to be the central feature of a square inspired by Antiquity. He designed a number of buildings for Catherine II of Russia, which were to influence architects like Starov, Volkov and Bashenov.

Château de Pierrefonds: interior courtyard

Perspective of the Facade of a Building for Catherine II

of the Sainte-Madeleine Church at Vézelay; from 1845, he worked with Lassus on the Notre-Dame Cathedral in Paris. Napoleon III commissioned him to restore the Château de Pierrefonds, in the forest of Compiègne. The author of important works of theory, he was regarded as an authority on the protection of historical monuments. Among his writings are the *Dictionnaire raisonné de l'architecture française du XIe au XVIe siècle* (1853–1868); the *Dictionnaire raisonné du mobilier français de l'époque carolingienne à la Renaissance* (1855–1857); and the *Entretiens sur l'architecture* (1858–1872). Viollet-le-Duc's importance to modern architecture lies in his rationalism and his insistence on logic in relation to buildings.

WAILLY Charles de (Paris 1730 – Paris 1798). Like almost all his contemporaries, was particularly impressed by the Thermae of Caracalla and of Diocletian in Rome, and studied with Peyre while on a journey to Italy. A friend of the Marquis de Marigny, he was admitted to the first class of the Académie d'Architecture. It was the start of brilliant career. He became deputy Inspector

WYATT James (Weeford 3.8.1746 – London 5.9.1813). One of the architects most in demand at the end of the 18th century. He became famous for the legendary Pantheon in London, a building constructed in a combination of the styles of the Hagia Sophia and the Pantheon of Rome (1769–1772). His buildings include royal palaces, five cathedrals, seventeen churches, eight college buildings and over a hundred country houses. The origins of his style were in Italy, where he studied Venetian and Roman architecture and experimented with various fashionable building styles. He was famous as a Neo-Classicist and Neo-Gothic, as a plagiarist of the Adam brothers and as a representative of the 'picturesque' style. His most admired works include Heaton House (Lancashire 1772), Heveningham Hall (Suffolk 1780–1784), Goodwood House (Sussex) and Dodington House (Gloucestershire, 1798–1808).

Illustration for Goethe's 'Werther' by Tony Johannot

Literature

The Romantic writer

'Romanticism is the art of presenting to people the literary works which, in the present state of their customs and beliefs, are liable to give them the greatest possible pleasure. Classicism, on the contrary, presents them with the literature which gave the greatest possible pleasure to their great-grand-fathers', wrote Stendhal in *Racine et Shakespeare* in 1823.

Before embarking upon a study of the subject matter or the style of the Romantic movement in literature, some of the facets of the literary temperament of the Romantic writer should be considered.

The Romantic saw himself as an innovator, at odds with tradition; he wanted to be himself, new, pristine, surprising (which did not, of course, rule out the fact that he had antecedents). He refused to accept the role of heir or successor, which distinguished him from his Classical or Renaissance counterpart. 'Let one recall the troubles of recent times, and one will see that, if but few romantics remain, it is because few among them have found Romanticism, but *they all sought it sincerely and faithfully*. Romanticism neither lies precisely in the choice of subjects nor in precise truth, but in a way of feeling' said Baudelaire.

This brings us to the revolutionary side of Romanticism: it explains the French 'mal du siècle' and its equivalents (Byronism, *Weltschmerz*) as well as the variations in intensity of this malaise: the disenchantment of Senancour or d'Amiel, the world weariness of Chateaubriand, the blatant dandyism of Byron or Pushkin's Onegin, the Promethean revolt of Shelley or of Leopardi. This desire to set oneself apart also justified the liberal political commitment of the Italians and French, and the radicalism of the Germans. René or Olympio, Faust or Don Juan, Oberman or Jacopo Ortis – all these heroes are the living portraits of their authors, as well as symbols of the Romantic temperament. The Romantic in himself is unique, even if he has brothers and sisters in literature; he is One, because he is Other.

There is thus both accuracy and artifice in the distinction between Romanticism and Pre-Romanticism. It would be going too far to call Goethe and the other *Stürmer* (Herder and Schiller), Bürger, Rousseau or Ossian (or rather Macpherson) Romantics; but it is true to say that Romanticism was nurtured by them; it drew inspiration from *Werther* and from *Faust*, as it did from Herder (1744–1803), Lessing, and Gray (1716–1771), with his famous *Elegy in a Country Churchyard* of 1751.

The French poets owed their existence to the discovery of Chénier in H. de Latouche's 1819 edition. But where would the Germans be without Jean-Paul Richter (1763–1825), the

Eugène Delacroix *Dante's Barque* 1822

Italians without Monti (1754–1828), the Russians without Joukovski (1783–1852)? If forced to choose and to draw up the list of the gods in the Pantheon of Romantic literature, that list would include Goethe (for *Werther*), Schiller (for his plays), Rousseau (for his egocentricity), and Ossian (for the Nordic and legendary aspects of his poems): Romantic sensitivity flowed directly from these masters. One would also need to go further back in time and add the names of all the 'Baroque' geniuses who are impossible to categorise, but who helped to determine the Romantic literary temperament: Dante, Petrarch, Shakespeare, of course, but also Ronsard, the *Minnesänger* and the popular storytellers (reinstated in particular by the Grimm Brothers). There was, of course no unity or common ground between all of these: however they were all inspirational figures themselves in breach of the official aesthetic and philosophical doctrines of their own time. Because they were once damned, they were later sanctified. Because they were misunderstood, they were glorified; because they were outsiders, they were adopted by those who felt themselves to be, and wanted to be, different. 'I am undertaking a venture for which there have been no precedents and which will have no imitators. I want to show ... a man ... and that man will be me' wrote Rousseau at the beginning of his *Confessions*.

It seems that the Romantic had never, at any time or in any place, been anything other than himself.

The different strands of Romanticism

There were, however, different generations and different Romantic schools. Thus in France, we can distinguish the generation of the founders and initiators of the movement: Chateaubriand, with his two very characteristic works, *Le Génie du Christianisme* (1802) and *René* (1804); Madame de Staël whose *De l'Allemagne* emphasised, as early as 1810 (though secretly, as it was banned) the originality of German letters. Similarly instigatory or catalytic roles were played by Nodier, Stendhal with *Racine et Shakespeare* which, in 1823–1825, advocated theatrical reform, and Lamartine, whose *Méditations Poétiques* in 1820 revealed a new kind of poetry.

The great generation, and the best-known, was that of Vigny, Hugo, Balzac, and Michelet, all born between 1797 and 1802, and who reached maturity, along with the French Romantic movement itself, at the time of the July Revolution. Finally, there were the young Romantics: Nerval, born in 1808, Musset (1810), and Gautier (1811), who perpetuated the movement until the period of the Second Empire.

In short, the span of French Romanticism can be set between *Le Génie du Christianisme* in 1802 and Hugo's *Contemplations* in 1856, even though there were Romantics writing after that date (Hugo himself), and indeed some aspects of Romanticism which lasted through to Surrealism. In Musset's *Lettres de Dupuis et Cotonet* (1854) can be traced the stages and mutations of the French Romantic movement.

In other countries there were also discernible phases and trends. In England, the generation of Burns and Blake, born around 1760, was the instigatory one. Then came the real founders of the movement: Wordsworth and Coleridge with his *Lyrical Ballads* of 1798, and finally the generation of the 'stars', who were famous throughout Europe: Byron, who wrote his celebrated *Corsair* in 1814 and died in 1824; Shelley and Keats, who died in 1821 and 1822 respectively; and Walter Scott, whose most resoundingly successful works spanned the period from 1814 (*Waverley*) to 1823 (*Quentin Durward*). English Romanticism was at its height while French Romanticism was still in limbo.

Similarly in Germany the Romantic movement was in full flower at the time of the Napoleonic Wars, if not just after; the *Hymns to the Night* by Novalis date from 1801, and *Des Knaben Wunderhorn* from 1806 (the first part) and 1808 (the second). Kleist committed suicide in 1811, and Hoffmann died in 1822. There was no single Romantic school in Germany, but there were Romantic circles in Jena, Heidelberg and Berlin. There were also very different national or regional trends; the Romanticism of the Jewish Rhinelander Heine had nothing in common with that of Novalis; Eichendorff's lyricism was far removed from the Swabian (Mörike) or Austrian (Lenau) poets, apart from the fact that they wrote in a common language, German.

There were any number of distinctions and nuances, but above and beyond them, there was a common consciousness and fraternity; Byronism, cosmopolitanism, troubadour or Gothic style, all attest to the fact that the Romantic recognised that he had brothers and allies, even though he wanted to be radically different, and saw himself as unique.

The Romantic character can also be defined by the way it was seen in the eyes of the

'Contemporary artists' 1833

outside world. For the audience of the time, the Romantic was a figurehead of national inspiration. Madame de Staël saw the first signs of the movement in this single characteristic:

'The name of romantic was recently been introduced in Germany to designate the poetry
which has its origins in the songs of the troubadours, which was born of chivalry and Christianity.... The literature of the ancients is, with the moderns, a transplanted literature;
romantic or chivalrous literature is indigenous to us, and it is our religion and our institutions
that have made it blossom' (*De l'Allemagne*).

Similarly, the inspiration of folklore – Scottish for example, for the British writers,
mediaeval or popular for the Germans – played a decisive role in the advent of the revival
movement. In other national schools, Italian or Polish for instance, it might perhaps be said
that Romanticism was *confined solely* to this national inspiration: it is certainly true of
Michiewicz and his *Ballads* (the famous *Konrad Wallenrod*, for example), and of Manzoni and

his *Promessi Sposi*. Romantic literature is thus a national literature, because of the nationalist temperament that the authors displayed to their audience.

This fundamental nationalism was at times, by force of circumstance, taken to extremes, for example in the famous politico-literary dispute about the Rhine, during the 1840s, when Musset disputed with Becker; or in the militant involvement of Eichendorff, La Motte-Fouqué and Körner against the French, in 1813. But the Romantics with their crusading spirit also openly declared their support for oppressed nations – Poland, Italy or Greece; thus Hugo and Mazzini, Mickiewicz and Byron, are drawn together. Internationalist and humanist conviction were upheld by Lamartine in the famous *Revolutions* (1831). Shelley in *Queen Mab* (1813), and Heine in the third volume of the *Reisebilder* (1830). These different attitudes should not be regarded as contradictions, but simply as manifestations of a very strong loyalty to the nationalist principle: even in the *Marseillaise de la Paix* (1841), Lamartine did not deny the existence of different native soils, but preached their confederation, and said of the Rhine:

Roule libre, et grossis tes ondes printanières,
Pour écumer d'ivresse autour de tes roseaux;
Et que les sept couleurs qui teignent nos bannières,
Arc-en-ciel de la paix, serpentent dans tes eaux!

Victor Hugo *Ruined Castle*

Throughout Europe, the Romantic found his roots in his native soil and his past.

To his audience, the Romantic writer was a committed, perhaps overtly partisan, writer, whereas in the past he had either had no party or supported the existing authority. In this respect, the Romantics were heirs of the 18th century; they were either liberal (the Italians and most of the English), or partisans of the Holy Alliance (the French during the 1820s, for instance); and they both spoke and wrote of their beliefs. This gave rise to Hugo's *Les Châtiments* (1853), a criticism of Louis-Napoleon Bonaparte, Pellico's *Le mie Prigioni* (1832), of Austrian tyranny in Italy, and *The Prisoner of the Caucasus: A Hero of our Time* by Lermontov, of the suppression of free speech in Russia. In the same spirit, was the political role Byron played in the struggle for Greek independence; Lamartine's role at the head of the French provisional government of 1848, or Pushkin's place at the heart of the Decembrist movement. Out of this capacity for fervent commitment to national and liberal causes Heine's famous *Die Grenadiere* were born, as was the patriotic German poetry of 1813 (Arndt, Körner), and the tone of Kleist's works. It was also the chief native force of the Polish Romantic movement, certainly of one of its major works, Mickiewicz's *Pan Tadeusz*; and of the flowering of Hungarian, Czech and Yugoslav literature after centuries of somnolence.

Art and literature

The Romantic writer was also an artist. He professed to love all the arts, and to favour a system of fine arts in which classes and categories would be less strictly divided and less mutually exclusive than they had been in the past.

Stendhal, for example, wrote about painting (*History of Painting in Italy*, 1817) as well as about music (*Lives of Haydn, Mozart and Metastase*, 1815, *Life of Rossini*, 1824); Hugo proclaimed 'Music is in everything, a hymn comes from the world' (*Que la musique date du XVIe siecle – Les Rayons et les ombres*, no. 35) and Eichendorff, whose words Schumann chose as an epigraph to his *Fantaisie* opus 17, wrote in *Wünschelrute*:

Schlaft ein Lied in allen Dingen
Die da traumen fort und fort
Und die Welt hebt an zu singen
Triffst-du nur das Zauberwort

Many heroes of the novels of the time were musicians: Wackenroder's Berglinger, Balzac's Gambara, Hoffmann's Kreisler, La Motte-Fouqué's Ondine. Haydn, Mozart and Beethoven inspired *Mozart and Salieri* by Pushkin, *Don Juan* by Lenau and Hoffmann, *Die Nachklänge Beethovenscher Musik* ('The Echoes of Beethoven's Music') by Brentano, and the *Lettres d'un Voyageur* by George Sand, not to mention the many novels, which have since disappeared, that had heroines languishing to the sound of a piano, an opera or a serenade! Finally, Hugo, Musset, Gautier, Blake, Pushkin, Kerner and Wackenroder all drew or painted with talent.

The influence of music and painting on the literary thinking of the time could be discussed further, but space prevents a full analysis here. However, the importance of plastic art to Keats should be remembered, as should the importance of music to Hoffmann and Stendhal, and painting and music to Nerval and Wackenroder, who could really be called 'total' artists. Thus it is clear that the Romantic artist nurtured his literary character, to a

significant extent, through enthusiasm for the other arts. Symbollically, it was at a performance of *Freischütz* in Paris in 1824, that Hugo met Devéria.

Nature and religion

A feeling for Nature is the second characteristic of the taste of the Romantic writer. That
taste first appears in the search for solitude, which led some, such as Chateaubriand, Lenau
and Byron, so far as to cross seas and seek the very limits of the so-called civilised world. More
often, this love of solitude drew the Romantics towards fields, woods, mountains and oceans.
But their motivation was not so much to enjoy the picturesque qualities of the setting and to
describe them – as did the *Stürmer*, Bernardin or Rousseau; it was more to dream, and to feed
their melancholy. Taken to the extreme, this resulted in a mistrust of the conventional and
touristic, as found in Chateaubriand, Pushkin or Heine, and most of the discerning spirits of
the time. Thus, the Alps were preferred to the Ocean, 'old companion' of the Vicomte;
Milanese Italy to the Neapolitan shores which were overrun by English people; and the Russian countryside and the North Sea to the museums and the most famous sites of Western and
Southern Europe. Other Romantics, such as Lamartine, Eichendorff and Mörike, preferred
the familiar landscapes of their native soil to famous 'sites'. Others loved the forest – witness
Hugo's forest, the forest of the *Knaben Wunderhorn* and of Dürer. Many will be familiar with the
acerbic lampoons of the Romantic picturesque contained in Flaubert's *Madame Bovary* and the
first books of Heine's *Reisebilder*.

Most of the time, the landscapes were completed by ruins of ancient edifices: moss-
covered churches or castles, such as those in Caspar David Friedrich or Philipp Otto Runge's
paintings or in the collection of engravings of *Picturesque France* by Taylor. It was this very
poetry of ruins and mists that inspired the Romanticism of many Italian poets, Foscolo, for
example, in his book of *Sepolcri* (Sepulchres), or of the *Génie du Christianisme* by Chateaubriand, who formally reinstated admiration for Gothic art in France. The charm of the past
and of places with strong historical associations was very far-reaching indeed, inspiring a
whole series of journeys to the Orient (*Voyages en Orient* by Lamartine, *Voyages* by Nerval,
Itinéraire de Paris à Jérusalem by Chateaubriand, *Rome* by Gogol).

Thus the Romantics not only observed Nature – most of them loved it (Leopardi and
Vigny being exceptions). Some, such as Atterbom, Shelley and Hugo, perceived it as the
kingdom of God – whether pantheist or monotheist mattered little. They spontaneously
placed their trust in this Supreme Being. Wordsworth explained in *The Prelude* how, after
seeking a refuge only within himself, he found an inexhaustible source of pure and ineffable
delights in Nature. Lermontov too, in *The Novice*, showed how the Caucasus, wild and burning, penetrated his inmost being and fed the devouring flame of his heart. But it is perhaps the
odes *To Autumn* and *To a Nightingale* by Keats that contain the most perfect and most typical
expression of this Romantic predilection for Nature; even though the poet adopted a 'classical'
form, by endowing objects with a conscious life he added infinitely more boldness, richness,
and sincerity.

It follows naturally that the third characteristic of the Romantic spirit should be the
consciousness of God or of religion. However, without exception, this had less to do with a
redeeming God than with a desire to expand the spirit, to experience more keenly the temporal and the transient. The great masters were the German Romantics: Novalis with his *Hymns*

Jean-Baptiste-Camille Corot *Souvenir de Mortefontaine.* 1864

to the Night, Wackenroder, but also Goether, chiefly in *Faust*, and the Dane Oehlenschlaeger, who mocked all enlightened religion. In France, the positions adopted were far more varied: Chateaubriand was probably the closest to Germanic mysticism, in *René*, *Le Génie du Christianisme* and even in the astonishing *Vie de Rancé*, which describes with bitter irony the life of a Trappist. This way, as has been suggested, have been born of Protestantism: in a priest as Romantic as Lammenais there was no langour, no inner light. For Vigny and Byron, religiosity could be repressed and give way to both hatred and despair, as in *Moïse* or *The Mount of Olives*. Some, such as Musset or Manzoni, expressed a nostalgia for the simple faith of childhood; while others, like Leopardi, Shelley and Michelet, saw God as no more than an empty word which, nevertheless, breathed astounding conviction and elevation of the spirit into their writing. But every one of them without exception found themselves, at one time or another, with a need to face the central question of spiritual life; thus religion, its substitutes and its different guises, constituted an essential source of inspiration for the Romantic artist.

Love as a Romantic theme

Love, even more than a feeling for Nature and religious aspiration, dominated the Romantic spirit. Madame de Staël was well aware of this when she wrote: 'To perceive the true grandeur of lyrical poetry, one must wander lost in reverie through the ethereal regions, forget the noise of the world by listening to celestial harmony, and consider the entire universe as a symbol for the emotions of the soul' (*De l'Allemagne*). It was not necessarily the case that love was used as a theme in the work of the Romantics: they did not all sing its praises; nor did they treat it from the literary and historical point of view. No one needed Romanticism to analyse the loving heart; its importance was more of a moral or sociological significance.

In such a society, finally at peace and tired of war and heroic action, as Musset described it in *La Confession d'un enfant du siècle*, the emotions of the heart and the nuances of passion became the chief preoccupation of men's innermost thoughts. Love, it might be said, became a reference point. Unheard of liberties and privileges were demanded in its name for the man or the woman in love. On the one hand, Schlegel's novel *Lucinde* (1799) caused a scandal by its 'immorality', but on the other hand, love acquired a moral and, so to speak 'propaedeutic' value in a society which was now based on the 'rights' rather than the duties of mankind: mystical love was confused with religion in *Heinrich von Ofterdingen* by Novalis. Love was the plea in defence of the passionate lover, in the work of Balzac, George Sand, Pushkin, Lenau; different forms of love and, above all, 'coup de foudre', or love at first sight, and its consequences, were themes in Stendhal, Goethe and Hugo (for instance Ruy Blas, 'a worm in love with a star'!). Finally, the idea of time being suspended by love, time standing still for lovers, was described by all the great lyric poets, from Lamartine to Byron. All this goes some way towards explaining why the Romantic writer so clearly preferred the image of the woman-as-angel: it recurs everywhere, although its most interesting face – and the most sublimated – is that of the Muse in Musset's *Nuits*. Because love was no longer perceived as a simple sensual impulse or an emotional whim, it acquired an inalienable value in the eyes of the Romantics.

This, then, was the Romantic spirit, in its tastes and attitudes towards itself and others. Its basic nature resides in its constant hunger and striving for the 'hereafter': '*Anhelo a otra cosa mejor*' ('I long for something other, something better') said Larra, and Goethe too was aware of this when he equated Classical with healthy, and Romantic with unhealthy. In the final analysis, Romanticism was a matter of temperament, a question of personality.

The literary forms

If the Romantic character had remarkable unity, could the same be said of the different fields in which the European artists worked? Is it possible to single out common traits which, above and beyond differences of national or individual temperament, unite all works of poetry, prose and plays?

It is generally held today that Romanticism signified, first and foremost, a poetic revival. This viewpoint may well be more than justified. The first half of the 19th century saw a flowering of exceptional talents, the abundance and brilliance of which has never been equalled in the history of literature. What would English poetry be without Byron, Keats and Shelley, French poetry without Hugo, Russian without Pushkin, German without Novalis and Eichendorff, Italian without Leopardi? What is more, between these different national streams there was an undeniable convergence of content, theme and form.

Across the many European nationalities, poetry, whatever was said about it at the time, was not particularly novel from a technical point of view: the Neo-Classical aspects of Lamartine's work have been underlined, but the same could be held of Leopardi, Pushkin, Shelley, Keats, who were all much influenced by traditional rhetoric. It is true of the Germans too, with perhaps the exception of Novalis: Eichendorff, Brentano and Mörike never did violence to the German tongue, nor used it to expressive ends that might have involved a dislocation of language. Thus, on the whole, there was no frontal breach of traditional language by the poets: Hugo's famous battles for the perfect rhyme and the proper word seem, with hindsight, to be no more than skirmishes.

On the other hand, from a typological point of view all the poets appeared to share a wish to jumble styles in order always to achieve a maximum expressiveness: everything could be said, and should be said, and very strongly, even if it did not amount to much. None of the poets had thus ever been exclusively a lyrical poet, as they all dreamed of having something nobler or more popular to say, whether it be in the form of the epic poem, philosophical or political poetry, or satire. This is evident from the fact that only a relatively small number of poems by Lamartine, Hugo, Mickiewicz or Shelley were lyrical, compared with the rest of their work, even their work in verse. Even among the lyrical poets reputed to be the most influential and the purest – Byron, Novalis and Pushkin – there is another inspiration beneath the lyricism: it may be satirical and political, in Byron's *Don Juan*, for example (in Canto X, the derisive picture of London which follows on directly from a picturesque evocation of the beauties of Greece), or philosophical and outrightly religious, as in the fourth *Hymn to the Night* by Novalis or in the *Geistliche Lieder* (Spiritual Songs) which followed and which the Protestant Church adopted in its service.

As for the other poets, such as Heine or Hugo, in their most mature work they were fond of combining the ironical or vindictive vein with the sentimental: thus Heine could call himself a 'defrocked romantic' and Hugo a 'seer' and a 'magus'. We thus arrive at a sort of interlocking, interconnecting representation of Romantic poetry, in which styles and accents 'dovetail' each with the other, both at the level of personal poetic temperament, and at that of the great 'productions' of which the period was so fond (*Le Corsaire, Les Châtiments, Eugene Onegin*).

Finally, almost all over Europe, poetry adopted similar subject matter. It began with the expression of a spiritual awakening: a return to the Bible, to religion or to illuminist or occult traditions. This gave rise to the preoccupation of the lyrical Romantics with the meaning of Man's life, his origins and his mysterious end: the title of Vigny's book, *Les Destinées*, bears witness to this. It also gave rise to the evolution in Romanticism from the inspiration of the Middle Ages and Christianity (for Madame de Staël and the Germans, for instance) to Utopia, humanitarianism, and even social and political revolution (which was quite typical of the Polish Romanticism of Mickiewicz, Krasinski and Slowacki).

This spiritual awakening led naturally to personal, even introspective, poetry, as in the *Poésies de Joseph Delorme* by Sainte-Beuve, or the verses of the Swabian Romantics (Gustav Schwab, Wilhelm Hauff) and the English rustic poets (Burns, Blake, and Clare). In most cases, this inspiration was invariably translated into highly rhetorical lyricism, as is the case with Hugo, Lamartine, Leopardi or Foscolo.

The third common theme was that of the writer's 'mission'. Whether he was a seer or prophet like Hugo or Novalis, a political guide or the voice of national identity like Lamartine, the Italians or the Poles, or firmly convinced of his own personal, moral and philosophical eminence like Shelley, he sang of the power of the ideal, progress, and a radiant future; thus Vigny's *Esprit pur*.

Thus universal theme of the 'wisdom' of the Romantic had its national variations. Notions of truth and the picturesque, concepts that were often to the fore, do not explain the movement in Germany or in Italy; similarly, the flexibility of the rules of metrics and prosody was not in evidence in the work of the Slavs, or that of the Italian and Spanish Romantics.

Perhaps, in the final analysis, it was Sismondi who provided the most apposite and witty definition of Romantic lyricism:

'The Romantic style appeals directly to our own heart; the Classical style, it seems, can only achieve this by way of folios, so that each emotion it inspires in us must be justified by a quotation from an ancient author' (*La Littérature du Midi de l'Europe*).

One of the most original characteristics of European Romantic poetry was the emergence of the lyrical epic – known, according to country, as ballads, lieder, romances or even simply as poems. These were works of varying length, most often in short verses, that scanned well and were frequently divided into equal stanzas. Rhyme, assonance, alliteration, repetition and refrain all played a large part. Their style aspired to be simple, concrete and consciously naive or popular. Their subject matter was either a private experience, full of pathos or even tragedy, an episode from national history, or a secular or religious legend. The fundamental preoccupations of the Romantic soul were expressed in these works: love of the past, of popular art forms, mystery and terror, and sometimes also a confusion of styles.

Some of these poems sprang straight from the imagination of their authors: most of Hugo's *Ballades*, for instance, or *The Rime of the Ancient Mariner* and *Kubla Khan* by Coleridge. Others drew on elements of folklore that the author remodelled according to his own temperament, like Heine's famous *Lorelei*. Others still developed episodes from very well-known legends, that of El Cid, or of the sagas and epics like *Die Niebelungen*. It should, however, be

Girodet-Trioson *Atala at the Tomb*. 1808

remembered that these rhyming pieces were descended from a form that had already been experimented with in the 18th century, with Ossianism and the German ballads. Bürger's *Lenore*, some ballads by Goethe (*The Sinner*) and by Schiller (*The Glove*), and the elegies of Young and Gray, all exerted considerable influence. In France, the influence of the troubadour style should also be mentioned: this sometimes adopted poetic forms, as, for example, in the *Chants galliques* by Baour-Lormian.

The legendary and folk element was particularly evident in Germany, especially in the work of Uhland, the best of whose many collections of ballads date from between 1805 and 1814 such as *Der blinde König* (The Blind King), *Graf Eberhard* and *Das Schloss am Meer* (The Castle by the Sea). But mention must also be made of Hoffman von Fallersleben (1789–1874), who taught at Breslau and who, in his *lieder*, provided simple lyrics for authentically popular airs. Brahms, whose feeling for simplicity never erred, set several of them to music, and others became really famous (*Alle Vögel sind schon da, Ein Männlein steht im Walde*). The goal of these poets was to realise the dream of Herder and Schlegel: real poetry should be the voice of the people, the expression of its ingenuous soul, rendered with a minimum of artifice. The ballads or romances of Chamisso and von Platen were, to a greater or lesser extent, built on this same idea, even though their subject matter was drawn from foreign sources.

The English and Scottish ballads or romances perpetuated the popular songs, as well as the rustic elegies of the previous century. Southey's ballads, published in 1797, were already Romantic by reason of their mediaeval setting, their imagery of sorcery and witchcraft, but they contained neither popular language nor ingenuous sentiments. It was Walter Scott who created the English language ballad with his *Minstrelsy of the Scottish Border* (1802–1803), folowed in 1805 by the *Lay of the Last Minstrel*, in 1808 by *Marmion* and in 1810 by *The Lady of the Lake*. These poems were the continuation, although much broadened, of the style set by Percy, who had rediscovered the old Scottish folk ballads at the end of the 18th century. But Scott's style evolved towards the ballad of personal inspiration (*Lay of the Last Minstrel*), then towards the narrative poem embellished with lyrical and popular elements (*The Lady of the Lake*); this was all but a novel in verse, or the style of the Byronic poem. The master-piece of the genre, however, was Coleridge's *The Rime of the Ancient Mariner* (1798).

The Spanish *romancero*, recently re-edited and completed, provided its country of origin and the whole of Europe at the beginning of the 19th century with a host of tales of love and death. Athough it is usual to distinguish between the 'historical romance' and the 'romantic legend' in Spain, both provided hyper-Romantic material in form as well as in content. The Duke of Rivas was one of the first, with his *Romances históricos*, to provide an example of Romantic poetry which had found its true national roots, as much in the use of the assonant octosyllabic verse as in its subjects – eighteen of them, drawn from every period of Spanish history, all filled with violence and passion. Rivas also wrote a poem which, although narrative and of vast length, gave pride of place to local colour and to the evocation of national spirit: *El Moro exposito* (The Moorish foundling). Some poets who were especially enamoured of historical accuracy concentrated on the realistic portrayal of past customs; others freely invented, within the setting provided by the *romancero*, a whole world of gallant knights and gentle ladies (like Mariano Roca de Togores, the two Bermudez de Castro brothers, José Joaquín de Mora, or even Espronceda) which was not untouched by the influence of Hugo and the Germans. Conversely, it is interesting to note that Heine, in his *Romanzero* as well as in some of his early works (*Don Ramiro*, for example) was inspired by this Spanish poetry.

Throughout Europe, the ballad, the romance and the epic lyrical poem were used in different ways, but without belying the essential characteristics of their typically Romantic poetic inspiration. In Italy, Berchet, Prati and others were composing *ballate* and *romanze*, whether to tell an invented love story in lyrical mood (*Il Trovatore* by Berchet), or to exalt national glories in view of the *Risorgimento*. In Holland, the future novelist J. van Lennep began his career by imitating the English ballads in his *Legends of the Netherlands*, which met with enormous success. In Denmark, Ingemann produced one of the masterpieces of Danish Romanticism with *Holger Danske*, a cycle of short poems in the style of the ancient *viser*.

The Slavs placed themselves willingly under the influence of Scott and the Germans. A few examples are: in Poland, the *Ballads* by Mickiewicz, and the *Songs of Janusch* by Wincenty Pol; in the Czech language, the *Muse of the Tatras* by Shafarik, and the *Garland of Popular Legends* by Erben. The Russians left only a few ballads as such: Lermontov's *Czar Ivan Vassilievich* is famous for the vivid colour with which it portrays the sentiments and the language of the old Russia. The cycle of the *Kozbar* by the Ukrainian Chevtchenko was a compilation of national ballads, and there was also Pushkin's famous development of the spirit, subject and metre of popular poetry in the poems *Russlan and Ludmilla* and *Poltava*. In Hungary, finally, the ballad constituted an essential form of national poetry. Kolscey inaugurated the style in 1814 and with Kisfaludy, Arany and Garay, it took on the form of the 'epic ballad'. These were short tales, full of blood or fantasy, about madness, murder and judgement. Arany was the undisputed master of the genre, because he knew so well how to express the force of destiny, how to describe beautiful women, how to envelop the action in a fearsome atmosphere, and enhance all this with the most musical of verse.

There is no doubt whatsoever that epic lyrical poetry found its most deservedly famous and most brilliant flowering in the Romantic period. It was a true meeting ground of styles and reflected all the various tendencies of the lyricism of the day, quite independently of the fact that ballads and romances represent something approaching the quintessence of that unique spirit.

On the surface at least, it was in the domain of prose that the continuity of the Romantic movement in relation to what had preceded it was most clearly marked. Although in drama and in verse the writers of the time may have suddenly experienced the revelation of a new eloquence, the same did not hold true for the novel, criticism, and history. The breach had already taken place with *La Nouvelle Héloise*, *Werther* and Richardson's novels. *Delphine* by Madame de Staël, *Lélia* by George Sand, and *René* by Chateaubriand were nothing more than applications of an already tried and tested formula. Moreover, the novel did not give rise to the impassioned taking of positions, to the battles which gave drama and poetry their revolutionary charm, even if it was more apparent than real. Also, the novel did not really attain maturity during the Romantic period: in *every* literature, it was doing little more than feeling its way towards realism, slowly and gradually experimenting with a formula of objective narration, in the third person. In this respect, the evolution of Balzac, from the influence of Walter Scott to the most personal and widely celebrated realism, is exemplary. This is evident from reading the preface to the *Comédie Humaine* alone. But it would be hard to say – even with hindsight – that Balzac and Stendhal were Romantics from the outset.

What, then, were the major modifications to the novel brought about by European Romanticism? In he realm of personal Romanticism, we find, first of all, the dominant role of the author himself – his ego – to the point where, whether by an artifice in the narration or in the eyes of the reader, the person of the author becomes confused with that of the hero: the identification, for instance, of Foscolo with Jacopo Ortis, Pushkin with Onegin, Byron with Don Juan (even if, in this case, it is in a verse novel), and Constant with Adolphe. This gave birth to the autobiographical novel as well as to the novel in verse; to cycles of novels (*Jocelyn* by Lamartine, the *Carthusian* by Eotvos) as well as to isolated works (*Oberman* by Senancour). The clearest continuity is to be seen in novels in the form of letters, such as *Oberman*, and in narratives in the first person addressed to a listener who is present in the book (*René*). These two narrative forms bear unmistakable witness to the extent of their inheritance from the 18th century. Love, analysed with even greater and more attentive complaisance, was still their mainspring.

Outward Romanticism, which we have called the commitment or the humanitarian ideals of the artist, had its place too: it inspired the historical novel or the novel of adventure with its exoticism of time and place: for example, Chateaubriand's *Martyrs*, Scott's cycles, *Liechtenstein* by Hauff or the *Guardians of the Crown* by Arnim. The best examples are those where personal commitment and intimate conviction feed the description, as witness the success of Manzoni's *Sposi*, Mickiewicz's *Pan Tadeusz*, and Gogol's *Taras Bulba*. In cases such as these, the feeling for Nature is reinforced by nostalgia for a homeland lost or enslaved, the depiction of landscapes, picturesque sights (containing ruins or monuments) and domestic life; the aim is ultimately the 'integral resurrection of the past' (Michelet).

This formula brings us to the Romantic view of history. History, like criticism, benefited from the exuberance of the novel form. It is certainly the case with history 'à la' Michelet, where the writer is biased and concentrates on epic themes; but it is also the case of the biographical critique, that used the man as the point of departure for an understanding of his work. Chateaubriand in his *Essai sur la littérature anglaise* showed the way for Sainte-Beuve; the *Cours familier de littérature* by Lamartine was inspired by novels about the life of an artist that abounded at the time. Similarly, the thesis novels by Victor Hugo, George Sand and the Germans (*Lucinde* by F. Schlegel, *Godwi* by Brentano) show an innate relationship with history, because the author was dealing here with the problematic interaction of love and society, the individual and the whole. Michelet's *La Sorcière* could perhaps be called a novel; Hugo's *Les Misérables* and Gutzkow's *Doubting Woman* are perhaps history.

Where are the boundaries? How can we set up a system of definition which would encompass all these styles? A response to these questions might be that the first rule of Romantic prose was osmosis. There was, indeed, interpenetration between fictional and historical styles. There is a contrast here with what we have seen to be the case with poetry, where the various accents and orientations all sprang initially from lyricism; in prose, different styles co-existed from the outset, but their boundaries tended to become blurred.

Consequently, the second rule might perhaps be that of totality: prose wanted to encompass all styles, almost in a single work. Hence the charm, in our eyes, of the *roman-fleuves* or erratic, often unfinished, works such as *Heinrich von Ofterdingen* by Novalis, where the prose poem co-exists with philosophical meditation, where lyricism and love go side by side with the esoteric purpose; or that of *Seraphita, Louis Lambert, La Peau du Chagrin*, in which Balzac is revealed as much as a poet of fantasy as a novelist of realism, a historian of French society as much as a disciple of Swedenborg or Saint-Martin; or even Sainte-Beuve's strange *Volupté*, which seems to be a combination of *René* and *Le Génie du christianisme*, both moral tract and work of fiction, both a poem in the style of Ossian or Werther and a covertly atheistic tome.

Of the various prose styles, the historical novel was perhaps the one that earned Romanticism, over an extended period of time, from 1815 to 1850, its greatest literary laurels. Here, the breach with the 18th century is very clear. Although writers had, long since, been setting fictional intrigues against the background of past centuries, the intrigue itself bore almost no relation to the historical period: the past was merely a setting designed to lift the reader out of his normal surroundings or to make the action seen more credible to him. La Calprenède and Mademoiselle de Scudéry paid scant attention to describing the historical and geographical setting in detail and with accuracy, nor did they trouble to show its relationship with the events and the intrigue of their story.

Eugène Delacroix *The Abduction of Rebecca* (after *Ivanhoe* by Walter Scott). 1858

In the second half of the 18th century, the *Antiquary Novels* were published in England. These were rather mediocre works of fiction, but their authors were at pains to display their knowledge of local history and antiques. The style met with little success.

In Germany, the *Ritterromane* and the *Räuberromane*, tales of knights and brigands, were even less prophetic of the new genre. At the beginning of the 19th century, however, with Ossianism and the troubadour style, the atmosphere was propitious to the evocation of unfamiliar surroundings, and there was a general trend towards the open air, moss-covered stones, and mediaeval or legendary lovers.

It was in Scotland that the movement was born. From the land, already famous for its pre-Romantic and Romantic poets, came *Waverley* by Walter Scott, in 1814. Intially published anonymously, but soon attributed to Scott, the series of Waverley novels appeared in rapid succession until the author's death in 1832, and met with ever increasing success. All the countries on the Continent raved about this new form of novel; Pushkin even described in *Onegin* now the new fashion had reached as far as the Russian steppes! In France, Scott was received with enormous enthusiasm and his entire works were excellently translated by Deffaucomprey.

The French writers, however, who were the first to experiment with this form of fiction, were never specialists in the historical novel. They all produced as least one work in the style, then went back to their own source of personal inspiration. During Scott's lifetime, works that appeared in France, between 1826 and 1831, included *Cinq-Mars* by Vigny, *la Chronique du temps de Charles IX* by Merimée, *les Chouans* by Balzac and *Notre-Dame de Paris* by Victor Hugo (who was to take up the form again much later with *Quatre-vingt-treize*).

Yet all these works were notably different from those of Scott, since each author, first and foremost, remained himself. Each had his own personal conception of history – something that was completely absent in Scott – at the expense of distorting the veracity of the central characters; each invented a plot far more complicated than any of those created by Scott (think of *Notre-Dame de Paris*!), and depicted passion verging on insanity, and extremely extravagant characters. So as far as the young French Romantics were concerned we cannot speak of imitation of Scott, but more of a personal tribute paid to him.

Dumas, from 1839 onwards, was more faithful to Scott in his series of well-known works which met with unfailing success. In every country and language, writers tried to compete with Sir Walter, because his new form of novel lent itself so well to the Romantic searching for a means of expression, to early or outward Romanticism. The historical novel appeared as early as 1820 in Italy, in 1824 in Denmark, in 1825 in Poland, in 1826 in Germany and in France, in 1828 in the Czech language, in 1829 in Spain, Holland and Russia, and in around 1840 in Hungary and in Portugal. In most countries, the style was the domain of specialist writers, most of whom are forgotten today and eminently forgettable, and of whom it could be said that their technique tempered their romantic ardour.

There were also noticeable differences from one country to another. In Germany, the *Bildungsroman*, or educational novel, came into fashion with Goethe: set in the past and full of local colour, the *Bildungsroman* verged on the historical novel without really being one. This was true of *Die Kronenwächter* (The Guardians of the Crown), that vast work by Arnim, which appeared only just after *Waverley*. The masterpiece of the genre is unquestionably *Liechtenstein* by Hauff: published in 1826, this book brought the customs, landscapes and history of Swabia in the early 16th century to life, under a sunny sky.

In Holland, the traditional national qualities of seriousness and close attention to reality and colour, lent some value to the works of Margarethe de Neufville, van den Hague, and more particularly to the novels of Drost, van Lennep and Mrs Bosboom-Toussaint. Van Len-

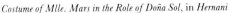

Costume of Mlle. Mars in the Role of Doña Sol, in Hernani

Costume of Frederic Lemaître in Ruy Blas

nep was even dubbed the 'Dutch Scott', because of the way Fate controlled the psychological thread of his novels.

In countries that were subjected to foreign occupation and where a national conscious- ness was dawning, the historical novel took on symbolic value. This was particularly true in Italy and Poland. In Italy, the inspiration of the historical novel, like the play, was drawn from the annals of bygone national splendour or misfortune. The complications of the plot and the violence of passion which characterise the works of Guerazzi (*Beatrice Cenci*, *Pasquale Paoli*) and Manzoni (*Promessi Sposi*) make these very Romantic novels. But the most important, first both in date and in value, is that of Manzoni. In his *Promessi Sposi*, his prime concern was respect for historical truth, even if, to some extent, this was to the detriment of the fictional interest. Manzoni's Romanticism was of a doctrinal nature; but for the precision of its landscapes or its period detail, and for its reconstruction of a society two centuries old, this novel must rank with the finest works of Walter Scott.

In Spain, the fashion for the historical novel lasted from 1830 to 1850. Larra wrote *El Doncel de don Enrique el Doliente* (1834), an adaptation to contemporary taste of the old story of Macias el Enamorado. Espronceda failed utterly with *Sancho Saldana* (1834) and did not try again. Patricio de la Escosura wrote a great number of successful stories of which the most curious is *El Patriarca del Valle*, a very complicated allegorical tale, in imitation of Eugene Sue's *Juif Errant*, which purported to portray Spain at the end of the previous century. Martinez de la Rosa also produced a historical novel: *Doña Isabel de Solís*, based on an episode in the struggle between the Catholic kings and the sultans of Granada. The best works of historical fiction, however, were *El Señor de Bembibre* by Enrique Gil, a story of love set against the fall of the Knights Templar, and *Doña Urraca de Castilla* (1849) and *Doña Blanca de Navarra* by Navarro Villoslada.

In Poland, where every branch of literature was infused with Romantic and nationalist spirit, the historical novel set out to revive the memory of past glories, and the brilliance of 16th and 17th century Polish society, for example in the work of Kraszewski and Niemcewicz.

In Russia, despite the strict censorship which even mistrusted allusions to history, the style of the historical novel was adopted with zeal, particularly by Zagoskin who, in 1825, published *Yuri Miloslavski*. But, as he did in every literary field, Pushkin produced by far the finest example with *The Captain's Daughter* (1835–1836), a fictionalised version of the Pugachov revolt, of which he wrote a historical account elsewhere.

In Denmark, Ingemann, who was known as the Danish Walter Scott, produced the best examples of the historical novel with *Woldemar the Victorious*, *Holger Danske* and *Prince Othon*. He brought a new element to the genre by borrowing events and details from popular poems (*viser*) and thus avoiding the psychology of Scott's works, which was at once too rudimentary and too modern for him.

So, in many countries, the great wealth of historical novels inspired by Walter Scott helped to bring about, more universally and with more ease than even the most successful plays or epic-lyrical poetry, a new taste for vivid, fervent and colourful literature.

It would be a mistake, however, to think that the list of literary types produced by the Romantic movement did not extend beyond the fields of the novel or of lyric-epic poetry; anyone following the development of historiography, literary criticism or travel journals in the period will notice that remarkable innovations took place in these three forms of prose writing during the first half of the 19th century.

The writing of history had, for centuries, been little more (with the exception of the works of Voltaire) than tales of battles or of the memorable achievements of the world's great men. Even under the pen of Hume or Voltaire, the narration was abstract, flat and devoid of any picturesque element. Historians, even the most conscientious, showed little interest in researching archives, or drawing inspiration from monuments, the arts or literature. All that was to change with Romanticism.

The tendencies of the emergent Romantic spirit were radically to transform the way that history was written. Historians began to look at the Middle Ages with different eyes. When he wrote his *Histoire des ducs de Bourgogne*, Barante meticulously followed the work of the ancient chroniclers so as to provide the reader with the most vivid and most detailed account possible. But in Europe it was Augustin Thierry who was the first to take an absolutely new direction. Under the influence of Chateaubriand's *Martyrs* and Scott's novels, he attempted to examine in depth the material, social and moral setting of the Merovingians, the Normans and the

Third Estate. To do so, he emphasised local colour and details of the customs and morality of the time, and tried to explain the major causes of events. In so doing, he set himself on the same plane as Scott, Hugo and Merimée; the historian had become a painter.

However, the archetypal Romantic historian was Michelet. Not only did he base his *Histoire de France* on archive documents, the first time this had ever been done, but he seemed to be able to commune with the men of the past – with their hearts, their way of thinking, and their deepest aspirations. An essay such as that of *La Sorcière* (The Witch), for example is quite remarkable in this respect. Less concerned than Thierry with local colour, what he sought to depict was the spirit of things and of people, which makes his approach more like that of Hugo and gives his finest writing an almost visionary and prophetic quality. For the first time, history acquired new meaning: it was like the work of a poet.

Carlyle, who was Michelet's contemporary and diametrically opposed to him in his moral and political views, had the same vivid imagination, passion, and the violent staccato style. Like Michelet, in fact much more so, Carlyle set himself up in opposition to the Age of Enlightenment and to Classicism. No one was more romantic than Carlyle, in the sense that his Romanticism constituted a reaction against the art and thought that Europe had inherited from Humanism; his two great works, *The French Revolution* and *Frederick the Great* can thus inspire as much exasperation as admiration.

The Romantic movement also had an innovative influence on literary history and criticism. There had certainly been no dearth of critical works in the preceding centuries, but, firmly under the influence of Aristotelian rhetoric, they confined themselves to an examination of how well works conformed with the prevailing rules: the discussion was always one of poetics. Critics never considered works from the point of view of historical relativity, and thus made some fatal errors of judgement, for instance in talking of the 'barbarism' of Shakespeare, in their ignorance of the real meaning of Renaissance or Baroque art, their disdain for all popular inspiration, and so on.

Madame de Staël in her work *De la Littérature* was the first to attempt to alter the course of criticism by basing it on variations in both institutions and customs. At the same time, her book was an outline for a history of literatures, an attempt to substitute external and scientific criteria for personal standards. If Madame de Staëk did no more than usher in a new tendency, it was the Germans who really launched it. Wackenroder and Tieck applied the notion of historical relativity to the Fine Arts in *Outpourings of the Heart of an Art-loving Monk* and in *Franz Sternbald* respectively. Friedrich Schlegel, writing about Homer, and his brother August Wilhelm writing about Shakespeare and Calderon, both clearly adopted this point of view (in their review, the *Athenäum*, 1798–1804).

This was followed a whole series of studies of comparative literary history: Chateaubriand in his *Essai sur la littérature anglaise*, Sismondi and Ginguené in their studies of the Italian literatures, Ampère on the Northern literatures, Villemain in his *Cours de littérature française* (1828–1829), all paint a wide picture in which, under the very clear influence of Madame de Staël, works of literature are put back in their historical and geographical context and compared with one another. There were also a great many essays of pure criticism, often by the young writers themselves, which adopted a new system of classification of literary values: Shakespeare, Dante, Petrarch, and also Virgil, Homer and Goethe, were the idols of Deschamps, Hugo, Hazlitt and de Quincey.

In France, Sainte-Beuve drew up a kind of systematic 'natural history' of great minds: a reconstruction of a literary period in *Le Tableau de la poésie française au XVIe siecle*; of a literary set in *Port-Royal*; of a career in *Chateaubriand* and, above all, of an author or of a single work in

Chateaubriand by the Ruins of Carthage

Portraits littéraires and *les Lundis*. Nothing could be more in contrast with the spirit of Classicism than this meticulous search for precise and significant detail, for historical value and for the relationship of the subject with the contemporary world.

Art criticism, which, despite Diderot's *Salons*, had remained a minor and all but disregarded medium, began to flourish with the accounts of concerts, plays, operas and exhibitions written by Nerval, Gautier, Heine and Hugo. Thus a whole secondary literature was born out of the Romantic movement, which provides us with occasional glimpses of the newly emerging system of the fine arts during this period.

Finally, travel journals and depictions of local mores also profited from this new perception of history. Unlike the classical traveller, who was mainly interested in the laws and institutions of foreign countries, the romantic traveller came to see the landscapes, the life styles and all that was picturesque, wherever he went. His sensitivity and his imagination sometimes embellished reality, as in the accounts of Alexandre Dumas. Their journeys were confined to Europe (Switzerland, Italy, Spain, the German countries) or to its borders, and

Illustration for Chateaubriand's 'Les Natchez' by Staal

the shores of the Mediterranean. France is particularly rich in travelogues, having produced accounts of the journeys of Chateaubriand, Lamartine, Gautier, Nerval and Hugo, which embody all those authors' finest traits as well as each one's personal brand of Romanticism.

Newer still were the picturesque descriptions of contemporary mores. They prolifererated in different lands between 1820 and 1850. *The Sketchbook* by the American Washington Irving; *Las Escenas Andaluzas* (Andalusian Scenes) by Estebanez Calderon, *Las Escenas Matritenses* (Scenes of Madrid) by Mesonero Romanos, the two most famous describers of Spanish life; all blend Romantic colour and fantasy with a meticulous concern for accurate detail that presages the trend towards realism. The Romantic elements in these, and other, contemporary works are to be found, in less concentrated form, in novels, poetry and drama. In a more subjective and more journalistic style, were the *Mémoires d'un touriste* by Stendhal and his fine descriptions of Italy (*Rome, Naples, Florence* and *Promenades dans Rome*) which are, at one and the same time, the intimate thoughts of a man of very romantic temperament, biting portrayals of mores, and somewhat whimsical travel journals.

The spirit of Romanticism did not leave its mark only on poetry and prose; it also deeply influenced the writing of drama. In France, it was in the medium of the theatre that Romanticism made its greatest impact, and the famous 'battle of Hernani' (1830) is still discussed today. But first we must examine the position of the theatre at the beginning of the 19th century.

At the time, there was little variety in either plays or repertoires; little to provide interest apart from a few traditional kinds of tragedy and comedy, and a few successful dramatists: Kotzebue and Iffland in Germany, and, in France, authors such as Legouve, Lemonnier, Baour-Lormian, Pixérécourt and Raynouard, who were mentioned in Stendhal's *Journal* and deserve to be remembered. Moreover, the repertoire of the European theatres varied in type. Although there were French theatres all over Europe, except in England, each country also had its own national traditions which, to a greater or a lesser extent, favoured the revival movement. Great Britain had always maintained a Shakespearean repertoire, and Germany had created a repertoire of the works of Schiller: this explains why the question of the reform of the theatrical stage barely arose in these countries. In the Latin countries, on the other hand, the theatre was dominated by weighty classical tragedy at one end of the spectrum, and popular farce at the other, with very little in between. Faced with the rigidity of a played-out repertoire and the sense of a great gap between the theatre and life – even between different forms of drama itself – Romanticism had an important role to play in re-shaping national theatre.

The existence of dramatic criticism, and of a theoretical consideration of drama were the first factors, both chronologically and in importance, that signalled the renewal brought about by the Romantic movement. It was August Wilhelm Schlegel who, with his translations of Shakespeare and Calderon, and his *Literature Course* in around 1810, explained the need for each country to draw upon its own inspiration and forms. In England in the 1820s, the Shakespearean criticism of Coleridge and Hazlitt preached respect for the entirety of the great dramatist's work. In France, Chateaubriand, Hugo and Stendhal did not, as is often mistakenly believed, recommend comparison and contrast between the heritage of Shakespeare and the heritage of Racine, but a fusion of the two in a new form of drama. On this point, moreover, they were merely making amends for the attitude of Voltaire who, in spite of his – perhaps calculated – feelings about the 'barbarism' of Shakespeare, recognised his *raison d'être*.

Thus, the Romantic movement in the theatre was an attempt at synthesis at every level. To take the level of style to begin with: Hugo's formula of the alliance 'between the sublime and the grotesque' is well known, but one could equally well cite Manzoni and his *Letter to M. Chauvet* (1823). At the level of subject matter, the famous demand for 'local colour' has been much misunderstood. It was not, in fact, a concern for meticulous detail, within the limits of realistic staging – which was to be the purpose of naturalist theatre – but more a concern for psychological and historical truth. 'Local colour is what essentially characterises the state of society that dramatic compositions aimed to depict' wrote Benjamin Constant in his *Reflexions sur la tragédie de Wallenstein*: that is to say, the dramatist, according to his subject matter, would choose a style to suit the historical situation that he was attempting to evoke. The historical play was only one of the means of providing local colour; it was the style appropriate to an evocation of the mediaeval or Renaissance periods, particularly in France. 'Honour is due to the tragic poets of our time who have finally found the noble audacity to abandon the fable and ancient history in order to offer us scenes from our own annals, or at least from modern records' Stendhal wrote in his *Lettres Normandes* (1820).

Thirdly, the desire for synthesis in the field of Romantic drama is marked by a particular concern to distinguish, among the famous 'unities', those which had become superfluous in modern times – the unities of time and of place – and that which was indispensable: unity of interest, centred on one character, around whom the action of the play revolved. This was the claim laid by the Italians, by Manzoni, but also by Berchet in the *Lettera semi-seria di Crisostomo* (1816); it was the great lesson to be learned from the theatre of Schiller, and in particular from the famous *Wallenstein* trilogy (*Wallensteins Lager*, 1798, *Die Piccolomini* and *Wallensteins Tod*, 1799).

Finally, at a generic level, the desire for synthesis went so far as to blur the border line between plays that could be staged and plays that were, so to speak, unplayable, or between the play and the dramatic poem. A very considerable proportion of the output of the Romantics consisted of unstaged, unstageable plays, written solely to be read. This was particularly true of plays written after 1830, even though the first was *Manfred* by Byron, written in 1817. It was certainly the case of *Correggio* by Oehlenschlaeger, *Savonarola* and *Don Juan* by Lenau, *Camões* by Garrett, and later by Joukovski.

In similar vein, Pushkin's 'little dramas' might be cited: *Mozart and Salieri*, for instance, and *Don Juan*; the collection of plays by Musset under the title *Spectacle dans un fauteuil* (Armchair Theatre) or the *Théâtre de Clara Gazul* by Merimée. Closer to the real theatre in their form, but also intended to be read rather than staged, were the most characteristic and Romantic plays of the German and Scandinavian authors. They drew their subject matter from international folklore (*Blue-Beard*, subtitled *A Nursery Tale*, by Tieck), from the legends of the Christian Middle Ages (the Sigurd trilogy by La-Motte Fouqué), and from the marvellous tales of the Orient (*Aladdin or the Miraculous Lamp* by Oehlenschlaeger, *The Blue Bird* by Atterbom).

Given this context, where are the 'historical plays', which represent the ultimate in Romantic style – *les Burgraves* and *Cromwell* by Hugo, *The Cenci* by Shelley, *Mazeppa* by Slowacki, *Lorenzaccio* by Musset, the *Count of Caramagnola* by Manzoni, *Kätchen von Heilbronn* by Kleist – to be placed? In spite of the variety of their sub-titles (tragedy, drama, dramatic scene, dramatic poem), what all these works have noticeably in common is that each represents an attempt at dramatic synthesis. Thus we see a synthesis of styles (in *Cromwell*), synthesis of an aesthetic and a quite separate subject (*The Cenci*), synthesis of poetry and drama, for the most part, synthesis of a style – drama – and a spirit – Romantic disenchantment, of which the finest illustration is perhaps *Lorenzaccio*. All the ambiguity of the Romantic theatre can be seen in this light.

A final observation that should be made is of the attempt to re-situate the Romantic theatre in relation to the global phenomenon of the theatrical arts. Unlike prose or poetry, the theatre of the Romantic movement was always fighting a battle on two fronts. On the one hand, or externally, it was in direct, and fierce, competition with opera and ballet. There is evidence of constant contact, of bridges between one art form and the other: thus Victor Hugo, in his famous Preface to *Cromwell*, dreamt of a total theatrical event, and could also regard the lyrical stage with envy; while as far as Henri Blaze de Bury, director of *La Revue des Deux Mondes* and author of *Meyerbeer and His Times* (1865) was concerned, it was 'grand opera' that had realised all the dramatic potentialities of both prose and verse drama, as he tried to explain to his contemporaries. One should also bear in mind that Rossini's great successes between 1815 and 1825, and the success of certain isolated works such as *La Muette de Portici* by Auber (1828), *Ossian* by Lesueur (1804) or even *Fidelio* (1814) or *Freischütz* (1821), all contributed very significantly to changes and developments on the dramatic stage.

On the 'internal' front, on the other hand, it is important to be aware that there were practically no 'born' dramatists. In noticeable contrast to both poetry and prose, most writers were only temporarily attracted to the theatre; this perhaps explains the existence of a parallel stream which never ceased to flow and which drew as much upon variety theatre and melodrama as upon properly so-called tragedies. It is curious, for example, that probably the greatest dramatist of the time, Büchner (1813–1837) was only very marginally influenced by the Romantic movement. It is no less disconcerting to note that, in Germany, from which the dramatic offensive had been launched, the most famous authors were all authors of 'tragedies': Grillparzer (1791–1872) with *Sappho* and *Medea*, Hebbel (1813–1863) with *Judith* and *Agnes Bernauer*, Otto Ludwig (1813–1865) with *Maccabees*, not to mention the extravagant Kleist, an otherwise confirmed Romantic, whose finest play, *Penthesilea*, plunged deep into the ancient springs of Greek 'dionysian' tragedy.

The historical or legendary drama is by far the most interesting form of Romantic theatre. Such plays were actually staged at the time and placed before the audience a wide historical canvas, which hovered between epic and legend.

Here, chronologically, the German Romantics led the way. They had no 'school' as such, no programme, no ideal in common. Thus the Prussian Kleist proved himself to be a Romantic in his choice of subjects, and his abundant use of local colour, as well as in his taste for the bizarre and extravagant. In *Die Herrmansschlacht* (the Battle of Arminius, 1808), the tale of the Germanic hero's victory over the legions of Varus contains a great number of transparent allusions to the patriotic struggle against Napoleon. *Kätchen von Heilbronn* (Catherine of Heilbronn, 1810) is subtitled 'a great historical drama from the times of chivalry' and contains all the elements that were later recognised and appreciated in the work of Victor Hugo. By comparison, the Austrian Grillparzer, with his more sober style and greater respect for form, embodies another aspect of the Romantic conception of drama: the poetic aspect. Often in emulation of Lope de Vega, he gave dreamy and nostalgic temperaments to his central characters, such as Leander in *Des Meeres und der Liebe Wellen* (Waves of the Sea and of Love, 1831) and Sapho in the work of the same name (1818). His plays evoke a strange world where action and dreams are intertwined.

Among the ranks of the authors of lesser stature, the name of Zacharias Werner should be mentioned. Werner's wild and eccentric Romanticism manifested itself in plays based on more or less authentical historical facts: the legendary order of the Knights Templar in *Die Söhne des Tals* (The Sons of the Valley, 1803), the colonisation of the Baltic regions in *Das kreuz an der Ostsee* (The Cross on the Baltic, 1806), and, above all, *Luther* (1807) which was much admired by Madame de Staël, Stendhal and the first French Romantics.

Such historical and national dramatic plays were extremely popular in Central and Eastern Europe from 1820. They provided the working models for such plays as *Boris Godunov* by Pushkin, *Bank Ban* by the Hungarian Katona, *King Fjalar*, a play written in Swedish by the Finn Runerberg, and *The Hill of the Elves* by the Danish dramatist Heiberg.

In the 1830s, it was French drama that gained the ascendant and was imitated by the Italians and the Spaniards. This latin form of Romanticism did not draw on legendary sources and excluded overly obscure symbolism, as well as all elements of the miraculous and the religious. On the contrary, the emphasis was placed on the depiction of mores, and on the dramatic and human interest. Alexandre Dumas *père* was a prolific, and prolix, example of this dramatic formula. Between 1830 and 1840, various of his plays were staged, including *Christine de Suède* (Christina of Sweden), *Charles VII chez ses grands vassaux*, *Catherine Howard* and *La Tour de Nesle*; all were vaguely entitled 'tragedy' or 'drama', and presented some of the less noble aspects of Romanticism.

'*Dishevelled Romantics at the First Performance of Hernani on 21 Feburary 1830*' by Grandville

Less skilful, but more authentic was *The Maréchale d'Ancre* by Vigny, in which history borders on the fictional and is blended with the ethical musings of the author himself. Of Hugo's works, his verse plays were the most popular: *Marion Delorme*, *Hernani*, *le Roi s'amuse*, *Ruy Blas* and even the *Burgraves* trilogy. With these works, Hugo offered a real alternative to replace classical tragedy. The differences between the two genres are evident: Hugo's boldness of style and verse, mixture of tones, and mournful lyricism, reveal a sincerity of which is still perceptible today. These plays represent the most typical examples of what one might call pseudo-historical drama, in the sense that its heroes were entirely fictitious characters, but

207

were placed within a historical context. It was a formula that resolved at a stroke the problem that had so tormented Schiller and that had provoked the birth of drama: how to reconcile historical truth with dramatic interest.

Spanish drama originated in emulation of the French theatre, but differed fundamentally from it in that its subject matter was almost invariably drawn from authentic national history or tradition (a characteristic shared with Italian drama). Added to this were its generosity and intrepid rhythm which corresponded perfectly to the national temperament: with this freedom of treatment, the Spaniards rediscovered a great many elements in common with the theatre of Alarcon, Lope de Vega and Calderon.

The theatre blossomed rapidly in the wake of the success of *Hernani*: as early as 1830, Martinez de la Rosa staged *Aben-Humeya or the Revolt of the Moors* in Paris, in French, and later, in 1836, in Spanish. It was also in France that Rivas conceived *Don Alvaro or the Force of Destiny*, in which he cleverly plagiarised *Hernani*; the play is most famous for the opera that Verdi based upon it, *La Forza del Destino*. The great period of Spanish drama spanned the decade between the mid-1830s and the mid-1840s. The three most famous authors were Hartzenbusch with his celebrated *Los Amantes de Teruel* (The Lovers of Teruel) which was rewritten twice and which is free of any declamation of passion, but simply full of melancholy; Gutierrez, with the brilliant *El Trovador*, *El Rey monje* (The Monk King), and *Simon Bocanegra*, which is more reminiscent of Dumas than of Hugo; and finally, Zorilla with *El Zapatero y el Rey* (The Shoemaker and the King) and *Don Juan Tenorio* (1844) which clearly evince the affiliation between Spanish Romantic drama and the Baroque theatre of Molina. Many of these plays appear to modern eyes to lean rather too heavily towards melodrama; yet the dream-like and nostalgic atmosphere they evoke and their at once brilliant and melodious form are beyond compare throughout the whole of Eurpoe.

Italy, by contrast, never produced its own national historical theatre. The form of the classical tragedy had, surprisingly, survived and flourished in the 18th century with Metastase and Alfieri; so it is not unexpected to find that the Romantic movement there produced far less innovative drama than in any other country. Besides, the repertoire was subjected to rigorous censorship and stagnated through a lack of productions.

The twelve tragedies by Silvio Pellico were cast in the classical mould, even though their author belonged to the Milan Romantic movement. The first of these, *Francesca da Rimini* (1815), was the only one to achieve any great success. After 1825, Tedaldi-Fores, Marenco and others staged several 'historical tragedies', undoubtedly under the influence of Manzoni's two published plays (*Il Conte de Caramagnola*, 1820, and *Adelchi*, 1822) and his *Letter to M Chauvet on the unity of time and place in tragedy* (1823).

The most important Italian dramatist of the time was Niccolini, whose works were banned by the authorities because of their nationalistic content, and were only staged in the theatre much later: *Nebuchadnezzar*, *Arnaldo de Brescia*, *Antonio Foscarini*. They were full of vigour and expressed in beautiful and striking language.

Thus it would be justified to say that drama and the theatre in Europe turned Romanticism to great advantage. Indeed, if the Romantic movement still retains a 'historical' dimension today, it is in and through the plays that it has left us.

These then are the works that are most characteristic of literary Romanticism. If, with hindsight, they afford us an image of the movement that is full of contrasts, and even of contradictions, it is perhaps because this reflects the nature of the Romantic period itself.

ANDERSEN Hans Christian (Odense 2.4.1805 – Copenhagen 4.8.1875). Born into a poor family, Andersen was self-taught and became a writer and story-teller almost by default, as he wanted to be an actor or playwright. In fact, his work took various forms: of gentle and melancholic nature, he began by writing some rather bland *Elegies*. Accounts of his many journeys followed: *Journey on foot from Holmen to the far East of Amager* (1828); *Travel Scenes* (1831); *A Writer's Bazaar* (1841); *In Sweden* (1849), and some plays, which met with little or no success: *Love on the Saint Nicholas Tower* (1829) and *The Mulatto* (1840).

Andersen devoted himself above all to prose. He wrote several novels: *The Improviser* (1833), *Only a Fiddler* (1837), *The Two Baronnesses* (1847), of which two were autobiographical: *To Be or Not to Be* (1857), *Lucky Peter* (1870) and, of course, the countless tales for which he is so famous. Their intentionally naive and simple style, their familiar fantasy, in the vein of Hoffmann, and their Nordic and folkloric character, are fine illustrations of Romanticism.

loneliness were expressed in epic poems and historical ballads, a style which he practised to perfection.

From 1854 to 1879 he completed the *Toldi* trilogy, while concurrently, with the *Death of Buda*, trying to create a great Hungarian epic in the style of the *Niebelungenlied*.

Portrait of Arnim

ARNIM Achim von (Berlin 26.1.1781 – Wiepersdorf 21.1.1831). Arnim's name is always associated with that of the Brentanos: either with Clemens, his friend and co-author of *Des Knaben Wunderhorn*, or Bettina, the sister and the confidante of Goethe and Beethoven, who later became Arnim's wife. Arnim was born into the old Prussian nobility. He studied the natural sciences at Halle, Jena and Gôttingen. He travelled frequently and made friends with the musician Reichardt and with Tieck, and was part of the literary coteries of Heidelberg and Berlin. After his marriage in 1811, he lived quietly on his Wiepersdorf estate, bringing up a large family and writing.

Calm by nature, Arnim had neither the formal talent nor the passion of the Brentanos. His historical novel *Die Kronenwächter* (The Guardians of the Crown, 1817 and 1854) is never-ending, but *Hollins Liebesleben* (1802) has more life. Above all, Arnim wrote captivating tales of fantasy: *Armut, Reichtum, Schuld und Busse der Gräfin Dolores* (Countess Dolores), and *Isabella von Aegypten* (Isabel of Egypt, 1811).

Portrait of Andersen

ARANY János (Nagyszalonta 2.3.1817 – Budapest 22.10.1882). This Hungarian poet was a travelling actor, a teacher and a civic official before he discovered his literary vocation. *Toldi*, the first part of an epic trilogy (1847), brought him to fame. Closely involved with Petöfi, he shared the latter's radical political views. After the failure of the 1848 Revolution, Arany had difficulty in finding his place in a changed society. His bitterness and

ATTERBOM Daniel Amadeus (Azbo, Ostergotland 19.1.1790 – Stockholm 21.7.1855). One of the leaders of the Swedish Romantic school grouped around the magazine *Phosphoros* (it is sometimes known as the phosphorist school). He was influenced by German idealist philosophy (particularly by Schelling), but also by the popular songs and legends which lent some of their freshness to his poems. His best known works are *The Harp of the North* (an anthology of popular songs) and, of his many poems, *The Isle of the North*.

BALZAC Honoré de (Tours 20.5.1799 – Paris 18.8.1850). For Balzac, who studied Law, was impatient to come to Paris and decided in 1819, against the advice of his family, to become a writer, the only path to follow was that of wild Romanticism. Under the influence of Walter Scott, Balzac, using the pen-name of Lord R'Hoone, conjured up a world of magic, of strange times and events (*Heritière de Birague, Clotilde de Lusignan, La Derniere Fée, Wann-Chlore*). Madame de Berny, his first love (later depicted in *Le Lys dans la Vallée*), does not seen to have modified his style, since Balzac continued to believe in the dark powers and unknown forces that he described in *la Peau du chagrin* (The Skin of Sorrow, 1831), *la Recherche de l'Absolu* (In Search of the Absolute, 1834), *Louis de Lambert* (1832), *Seraphita* (1835), as well as in two philosophical tales: *le Chef-d'oeuvre inconnu* (The Unknown Masterpiece) and *les Proscrits* (The Proscripts). It was Walter Scott who inspired his first masterpiece, *Les Chouans* (1829). When he was writing under the influence

Portrait of Balzac by David d'Angers, 1843

of Scott and Swedenborg, there was no mistaking his Romanticism.

Balzac's work always concealed a marked predilection for the irrational behind its apparent realism. There is a shadowy area even in his most type-cast characters: Goriot, Grandet, Vautrin, Madame de Mortsauf and Cousine Bette are related to Dostoyevsky's heroes, madmen and maniacs whose derangements are similar in nature, but differ in their field of application from those of Baltazar Claës or Louis Lambert. As far as the setting or the plot of Balzac's novels is concerned, it is clear that, even when he seemed to be describing a real event, of everyday life, the author, more often than not, suffused it with a magical halo, lifting it out of the commonplace and into the realm of mythological adventure. In *Beatrix* (1839), for example, which appears to be a fictionalised account of the love affairs of Liszt, of Marie d'Agoult, and George Sand, the 'Breton' aspect of the book makes it almost a romance of chivalry. Thus, Balzac's 'realism' is based on an essentially irrational psychology and philosophy.

Taking this further, when he set out to paint the 'social species' and, between 1834 and 1842, conceived his plan for the *Comédie Humaine* (Human Comedy), Balzac was thinking like a poet, or, if one prefers, like a romantic historian. He turned socio-economic observation into an epic form.

Most surprising of all is not the fact that Balzac revealed himself as a Romantic, but, on the contrary, that with his Romantic ideology and imagination, he was capable of depicting scenes of great realism, as in *Les Paysans* (The Peasants, 1844), *Le Médecin de Campagne* (The Country Doctor, 1833) and *César Birotteau* (1837).

BERCHET Giovanni (Milan 23.12.1783 – Turin 23.12.1851). Berchet's formation as a writer, in his native Milan, consisted of a reading of the classics as well as of the work of foreign poets. He was one of the figureheads of Italian Romanticism. He militated for a literary renewal aimed at awaking the aesthetic and moral consciousness of his country and thence its national ideal. He was the first theoretician of the new movement and expressed his views in the *Lettera semi-seria de Grisostomo* (1816). He showed the way by translating and adapting into Italian two German ballads by Bürger: *Lenore* and *Der Wilde Jäger* (The Savage Huntsman), which were of major importance to the whole European Romantic movement. The Director of *Conciliatore*, Berchet used it as the mouthpiece for Romantic ideas: patriots and liberals contributed to the review, which was soon banned by the Austrians.

Forced into exile, Berchet nonetheless continued to be the voice of patriotism and Romanticism: in London, in 1824, he published *The Refugees of Prague*, the *Romanze* and, in 1829, the *Fantasie*. Berchet's poetry, always inspired by love of his country, contributed strongly to keeping the flame of the *Risorgimento* alive.

BLAKE William (London 28.11.1757 – London 12.8.1827). Blake was born and died in London and began his career as a craftsman-engraver who lived modestly from the sale of his engravings and his illustrations of the poems of Dante and Young in particular. From childhood, Blake had had visions: he claimed to have seen God and winged angels. Later, he maintained that his poems and drawings were dictated from Above. It was this leaning towards the supernatural and the irrational, and his complementary talents, that made Blake a Romantic artist, and one whose work has passed the test of time.

His first collection of poems, *Poetical Sketches*, appeared in 1783. Blake printed and illustrated the next volume himself, in spite of the total lack of success of the first work. The *Songs of Innocence* (1789) express the fresh and lyrical view of the world as seen through the eyes of a child. The *Songs of Experience* (1794) which followed, contain a more disturbing note.

But Blake's major works reveal a very strange and complex character and are very obscure, as for example *The Marriage of Heaven and Hell* (1790) and *America* (1793). He even produced prophetic works such as *The Book of Urizen* (1794), *The Song of Los* (1795), *Jerusalem* (1804) and *Milton* (1804). Through his use of symbols, Blake, in these works, attacked all forms of tyranny. To the power of reason (Urizen), he contrasted intuitive vision (Los) and proclaimed its superiority.

BRENTANO Clemens (Ehrenbreitstein 8.9.1778 – Aschaffenburg 28.7.1842). Born in Frankfurt, Brentano studied in Jena from 1797 and it was there that he published *Godwi*, a novel of adventure and education in 1800. He wrote love poems, a comedy, *Ponce de Leon*, and *Die lustigen Musikanten* (The Merry Musicians) on which Hoffmann based a romantic opera that was staged in Warsaw in 1805, then in Mannheim. Brentano went to Heidelberg only briefly, but it was there that he met Arnim, and there that the two of them published the significantly titled *Zeitung fur Einsiedler* (Newspaper for hermits) and formed the second Romantic literary circle, around Creuzer and Görres, at the University. During this time, they researched and collected the popular songs that they adapted and published under the title of *Des Knaben Wunderhorn* (1806–1808). Afterwards, Brentano went, after some detours, to Berlin. It was the meeting place for the last literary circle which included Chamisso, La Motte-Fouqué, Hoffmann, Kleist and the Eichendorff brothers. Although he had little inclination towards militant patriotism, Brentano nonetheless participated in Kleist's *Abendblätter* and the meetings of the *Christliche Deutsche Tischgesellschaft* which held banquets attended by the whole German intelligentsia. This society advocated the Christian and German unification of the nation under Prussian rule. The epic cycle of the *Romanzen vom Rosenkranz* (Romances of the Rosary) dates from this period, as do the dissertation on the Philistine, Brentano's major dramatic work: *Die Gründung Prags* (The Foundation of Prague) and the lovely story of Kasperl and Annerl. Brentano retired from the world after his conversion to Catholicism in 1818.

Portrait of Charlotte Brontë

BRONTË Charlotte (Bradford 21.4.1816 – Haworth, Yorkshire 31.3.1885) and *Emily* (Bradford 20.8.1818 – Haworth 19.12.1848). The three sisters Anne, Charlotte and Emily wrote poetry, the publication of which in 1846 at first went unnoticed. In 1847, Charlotte's novel, *Jane Eyre*, met with instant success. In it, she fictionalised her experiences as a governess, which she enveloped in an atmosphere of mystery, fear and injustice. Charlotte's two subsequent novels, *Shirley* and *Villette*, confirmed the success of *Jane Eyre*. In Emily's novel, *Wuthering Heights*, also published in 1847, the depiction of Romantic passion set within the unchained power of the elements reached its height. In 1848, Anne died, and the following year Emily and their brother Branwell also succumbed to tuberculosis. Charlotte decided to settle in London where she moved in a circle of minor Romantics which included Thackeray. She died in 1855, a year after her marriage to a clergyman.

Portrait of Emily Brontë

1838, and the *Last Poems* in 1862. She was much influenced by the style of Shelley, but this was not enough in itself to make her a truly Romantic writer: in her dates and in her style, she is more representative of Victorian literature.

Portrait of Elizabeth Browning

BROWNING Elizabeth Barrett (Coxhoe Hall, Durham 6.3.1806 – Florence 29.6.1861) and *Robert* (Camberwell, London 7.5.1812 – Venice 12.12.1889). Elizabeth Barrett's precocious talent was revealed by the publication of her poem *The Battle of Marathon* when she was only fourteen. She is best known for her romantic and secret marriage to Robert Browning, after which they lived in Italy. Her major works include the *Poems* (1850), her first collection having been published in

As for Robert, his first works, *Paracelsus* (1835) and *Sordello* (1840), a poem full of detailed allusion to mediaeval Italy, earned him his reputation as an obscure poet. In 1840, his historical drama *Stafford* was staged without success. His best poems, written after 1840, show the development of his dramatic monologue technique Browning concentrated on recreating the Italy of the Renaissance, but his work is at times somewhat indecipherable.

Portrait of Robert Browning

BÜRGER Gottfried August (Molmerswende, Harz 31.12.1747 – Göttingen 8.6.1794). Burger is probably the most famous member of what was known as the Göttingen circle. This was a circle of, as they liked to be known 'Bardic' poets which had gathered around the University of this small German town towards the middle of the 18th century. Adopting the style of Klopstock, that is to say a sentimentalist inspiration and a still very conventional poetic technique, these poets, together with the somewhat later *Sturm und Drang* movement, contributed to the birth of German Romanticism. Bürger, who led a both scandalous and wretched life, was undoubtedly their leader. He expressed his unhappy or guilty passion with warmth and forthright simplicity (in his *Molly Lieder*). Bürger is, above all, famous for his ballads, which are dramatic, fantastic and hallucinatory, unquestionably inspired by the Scots and by Percy, but Germanised with perfect metrics and prosody. *Lenore* is the most important, but not the only masterpiece of the genre: it deeply marked the minds of the young Romantics, Hugo Joukovsky, Chateaubriand, and before them, Goethe Schiller and the Schlegels, who read and re-read th moving story of the faithful fiancée carried into the grave by her phantom beloved.

BURNS Robert (Alloway, Ayrshire 2.1.1759 – Dumfries 21.7.1796). English and Scottish Romanticism looked for its sources of inspiration to popular art. This probably explains the immediate success of *Poems chiefly in the Scottish Dialect* by Robert Burns, the first edition of which was rapidly sold out. Although he was in great demand in Edinburgh cultural circles, Burns preferred to retire to the country and married his companion Jean Armour. Having failed to turn farming to profit, he became an exciseman in 1789. He composed another fifty or so poems of popular inspiration, and worked in a variety of styles – satire, little love poems, and narrative poems at which he excelled, including *Tam O'Shanter* (1790). But his fame is due above all to his lyrical works, a great number of which have been set to music. In his poems inspired by everyday reality, he wrote with a mixture of tenderness and humour (*To a Mouse*, for example). Two of his songs in praise of Scotland are still very popular today: *Auld Lang Syne* and *Scots Whahae*, in honour of the national heroes Bruce and Wallace.

Portrait of Byron

BYRON George Gordon, Lord (London 22.1.1788 – Missolonghi, Greece 19.4.1824). Educated at Harrow, the bastion of the English aristocracy, and at Cambridge, Byron travelled between 1809 and 1811 to Spain, Albania and Greece, which were to become his second homes. His scandalous private life, his incestuous relationship with his sister, and his marriage in 1815 which lasted no more than a year, have made him a legendary, almost mythical, figure.

In 1816, he decided to leave England for ever and carried his scorn, arrogance and defiance of conventions across Europe. He lived in Switzerland and Italy, before deciding to go to Greece to support the independence movement there. He died of a fever at Missolonghi in 1824.

Byron's first works were in quite traditional style. *Hours of Idleness* (1807) contained nothing revolutionary and when the work was criticised in the *Edinburgh Review*, Byron responded with a satire, in which he proclaimed himself a disciple of Pope and vigorously attacked Wordsworth and Coleridge. The first two cantos of the famous *Childe Harold's Pilgrimage* met with great acclaim when they were published in 1812, by reason of their exoticism and their novelty. The vein of Byron's work altered from then on: Cantos III and IV (1816–1818) were more sombre, expressing, though still in a traditional form, the poet's weariness of life, his melancholy and homesickness, and his emotions at the sight of particular ruins or landscapes. These were the key texts of European Romanticism.

Flattered by his success, Byron then launched into exotic and sentimental, even erotic, tales in verse: *The Giaour* (1813), *The Bride of Abydos* (1813), and *The Corsair* (1814) which made fashionable the eternal character of Don Juan. Byron's masterpieces were written during his exile. In *Manfred* (1817), an unfinished play, he defied society by glorifying incest, and in *Cain* (1821) it was God that he challenged: his heroes were tormented and rebellious men, torn between good and evil.

Finally came the works in which Byron blended satire with Romanticism: *Beppo* (1817), an ironical depiction of Venice, and *The Vision of Judgement* (1822), a violent pamphlet against the official and conservative poet Southey, works which presaged his long, unfinished, poem *Don Juan* (1819–1824).

CHAMISSO Adalbert de (Boncourt 30.1.1781 – Berlin 21.8.1838). A writer and scientist of French origin, Chamisso was one of the victims of the Terror who found refuge in Prussia and played an important part in that country's development. It is ironic that a Frenchman should have made a literary contribution to the German Romantic movement. He learned Greek, Latin and the natural sciences, became a page to the Queen of Prussia in 1797, and then an officer. During the summer of 1810, he became involved with the poetess Helmine von Chezy, who was to write the libretto for Weber's *Euryanthe*.

Between 1811 and 1814, he wrote the two works which brought him fame. In fact he was the author, among other poetical works, of *Frauenliebe und Leben* (The Love and Life of a Woman), a text which, if it appears rather antiquated today, was adopted and immortalised by Schumann in the *Lieder* cycle of the same name. Also in 1814, Chamisso published *Peter Schlemihls wundersame*

Geschichte (The strange Story of Peter Schlemihl), the fantastic tale of a man who has lost his shadow. It was after these two successes that Chamisso embarked on a journey around the world from 1815 to 1818.

On his return, he was appointed director of the Botanical Gardens in Berlin. He was a member of the last Romantic circle (appropriately known as the Berlin circle) and devoted the rest of his life to the natural sciences.

Portrait of Chateaubriand by Girodet-Trioson. 1841

Portrait of Chamisso

CHATEAUBRIAND François-René de (Saint-Malo 4.9.1768 – Paris 4.7.1848). Chateaubriand's attitude and intellectual approach as revealed in *René* (1802) and *Mémoires d'Outre-tombe* (Memories from beyond the Grave) are eminently Romantic, and characterised by a general rejection of the established order.

In fact, it was his rejection of the Old World that led him to the discovery of picturesque America and to write *Atala* (1801), *Les Natchez* (1809) and *Les Martyrs* (1809). It was his rejection of the Revolution that led him to emigrate, to find his faith and to become the poet and apologist of the *Génie du christianisme* (1802). He also refused to support either Napoleon or Louis-Philippe, thus taking on the character of the eternal proscript. Similarly, in the literary field, it was through his rejection of the 18th century, which had, however, marked him deeply in his *Essai sur les Révolutions* (1797), that Chateaubriand turned towards the powers of mystery and the irrational. It was the eponymous René who made world-weariness, one of the aspects of Romanticism, so fashionable. But Chateaubriand was a writer of many facets: the poetry of history, political passion, exoticism and cosmopolitanism were to inspire pages as different as the *Itinéraire de Paris à Jerusalem* (1811), *Voyage en Amerique* (1827), and his political pamphlets or literary essays (*la Monarchie selon la*

Charte 1816, *Essai sur la littérature anglaise* 1836, *Lettre à M de Fontanes sur la campagne romaine*).

These sources of inspiration were allied to a very personal style in the *Mémoires* and the *Vie de Rancé* (1844). It was perhaps in this work that he expressed most violently his hatred of life; the reality of Romanticism that has been vulgarised by literary history is clearly revealed. Chateaubriand was a man driven to despair, more authentic, perhaps, than Byron, more personal, in any event, than any other European Romantic.

COLERIDGE Samuel Taylor (Ottery Saint Mary, Devon 21.10.1772 – London 25.7.1834). After the death of his father, Coleridge was admitted, in 1782, to Christ's Hospital School in London. He started writing poetry at fifteen and went up to Cambridge in October 1791. He was to become famous there for his Greek verse, his francophile opinions and his unitarian Christianity. In 1794, he went to Oxford where he met Robert Southey; together they dreamed of founding an ideal republic in America. Coleridge's marriage in 1795 put an end to such schemes. He and his wife settled near Bristol in a cottage overlooking the Irish sea. Years of domestic happiness and professional activity followed: Coleridge founded a review, gave lectures on Shakespeare that evinced penetrating critical insight, and wrote many poems that were full of imagination and delicately expressed emotion. But his disappointment at the poor reception accorded his works induced him to start taking drugs. After a journey to Germany with Wordsworth, the two friends went to live close to one another in the Lake District. There, Coleridge fell in love with Wordsworth's sister-in-law, Sarah Hutchinson. At around the same time, in 1805, he abandoned poetry to devote himself to a variety of other work: criticism, philosophy, metaphysics, politics and theatre. He attempted in vain to give up drugs. In 1816, he settled in Highgate at the home of Dr. Gilman where he held a sort of literary salon, admission to which was much sought after. He grew weaker and weaker, and died in 1834.

Coleridge's poetical inspiration was very different from that of Wordsworth, even though together, with the *Lyrical Ballads*, they founded the English Romantic movement. Coleridge's poetry is dominated by hallucination and dreams. His masterpiece is *The Rime of the Ancient Mariner* (1798) which tells the strange story of a mariner who sails the world on a phantom ship. *Christabel* and

Portrait of Coleridge

Kubla Khan, in fantastic and magical style, were never completed. Coleridge's critical work was also important: *The Friend*, published weekly in 1809–1810, was devoted to religious and philosophical problems, whereas the *Biographia Literaria* (1817) contained thoughts about politics and philosophy, personal memoirs and literary criticism.

CONSTANT Benjamin (Lausanne 23.10.1767 – Paris 8.12.1830). Constant based an autobiographical volume, *Adolphe* (1816), on his long relationship with Madame de Staël, whom he followed more or less everywhere during their common exile. But apart from a disenchantment that was much more superficial than that of René or of Oberman, this work, which belonged to the grand tradition of the moralists and Classicism, was not really a manifestation of Romantic art. The same is true of his *Cahier rouge* (Red notebook), an elegant and cynical account of his youth, and of his *Journal intime*.

Portrait of Benjamin Constant

It was in his journalistic and critical activities that Constant was most in tune with the new art. From his many *Mélanges de littérature et de politique*, one could cite his translation of Schiller's *Wallenstein* and his *Réflexions sur la tragédie*. In these works, as in Madame de Staël's *De l'Allemagne*, is to be found a manifesto of the Romantic theatre.

DESCHAMPS Antoine (Paris 12.3.1800 – Paris 29.10.1869) and **Emile** (Bourges 20.2.1791 – Versailles 22.4.1871). These two brothers – translators and illustrators of new works and friends of Hugo – were important figures in the French Romantic movement.

Antoine, known as Antony, collaborated with his brother on an elaboration of the doctrines of Romanticism at a time when the movement centred around the newspaper *La Muse française* (1823), as well as on the literary salon opened by the two brothers. Antony's major work is a verse translation of the *Divine Comedy* (1829). He also published political *Satires* (1831–1834) and *Etudes sur l'Italie*. He illustrated several Romantic books and was also a painter.

Mental illness obliged him to spend most of his life in a Passy sanatorium, where Nerval was also a patient. Sections of *Dernières paroles* (Last words), 1835, and of *Resignation* (1839) discreetly mirror his slow mental decay.

DUMAS Alexandre (Villers-Cotterets 24.7.1802 – Puys 5.12.1870). The son of a general in the armies of the Republic who died in 1806, Alexandre Dumas knew hardship in his youth. His education was never completed; he had to earn his living as a clerk in the offices of the chancellery of the Duke of Orléans. At the same time, he wrote poems and short stories, until the immense success of his historical play *Henri III et sa cour* (1829) elevated him to the rank of one of the masters of theatrical Romanticism. The plays that followed, principally *Antony* (1831), *Charles VII chez ses grands vassaux* (1831), *La Tour de Nesle* (1832), *Catherine Howard* (1834) and *Kean* (1836), had the same rudimentary but effective dramatic stimuli, the same passion and feeling for dialogue. In 1838, with *le Capitaine Paul*, Dumas also embarked on a very fruitful career as a novelist, with his famous 'series': *The Three Musketeers, Twenty Years After, The Vicomte de Bragelonne* (1844–1847), *The Count of Monte Cristo* (1844–1845), and *la Dame de Montsoreau* (1846).

Dumas was also a leading light in the field of serialised

Portrait of Alexandre Dumas by A Devéria

novels and of 'industrial' literature. But today, it is his *Mémoires* and his various travel journals that are the most interesting to read. Dumas, who spent a fortune almost as fast as he made it, died in near-poverty at the beginning of the war of 1870.

EICHENDORFF Josef von (Lubowitz 10.3.1788 – Neisse 26.11.1857). This Silesian-born provincial civil servant lived a peaceful life that was devoted to his family and to letters.

After studying in Halle, he went to Heidelberg; there he made contact with the Romantic circle around Brentano and Creuzer. Later, he went back to Berlin and met Adam Müller and Brentano again (1809). Then, in Vienna, he made friends with Schlegel and Körner, whom he was to follow into the Lützow Commando in 1813. Finally, after 1816, he became a ministerial counsellor, first in Danzig, then in Koenigsberg and in Berlin. Eichendorff's first book *Ahnung und Gegenwart* (Presentiment and Present Time) was published in 1815. It is an interesting account of the years of war against Napoleon in Germany. His best-known work is *Aus dem Leben eines Taugenichts* (The Life of a Good-for-Nothing) which appeared in 1826. It is a novel which extols the joys of wandering (*Wandern*) and reverie, sentiments that were typical of the Romantic years in Germany. Eichendorff's poems, and he wrote a great many, were set to music by some of the greatest composers, as was only fitting, since his art was very musical and all painted in half-tones.

EÖTVÖS Joszef (Buda 13.9.1813 – Buda 2.2.1871). Eötvös is the principal representative of the Hungarian Romantic novel, even though his later work, after the revolution of 1848, tended towards realism. His philosophical novel *The Carthusian* (1839) was a turning point in Hungarian literature, and discernibly influenced by Chateaubriand and even Rousseau, both of whom were much admired in Hungary at the time. After this masterpiece, 'true poetry in prose' as the contemporary poet Erdelyi described it, Eötvös turned to political novels: *The Villiage Notary* and *Hungary in 1514* which, after the manner of Walter Scott, describes the situation of Hungary at the height of its political and artistic glory, just before the battle of Mohacs, which subjected the country to the yoke of the Turks.

ESPRONCEDA José de (Almendralejo 25.3.1808 – Madrid 23.5.1842). An undisciplined schoolboy, a conspirator as soon as he left college, imprisoned in 1824, then exiled to Gibraltar, Lisbon, London and Paris, Espronceda carried arms with the insurgents of 27–29 July 1830, and with the guerilleros of Chapalangara. His was a rebellious, passionate and generous spirit, and he possessed a totally unfettered and unstoppable poetic imagination.

The *Pelago*, a poem written in his youth, was followed by his lyrical poems, collected and published in 1840, which touched on all subjects and took on all forms. There were poetic meditations (*To Night, To the Sun*), picturesque and narrative songs (*The Pirate, The Cossack, The Beggar, The*

Condemned Man, The Executioner), drinking songs (*A Jarifa*), and historical subjects (*Torrijos, Joaquin de Pablo, the Messenians*). The external influences of Byron, Lamartine and Hugo, and also of Bernager and Casimir Delavigne are evident: nevertheless, Espronceda's voice remained an extremely personal one.

The Student of Salamanca, based on an old theme, is even more original and perfectly illustrates the fertility of Espronceda's imagination. But his master work is the *Devil-World* (1841), an unfinished philosophical poem, a synthesis of humanity in which Nature is contrasted to the rules and conventions of Society. Moments of admirable inspiration (like the prologue, the songs of death and immortality, and the superb elegy *A Teresa*) are interspersed with extravagant fantasies aimed at shocking the Philistines. Here too, foreign influences are evident: Byron and Musset, *Don Juan* and Voltaire, *Ahasverus* and *Faust*.

FOSCOLO Ugo (Zante 6.2.1778 – Turnham Green, near London 10.9.1827). Son of a Venetian father and a Greek mother, Foscolo was born in Illyria and died in exile in England. He studied in Spalato (Split) and Venice, where he read the classics and foreign literature which already bore evidence of burgeoning Romanticism. Foscolo had a tumultuous love life with a succession

Portriat of Foscolo

liano, employed at the Chancellery of Milan at the time of the Kingdom of Italy, a volunteer in the Italian division at the Camp de Boulogne (1806), and a teacher at the university of Pavia in 1808. He was finally proscribed by the Austrians and became a political refugee in England, where he lived on a modest income from translations and Italian lessons. In his life and loves, Foscolo came to know only too well the unhappiness that he so often and so magnificently evoked in his work. He embraced a great number of styles in his writing: verse and prose, novel and tragedy, studies and translations. Two works stand out: *Le Ultime Lettere di Jacopo Ortis* and his collection of poems *Dei Sepolcri* (Of Graves).

The idea for the first, a novel, came to Foscolo after the suicide of a Paduan student called Ortis. *Of Graves* was inspired by the fashion for graves that flourished in Europe throughout the second half of the 18th century and was especially pronounced in English literature. The poem, divided into three parts, describes the civic and family aspects of death, the social aspect of graves and the cult of the dead and finally the famous men and the unsung heroes who gave their lives in Ancient times for love of their country.

GAUTIER Théophile (Tarbes 31.8.1811 – Neuilly-sur-Seine 23.10.1872). Théophile Gautier's participation, sporting his legendary red waistcoat, in the battle of *Hernani*; his attendance at literary coteries; the content and inspiration of his first poems (*Poésies*, 1831); and the

Portrait of Théophile Gautier

of distinguished women (Antoinette Farani-Arese was to inspire the ode *All'amica risanata* (To a Cured Friend) in 1802). His career was no less turbulent: he was, in turn, a light cavalryman at the time of the Cispadane Republic (*A Buonaparte liberatore*), a journalist with the *Monitore ita-*

mediaeval bric-à-brac that fills *Albertus* (1832), would seem to characterse him as a caricature of facile and outdated Romanticism.

But this bohemian did in fact have a sense of historical

values, which he defended, particularly in his critical articles (he was a defender of Wagner and of Weber). This 'Jeune-France' openly mocked the excesses of the movement in *Les Jeunes-France, roman goguenard* (a facetious novel) in 1833. He was thus accused of the reverse: Gautier has been made a champion of art for art's sake. He did in fact defend it in the *Préface de Mademoiselle de Maupin* (1835) and practised it in *Emaux et Camées* (Enamels and Cameos, the complete collection dating from 1852). In fact, he tried in vain to conceal an anguished soul haunted by the eroticism that his many fantastic tales (*Omphale*, 1834; *la Pipe d'Opium* 1838, and others) all too evidently revealed.

GOETHE Johann Wolfgang von (Frankfurt-am-Main 28.8.1749 – Weimar 22.3.1832). Goethe was one of the most influential representatives of the *Sturm und Drang*. Between 1770 and 1775, events such as his stay in Strasbourg and his meeting there with Herder, his discovery of Gothic art, the love inspired by Frédérique Brion, the visit to Wetzlar where he fell in love with Charlotte Buff, and his reading of Shakespeare, Ossian, Homer, Rousseau and Richardson, all accentuated the sense of a renewed Beauty in his naturally passionate temperament. This makes it easier to understand the great hymns dedicated to Mohammed and to Prometheus, the poetry of popular inspiration, the plays (*Goetz von Berlichingen*, *Egmont*, *Faust*) and, above all, *Werther* (1774). These works present us with heroes tormented by passions that are both metaphysical and carnal and, far more, they are works characterised by innovations of form that were of capital importance for subsequent literatures and especially for those of the North.

Chateaubriand was the first to acknowledge his debt to Goethe in *René*. Madame de Staël and the whole Coppet group all but venerated the man who was by then the god of Weimar. Bettina Brentano boasted of her intimacy with him and Heine left a moving account of a visit to Weimar. Although Goethe was not a Romantic in the strictest sense of the term, his relations with the European Romantic movement were very close. His novel *Wilhelm Meister*, with the romantic characters of the harpist and Mignon, was the ideal of fiction for Novalis and Friedrich Schlegel; his *Elective Affinities* was based on the Romantic philosophy of Nature; the act devoted to Helen in the second *Faust* represented the symbolic marriage of Classicism and Romanticism, while the character of Lynceus was modelled on Lord Byron.

Although he repudiated Romanticism, Goethe integrated into his work, and sometimes anticipated, the new forms, visions and conceptions of the Romantic age.

GOGOL Nicolas Vasilievich (Sorochinski 31.3.1809 – Moscow 4.3.1852). If one limits one's reading of Gogol to his early works, from the *Ukranian Stories* (*The Vigils of the Hamlet*, 1831; *Mirgorod*, 1835) to the *Petersburg Stories* (*The Nose*, *The Portrait*, *The Diary of a Madman*), one can gauge how deeply his talent was influenced by German Romanticism, Hoffmann especially, and by Ukranian Romanticism which manifested itself in the work of Russian, as well as Polish, authors.

Some of Gogol's stories have a disturbing note: the theme of demonic possession in *A Terrible Revenge*, for example. It was to degenerate into a feeling of real anguish in *Mirgorod*, which indisputably placed its author among the ranks of the Romantics. In yet another aspect of his work, Gogol was a 'realist' storyteller (*Taras Bulba*), influenced by Pushkin and by the style of Walter Scott.

Portrait of Gogol by Moller

GUTIERREZ Antonio García (Chiclana-Cádiz 5.7.1813 – Madrid 26.8.1884). Gutierrez had a more vigorous and more passionate dramatic temperament than his compatriot Hartzenbusch. But, like him, he made Spanish Romantic drama famous. *El Trovador* (1836) was one of the most brilliant successes of the century and is a typical example of a Romantic play. It was almost effortlessly transformed into opera by Verdi for his famous *Il Trovatore*. Later plays met with almost equal success: *El Rey monje* (1837), *Simon Bocanegra* (1843), also adapted into an opera by Verdi, *Verganza catalana* (1864) and *Juan Lorenzo* (1865). Gutierrez left sixty-two works for the stage, which included some comedies, and some poetry.

HARTZENBUSCH Juan Eugenio (Madrid 6.9.1806 – Madrid 2.8.1880). Hartzenbusch's great triumph was the fine play *Los Amantes de Teruel* (1837), in which he skilfully rejuvenated a somewhat overworked subject.

Doña Mencia followed in 1838, then *Don Alfonso el Casto* (1841), *La Jura en Santa Gadea* (1845) and *La Madre de Pelayo*. In addition, he wrote some less successful comedies and even some fairy-table plays (*Los Polvos de la Madre Celestina, La Redoma encantada*). His *Fables* (1844 and 1861) were also popular and although his *Ensayos Poeticos* (1843) are forgotten today, as are his short stories, the range of his work goes to show that he was familiar with every branch of literature.

HAUFF Wilhelm (Stuttgart 29.11.1802 – Stuttgart 18.11.1827). Poet, novelist and story-teller, usually classed as belonging to the Swabian Romantic school. His brief literary career was rich in interesting works: poems of popular lyricism; a historical novel in the manner of Walter Scott, *Liechtenstein* (1826), in which Hauff lovingly recreated the Swabia of bygone times; and artistic short stories in which he distanced himself from Romanticism and approached realism, such as *The Beggarwoman of the Pont des Arts, The Jew Süss*, and *Portrait of the Emperor*. On occasion, Hauff could imitate Hoffmann, blending fantasy with humour in *Extracts from Satan's Memoirs* or *Fantasies in the Municipal Cellar of Bremen*. The Orient as well as Germany (*The Spessart Inn*) served as the setting for his tales, for which he took the brothers Grimm as his models.

HEINE Heinrich (Düsseldorf 13.12.1797 – Paris 17.2.1856). The nephew of a rich Jewish banker, young Heine soon left his native Düsseldorf for Hamburg. His law studies in Göttingen and Berlin had been of no interest to him; in Hamburg, he was hardly more impressed by commerce and finance. In 1825, he converted to Protestantism in the hope of obtaining employment as a civil servant. While in Hamburg, he came to know the North Sea and his love of Nature went hand in hand with a hopeless love for his cousin, an unhappy love, but one that produced the beautiful series of *Nordsee* poems. Heine was also concerned with politics. His *Reisebilder*, satirical travel scenes of Germany and the whole of Holy Alliance Europe, made him a spokesman and a leader of the left wing tendency in German literature (Jung-Deutschland).

The latter years of Heine's life were spent in France. In the wake of the failed revolutions in Germany, he emigrated to Paris in 1831. There he was to live the life of a 'European': he preached peace between the two countries, and set out to demonstrate their complementarity, at a time when the dispute over the Rhine was already beginning. There was also authentic Romanticism in his lyrical poems (*Intermezzo* or *Heimkehr* – Homecoming – for example) as well as a 'boulevardier', Voltairian spirit in his prose and humorous writing (*Lutezia* or *Deutschland, ein Wintermärchen* (Germany, a Winter Tale). Heine was then attacked from all sides, by the German radicals and socialists (Börne, Ruge) as well as by the German kings who, in 1835, banned his works in their countries. After

Portrait of Heine by Charles Cleyre

the death of his wife, Mathilde Mirat, he found consolation for his setbacks and his sorrows with his new companion, Catherine Selden. From 1848 until his death, Heine was completely paralysed; he resorted to morphine to lessen his pain. In this period, he wrote the *Romancero* and *Lazarus*, collections of poems inspired by passion and fantasy.

HOFFMANN Ernst Theodor Amadeus (Konigsberg 24.1.1776 – Berlin 25.6.1822). The Prussian-born Hoffmann was a great lover of music, that of Mozart in particular. He even changed his third name from Wilhelm to Amadeus in homage to the composer. After very advanced legal and musical studies, his first post was as a legal adviser at Glogau in Silesia (1793), and he was then transferred to Berlin (1798–1800). His next expected appointment, in Posen (Poznan), and the promotion he had been expecting was withheld from him for intemperance and disrespect to his superiors. He was 'exiled' to a distant post in central Poland. When the country was occupied by Bonaparte's troops in 1806, he decided to embark upon a musical career: he became a conductor and Director of Music at Bamberg. Then he went to Leipzig, where he contributed articles on music to the Leipzig *Gazette*. Whether or not his caricatures of the French were regarded as proof of patriotism, he was reinstated in his former position and appointed legal adviser in Berlin in 1816.

Hoffmann was a very fine music critic, but perhaps a less successful composer, in his opera *Undine* for example, but he is famous above all as the master fantasy story-teller. All his heroes and heroines were attributed with some terrifying or mysterious characteristic. The real world, for Hoffmann, was not the world we see: reality was an apparition that the merest breath of wind could blow away. Hoffmann's tales are, of course, also known for

Offenbach's famous opera based upon them, first performed in 1881.

HUGO Victor (Besançon 26.2.1802 – Paris 22.5.1885). There is sometimes a temptation to ask which of Hugo's many faces was the true one: that of the young legitimist Royalist of 1820; the wild and provocative Romantic of 1830; the Romantic 'arrivé' of 1840, friend of the Duchesse d'Orléans; the Guernsey proscript, or the Senator-for-life of the Third Republic who believed in Progress, Fraternity and Secularity?

We might also ask which was the real poetry of Hugo: that of the years 1830–1840, of his exile (*les Châtiments*, 1853, *les Contemplations*, 1856), or of his years of triumph (*Toute la lyre*, *la Fin de Satan*), written after 1859. Finally, was Hugo a Romantic throughout his career, and are there connections between his Romanticism and the other movements that, at one time or another, existed around him?

Henri Guillemin, Hugo's biographer, has done much to dissipate some of the myths that have grown up around him. He outlined Hugo's attitude towards three essential questions: God, love and money. Although he had not been baptised, Hugo had a deeply religious temperament and a perpetually superstitious side to his character. This may well explain his early rejection of Catholicism, the séances at Marine Terrace, and the religion of Humanity, which the Third Republic was to make its own. Hugo was not revealing his true faith in 1820 or in 1830: on the contrary, he concealed it. It was the coup d'état of 1852 which brought Hugo back to his natural belief in the people, the great geniuses of Humanity.

As far as money was concerned, his impoverished life as a young man when he lived in humble lodgings in the rue du Dragon around 1818, may explain his subsequent attitude towards wealth; he became adept at managing the financial aspects of his talent. and loved pleasures that were solid and discreet.

As for love, his affairs of the heart are all but legendary, from Juliette Drouet to the amorous adventures of his eighties. But we may not be so aware of how much he was inspired by his first love, his wife, Adèle Foucher. 'How great is your power over me, since your image alone is stronger than all the effervescence of my age?' It is only necessary to read the confidences scattered in the fragments of *Tas de Pierres* (Heap of Stones) to know that it was Adèle who, first, betrayed her 'illustrious poet'. *Victor Hugo raconté par un temoin de sa vie*, an account by a 'witness to his life', is thus highly misleading; the real face of Hugo is that of an adolescent in love with the absolute who also has a sense – or a need – of sin, just like Baudelaire. Authentic Romanticism, that is to say the need to love for eternity and to express it, is as evident in the famous *Tristesse d'Olympio* (1840) as it is in *Les Misérables* (1862) or *l'Art d'être grand-père* (1877).

As for most of the Romantics, the dream, in Hugo's work, is not only a great source of inspiration, but is also apparent in every aspect of his intellectual and aesthetic personality.

We are familiar with his depiction of fantastic cities emerging out of night and mists: the attraction of the irrational and mysterious for Hugo is expressed throughout his work, in *The Rhine*, an account of a journey (1840), as well as in the early poems (*les Orientales*, *les Ballades*, 1822–1829), or the later ones; in the famous night of *Eviradnus* (*la Légende des Siècles*) which is erotic and macabre, or in the *Quatre-vents de l'Esprit*. Dreams, or as he himself called them 'the slope of reverie' (in *Feuilles d'automne*, 1831) are the very substance of Hugo's lyricism, whether they are visions of the Beyond or in hallucinations, or inspired by another art form like painting (in 'A Albert Dürer' from the *Voix intérieures*, 1837), the music of Beethoven, Schubert and Weber, or legend, as in the marvellous night of 'Booz endormi' in the *Legende des siècles*.

But this unreality is not always evoked in the same manner: after the visual approach of his first works, Hugo became more and more visionary. In addition, he had such a magical mastery of the verb that it fundamentally distinguished him from *all* the other Romantics, in France and elsewhere.

Bust of Victor Hugo by David d'Angers

It is thus pointless to try to compare the Hugo of the *Odes* (1822) with the Hugo of *Toute la lyre* (1888). If Romanticism resides in the soul and in dreams, then Hugo, in his verse and in his prose, was truly a great Romantic poet.

KEATS John (London 29 or 31.10.1795 – Rome 23.2.1821). The son of a postmaster, Keats initially studied medicine, but abandoned his studies for poetry. He was friendly with and encouraged by men of letters and in 1817, published his first collection of poems in an Ollier edition. In *Sleep and Poetry*, he announced that his art was to be one of evocation and imagination. In 1818, *Endymion* (A poetic romance) was published: it was both a symbolic and a narrative poem, and was violently attacked by the conservative press. Mourning the death of his brother Tom from tuberculosis, Keats was soon, like Tom and their mother, suffering from the disease himself. His passionate love for Fanny Brawne, whom he met in 1818, was a source of inspiration, but also of despair since marriage proved impossible. During this period, the poet's *Letters* are evidence of a talent as a letter-writer as great as his talent for poetry itself. His health deteriorated rapidly but he continued to write. He left for Italy, intending to spend the winter of 1820 there. He died in Rome in February 1821, in his twenty-sixth year.

The poems he wrote between 1817 and 1820 show a rapid evolution that is absolutely unparalleled. *Endymion* already contained the main characteristics of his poems: the personal element was suppressed, sublimated, in favour of a sensual delight in the beauty of form. The supreme faculty is imagination, as it was with Coleridge, but it is held in check by the sense of the dramatic and the perfection of the verse. Hence Keats' taste for Greek mythology, which lent itself to this alliance of delight and severity. He was also greatly influenced by the English classics. *Endymion*, for instance, had elements of Spenser and Chaucer in its search for a rigorously beautiful and controlled sense of the miraculous. In *Isabella*, Keats abandoned obscure symbolism for simple narration in the style of Boccaccio. The poems written in 1819 are undoubtedly his finest work. *The Eve of Saint Agnes* tells the story of the passionate love of Porphyro for Madeleine, set against a rich background of mediaeval magic which protects the lovers from a cold and hostile outside world. The ballad of *La Belle Dame Sans Merci* traces the seduction of a young knight by a fairy, with the same sense of mystery and unreality as in Coleridge. *Lamia* is a symbolic tale: beneath the story of a young man enslaved by an artificial beauty, Keats exposes the relentless antagonism between imagination and philosophy. The five *Odes* (to a Nightingale, on a Grecian Urn, to Autumn, on Melancholy, to Psyche) are deservedly Keats' most famous work, and unequalled in English literature.

KLEIST Heinrich von (Frankfurt-an-der-Oder 18.10.1777 – Wannsee 21.11.1811). Destined for a military career, Kleist resigned as an officer in 1799, weary of a life in which it did not seem to him possible to reconcile literary and military glory. He made a first journey to France in 1801, with his sister Ulrike, to spread Kant's philosophy. From there, he went to Switzerland where he continued to work on a play he had begun, *Die Familie Schroffenstein* (The Schroffenstein Family), and in which atrocity is heaped upon atrocity. He also started the famous comedy, *De Zerbrochene Krug* (The Broken Pitcher). Back in Germany, he stayed at Ottmannstadt (1803) and read his unfinished play *Robert Guiskard* to Wieland, the 'Voltaire of Germany'. He returned to France where he was almost arrested for spying. In Potsdam, he accepted a post in the administration of the Koenigsberg estates; it was there that he wrote *The Marchioness of O*, a short story, and *Amphitryon*, in imitation of Molière and

Portrait of Kleist

Plautus. He also started *Penthesilea*, the 'dionysian' play much liked by Nietzsche. Arrested again for spying in 1806 by the occupying powers, he was interned in France. On his release he went to Dresden where he published two stories: *Das Erdbeben in Chili* (Earthquake in Chile) and *Die Verlobung in St Domingo* (the Betrothal in St Domingo). In 1809 Kleist sent *Die Hermannschlacht* (the Battle of Arminius), a militantly Prussian play, to the theatres of Vienna. His contemporaneous novel *Michael Kohlhaas* was of similar inspiration. In 1810, two stories *Das Bettelweib von Locarno* (Beggarwoman of Locarno) and *Die heilige Cäcilie* appeared, and *Kätchen von Heilbronn* was staged in Vienna. Kleist's last play was *The Prince of Homburg*. He also wrote *Der Findling* (the Foundling) and *Der Zweikampf* (The Duel), one of his most Romantic works. It was on the shores of the Wannsee near Berlin that

Kleist committed suicide, with his companion Henriette Vogel.

KRASINSKI Zygmunt (Paris 19.2.1812 – Paris 23.2.1859) Krasinski's whole life was marked by the conflicts between duty and emotion, class consciousness and patriotism. Born into a noble family related to the Radziwills, he was constantly subjected to the forces of family and tradition. In obedience to his father, one of Napoleon's generals, he did not take part in the 1830 insurrection, nor did he emigrate. His life, rich in personal drama, was filled with dreams and ideas rather than actions. With his lyrical talent and metaphysical spirit, he could translate the most abstract of ideas into images. His play, *la Comédie non divine* (1833), was deeply pessimistic. He condemned both the decadent old world represented by Count Henri, and the Revolution represented by Pancrace. The same pessimism is evident in *Irydion* (1822–1836), half drama, half story, in which, like Mickiewicz, he dealt with the problems of treason. The work was influenced by Chateaubriand's *Martyrs*. In common with the philosopher Cieszkowski whose theories, in Krasinski's eyes, completed Hegelian philosophy, he imagined that a martyred Poland would be placed at the head of nations. The same inspiration reappears, together with feelings of love, in *Dawn* (1841–1843). Attacked by Slowacki and the whole emigré community, Krasinski defended himself in a series of poems of uneven value, the *Psalms* (1845). He then devoted the last ten years of his life to political writing.

LAMARTINE Alphonse de (Mâcon 21.10.1790 – Paris 1.3.1869). The salient dates of Lamartine's life and career provide quite a good summary of the history of French Romanticism.

Lamartine, who had strong ties with his native region (to which he devoted his works *Milly ou la terre natale*, 1827, *la Vigne et la maison*, 1857), was almost the oldest of the so-called Romantic writers. He was born at a time when the generation of the fathers of Romanticism was being formed: Stendhal arrived in Paris in 1799, and Chateaubriand wrote *Atala*, *René* and *le Génie du Christianisme* around 1800. Like everyone else, Lamartine read Chateaubriand and was to have a love of Italy in common with Stendhal: like Stendhal, he was a diplomat there, but between 1820 and 1830.

In 1820, *Les Méditations* were published, followed, ten years later, by the *Harmonies*. The whole of Romantic poetry was born between these dates, but Lamartine was the first to win public acclaim. This was probably because his first collection, which included the famous poems *l'Automne*, *l'Isolement*, *le Lac*, and *la Vallon*, summarised what was expected of the new movement rather well. The work as a whole did not revolutionise techniques (it had none of the audacity for which Hugo was

to criticise Chénier), nor did it contain significant innovations to traditional themes. Yet, in the way in which the unknown thirty year-old poet spoke of love, religion and Nature, his contemporaries heard a new voice. His views translated a hesitant and painful quest, in which love, religion, and a sense of the emptiness and futility of life were intermingled in the most intimate and lifelike manner.

Portrait of Lamartine by Chassériau, 1844

In 1848, the most Romantic of all the revolutions of the 19th century witnessed the personal triumph of Lamartine as leader of the provisional government, and he carried with him the hope of realising the generous ideas of a whole movement of opinion.

But with the advent of the Second Empire, Lamartine withdrew into virtual isolation, able only to draw up a sort of general aesthetic of the Romantic movement with his *Cours familier de littérature*, between 1856 and 1869. Meanwhile, the nature of his melancholy was changing: more bitter than that of 1820, it inspired other, infrequent and secret poems, but just as fascinating as his early compositions.

Lamartine's personal disintegration, be it political or poetical, can be likened to the final disintegration of the Romantic epic.

LA MOTTE-FOUQUÉ Friedrich, Baron von (Brandenburg 12.1.1777 – Berlin 23.1.1843). La Motte-Fouqué was the originator of the so-called *Pole Star* poetico-literary society. In 1840, he edited the *Newspaper for the German Nobility* and was a member of the Berlin Romantic circle. He left an immense body of work, having written steadily over the years in every literary genre. The only work of his that is read today is *Undine*, a tale of fantasy, on which Hoffmann based an opera and which Giraudoux adapted for the French stage. An enchanting work according to Goethe, and thought a marvellous and charming work by Heine, it shows clearly the author's nostalgia for the mediaeval world, which seemed to him both more simple and more mysterious, closer to Nature and its powers and, above all, closer to poetry. Compared with *Undine*, La Motte-Fouqué's interminable novels of chivalry, and his dramatic *Sigurd* trilogy, appear as obsolete and second-rate.

LENAU Nikolaus Niembsch von Strehlenau known as (Csatad, Hungary 13.8.1802 – Oberdobling 22.8.1850). An alcoholic, gambler, seducer and obdurate traveller, Lenau seemed to be cursed as a man and as a poet. The important stages of his career included his stays in Vienna, in Stuttgart, then in America (1832-1833). On his return, he fell madly, almost masochistically in love with Sophie von Lowenthal, who scorned and mocked his feelings. From 1844, the first signs of the insanity that was to bring him to end his days in an asylum, began to appear.

Lenau was a Southern German Romantic, in that he belonged to both the Austrian and the Swabian schools. He sang the praises of the roses of Tokay as well as of the reeds of the puszta. The most characteristic trait of his Romanticism was his expression of *Weltschmerz*, far more radical than that of Heine. In fact, Lenau stands at the borderline between Romanticism and Symbolism. He might be likened to Verlaine or to Baudelaire.

LEOPARDI Giacomo (Recanati 29.6.1798 – Naples 14.6.1837). Leopardi ranks among the greatest and most famous representatives of Italian Romanticism. Intended by his family for the prelature, gifted with great sensitivity and a prodigious intelligence, he took refuge in his studies and spent days and nights on end in his father's library. At the age of eleven, he had exhausted and surpassed the knowledge of his teachers; he taught himself Greek, Hebrew, Spanish and English, perfected his French and composed his first poems. He was only eighteen years old when his work began to be published in the Milanese journals. It was at this time that he became a friend of Pietro Giodani, an illustrious scholar, under whose influence he developed his liberal ideas. These were to be translated into sublime poetry such as *All'Italia* (To Italy) and *Sopra il Monumento di Dante* (On Dante's Monument).

Suffering from poor health, misunderstood, he dreamed of escape and of dying, and in haughty and despairing solitude wrote poetry in which he poured out the torments of his desolate soul: *Alla luna* (To the moon), *L'infinito* (The Infinite), *La sera del di de festa* (The evening of the feast day), *L'Ultimo Canto di Saffo* (Sappho's Last Song).

In 1822, he went to stay in Rome but returned dis-

appointed a few months later. He spent another two years in his native town of Recanati. Two poems of remembrance date from this period: *Il Risorgimento* (The Revival), *A Silvia* and many other works which are real anthology pieces: *Le Ricordanze* (Recollections), *La Quiete dopo la tempesta* (The Calm after the Storm), *Il Sabato del Villagio* (Village Saturday), *Il Passero solitario* (The Lonely Sparrow), *Canto noturne* (Nocturnal Song).

But he was dragged out of the 'wilderness' by his friend Colletta and spent time in Florence and, from 1833, in Naples. It was there that he lived the last years of his life in a milder climate that inspired him to write *La Ginestra* (The Gorse) which is considered to be his spiritual testament.

LERMONTOV Mikhail Iurievich (Moscow 15.10.1814 – Pistigorsk, Caucasus 27.7.1841). Lermontov is often compared to Pushkin and was indeed his emulator and friend, but there are several points of difference between these two poets who both represent Russian Romanticism so well.

Although they were both influenced by French literature, Pushkin's experience of it was confined more to the pre-

Portrait of Lermontov by Toidze

Romantic writers of the end of the 18th century and even the neo-Classicists of the early 19th; Lermontov by contrast was fired with enthusiasm for Stendhal and Vigny. The same is true of the influence of Byron: it was logically and chronologically limited for Pushkin, while for Lermontov it was no truly intimate experience, a revelation. Yet his was no slavish imitation, even in his most 'Byronic' works: the minor poems of 1835 and 1836, the two great poems *The Novice* (1840) and *The Demon* (1841) and, of course, the famous novel *A Hero of Our Time* (1839).

In any attempt to analyse the characteristic features of Lermontov's Romanticism, one is immediately struck by the spiritual duality in all his works: the outpouring of personal feelings is set against the striving for a universalisation of emotion. But his work differs from that of Pushkin in that this dichotomy is never resolved nor transcended during the author's literary evolution. Balance between idea, image, word and rhythm is only rarely achieved. Sometimes the intellectual element dominates at the price of ratiocination; sometimes, on the other hand, and more frequently, the central element is emotion: whence the seemingly unnecessary heaping of image upon image, the excessive musicality of *The Demon* for instance, and the confusion of motives in *The Prayer* or *Glory*. Attempts to control the confusion and contradictions, as in *Meditation* or *Death of the Poet*, merely leave an impression of desperation.

The only options available to the poet were those of silence or revolt. Lermontov chose revolt, in *Death of a Poet* for example. In *Meditation*, he went so far as to indict society in the name of his generation: 'Farewell, vile Russia' he cried. But contempt and revolt were no more than the symbols of an incurable loneliness which could not even find solace in the heart of Nature. Only the Caucasus, wild and still unexplored in places, inspired Lermontov, in the course of two successive exiles, to write the poems that have become famous: *In the Caucasus, Morning in the Caucasus* and especially *The Quarrel*.

MACPHERSON James (1736–1796). An extraordinary literary hoax attributed the so-called 'Ossian' poems to Ossian, son of the legendary bard and warrior Fingal who lived, it seems, in the 3rd century; in fact, they were written by a Scottish schoolmaster, James Macpherson. Macpherson was unquestionably familiar with the literary forms and styles of the past and exploited the resources of the old legends of the North, of mists and picturesque landscapes. *Fragments of ancient poetry translated from Gaelic and Erse* (1760), followed by *Fingal* and *Temora* (1762) were received with enthusiasm throughout Europe and read by entire generations of Romantics: Goethe, Herder, Schiller, Chateaubriand, Foscolo, Tieck, Byron, Pushkin, Manzoni. Ossianism became a

real fashion, infinitely more significant in the genesis of the European Romantic movement than either Ossian himself or Macpherson.

MANZONI Alessandro (Milan 7.3.1785 – Milan 22.5.1873). Manzoni was one of the mainsprings of the European Romantic movement. Although he was not as charismatic as Leopardi, he was none the less much the more famous. Although he was as much a theoretician as Berchet, he provided a better formulation of the literary rules that were to contribute so greatly to the integration of Italian Romanticism into the international movement. Although he was less committed than Foscolo or d'Azeglio, he nevertheless became a living symbol of the political *Risorgimento* and the aesthetic revival.

When he left college, Manzoni joined his mother, Giulia Beccaria, daughter of the famous jurist and philosopher, in Paris in 1805. There he familiarised himself with all the cosmopolitan trends in what was at the time the first capital of Europe, and learnt the importance of international exchanges, both on a political and on an artistic level.

During this period, Manzoni received a visit from Foscolo and, probably influenced by him, wrote three poems, *In morte di Carlo Imbonati* (On the death of Carlo Imbonati) in 1806, *Il Trionfo della libertà* (The Triumph of Liberty) in 1801, and *l'Adda* (1803). His third important en-

Portrait of Manzoni

counter was with Henriette Blondel, the daughter of a Geneva banker, who converted to Catholicism in order to marry Manzoni. He remained cosmopolitan, profoundly Italian and deeply religious. The work which followed seemed to follow logically from this triple commitment. In 1810, he settled in Italy for good: he lived part of the time in Milan, part of the time in his villa at Brusuglio, and spent all his time writing.

His philosophical commitment gave rise to a series of sacred hymns: *la Risurrezione* (Resurrection), 1812; *Il Nome de Maria* (The Name of Mary), *Il Natale* (Christmas), 1813, *La Passione* (The Passion), 1814; and *La Pentecoste* (Pentecost), 1821. Like Novalis and the French Romantics of 1820, Manzoni was first and foremost a Catholic poet.

The patriotic commitment inspired by Foscolo produced the ode *Marzo 1821* about an attempted revolution in the Piedmont, and the beautiful stanzas, vibrant with emotion, of the *Cinque Maggio* (Fifth of May), on the death of Napoleon on Saint Helena. Like his counterparts in Italy, France, Germany and the Slav countries, Manzoni was a liberal poet.

His renewed aesthetic consciousness inspired a series of masterpieces like *Il Conte de Caramagnola* (The Count of Caramagnola) 1820, and *Adelchi* (1822). Drawing his subjects from the Middle Ages, Manzoni welcomed the new theories which created Romantic drama and later explained the necessity for them in a famous text written in French: the *Letter to Monsieur Chauvet on the unity of time and place in tragedy* (1823). With their patriotic intent, these two plays were aimed at contributing to the national Renaissance of Italy and the choruses, very different from those of Ancient tragedy, were intended to express the political ideas of the author.

Finally came Manzoni's masterpiece: *I Promessi Sposi* (The Betrothed) which tells of two lovers separated by the arbitrariness of political and foreign power. The novel was also a political work and of paramount significance in European literature. Inspired by, among others, the *History of Milan* by Ripamonti, it brings back to life the sad period of the Spanish occupation in the 7th century. Its influence in Italy, as well as its intrinsic qualities which make it one of the great historical novels of European Romanticism, place Manzoni among the leaders of the new literature on the basis of the *Sposi* alone.

MERIMÉE Prosper (Paris 28.2.1803 – Cannes 23.9.1870). No one could have appeared further removed from Romanticism than this son of a Parisian bourgeois family; yet Merimée embodied many of the traits of a true Romantic, in the Second Empire period.

A great lover of the plastic arts (he would have liked to be a painter, like his father), friend of Stendhal and Musset, general inspector of historical monuments, he travelled across France to draw up an inventory of monuments and archaeological remains, assisted by the young Viollet-le-Duc. The frenetic aspects of his first work, a manuscript found in Spain: *le Théâtre de Clara Gazul* (1826), can best be explained in terms of a very 'Jeune-France' taste for mystifying the bourgeois, and also in terms of the temptation of exoticism and rhetori-

cal virtuosity. The same is true of *la Guzla* (1827), a collection of what purported to be translated Illyrian songs, but which was in fact a skilful synthesis of original elements and a pastiche of romantic folklore and populism. But Merimée's unique talent – his mocking Romanticism – can be deceptive: his work reflected a conflict between Nature and Culture, between the instincts and reason, which foresaw the limitations of the new aesthetic.

Portrait of Merimée

Merimée was really at his best in a different genre: in *la Chronique du règne de Charles X* (1829), he rejected elaboration and the dangerous temptations of the novel *à la* Walter Scott and assiduously verified every last detail of his reconstruction of the past. Similarly, he was at his best in short stories, including those published in *la Revue de Paris* and *la Revue des Deux Mondes* from 1829: *Mateo Falcone, Tamango, la Partie de tric-trac, Colomba, les Ames du purgatoire*, among others, and *Carmen* (1845), *Lokis* (1869), *la Chambre bleue* (1873). In these texts, the element of fantasy serves to dissimulate the violence, cruelty, the taste for blood and for love, to which Merimée reduced human nature.

MICHELET Jules (Paris 21.8.1798 – Hyère.9.2.1874). Michelet is the only great Romantic historian still in public favour today. He could even be called 'modern', perhaps because of his democratic and populist con-

Portrait of Michelet by Lafosse, 1862

contemporary of Pushkin, Heine, Leopardi and Vigny. Deeply marked as an adolescent by the tragic spectacle of the retreat of the Grande Armée, he made an early political and philosophical commitment. This first part of the author's life, which can be called his 'Lithuanian' period, saw the composition of the *Ode to Youth* (1820), which showed the influence of Schiller, and his first collection of poems: *Ballads and Romances* (1821), a veritable manifesto of Polish Romanticism. Although, in its recourse to legend and fantasy, it was of German inspiration, the collection was soon followed, by popular demand, by a second (1823) which included *The Farewells*, an unfinished lyrical drama that is of great importance in Mickiewicz's work.

victions as well as the seductiveness of his powerful and poetic imagination. He said 'I was born, like a weed without sun, between two of the paving-stones of Paris'. He observed the working classes of the city and felt solidarity with them and, in 1831, with *Introduction à l'historie universelle*, he discovered the importance of the notion of peoples in his conception of history.

But this historian (*agrégé* in 1831, professor at the Ecole Normale in 1827, then at the Sorbonne in 1834 and at the Collège de France in 1838) was also a 'philosopher', in the 18th century sense: a defender of the Rights of Man, pamphleteer, and 'crusader': witness the verve and conviction of his well-known pamphlet *les Jésuites* (1843).

Michelet was interested in everything, stirred by all that was repressed and humiliated, and interested as much by the Knights Templar whose *Trial* he retraced, as by the Protestant religion (*Mémoires de Luther*, first two volumes 1835), or *les Origines du droit français* (The Origins of French Law), 1837.

But the finest sources of inspiration were those which inspired his passion: political passion in the *Histoire de la Révolution* (1847), and amorous passion in *Amour* (1858) and *la Femme* (1859).

It was to these subjects that Michelet's glowing style was best suited. Like Hugo, he clung to his undying Romanticism until the time of the Second Empire (under which he was dismissed). His finest texts are those which rise above and beyond history, like the *Bible de l'humanité* (1864) and the surprising *Sorcière* (The Witch), 1859.

MICKIEWICZ Adam (Zaosje, near Novogrodek 24.12.1798 – Constantinople 26.11.1855). Michiewicz is one of the most interesting representatives of the European Romantic movement. He was born in Lithuania, a

Portrait of Mieckiewicz after Wankowicz

A 'Russian period' followed. In 1823, Mickiewicz w. imprisoned for his subversive activities and exiled Russia: 'Lithuania, my country, only he who has lost yo knows how to cherish you' he wrote later in *Pan Tadeu* In Petersburg, where he lived, Mickiewicz becam friendly with a whole circle of worldly and cultured pe ple, and particularly with Pushkin and Joukovski. Th *Sonnets of the Crimea* (1826) and *Konrad Wallenrod* (182 date from this period, as does the enthusiastic receptic Mickiewicz's works received in Poland. Thereafter, tl poet was regarded as the founder of the school: in 182 the first complete edition of his works in two volumes w published (with the addition of new works, such as tl oriental poem *Fanny*). In that same year, Mickiewi went abroad: to Germany (where he visited Goethe Switzerland, Italy and then France. He settled in Paris 1832, after the failure of the Polish insurrection of 183 in which he took no part because he failed to get there time!

This was the beginning of the third period of Mickiewicz's career: the years of Dresden and Paris. Leaving behind the inspiration of Byron and Pushkin which had strongly influenced ever such a deeply personal work as *Konrad Wallenrod*, Mickiewicz attempted to become a uniquely national and patriotic poet. The theme of a crucified Poland inspired the *Books of the Polish People and their Pilgrimage* (1832), and also the famous verse novel *Pan Tadeusz*. Three very Romantic themes run through this epic work: Pan Tadeusz's hesitant two-fold love for Telimene and Zosia, a dispute about a ruined castle, and the clandestine and patriotic activity of Father Robak. If, until then, all Mickiewicz's poetry was purely Romantic, then *Pan Tadeusz* marked the beginning of a Romanticism that was different both in form and content. It is a novel in verse, like Pushkin's *Onegin* and the great works of Byron, but in its richness of description is reminiscent of the style of Walter Scott. Instead of a spirit of exaltation, the poem has a serene and lofty tone, and speaks of the Polish national 'genius', and the myth of a great nation. From 1836, he inspired and directed the Polish movement in exile. In financial straits, he wrote a French drama: the *Confédérés de Bar* (1836). He taught in Lausanne in 1840–1841 and also at the Collège de France from 1840 to 1844, where his Slav literature course was renowned. He became increasingly prey to politiconational mysticism. He died suddenly of cholera in Constantinople in 1855, as he was preparing to land on the Russian coast, at the head of a legion of Polish volunteers, to liberate his country from slavery.

al downfall – the almost masochistic complaisance of his life and work – was, in a sense, more authentic than the world weariness of, say, Oberman, René or Olympio. Furthermore, possibly under the influence of alcohol, Musset has visions, and disturbances of hearing; we know from his personal papers and from the testimony of

Portrait of Musset by David d'Angers

MUSSET Alfred de (Paris 11.12.1810 – Paris 2.5.1857). Musset was a dandy, a child prodigy who, when he made his literary debut at the Cénacle of the rue Notre-Dame-des-Champs at the tender age of eighteen, astounded everyone, and published a boisterous work (*les Contes d'Espagne et d'Italie*). He was so talented (he wielded the paintbrush as skilfully as the pen) that he delayed in deciding on his choice of artistic career, and rather squandered his gifts and his life, without really achieving anything exceptional.

The themes of his poems were those universal at the time: love, pain, and world weariness (for example *Rolla*, the *Nuits* cycle, and *le Saule*), while the style of the poems was sober: apart from the cult of the proper word and a great propensity for enjambement, he used no daring images; his verses were limpid, melodious, and sometimes rather dull.

The same holds true of his plays and novels: *la Confession d'un enfant du siècle* (1834), an autobiographical work; *Lorenzaccio* (1835); *les Caprices de Marianne* (1833); and *On ne badine pas avec l'amour* (1834), all revealed a rather superficial Romanticism. Nothing in these works signalled a progression of the art, nor was there anything really new in their inspiration or themes. Yet the poet's person-

his friends, that he was haunted by the music of Schubert, and thought he saw and heard coloured notes. In this light, the apparitions that haunt the *Nuits* should be taken seriously, and it becomes easier to understand the ideal of euphony and eurhythmy for which he was striving.

Therein, perhaps, lies the key to Musset. He and Lamartine were the only poets who claimed a musical conception of their work, but among the poets of his time, Musset alone possessed the musicality and the simplicity with which one normally associates the English and German Romantics.

NERVAL Gérard de (Paris 22.5.1808 – Paris 25.2.1855). Under his real name Gérard Labrunie, this scholar of German made a powerful contribution to Romanticism in his translations (of *Faust* in particular, 1827–1830); and with his accounts of his travels in Germany, Holland and Austria (published in one enchanting volume, entitled *Lorely* in 1852). The very nature of his talent, so distinct from that of the other French Romantics, contributed to introducing France to the dream, mysticism and the cult of night, which were the chief themes, and the source of inspiration, of German Romanticism. He used the experiences of his life as a basis for myths and legends. From his childhood years spent in Valois, he retained the memory of an idealised Valois, the legends, landscapes and rustic amourettes of which were brought together in *Sylvie* (1853), a short novel which, though simple in form, is of great charm and consummate artistry. His memories were also the basis of a whole volume of *Promenades et Souvenirs* (1854–1855), and of the tale of a real quest for the past (*les Nuits d'octobre*, 1852); this is a kind of geography of a magical land, France, a land of love, mists and the voices of women singing. The difficulty of analysing Nerval's work stems from the fact that the author was constantly shuffling chronology and reality and re-ordering them in a poetic world that was very much his own, and ruled by eternal, idealised and inaccessible Woman. After his stay in Valois, Nerval decided to embark on a career as a man of letters.

Gustave Doré *'La rue de la Vieille Lanterne' illustrating The Death of Nerval*

By turns a librettist of comic opera (*Piquillo, les Monténégrins*), a theatre and music critic, he even became the patron and founder of a newspaper, *le Monde dramatique* (1835), for love of Jenny Colon, an opera singer, who was the main inspiration for the portrait of *Aurélia* and the esoteric verses of the *Chimères*. 'My only star is dead and my spangled lute bears the black sun of melancholy' cried the poet's *alter ego*, the disinherited Desdichado.

After Jenny's untimely death, Nerval tore himself away from bohemian literary life (which he described in *les Petits Châteaux de Bohème*) and withdrew into himself. There was nothing legendary about his life now: he eked out a living as a tutor, solicited copy work and travelled to find inspiration as well as revenue. But beneath his appearance as an agreeable, un-eccentric man of letters, Nerval was suffering inner torments which came to a head in February 1841.

After his first attack of insanity, followed by eight months of confinement, dreams began increasingly to spill over into real life for Nerval. He took up research into alchemy, mysterious religions and all things esoteric or para-psychological, the record of which paralleled the course of his illness, which stemmed from an unrequited and desperate need for love. He experienced repeated attacks of madness, interspersed with periods of respite and literary creation in which the poet found his most poignant voice. Nerval committed suicide on an icy February night in 1855.

His series of short stories *les Filles du feu* (1854) and *Aurélia* (1855) are among the most original works of French Romanticism.

NODIER Charles (Besançon 29.4.1780 – Paris 27.4.1844). Nodier is known as one of the initiators of Romanticism, but it is often forgotten that he started, in the *Journal de l'Empire* in 1812, by defending the Neo-Classical aesthetic. Nodier was a well-known Anglophile: he visited Scotland and Walter Scott in 1821 and tried to introduce Scott's style to France. But it should be remembered that he was first influenced by Wertherism and by the experience of a hopeless love affair in 1800, and that his first novels were *les Proscrits* and *le Peintre de Salzbourg*. In fact, Nodier followed many fashions: Wertherism, as mentioned, but also a 'black' style, in a story of brigands, *Jean Sbogar* in 1818 and *Smarra*, inspired by the Illyrian tales, and also the Scottish whimsical style with *Trilby* in 1821. He was also seemingly following fashion when he opened his famous salon, where the whole young Romantic school met in 1824, and where his daughter Marie enchanted the assembled company with her delightful voice.

Portrait of Nodier

1800. His works also include a great number of philosophically or scientifically inspired texts, collected in the *Encyclopaedia*. Novalis was only twenty-nine years old when he died prematurely in 1801. He was an important figure in the so-called 'Jean' Romantic circle. In the *Encyclopaedia* he left the fragmented outline of a grand philosophy of Nature. His poetical mysticism and his love for Sophie von Kuhn found their finest expression in the *Hymns to the Night*, with the preeminence of night over day, and the attraction of mystical darkness. Novalis, in fact, accepted death with serenity because he believed that it would reunite him with Sophie, and that his earthly existence was no more than a pale prelude to a more genuine wedding.

However, after a profound crisis in 1830, he found his own style in another series of tales: the heroes of *la Fée aux miettes*, *le Songe d'Or* and *Jean François les bas bleus* are carried away by their chimera, proving that the fantastic exists only within certain exceptional beings. This individual vein of fantasy, that can be likened to that of Hoffmann, was also to be illustrated by Théophile Gautier and Maupassant.

Portrait of Novalis, 1845

NOVALIS Friedrich von Hardenberg known as (Wiedersteht 2.5.1772 – Weissenfels 25.3.1801). From 1790, Novalis studied philosophy at Jena under the influence of Schiller who was teaching there, then law at Leipzig and Wittenberg in 1792. It was in Leipzig that he met Friedrich Schlegel. In 1795, in Gruningen, Novalis met Sophie von Kuhn who later became the mystical fiancée in the *Hymnen an die Nacht* (Hymns to the Night). She was only thirteen and died two years later at the same time as one of the poet's brothers. Novalis returned to Jena: he studied theology and metallurgy with the famous mineralogist Werner, who taught at the mining school in Freyberg. Their meeting was to be decisive for the evolution of Novalis' thinking. In 1798, he became engaged to Julie von Charpentier, and then converted to Catholicism. This was the high point of Novalis' Romantic idealism. He wrote the *Hymns to the Night* in 1797, and then an unfinished esoteric novel *Heinrich von Ofterdingen*, and *Die Lehrlinge zu Sais* (The Apprentices to Saïs) in

OEHLENSCHLAEGER Adam Gottlob (Vesterbro, near Copenhagen 14.11.1779 – Copenhagen 20.1.1850). This Danish writer who, like some of his fellow-authors and compatriots, also wrote in German (like Andersen, Baggesen etc.), differed from them in that he was an eminently national poet. Therein lay his Romanticism: his inspiration was drawn entirely from the history and ancient literature of Denmark. He had friends in the Romantic movements of many countries and spent time in Paris, Germany and Italy.

After his travels and under the influence of a Germano-Norwegian professor called Steffen, a great admirer of Goethe, Oehlenschlaeger turned to literature. From then on, he was surrounded with honour and glory and was proclaimed the prince of Scandinavian poets. He was a Professor at Copenhagen University and a State counsellor. His works include historical dramas and tragedies in the 'gothic' style: *Palnatoke, Axel and Walborg, Hakon*

Jarl, Charlemagne; poems, based for the most part on the myths and legends of the North: *Helgi, the Gods of the North*, or sometimes on foreign literature, like the Oriental tale of *Aladdin*; ballads and romances, idylls and *Poetic Art*. He also wrote comedies, opera libretti, travel journals and memoirs.

PELLICO Silvio (Saluces 25.6.1789 – Turin 31.1.1854). Pellico belongs to the Romantic movement by virtue of the role he played at the *Conciliatore* and his role as a writer as the author of a historical tragedy *Francesca de Rimini* (1816) and two volumes of poetry (*Poesie inedite*, 1837). However, his extraordinary life in captivity also contributed to the particular interest of Italian Romanticism. Arrested in 1820 for 'carbonarism' or membership of a liberal patriotic and anti-Austrian secret society, he was condemned to death, then had his sentence commuted to fifteen years' imprisonment. It was these years in Austrian gaols that Pellico described in the famous *Le mie prigione* (My prisons). Published soon after the author was released in 1832 this work, according to Balbo, did Austria more harm than any lost battle.

PETÖFI Sandor (Kiskoros, Hungary 1.1.1823 – Segesvar, Hungary 31.7.1849). The importance of Sandor Petöfi is inseparable from the Hungarian revolution of 1848. Preferring the democratic patriot Kossuth to the noble reformist Szechenyi, the Hungarians took advantage of the unrest in Europe in 1848 to rise up against the centralising Germanism of the Habsburgs. It was an exalted and desperate period in Hungarian history because revolutionary and patriotic hopes were quickly followed by counter-revolution and the repression imposed by emperor Franz-Josef with the assistance of Czar Nicholas I. The Hungarian independence movement was definitively crushed on 13 August 1849 at Vilagos.
A knowledge of these facts is necessary to an understanding of Petöfi's Romanticism. If Kossuth was the spirit and the arm of the revolution, then Petöfi was its voice. A man of intense sensitivity, a patriot and democrat, the poet had a short and tumultuous life, which was reflected in his works. By turns a student, soldier, actor, editor of Vörösmarty, he married for love in 1847, and his career would probably have continued on a happy path if the revolution had not put everything into question. It was under the influence of revolutionary events that Petöfi wrote his famous *National Song* and decided to turn from words to direct action: he enlisted in the insurgent troops and died at the battle of Feheregyhaza on 31 July 1849. His first volume of *Poems* (1844) had been wildly success-

ful. His work had all the characteristics and qualities of popular poetry: spontaneity, boldness, naivety, militant spirit, and a striking lack of rhetoric. The epic form interested him less, but he did write the extraordinary *Janos Vitez* (John the Valiant) in 1845. Petöfi was sometimes prone to bombast and turgidity when writing in this style, but in the lyrical and symbolic poetry that typifies Hungarian Romanticism, he was without equal.

POE Edgar Allan (Boston 19.1.1809 – Baltimore 7.10.1849). Poe's fantastic Romanticism was quite unique and his life as a fated poet was just as Romantic in itself. The son of an actor, orphaned at a very early age, condemned to poverty and excesses of every kind, Poe never experienced anything other than misfortune and unhappiness, and seemed to take perverse pleasure in that fact. The publication of his first poems left him with high hopes; he joined the staff of the *Southern Literary Messenger*, in which he published most of the stories that have since become so famous as the *Tales of Mystery and Imagination*. He then lost his job and lapsed completely into alcoholism. The plots of his stories were rigorously constructed, while his fantastic subject matter verged on the horrific, very much in tune with the blackest tastes of the time.

PUSHKIN Alexander Sergeyevich (Moscow 6.6.1799 – Saint Petersburg 10.2.1837). Pushkin was the incarnation of Romanticism. He took part in all the exploits of the Petersburg gilded youth, then in the political insurrection that was to give birth, a few years later, to the Decembrist movement. His exile to southern Russia, where he was sent for four years (1820–1824) on account of some seditious poems, followed by virtual house arrest at the family residence in Mikhailovskoe until the death of Czar Alexander I (1826), were eminently Romantic. So was the fact that he was totally misunderstood, both from a literary point of view (the new Czar Paul I was not in the least impressed by his work) and from a sentimental point of view (his wife Natalia, a superficial society woman, gave him no peace and caused him to fight a fatal duel). Thus, Pushkin's life conformed with all the Romantic criteria of the time.
As regards his writing, Pushkin, while deeply indebted to European Romanticism, gradually distanced himself from it in various ways. There seem to be two quite distinct periods in his work: the first extends from the 1820s to his third exile in the 1830s; the second, which can be described as his mature period, covers the last twelve years of his life. The first period can be qualified as that

Portrait of Pushkin's wife, Natalia Goncharova by Brüllow

Portrait of Pushkin by Tropinine, 1827

in the verse novel *Eugene Onegin* (1823–1830), conceived as the Russian counterpart to Bryon's *Don Juan*. Initially perceived as a both Romantic and satirical work, the poem tells of the wasted life of a young dandy.

In exile once again, Pushkin's talent reached its pinnacle. Now he drew his inspiration from the timeless geniuses of world literature – Shakespeare, Dante, Petrarch – and also from Karamzin, author of the famous *History of the Russian State*. His heroes were still Romantic in spirit, in their devouring passions and their love of solitude, but now the poet tended to depict the universal and to contrast overly subjective values with concrete and objective ideals. In parallel, lyricism was supplanted by the epic style, tales of fantasy or outright realism. This was true of *Poltava*, a lyrico-epic poem (1828) about the Russian victory over the Swedes, and of *Boris Godunov* (1825). Pushkin continued to write poems, but in concise style now: the short poems, masterpieces of harmony and simplicity, of the so-called 'Mikhailovskoe' cycle, including the famous text dedicated to A. Kern (1825): 'I remember that marvellous moment'; the poems to Nature – *The Storm*, *The Road in Winter*, *Autumn*; and the more general poems – *The Poet*, *The Crowd*, *To André Chénier*, *The Prophet*.

The short tragic pieces that he wrote between 1830 and 1833 (*The miserly Knight*, *Mozart and Salieri*, *Don Juan*) represent, perhaps, together with *The bronze Horseman* (1833), the height of his achievement. In spite of Romantic arguments or colouring, Pushkin was dealing with universal themes: avarice, envy, seduction, and he dealt with them in an original way by relating them to a global questioning of the meaning of life, destiny and freedom. Thus the figure of the demon, so dear to the author, evolved. His attitude towards it went from positive to negative, as witness his fantastic and popular narratives: *The Queen of Spades* (1833), the *Tales of Belkina*, and *Stories*. Finally, Pushkin turned to the prose novel, at a time when the style had stabilised once more, in the wake of the novelty of Walter Scott, Hugo and Merimée: he wrote *Dubrovski* (1832), the story of a nobleman ruined by an iniquitous trial who becomes a bandit, and *The Captain's Daughter* (1836), based on his *History of the Pugachov Revolt* (1833).

of his discovery, in the Caucasus, of the Orient, of adventure and of Byron. The poems written from 1820 to 1825 reflect Pushkin's admiration for and debt to the author of *The Corsair*: he himself recognised that the *Prisoner of the Caucasus* (1820–1821) bore the influence of Byron. The same oriental and Byronic theme was to be found in *The Fountain of Bakhtchisarai* (1823), *The Tziganes* (1823), and particularly in *The Demon* (1823), in which a young man is assailed by doubt in the shape of a demon reminiscent of Goethe's Mephisto. The Byronic influence culminated

RIVAS Angel de Saavedra, Duke of (Cordoba 10.5.1791 – Madrid 22.6.1865). The Duke of Rivas' first poems and early plays (*Doña Blanca*, *Ataulfo*, *Aliatar*) were purely Classical in style. The influence of Quintana and

Gallego was still in evidence in compositions such as *la Victoria de Bailen, Napoleon destronado* (1814). Exiled as a liberal to Paris (1822), then to England (1823), Rivas wrote a new tragedy, *Lanuza* (1822), and occasional poetry. He spent five years in Malta, where he wrote *el Faro de Malta, las Estrellas*, and the outline of a highly original poem, *el Moro expósito*. In Paris once more in 1830, Rivas was won over to the new art: he wrote his *Don Alvaro*, which was staged, together with his comedy *Tanto vales cuanto tienes*, after his return to Spain in 1834. He became a peer of the realm and Minister of the Interior in 1836, but had to flee the following year after the Granja revolution. He returned in 1837, and became ambassador to Naples and then to Paris (1859) before he retired from public life and died heaped with honours.

Apart from many lyrical poems written throughout his life, Rivas' three major works are *el Moro expósito*, the *Romances históricos*, and *Don Alvaro*. In *el Moro expósito* (the Moorish Foundling), which tells the ancient legend of Mudarra the foundling and the children of Lara, and in the *Romances históricos*, nationalist inspiration is evident. The eighteen stories are all based on subjects drawn from Spanish history from the reign of Don Pedro to the war against Napoleon.

Don Alvaro o la fuerza del destino, a play in prose and verse, was for Spain what *Hernani*, five years earlier, had been for France. It is famous for the opera that Verdi based upon it (*la Forza del destino*).

ROUSSEAU Jean-Jacques (Geneva 28.6.1712 – Ermenonville 2.7.1778). Rousseau, who in all respects belonged to the 18th century, especially for *la Nouvelle Héloïse* (published in 1761), which was imitated by Richardson, and the *Confessions* (1782–1788), which were a counter-argument to Saint Augustine, exercised a significant influence on the Romantics, especially in France. Chateaubriand acknowledged his debt to Rousseau for his cult of the individual, his sensitivity and his love of wild and melancholy Nature. The same was true of Madame de Staël, Stendhal, Musset, and even Lamartine. In Germany, Rousseau's principal influence was on Goethe and Schiller, neither of whom were Romantics. Rousseau in fact exemplifies what separated Romanticism from its closest antecedents. If what has long been known as pre-Romanticism augured, chiefly in its themes, the great and sweeping renewal that came with the 19th century, it differed from it in two vital respects: artistic technique and consciousness. Rousseau's language, style, and conception of life and art are the very antithesis of those of Chateaubriand who, at least at the outset, was closest to him.

SAINTE-BEUVE Charles-Augustin (Boulogne 23.12.1804 – Paris 13.10.1869). Sainte-Beuve was the great literary critic of the Romantic era. In 1826, he joined the staff of *le Globe* and was a friend of Victor Hugo who invited him to join his circle. In 1828, Sainte-Beuve published a *Historical and critical tableau of French poetry and French theatre*, followed in 1829 by *Life, poetry and thoughts of Joseph Delorme*. The central character (the voice of the author himself) indulges in complaisant self-analysis and his thoughts reflect his disenchantment. In the same spirit, he also wrote the *Consolations* (1830), a collection of poems favourably received by Hugo and Lamartine.

A feeling of personal failure followed: his affair with Madame Hugo introduced a disturbing malaise into his private life, which Sainte-Beuve tended to confuse with the essence of the Romantic movement itself. *Volupté* (1834) searched for the causes of a vain existence with a complaisance which his contemporaries found suspect: in it, he analysed with cruel lucidity the distance between self and self which is both a perpetual flight and a desperate attempt to control one's fate. In any event, Sainte-Beuve distanced himself from the fashionable school, which served to strengthen his critical activity (in particular *Chateaubriand and his literary group*, 1861).

SAND George (Paris 2.7.1804 – Nohant 2.6.1876). Under her real name of Aurore Dupin, George Sand spent most of her childhood in Nohant, in the Berry, with her grandmother Dupin, daughter of the famous Maréchal de Saxe and widow of the financier Dupin de Francoeuil, in a family atmosphere where artistic tradition did not preclude originality. Orphaned in 1808, she was deeply marked by her early childhood years, which would provide the material for her novels, and her lyricism as well as her realism. She was very young when she started scribbling stories. From 1817 to 1820, Aurore was educated to be a fashionable young lady in a Paris convent; then she returned to Nohant for two more years of freedom to play, dream, write, read and make music. An arranged marriage in 1822 with baron Dudevant proved unhappy; the couple were legally separated, a relatively rare event at the time. Aurore settled in Paris, where, to earn a living, she became a novelist and journalist. She produced her first book in collaboration with Jules Sandeau: *Rose et Blanche*. In 1831 she published *Indiana*, under what was to become her pseudonym. She lived through the July monarchy, forming famous liaisons, for example with Musset and Chopin, and the Second Empire and the Commune saw her becoming more and more radical in outlook. She died in the first years of the Third Republic, the object of near-veneration.

George Sand's immense body of work is traditionally di-

great theme of resistance to tyranny and oppression, which is expressed in all his plays, in his poetry and in his historical works, became one of the fundamental themes of the whole European Romantic movement. Finally, his mastery of a form like the ballad, and of such a medium as drama, had a direct influence on the development of the theatre and of the new poetry.

However, the similarities end there. Schiller's love of Greek Antiquity, his aesthetic doctrine inspired by Kantian philosophy, and, more generally, the fact that he had a constant and determined desire to be 'classical' in the strictest sense of the word, make it impossible to place him fairly and squarely as a Romantic. The author of the treatise on *Grace and Dignity*, of the *Letters on the Aesthetic Education of Man*, and of the essay on *Naive Poetry and Sentimental Poetry*, who wrote at the beginning of *Nänie* (1796) 'Even beauty must die!', rejected Romanticism.

Portrait of George Sand by T Kwiatowski

vided into four periods. From 1831 to 1840, she wrote romantic novels in the current taste, in which love battles against prejudice and purifies itself or dies in triumph (*Indiana, Valentine, Lélia, Mauprat*). 1840 to 1845 was the period of the socialist and mystical novels written under the influence of Lamennais and Pierre Leroux (*Spiridion, Consuelo, le Meunier d'Angibault*). A period of exclusively pastoral novels followed (*la Mare au diable, la Petite Fadette, les Maitres sonneurs*). Finally she returned to a worldly romantic vein with *les Beaux Messieurs de Bois-Doré, le Marquis de Villemer*, and at the same time wrote her autobiography: *Histoire de ma vie*. In the work of George Sand, we find all the aspirations of the Romantic era, depicted with great sensitivity.

SCHILLER Friedrich von (Marbach 10.11.1759 – Weimar 9.5.1805). Friedrich von Schiller and his friend Goethe symbolised Weimar Classicism; yet although Goethe certainly did not belong to the Romantic movement, the same is not strictly true of Schiller. Like Goethe he was a representative of the *Sturm und Drang* movement, born towards the middle of the 18th century, but the effects of it were far more prolonged in his work than in that of Goethe, lasting into the early 19th century. Thus Schiller's great plays: *Wallenstein* (1796–1799), *Maria Stuart* (1799–1800), and *William Tell* (1803–1804) are contemporaneous with Novalis' *Hymns to the Night* (1800), with Tieck and Wackenroder's first works, and the activities of the Jena circle. Furthermore, Schiller's

SCHLEGEL August Wilhelm (Hannover 8.9.1767 – Bonn 12.5.1845). A theoretician of early Great Romanticism (that of the so-called Jena group), famous translator of Shakespeare (with Tieck), of Calderon, and of Italian, Spanish and Portuguese poetry, A.W. Schlegel also knew Sanscrit and ancient Provençal. His was a brilliant mind that suffered from the decline of Romanticism

Portrait of August Wilhelm Schlegel

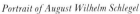

and the oblivion to which his last years were consigned. It was in Göttingen that he met Bürger, whose ballads, especially *Lenore*, met with such immense success in the European Romantic movement. Schlegel taught at Jena from 1798 to 1800, founding the first Romantic circle there and inspiring the famous journal of art and aesthetics: the *Athenäum*. From 1801 to 1803, he taught in Berlin. Then he met Madame de Staël and, mainly to escape from administrative and political concerns, agreed to become her children's tutor. He travelled Europe with her, fleeing Napoleonic persecution, and visited Geneva, Rome, Paris, and Sweden (1812). During the wars of independence, he enlisted in the German army (1813), and was on the political staff of the Crown Prince of Sweden. The Restoration brought him back to Coppet, but he returned to Germany when Madame de Staël died (1817). He left a volume of poetry, published in 1810, but is known above all for his *Literature Course*, which he taught in Vienna and in Berlin, and in which he strongly criticised French tragedy.

Portrait of Friedrich Schlegel

SCHLEGEL Friedrich (Hannover 10.3.1772 – Dresden 11.1.1829). Better known than his brother August Wilhelm, Friedrich Schlegel was as much a theoretician as a practitioner of the early German Romanticism of Jena. Destined by his father for a commercial career, he studied law at Göttingen, but soon moved towards literary studies and went to Leipzig where he met Novalis (1791).

He concentrated first on Ancient literature, which he worshipped at the time: *Wert des Studiums der Griechen und*

der Römer (1794). He settled in Jena in 1796, started to turn away from Antiquity and broke with Schiller. He founded the *Athenäum* with his brother. It contained pieces of criticism as well as doctrinal articles on the renewal of art and the evolution of tastes. Then he went to Berlin where he became a friend of the philosopher Schleiermacher and where he married Dorothea Veidt, daughter of the philosopher Moses Mendelssohn, after her divorce. In a novel that caused a scandal (*Lucinde*, 1799), Schlegel asserted that sensuality refined by the cult of beauty should be man's ideal. Schlegel's conversion to Catholicism, in 1808, caused as much of a stir as his thesis on Hindu language and philosophy in the same year. He then served the anti-Napoleonic Austrian government: he was private secretary at the Vienna chancellery, on Archduke Charles' staff at Wagram, and was on the editorial staff of several patriotic journals. Despite these activities, he also published some *Poems* in 1809. His *History of Ancient and Modern Literatures*, published in 1815, is an additional monument to Schlegel's criticism and Romantic aesthetic. A counsellor of the Austrian legation to the *Bund* in Frankfurt, he returned to Vienna in 1818 and founded the newspaper *Concordia*. He was a great instigator of mediaeval studies, of classical philology and of comparative literature, while his novel *Lucinde* was a dominant influence of the time in its sensitivity and sentimentality.

SCOTT Walter (Edinburgh 15.8.1771 – Abbotsford, Roxburghshire 21.9.1832). Initially, there was nothing to indicate that Scott would become a prolific novelist. However, he was fascinated very early on by the legends and traditions of Scotland. He made a reputation for himself with his poems and contributed regularly to literary journals, particularly the famous *Quarterly Review*.
Scott produced both verse and prose. In 1802 he published a collection of Scottish ballads, in keeping with contemporary taste (*Minstrelsy of the Scottish Border*) closely followed by a volume of poems: *The Lay of the Last Minstrel* (1805) which was an immediate success. He then produced a series of narratives in verse (*Marmion, the Lady of the Lake*).
It was the success of *Waverley*, published anonymously in 1814, that made Scott decide to concentrate on the novel. Over the next fourteen years he wrote twenty-seven novels of which the most famous are *Guy Mannering* (1815), *The Bride of Lammermoor* (1819), *Ivanhoe* (1819) and *Quentin Durward* (1823).
In all these works, Scott meticulously portrayed the mores, characters, customs and events of days gone by. The novel was already an almost nationalistic undertaking. More often than not, his themes were insurrection, romantic love, clan rivalry, and his narratives were

Portrait of Walter Scott

always set against imposing backcloths, such as the Scottish moors, Kenilworth Castle, etc. His imaginative power went hand in hand with highly skilful staging and great realism of detail.

Portrait of Senancour

SENANCOUR Etienne Pivert de (Paris 16.11.1770 – Saint-Cloud 10.1.1846). Senancour's work was a reflec-

tion of his life: desolate and solitary. After many peregrinations, and a number of bereavements and disappointed loves, Senancour passed his life isolated and abandoned. He was interested in illuminist doctrines, but vehemently hostile to Christianity.

This disenchanted existence was the subject of his major work, the novel *Oberman* (1804). In it, the author poured out the long story of his unhappy love-life. Like him, the hero feels out of place among his fellow-men and dreams of an impossible happiness. Oberman suffered from a more metaphysical and more desperate malady than René.

At the same time, *Oberman* revealed the author's penchant for spiritualism and transcendental doctrine; as his name indicates, Oberman was a man of high ideals, who discoursed on Pythagoras and meditated on Swedenborg. This was even more strikingly evident in *Aldomen* (1795), another autobiographical novel, and the *Libres Méditations d'un solitaire inconnu* (1819).

The work of Senancour was unique in the French Romantic movement: he is perhaps closest to Novalis, Jean-Paul Richter and the abstract writers of the Romantic era.

SHELLEY Percy Bysshe (Horsham 4.8.1792 – at sea off Viareggio 8.7.1822). Shelley's life was almost as full of incident as that of Byron. He too was the son of a noble family and his predilection for tales of fantasy manifested itself early in his childhood. After Eton, he studied at Oxford, but was expelled after the publication of his tract entitled *The Necessity of Atheism*. At the age of nineteen, he eloped with the sixteen year-old Harriet Westbrook; three years later he fell passionately in love with Mary Wollstonecraft, daughter of the philosopher Godwin, and left Harriet. He went to Switzerland where he and Byron became friends, married Mary after Harriet's suicide (1816) and settled in Italy (1818). It was there, caught in a squall while sailing in the Bay of Spezzia, that Shelley drowned in 1822.

Even in his early work, Shelley depicted a complete philosophical and moral system: *Queen Mab* (1813) was an expression of his revolutionary faith in Godwin's atheist doctrine. *Alastor* (1816) was an evocation of the poet's loneliness and his taste for death. *Hymn to Intellectual Beauty* (1817) denoted a period of Platonism. *The Revolt of Islam* (1818) combined a story of incest with a statement of the ideals of liberty and justice. Shelley's Romanticism was not merely lyrical and sentimental, it was also ideological and prophetic, as that of Hugo and Lamartine was later to be.

Shelley's masterpieces date from his years in Italy. They include the famous poetical tragedy *The Cenci* (1819); *Prometheus Unbound* (1820), a philosophical drama and sublimation of his political preoccupations; *Epipsychidion* (1821), a vast love poem in honour of the ideal Woman;

Adonais (1821), a touching elegy on the death of Keats and also a personal confession; and finally, *A Defence of Poetry*, in which Shelley expressed his poetic ideal and his conception of the poet's role. His best-known works are the short lyrical poems, published after his death: *Ode to the West Wind, To a Skylark, Autumn* and *The Hymn of Pan*.

SLOWACKI Juliusz (Krzemieniec, Poland 4.9.1809 – Paris 3.4.1849). If Mickiewicz inaugurated the Romantic movement in Poland, it was undoubtedly in Slowacki

Portrait of Slowacki

that it reached its apotheosis. Isolated, overflowing with imagination and wildly egocentric, he died at the age of thirty-nine of tuberculosis after a brief career that resulted in a body of work at once lyrical, dramatic and epic. The period of his adolescence was influenced by the young Mickiewicz and by Byron: this is evident in his stories (*Hugo*, 1829, *Jan Bielecki*, 1830) and in his plays (*Mindowe*, 1829, *Maria Stuart*, 1830). His heroes were all solitary figures, misunderstood and subject to tumultuous passions.

When Slowacki left Poland for Paris in 1831, after the 1830 insurrection, and started to meditate on the misfortunes of his country as well as on his own attitude towards it, it was the influence of Shakespeare that asserted itself in *Kordian* (1833), an autobiographical drama in verse. It contained a whole literary syllabus on the role of poetry: it should revive history and, in evoking great moments from history, serve to tear the Poles away from exaggerated rationalism, as well as world-

weariness. Slowacki's messianic plan was manifest here as well: Poland was the chosen nation, with a duty to sacrifice itself for others. *Balladyna* (1834), a both poetical and political tale, with its many reminders of Shakespeare, was imbued with the pessimism that was one of the constants of Slowacki's work. This pessimism was, however, attenuated by visits to Switzerland, Italy and the Orient in 1836–1837, which opened up a new world to him, as witness the idyll *En Suisse* (1835), in which his love for Maria Wodzinska is complemented by the beauty of the Alps. The idea of purificatory sacrifice dominated *Anhelli* (1838), a prose poem of political inspiration: the torments endured by political prisoners in Siberia culminate in the announcement of a glorious resurrection. Slowacki was to move away from Romanticism with the parody poem *Beniowski* (1841) in the style of Byron's *Don Juan*, and with *Fantazy* (1841), reminiscent of Musset.

The final phase of the poet's evolution was marked by Darwinian scientism. Although already consumed with tuberculosis, Slowacki did not miss the 1848 revolution, and in fact, took part in it in Poznan. A strange figure of contrasts, misunderstood by his contemporaries, Slowacki was to enchant the modernists of 'Young-Poland', half a century later.

STAËL Madame de (Paris 22.4.1766 – Paris 14.7.1817). Germaine de Staël-Holstein, daughter of Necker, belongs, with Chateaubriand and Senancour, to the generation of artists who began the French Romantic movement of 1820 and 1830.

Brought up at the Philosopher's School (she met the celebrities of the day in her mother's salon: d'Alembert, Diderot, Marmontel) Germaine Necker had a very strong penchant for Jean-Jacques Rousseau: her first work was a *Letter on the Works and the Character of J-J Rousseau* (1788). During the Revolution, having become the wife of the Swedish ambassador and the mistress of one of the first revolutionary ministers, Monsieur de Narbonne, she opened a salon on the Rue du Bac. But her independence of spirit, judgement and candour made her suspect: she had to leave for Coppet, her father's estate. There she founded what was gradually to become the 'société de Coppet', a meeting-place for the modernist intelligentsia of Europe. Coppet was a hotbed of Romanticism and liberalism. Her *On the Influence of the Passions on the Happiness of Individuals and Nations* (1796) and *On Literature Considered in its Relation to the Institutions of Society* (1800) date from this period.

In 1803, Madame de Staël, who had just published *Delphine*, a novel original in its feminism and musical form, was reported to the Bonapartist authorities. Followed by Benjamin Constant, she left France and travelled to Germany (where she met Goethe, Schiller and Wieland in Weimar), Italy and Russia. They were difficult but fruitful years, in that Madame de Staël, by her contacts with all the European intellectuals, acquired new ideas that

Portrait of Mme de Staël

would, in time, be the basis of the Romantic movement. *De l'Allemagne* (1810), destroyed by order of the Emperor who found it anti-French, was an anti-Classical work which celebrated the poetry of chivalry and German nature and philosophy, on which the early years of French Romanticism were based.

Diary, his *Souvenirs d'égotisme* are akin to the works of Amiel, Senancour and Kierkegaard.

Stendhal was also a Romantic in his literary and artistic tastes: Shakespeare, Rossini, Cimarosa, Mozart, Italian painting and literature (Monti, Pellico) and English literature, which he constantly championed, and in his theory of modern beauty, which he saw as different from that of fifty or sixty years before. He developed these ideas in his *Lives of Haydn, Mozart and Metastase* (1815) and *Life of Rossini* (1824).

In consequence, Stendhal contributed to the creation of the Romantic movement as such (he himself referred to 'romanticisme'). In Milan he was friendly with the liberals, while in Paris he mixed with Delécluze and all the old Bonapartists: it was the left wing of French Romanticism which championed the theatrical revival, and *Racine et Shakespeare* (1823–1825) was, in this respect, an important contribution to the Romantic cause.

Portrait of Stendhal by De Dreux d'Orcy

STENDHAL (Grenoble 23.1.1783 – Paris 23.3.1842). Henri Beyle, known as Stendhal, is famous above all for his two novels: *Le Rouge et le Noir* (1831) and *La Chartreuse de Parme* (1839). His love of Italy, which he knew as a tourist under the Restoration, as a diplomat under Louis-Philippe and as a soldier of Bonaparte under the Directoire, inspired *Rome, Naples et Florence* (1826, 2nd edition), *Promenades dans Rome* (1829) and *Chroniques italiennes* (1839).

Stendhal's romanticism manifested itself in his life, his morals, his self-confessed 'egotism', and a perpetual quest for happiness, love, improvisation and spontaneity. Thus he was inspired to write such monuments to love and Romantic sensitivity as *De l'amour* (1822), inspired by his hopeless passion for Metilde Dembowski, and his posthumous autobiography: *la Vie de Henri Brulard*. His

With the advent of Realism, there was a tendency to ignore Stendhal's Romanticism and to see only the critical side of his novels. However, it would be wrong to confuse cause and effect: it was not Stendhal who was a precursor of Realism, but rather Realism that adopted and developed, albeit in an entirely new direction, an aspect of French Romanticism that was partisan, irreverent and progressive. Realism was born of the liberalism of the years 1830–1840. Stendhal was a liberal, but his Romanticism was as much born of temperament as of conviction.

TIECK Ludwig (Berlin 21.5.1773 – Berlin 28.4.1853). The same haziness of definition surrounds the figure of Tieck as that of all the precursors of the movement who lived long lives. Of modest origins, Tieck was fired at a very early age with enthusiasm for Goethe and the theatre. A degree of mental strain, intense sensitivity, the

Octavianus (1804). A bewitching atmosphere reigns in Tieck's work: the atmosphere of the primeval forest and of magical moonlit nights.

Portrait of Ludwig Tieck by David d'Angers

death of two childhood friends and his battle with his family background gave his character a shadowy side, that verged on neurosis. He lived in Jena from 1796 to 1800, and was instrumental in forming the first group of Romantics there, with Novalis, the Schlegels, and, in part, Arnim and Brentano.

Tieck was, above all, a prolific story-teller: his favourite genre was the fantastic, humorous, satirical or romantic tale, in which he disguised his underlying meaning in a cloak of fantasy. The early, somewhat rationalist, stories criticised the Wertherist fashion. Then, influenced by Wackenroder, Tieck discovered the poetry of German history: it inspired, among others, *Magelone* and *Melusine*. The stories that followed were both poetic and terrifying: *Der blonde Eckbert* (1796), *Vom getreuem Eckbert* (Faithful Eckbert), 1799, and *Der Runenberg* (1802), where the characters are prey to repressed passions and Nature is mysterious and magnificent. For Tieck the sentimental novel was an object of derision, yet his *William Lovell* (1795–1796) is reminiscent of the innumerable letter-novels of the European 18th century. Tieck's major novel is probably *Sternbald* (1798), which, in the style of *Wilhelm Meister*, recounts the travels and adventures of a young artist.

Finally, he produced a whole series of stories that were either satires of the pedantic literary world of the time such as *Prinz Zerbino* (1799), or large frescoes which brought together all the themes of Germanic Romanticism, such as the two dramas *Genoveva* (1800) and *Kaiser*

UHLAND Ludwig (Tübingen 26.4.1787 – Tübingen 13.11.1862). The son of an old Wurtemberg family, Uhland is considered to be the leader of the Swabian Romantic movement. He studied law at Tübingen. A Francophile, he went to Paris in 1810, then, in 1812, joined the Ministry of Justice in Stuttgart, where he displayed a liberal spirit. A magistrate, then a deputy to the Wurtemberg Diet, he later went to the University of Tübingen (1829), where he taught German language and literature. He resigned to be able to represent Wurtemberg at the Confederation in Frankfurt in 1833. Disappointed, he cancelled his mandate in 1839. With the outbreak of the revolutionary events of 1848, he accepted a seat in the Frankfurt Parliament. An unrepentant liberal, friend of Kerner and Gustav Schwab, he was the most typical illustration of Swabian Romanticism: his lyrical poetry had assimilated the tone and themes of the *Volkslied* so well that many of his poems were adopted by the people (for example the famous *Kapelle*, or *Ich hatt' einen Kamaraden*). But he also wrote epic and dramatic works: *Graf Eberhard*, *Ernst von Schwaben*, *Ludwig der Bayer* or charming melodramas like *Das Schloss am Meer* (The Castle by the Sea), which inspired Richard Strauss to compose his work of the same name.

VIGNY Alfred de (Loches 27.3.1797 – Paris 17.9.1863). Vigny's career was typified and dogged by misunderstandings. He was born into the nobility and belonged to a family that was ruined by the Revolution. His youth, as he himself was to recount it, was blighted by an atmosphere of regret and suspicion.

Under the Restoration, in 1814, he enlisted in the army, only to discover before long that military glory was not for him, nor for his class. He dreamed of being a poet: in 1822 he published his first volume of poetry (*Moïse*, *Eloa*, *le Déluge*, among others).

But, although he wrote perhaps the first French historical novel, in imitation of Walter Scott, *Cinq Mars* (1826); although he may have produced the first French Romantic play, with *Le More de Venise*, emulating Shakespeare and staged in 1829 (before *Hernani!*); although he was regarded by the literary circle of the rue Notre-Dame-des-Champs as a leader of the young school, it was Hugo, and Hugo alone, who was to embody the burgeoning Romantic movement.

There was misunderstanding in his personal life too: his

Portrait of Alfred de Vigny by A Devéria

for example *The Awakening of Arpad*. But it was as a critic and as a leader that Vörösmarty played his most important role: he foresaw the future of Romanticism in Europe and urged Hungarian writers to adopt its banner. His *Call to the Hungarian Nation* (1837) became the favourite hymn of all Hungary.

marriage of love to the Englishwoman Lydia Bunbury turned to pain when his wife became frigid and he had to resort to the company of other women.

And finally, he was misunderstood by history, because his very pure, inspired verses áre no longer read and part of his poetry collected under the title of *Destinées* was not published until after his death, in 1864, and received neither the reaction nor the reception that it deserved. 'I have said what I know and what I have suffered' Vigny wrote in his *Diary of a Poet*, a few months before his death. It is regrettable that this connaisseur of German Romantic philosophy, this most intensely personal of Romantic writers, should never have been recognised for his true worth, as one of the most complete embodiments of the Romantic spirit.

VÖRÖSMARTY Mihály (Nièk, Hungary 1.12.1800 – Pest 19.11.1855). 1825 was a famous year for Hungary: it marked the sitting of the liberal Diet and it was also the year that saw the publication of Vörösmarty's epic, *Zalan's Flight*. Socio-economic renewal was thus connected with a renewal of literature: Reformism went hand in hand with Romanticism.

In this context can be found parallels between events as apparently dissimilar as the foundation of the Hungarian Academy of Sciences, the launching of the literary review *Aurora* (1822), the political activity of Count Szechenyi, and the literary activity of Kisfaludy and, especially, Vörösmarty. Vörömarty was the greatest Hungarian lyrical poet. He wrote some fine love poems and poems of nationalism, and also some rather less interesting plays,

WACKENRODER Wilhelm Heinrich (Berlin 13.7.1773 – Berlin 13.2.1798). Wackenroder was the first theoretician of German Romanticism. His meeting with Tieck, who became his friend and faithful collaborator, played a decisive role in his life. Wackenroder began, in 1793, by studying law at Erlangen, in accordance with his father's wishes. He used the opportunity to visit the masterpieces of German history in the region (Nuremberg, Dresden, Bavaria). In 1796, his first work was published by Unger in Berlin: *Herzensergiessungen eines Kunstliebenden Klosterbruders* (Outpourings of the Heart of an Art-loving Monk). In 1797, through Tieck, he met Friedrich Schlegel and participated in the Jena school, the first German Romantic doctrinal school. After a long and rather mysterious illness, he died in 1798.

If there was nothing particularly outstanding about Wackenroder's life, the reverse was true of his work. *The Outpourings* were the first expression of the Romantic ideals: they combine 'musical' emotion with religious ecstasy, and the grave and virile qualities of the old Nuremberg artists with the grace of the Italian quattrocento. Wackenroder had nothing but contempt for modern artists; his gods were Dürer, Raphael and all the musicians of the past. For him, the only kind of art that could truly express the sublime was music. This idea was developed in *Phantasien über die Kunst* (Fantasies about Art), published by Tieck in 1799, after the death of his friend. Thus, for the first time in German literature, music took its place beside the plastic arts and poetry, as one of the great symbols of spiritual life.

WORDSWORTH William (Cockermouth, Cumberland 7.4.1770 – Rydal Mount, Westmoreland 23.4.1850). Wordsworth was, together with Coleridge, the leader of the Romantic school with manifested itself in England much earlier than in any other country.

He was eight years old when he lost his mother. He was sent to boarding-school and from there went to Cambridge from 1787 to 1791. He spent his holidays in Yorkshire, fell in love with its picturesque landscapes which were to prove one of mainsprings of his Romanticism, and in 1790 travelled in the French Alps. He was also inspired by revolutionary ideas.

Back in England, he devoted himself to poetry and lived in the country with his sister, Dorothy, who helped him to find his faith in Nature once more. A legacy of nine

Portrait of Wordsworth

hundred pounds provided by one of his friends ensured his means of support. Living quite close to Coleridge, Wordsworth gained confidence in his own talent. Their friendship and their respective work, one influenced by the other, laid the foundations of the Romantic school which was born with the publication of the *Lyrical Ballads* in 1798.

In 1799, he settled in Grasmere in the Lake District, and in 1802 married his cousin Mary Hutchinson there. From then on, and for the rest of his days, he lived a quiet and peaceful existence, without a trace of his former revolutionary spirit. His poetry grew in power and in beauty, though it lacked the spontaneity and the freshness of the poems of his youth.

The distance he had travelled can be measured by comparing the *Descriptive Sketches* of 1793, which evoke a new theme, the Alps, yet in a conventional style, with the *Lyrical Ballads*. The latter represents, above all, a deliberate attempt to revolutionise poetry by abandoning the poetic diction of the 18th century. Wordsworth advocated the use of everyday language and simple, true images.

In 1805, he was working on a long autobiographical poem, *The Prelude*, only published in its entirety in 1850, which was perhaps his most masterly work. The later works, in particular *Intimations of Immortality* (1803–1806)

and *Ode to Duty* (1805) still have some of the vigour of his early work, while their philosophical content announces the poetry of his mature years (in particular *The Excursion*, 1814, and the volumes of 1815 and 1842). Today, Wordsworth is best known for some descriptive passages in *The Prelude*, a few odes and sonnets, and for his poems about Nature, which express beautifully the impressions of a simple and pious spirit.

ZORRILLA José (Valladolid 21.2.1817 – Madrid 23.1.1893). After studies in Toledo, Valladolid and Madrid, Zorrilla published four volumes of poetry in 1837–1838, followed by several more, such as *Vigilias del estio, Recuerdos y Fantasias, Los ecos de la montaña, El cantar del romero*; and also historical or fantastic legends in verse, such as the *Leyenda del Cid*. From Zorrilla's ardent and abundant output, must be singled out, firstly, the collection entitled *Cantos del trovador* (1840–1841) in which he gave his vivid imagination and his sense of history and local colour free rein; and secondly, the sadly unfinished poem *Granada*, in which the poet proposed to paint a vast record of Arab civilisation in Spain.

Zorrilla's lyrical poems are all characterised by a double inspiration: religious and national. To bring Spain's past back to life, the author drew mainly on legend, and here we find his masterworks: *Recuerdo de Toledo, El Montero de Espinosa, El Capitan Montoya, Margarita la tornera, La Azucena Silvestre*, and *La Pasionaria*. Zorrilla's poetry is, on the whole, marvellously flowing and melodious, although it does not always escape cliché or discordant metaphor.

Zorrilla was also a very great and prolific dramatist, leaving a large and varied body of plays. They include half a dozen real cloak-and-dagger plays, in three acts and in verse, according to the old formula (*Ganar perdiendo* in 1839, *Cada cual con su razon* in 1839, *Lealtad de una mujer y de una noche* in 1840, *Mas vale llegar al tiempo que rondar un ano* in 1845, and *La mejor razon la espada*); fourteen historical plays, of which the best known are: *El Zapatero y el Rey*, in two parts (1840 and 1842), *El Punal del Godo* (1843) about Don Rodrigo, the last Goth king, and a fantasy-religious play *Don Juan Tenorio*. This incarnation of the legendary Spaniard was, despite its critics, the greatest theatrical success of the 19th century in Spain. It is still performed today. Zorrilla naturally drew his inspiration from Molina, but also from *Don Juan de Marana* by Dumas. It is a combination of romantic adventure, pseudo-Christian miracles, sensuality and mysticism, with some stylistic affectations.

Music

The tastes of the time

It is very important to realise from the outset that the music of the Romantic era only corresponds in some small degree to out idea of what romantic music should be. The European audiences of the time were essentially eclectic in their tastes. In his *Mémoires*, Berlioz recounts the difficulties he experienced in trying to get his music performed, whereas it seems to us today to correspond perfectly with the aesthetic of the day. There were national differences too: Berlioz described his triumphs in Germany and in Russia, whereas Germany, as is well known, had some difficulty in accepting the music of Schumann, apparently the most Romantic of German composers. As in the field of literature, in music too there were battles and triumphs: 18 June 1821, the date of the first performance of *Freischütz* in Berlin, is a key date in the history of Romantic music, and one that was recognised as such by the contemporary press and public.

On the other hand, the creation in October 1814 of *Gretchen am Spinnrade*, one of the pinnacles of Romantic art, by the seventeen-year-old and still unknown Schubert, went completely unnoticed.

So, which composers were actually appreciated by the audiences of their own time? The answer is, indisputably, the composers of opera.

During the course of an initial period which lasted approximately until the early 1830s, the European repertoire consisted of French, German and Italian operas. The French were represented by more or less direct heirs of the 18th century tradition, such as Grétry, Lesueur, whose *Ossian ou les Bardes* in 1804 was a great success, and by composers moved by a new inspiration: Boieldieu with *La Dame Blanche* (1825) inspired by Walter Scott; Méhul with *Joseph* (1807) which gained the approbation of Weber and Wagner, and Auber, whose *La Muette de Portici* (1828) – more commonly known as *Masaniello* – was triumphantly received throughout Europe. We should also include in the French repertoire some composers of other nationalities who were writing in the style of 'grand opera': Gluck, firstly, whose works were staged over a very long period of time, Sacchini with *Oedipe*, Cherubini with *Médée* (1797), and Spontini with *Fernand Cortez* (1809) and *La Vestale* (1807). Nor should the *opéras comiques*, or *opera buffa*, be forgotten, such as those by Cherubini: *Lodokiska* (1791) and *Les Deux Journées* (1811).

The Italians were represented by Rossini, of course, but also by his predecessors: Paer, Paesiello, Mayr, Cimarosa. Cimarosa's works included *Il Matrimonio segreto*, the *Orazi, Nemeci generosi*, the *Maestro di capella* and *Traci amanti*. Rossini was appreciated chiefly for his 'serious' operas: *Tancredi* (1813), the work that made him famous, *Elisabetta, Regina d'Inghilterra* (1815), *Otello* (1816), *La Donna del Lago* (1819) and *Maometto* (1820), better known by the title under which it was later staged in Paris, *Le Siège de Corinthe* (1826). Apart from their intrinsic musical novelty, these works were remarkable for their libretti, drawn from authors like Walter Scott and Shakespeare. Then there were Rossini's more light-hearted operas, which are most popular today: *Il Barbiere de Seviglia*, the first night of which, in Rome in 1816, was a notorious fiasco, *La Cenerentola* (1817), *La Gazza Ladra* (The Thieving Magpie, 1817), and *L'Italiana in Algeri* (1813). These *opera buffa* were revived at more or less the same time all over Europe, between 1820 and 1828, and their success has endured the test of time. The years that Rossini spent in Paris were important: it was for the stages of the French capital that he created *Le Comte Ory* (1823), *Le Siège de Corinthe*, *Moïse* (1827) and *Guillaume Tell* (1829). This last work brilliantly represents both the qualities and the defects of 'grand opera': its grandiose proportions (nearly five hours of music), rich and varied orchestration, dramatic recitatives, vast scenic choruses, diversity of forms and pieces of vocal bravura, all staged with great pomp and display. It corresponded perfectly with the musical taste of its time.

German operas too held a place of honour – those of Mozart in particular. The first three decades of the 19th century witnessed a magnificent rehabilitation of Mozart; not only in Austria, where his grand operas were revived, between 1800 and 1810, in polished productions, at the theatre of the Carinthia Tor and at the Burgtheater in Vienna, but also in Berlin, where *Magic Flute*, with sets designed by Schinkel, was staged in 1824, and in Paris where the greatest singers, Garcia, Rubini, Maria Malibran and Henriette Sontag insisted on performing the leading roles. There was also Weber, famous above all for *Freischütz* (1821). As proof of Weber's international success, it should be remembered that *Euryanthe* (1823) was written for Vienna, and that it was on the invitation of Covent Garden that he wrote *Oberon*: Weber died in London soon after conducting the first performance of his work in 1826. By comparison with Mozart and Weber, the other German composers were only really successful in their own country: they were Marschner, Hoffmann, Spohr and Lortzing. Even Beethoven's *Fidelio* did not achieve celebrity: the German company which came to perform it in Paris in 1830, only met with a 'succès d'estime' in the eyes of writers like Hugo, or George Sand. As for the authors of *opera buffa*, Nicolai or Lortzing for instance, they were completely unknown outside the German countries.

The next distinct period more or less spanned the years from 1830 to 1840. Compared to the preceding period, it is much easier to characterise, by the addition of the names of Bellini, Donizetti and Meyerbeer to those of the older composers. Moreover, the Romanticism of this period corresponds more to our present-day conception of what it should be: melodramatic aesthetics, sumptuous stage production, generous and brilliant vocal score and powerful orchestration: it was opera aimed at the utmost expressiveness, and dramatic suspense. This is perceptible in *Norma* by Bellini (1831) as well as *Lucia di Lammermoor* by Donizetti (1835), and *Les Huguenots* by Meyerbeer (1836). The composers set to music themes with guaranteed success: Bellini borrowed the subject of *Montecchi e Capuletti* (1828) from Shakespeare, and *Puritani* (1835) from Walter Scott. Donizetti turned to Shakespeare for *Anna Bolena* (1830), to Hugo for *Lucrezia Borgia* (1833), to Walter Scott for *Lucia*, and to Schiller for *Maria Stuart*. Meyerbeer worked exclusively with Scribe, who either wrote an original libretto in the fashion of the time, as for *Robert le Diable* (1831), or drew his inspiration from Merimée, for *Les Huguenots* (1836). It cannot be over-emphasised that the success of these new operas rested first and foremost on a particular type of libretto, which was served by music evolving in its dramatic intensity. For years, the stages of Paris, Berlin, London, Vienna, Milan and Venice were uninterruptedly filled with *Beatrice di Tende*, *La Somnambula*, *Roberto Devereux*, or *Don Pasquale*, *L'Elisire d'Amore*, and Meyerbeer's three grand operas: *Robert le Diable*, *Les Huguenots* and *Le Prophète* (1849).

The revolution of 1848 inaugurated, in opera, a repertoire which, although not accepted at first, gradually became the great Romantic repertoire: that of Verdi and Wagner. Wagner, of course, had his setbacks: witness the notorious Paris premiere of *Tannhäuser* in 1861 and the violent criticism aroused by the Munich performances of his works, particularly *Tristan and Isolde*, which was first performed in 1865.

Once again, it was a particular group of operas that were performed in theatres throughout Europe: Verdi's 'trilogy' of *Rigoletto* (1851), *Il Trovatore* (1853) and *La Traviata* (1853). Of Wagner's works, *Lohengrin* (1850), *Tannhäuser* and *The Flying Dutchman* were more popular than *Tristan and Isolde* or the *Ring* cycle: it was not until the early years of the 20th century that the *Ring* was included in opera repertoire, even in Berlin and Vienna.

In short, although opera was indeed the musical medium that Romantic audiences preferred, those audiences, for the most part, liked a great variety of works, some of them very far removed from what we today would think of as 'Romantic'. The real opera of the 'Romantic years' (1815–1848) was that of Rossini and Weber, followed by that of Meyerbeer, Bellini and Donizetti. It was a time of exhilarating discoveries when, suddenly, the petulance of Rossini and the poetry of Weber enchanted audiences who had, until then, been gently nodding through Gluck's 'lyrical tragedies'.

The 'concert music' of the Romantic era has its share of surprises too. We tend today to think of Chopin, Berlioz, Liszt, Schubert or Schumann as the gods of that period in music.

Liszt conducting a concert

Scene from *The Flying Dutchman* by Wagner at the Lyceo

Der Freischütz by Weber, Act II

Yet, in fact, the reverse was true: the first half of the 18th century was characterised by programmes that were extremely conservative. In parallel, there was a change of structures. Private commissions and patronage were replaced by State establishments; Conservatoires were founded for the teaching of music and 'limited companies' were set up to produce concerts: in 1813, in Vienna, the *Society of the Friends of Music* was founded, while the concerts of the *Société des Concerts du Conservatoire* in Paris began in 1828. In the field of symphonic music, Paris was to retain its preeminence for many years: Wagner related in his *Memoirs* that it was only when he heard it performed at the Société des Concerts that he really understood Beethoven's *Ninth Symphony*.

As far as the repertoire was concerned, until about 1830 the works of Haydn and Mozart filled concert halls everywhere. Then Beethoven took pride of place, sharing the programme with small doses of carefully chosen works by contemporary composers. As an illustration, the programme of the first concert of the Société des Concerts on 9 March 1828 was as follows: the overture to *Les Abencérages* by Cherubini; the Kyrie and the Gloria of the *Messe du Sacre* by the same composer; a duet from Rossini's *Semiramis*; the fourth violin concerto by Rode, and the Third Symphony, *Eroica*, by Beethoven. Similar programmes were being performed almost everywhere in Europe.

It is, in any case, worthy of note that Beethoven became the object of a real cult after his death in 1827. It was a cult that had certainly started earlier, in the opening years of the century, with, for example, E.T.A. Hoffmann's articles in the *Allgemeine Musikzeitung*, and with Brentano's poem *Nachklänge Beethovenscher Musik* (Echoes of Beethoven's Music), but it gathered momentum until the end of the 19th century and beyond. French writers made a particular contribution to it: George Sand in her *Lettres d'un voyageur* spread the image of a 'pastoral and rustic' Beethoven, Berlioz in his famous accounts of the *Débats* credited the opinion of a Shakespearean Beethoven, and Hugo in *William Shakespeare* eulogised the visionary aspect of the composer:

'Those dazzling symphonies, tender, delicate, profound, those miracles of harmony, those radiant resonances of note and song, emerge from a head in which the ear is dead. It is as though one were to see a blind god creating suns.'

This probably gave rise to the tendency to see Beethoven as a Romantic, which, in the strict sense, he never was.

There were other forms of music that were, at the time, successfully performed more or less all over Europe. There were the seemingly 'gothic', mediaeval works: thus there was a revival of J. S. Bach, presided over by Mendelssohn from the time of the famous performance of the *Saint Matthew Passion* in Berlin in 1829; and also a cult of 16th century religious music – Wackenroder, Hoffmann and Hugo all extolled Palestrina. This explains the success of an institution like that of Choron in Paris during the years of the Restoration, and the reason for the continued popularity of Handel in England. Such enthusiasm inevitably left its mark on the work of contemporary composers: Mendelssohn, Schumann, Liszt and Brahms tried their hand at writing fugues in the style of Bach, as well as chorales and even masses inspired by plainsong. Compared with these durable favourites, the 'contemporary' performances of music seem of only secondary importance to us: the paraphrases, transcriptions, variations and concertos by virtuosi of the piano or the violin only lasted from the time of Paganini to Liszt's last concerts, in the mid-1840s. Such was the real concert music of the Romantics. It was not until much later that Schumann, Liszt and even Schubert were acknowledged as Romantic composers.

Portrait of Paganini by Delacroix   *Portrait of Tamburini* in *I Puritani* by Bellini

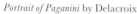

The interpreters of Romantic music

Many of the performers of the music preferred by the Romantic era are worthy of note. The Romantic age was the golden age of virtuosi.

There were the violinists: Viotti, who trained some remarkable pupils in Paris; Kreutzer, to whom Beethoven dedicated his famous Sonata; Rode, who was also a successful composer; and Habeneck who gradually spent more and more time conducting, at which he excelled (he was also the head of the Société des Concerts du Conservatoire). The most attractive figures were those of Baillot and Paganini. The former played a role that is all but forgotten today: a teacher at the Paris Conservatoire, soloist, first violin of a quartet that he founded and which became famous, it was Baillot who travelled throughout Europe to give legendary performances of chamber music by Haydn, Mozart, Beethoven, Boccherini and Onslow. Fétis, a stern critic of the day, praised Baillot's musical sensitivity, intelligence, taste, culture and artistic and moral integrity. His favourite pupil was Beriot, the husband of Maria Malibran. Paganini was the very incarnation of the Romantic virtuoso, a heroic, mysterious figure. Travelling to give concerts all over Europe, he exerted a decisive influence on Liszt, as well as on Schumann, Brahms and many other composers. Writers evoked him in their work: Heine in the *Florentine Nights*, and Gautier in a poem entitled *The Soul of Paganini*. His great technical prowess considerably advanced the art of the violin.

Portrait of Giuditta Pasta in Semiramis by Rossini

Portrait of Adolphe Nourrit in *William Tell* by Rossini

There were also a great number of pianists. The first to appeal to the public were Steibelt, Pleyel, Moscheles, Stephen Heller and Kalkbrenner. Their compositions are still occasionally performed today. It was perhaps Stephen Heller, born in Hungary, who inaugurated the movement of rapprochement between music and letters that was so characteristic of the period. He drew his inspiration from the heroines of Jean-Paul Richter and dedicated his works to them: his *Impromptus* op. 7, for example, to Liane von Froulay. These pianists also forced technique towards ever-increasing levels of difficulty, and developed virtuosity for its own sake. Sometimes this striving for ever greater feats of prowess rendered great services to music generally, by giving wider hearings to orchestral works transcribed for solo piano. Moscheles, for example, transcribed Beethoven's *Fidelio* for piano in 1814 and may have contributed to bringing to the attention of French audiences a work that was only rarely performed at the Opéra.

Then there followed the generation of pianist-composers that we know and admire: Liszt, Chopin, and Schumann, all born around 1810. There were also those whose names are known because of their rivalry with the leaders: Thalbert, of course, but also Marie Pleyel, the Egeria of Berlioz and of Nerval, and Dreyschok, who inspired Heine to speak sarcastically of his 'brutality'. Although there had been famous 'quarrels' in the preceding centuries (quarrels about sonnets in the 17th century, quarrels between the supporters of Gluck and the supporters of Piccini in the 18th century), in this period the jousting and rivalry for public favour was now confined to the performers, which in itself was a sign of the times.

Finally, the human voice offered some incomparable 'stars'. Romanticism marked the end of an interpretative style, the *bel canto*, that is to say a sparkling, light and flowing style of singing, which is hard for us to imagine today. Even the singers of Rossini and Bellini could not match the prowess of the castrati and some of the *prime donne* of the late 18th century. Stendhal in his *Vies des musiciens* solemnly deplored the decadence of the *canto spianato*. This singing style, which neglected dramatic truth in favour of virtuosity, corresponded perfectly to the Romantic mentality, and led to all the ornamentations and embellishments that German music and also the music of Verdi so firmly proscribed.

The French school of singing of the Romantic years has been all but forgotten. The names of Madame Branchu and Dérivis, who interpreted Gluck, Salieri and Spontini at the Académie de Musique, may be familiar. But the undisputed star of French opera was Adolphe Nourrit. He made his debut in 1821, at the age of nineteen, in the role of Pylade in *Iphigenie en Tauride* by Gluck. Nourrit dominated the musical life of Paris until 1837; he created all the leading roles in *La Muette de Portici*, *William Tell*, *Robert le Diable*, *La Juive*, and *Les Huguenots*. From 1834, he also introduced Schubert's work in France. He even collaborated in the libretto or in the dramatic development of some operas. He died an unhappy man after being replaced at the Opéra by his rival Duprez, who had neither his intelligence nor his finesse. There was also Madame Cinti-Damoreau, who created *Le Philtre* and *Le Domino-noir* by Auber and, finally, the famous Cornélie Falcon who played the role of Alice in *Robert le Diable*, Aurélie in *Gustave III* and created the part of Rachel in *La Juive*.

Separate from any school, and perhaps a school in itself, was the famous Garcia family, originally from Spain, but who lived in Paris from 1801. The father, Manuel, who also wrote zarzuelas, made his debut in Paër's *Griselda*. In Italy, he created the tenor roles in *Elisabetta* and *Il Barbiere* by Rossini. But his greatest triumphs were in Paris, where he gave some unforgettable performances in Mozart operas, in particular as Almaviva and as *Don Juan*. Manuel Garcia was also the tutor of his two astonishing daughters: Maria, la Malibran, who died as the result of a riding accident in 1836, and Pauline, wife of Viardot, director of the Théâtre Italien, and friend of Turgenev. The two sisters dazzled the audiences of Europe and America from around 1830.

The brilliance of the Italian school of singers is legendary. Pride of place must certainly go to Giuditta Pasta, who was born in Milan and was a friend of Stendhal; before la Malibran, and for different reasons, she symbolised all the generosity and the demanding perfection of Romantic singing. She was a great dramatic soprano of considerable versatility (whereas Malibran was a mezzo). She sang all the Rossini roles, although she had to vie for them with the composer's wife, Isabella Colbran. Bellini wrote *Norma* for la Pasta, and the lyrical duets of Pasta and Malibran have passed into opera legend. La Pasta was also a remarkable actress; she had great respect for the music and had mastered all the theatrical demands of her art. Her greatest role was probably that of Tancredi (while la Malibran's was Desdemona).

Giulia Grisi, the beautiful soprano and actress, prolonged the myth of the Romantic soprano, although she lost in creative originality what she gained in perfection. She sang almost everything with equal success.

Finally there was the German school. The singers whose style was probably closest to our present conception of singing in this period were Henriette Sontag, with her remarkable interpretations of Mozart (the role of Donna Elvira, for example), Wilhemine Schröder-Devrient, an excellent Fidelio who became Wagner's ideal of the perfect singer, and Jenny Lind, 'The Swedish Nightingale', who can be included in this school: they were all greatly concerned with

Portrait of La Malibran

Portrait of Cornélie Falcon in *La Juive* by Halévy

dramatic expression and scorned easy effects.

By comparison with these female voices, the men did not leave such a great impression behind them. Only a few of their names have remained legendary: Rubini, an excellent tenor for whom Bellini and Donizetti wrote tenor leads, famous also for his extravagant mannerisms; Enrico Tamberlik, the superb Italian tenor; the baritone Tamburini and the bass Lablache. There were very few Germans: the tenor Tichatschek, friend of Wagner, who created the roles of Rienzi and Tannhäuser, and Ludwig Schnorr von Carolsfeld, who was the first Tristan. In France, the only famous singer was the baritone Victor Maurel.

These, even more so than the musicians, were the stars of Romantic opera and concerts. The singer and the prima donna were real celebrities, so much so that they became the heroes and heroines of the literature of the day.

It would be true to say that, during the Romantic years, the orchestras and the conductors did not enjoy anything like the prestige that they do today. The first was probably the orchestra of the Société des Concerts du Conservatoire de Paris, founded in 1828 under the conductor Habeneck. Their performance of Beethoven was, according to Berlioz and Wagner, excellent. In fact, they did little more than follow the tradition of symphonic music in Paris which had been propagated by the concerts of sacred music under the Ancien Régime, the concerts at the Opéra and the public rehearsals at the Conservatoire under the Empire, and the rue de Cléry concerts during the Consulate. The preferred programme was always Haydn, Mozart and Beethoven.

In the German-speaking countries too, famous symphonic societies were born. In Vienna, Nicolai founded the *Philharmonische Konzerte* in 1842: this existed periodically until 1860, when the famous Vienna Philharmonia was formed. Its conductors were, in turn, Otto Nicolai, until 1847, Karl Eckert until 1860, Otto Dessoff from 1860 to 1875 and Hans Richter from 1875 to 1898. The Vienna concerts were devoted to Beethoven, Mozart and Brahms more than Schubert or Bruckner. In Berlin, various promenade concerts were given and the Philharmonia was only founded provisionally in 1867 with elements of the Bilseschen Kapelle, until 1882 when it came into being definitively under the leadership of Ludwig von Brenner. It was only then that the orchestra took the name of Berlin Philharmonic; its conductors were J. Joachim, and then Hans von Bülow. Mention should also be made of the concerts given by the orchestra of the Berlin Opera, which welcomed such illustrious artists as Mendelssohn in 1843–1844 and Wagner in 1865–1866. In Vienna and Berlin there were also choral societies of great musical virtuosity. It was in Berlin that Mendelssohn directed the performance of the *Saint Matthew Passion* by Bach in 1829. Brahms was the director of the Vienna choir.

In Italy, symphonic concerts were neither fashionable nor popular at the time. If one is to believe Stendhal, the symphonies of Mozart and Beethoven could not be successfully, or even correctly, performed, because they posed too many problems for local orchestras. Italian orchestras did, however, enjoy a great reputation for opera. The two leading orchestras were those of San Carlo in Naples and of La Scala in Milan. However, the Milan musicians, admirable in their playing of gentle melodies, seemed to lack some of the power and brio necessary in the more sustained passages. The execution of the Naples orchestra was unfailingly resolute; it was as powerful as the French orchestras, but lighter than the Viennese. Stendhal went so far as to say: '... in a perfect orchestra the violins would be French, the wind instruments German, and all the rest Italian, including the conductor.'

Nevertheless, it would be a fallacy to think that Romanticism consisted of no more than the repertoire and virtuosi. The various audiences and national centres should also be mentioned. Italy was, above all and at all levels, the land of song. Every town of any size at all had its own opera house – Rossini, Bellini, Donizetti and Verdi all had their beginnings in these little theatres. There was a system of classification of what were known as the theatres *di cartello*, and to have appeared in one of them conferred a certain rank on a singer. La Scala, San Carlo, and theatres of Turin, Rome and La Fenice in Venice were permanently *di cartello*; Florence, Bologna, Genoa, Siena, Bergamo, Reggio and Livorno were only *di cartello* for certain seasons, either during carnival, or in the Autumn. On the whole, the leading Italian musical centres were Milan and Naples, followed by Rome and Venice. It was after the first performance in Rome of the *Barbiere* in 1816 that Rossini achieved international renown. Donizetti presented his first opera, *Enrico di Burgogna* at La Fenice in Venice in 1818, but he only became really famous after his *Anna Bolena* in Milan in 1822. Bellini made his debut in Naples, Verdi in Milan.

The most remarkable feature of Italian musical life was its nationalism, which had various effects. On the one hand, Italian opera became one of the touchstones of national consciousness: Verdi played a catalytic role in this respect. It should also be remembered that La Scala, probably by reason of the Austrian presence in Milan, was the cradle of Italian Romanticism. Stendhal in *Rome, Naples et Florence* described the impassioned and fascinating atmosphere in the boxes at La Scala, where Ludovico di Breme, Monti, Berchet and Pellico would discuss new ideas and blaze with passion, as did the entire audience, to the accents of Italian music.

On the other hand, such excessive specialisation entailed a total ignorance of all non-Italian music. It was only when he came to Vienna in 1820 that Rossini discovered Beethoven, and in Paris Spontini heard the music of Gluck and Mozart for the first time in 1839. The difficulties that Liszt encountered when he gave his concerts in Milan in 1838 are well-known; he found it quite impossible to play anything but paraphrases of Rossini! Not one Romantic composer was officially performed in Italy, despite the fact that Berlioz, Liszt and Mendelssohn all lived for a time in Rome.

Music's other homeland was obviously Austria and its capital Vienna. In fact, for a long time Berlin and Munich were of little significance. Despite the presence of Spontini and Meyerbeer, the opera and symphonic concerts played in Berlin did not reach an international audience until towards the end of the century. Dresden at the time of Weber (1817 to 1826) and also of Wagner (1842 to 1848), Weimar when Liszt was Director of Music there (1848–1858), and Leipzig, where Mendelssohn revived the tradition of J. S. Bach, were all more important musical centres than Berlin. Munich only came to prominence during the brief period that Wagner spent there, at the invitation of Ludwig II of Bavaria. So, although there were musical centres in Germany, they were only temporary, and devoted to a certain type of music (either opera, or orchestral).

Vienna, by contrast, benefited from great continuity in the musical field. From Beethoven to Brahms, there was always at least one leading composer in residence, even if the city did not always accord him the honour he deserved. It should not be forgotten, for example, that Schubert only met with a certain *succès d'estime* in his own country; and that for his *Lieder*; that Schumann failed miserably there; and that Italian operas were much preferred to German ones. But it would be equally misleading to deny that it was in Vienna that the musical careers of Liszt and even Chopin were decided; that Beethoven was an object of lasting reverence and honour there; and that the battles of Wagner and Bruckner against Brahms created a very lively musical climate in the city. Vienna may not have been the capital of modernism, but it was certainly a centre of musical life during the Romantic period.

In comparison with Italy, Germany and Austria, London and Paris could perhaps be characterised by their universalism. In these relatively wealthy capitals, with their freer, more varied, and perhaps more demanding audiences, musical life rapidly became very similar to what it is today. Capitals of opera as well as symphonic music, indispensable springboards for aspiring artists, havens of tried and tested values, London and Paris were the true capitals of Romantic music.

London had a reputation for enriching its 'stars'. Chopin, in letters written during his visit to England in 1848, explained that the aristocrats and industrialists formed the basis of a society of music 'consumers'; he also described the roles of money and profit in the musical world. We know of the role of patron and impresario played by the piano manufacturers, Broadwood for instance. Because of this, London was host to all the great artists: Berlioz conducted opera and several concerts there, Liszt was accorded a royal reception, Mendelssohn, in the Handel tradition, created his oratorios (*Saint Paul* and *Elijah*), and Weber was commissioned to compose *Oberon* for Covent Garden.

In Paris, the most notable fact was probably the development of a bourgeois audience for modern art. Doctor Véron, the famous director of the Paris Opéra during the reign of Louis-

Philippe, charted this evolution: in his *Mémoires d'un bourgeois de Paris*, he claimed to have staged a great number of ballets and operas by Meyerbeer to satisfy the demands of this new audience for pomp and dazzling spectacle. This same development would also explain the proliferation of concert societies, popular concerts (the one by Musard has remained famous), musical reviews, and music publishers. It is worthy of note that a Berliner such as the publisher Schlesinger, a Rhinelander (Habeneck), a Hungarian (Liszt), a Pole (Chopin), and a Belgian (Fétis) should all have come to make their careers in Paris. The pillars of musical life were the Opéra, the Théâtre Italien, the Société des Concerts, the Conservatoire, the *Revue Musicale* and the *Gazette Musicale*, and the houses of Erard and Pleyel. Paris was perhaps the foremost of the capitals of musical Romanticism.

The musicians of the Romantic Movement

In any attempt to define Romanticism intrinsically rather than extrinsically, the first problem encountered is that of chronology. There were different, and quite distinct, Romantic generations and nothing could be more misleading than to reduce the character of Romanticism to just one of them or to imagine that one generation typified the whole movement.

The 'first generation' was that of Beethoven, Weber, Rossini and Schubert – in other words, a generation which ceased to produce work after 1830, even though it included composers whose dates extended beyond this period. Beethoven died in 1827, Schubert died prematurely in 1828, as did Weber in 1826, while Rossini did not write another opera after *William Tell* (1828). Theirs was the generation of founders: Beethoven, with his profound transformation of the sonata and the symphony, prepared the way for their modern forms; Weber and Rossini, each with his own genius and national temperament, inaugurated the Romantic opera; and Schubert, finally, perfected new forms (the *Lied*) and created the first masterpieces of the new music in every field (except opera): *Gretchen am Spinnrade* dates from 1814, and the *Unfinished Symphony* from 1822, the same year as the *Wanderer-Fantaisie*. In short, and even without going into further detail, it is easy to see that Romantic music would not have existed had it not been for Beethoven, Weber, Rossini and Schubert.

This said, the fact remains that there are unanswered questions. For example, how can Beethoven's 'Romanticism' be defined? By taking the word of Hoffmann, Balzac and Wagner, we tend to see him as the father of the new aesthetic, but this may be something of an overstatement. It should be remembered that Beethoven's aesthetic world was that of the late 18th century. Some reservations must thus be expressed as to Beethoven's 'Romanticism,' whether from a moral point of view, if we consider his humanism and idealism, or from a literary point of view – to recall the works by Gellert, Hölty and Bürger that Beethoven set to music – or from the musical point of view (by reason of his admiration for Mozart, and the esteem in which he held Cherubini). Nevertheless, even though none of his works was 'Romantic' in the strict sense of the word, he was one of the founding fathers of musical Romanticism.

First, he demonstrated a deep-seated individualism: in the domain of social or human relations, it took the form either of misanthropy or of egalitarianism. Unlike Goethe, or even Mozart, he never paid much attention to established authority: the same attitude is applied to his art, and is evident in the virtuosity and the intrinsic musical difficulty of his works. Beethoven set the rules to one side and bent them to his service, whereas Mozart or Haydn had subjected themselves to the rules, the better to overcome them. The difficulties that arose from the first performances of his symphonies and quartets proved that Beethoven was not writing for society, or for the salons, but for the progress of the art itself. This single-minded attitude of the artist to his creation was revolutionary. It was the individualism expressed in the last piano sonatas and the last quartets that was Romantic.

If Beethoven was a borderline example of the first generation of the founding fathers of the Romantic movement, the role of the other composers was more clearly defined. Rossini and Schubert could be characterised by their boldness. They were in constant quest of originality, whether in a particular genre, as when Schubert 'invented' the *Lied*, on the level of detail, as in Rossini's instrumentation, or with Rossini again, in the various provocations that he hurled at his audience (for instance by composing another *Barber of Seville*, even though Paesiello had already written one). Their disdain for fashionable society led to confrontation as well as admiration. It is often overlooked that both Rossini and Schubert wanted above all to write the music that they themselves enjoyed and that their audiences sometimes reacted very differently. A last feature of this first Romantic generation was its nationalism. Weber was the best example of this: he worked in turn as a writer, conductor, poet and composer, and all for the greater glory of German art. From this viewpoint, one could refer to the battle of *Freischütz*, as one does to the battle of *Hernani*. But Weber was not alone. Rossini was every bit as nationalistic, in his faults as well as in his most striking qualities. This can be measured by his scorn for dramatic impetus and for Shakespearean tragedy as demonstrated by the score of *Otello*, and also by the somewhat laboured buffoonery of *La Gazza Ladra*. Stendhal, writing about the overture to this opera, said that it showed 'a total absence of subtlety ... complete absence of refinement and elegance'. In fact, this is where one becomes most aware of the breach between Cimarosa and Rossini. There was an 'Italian-ness' in Cimarosa, but it was more or less shared by Mozart; the Italianism of Rossini was as patent and polemical as Weber's Germanism.

However, it should not be thought that this generation sprang up in a musical void. Alongside these artistic ventures should be set those of a French school, formed at the very end of the 18th century. The school was represented by Boieldieu, Lesueur, Méhul and Auber and its operas formed the outline of a new musical direction. There is no doubt that Spontini, who lived in Paris from 1803 until 1820, served as the model for the school. It is significant that one of the first articles ever written by Victor Hugo was a critique of *Olympie* by Spontini (1820). In his earlier works, *La Vestale* (1807) and *Fernand Cortez* (1809), Spontini had already rejected the classical conception of opera, with its themes of love or of mythology. In its place, he created the grandest of grand opera, based on historical subjects, sustained by a powerfully resonant score, with striking crescendos and broad vocal ensembles. Spontini created a new type of opera, one that inclined towards melodrama.

Boieldieu, too, was well aware of the transformations of public taste. His *Dame Blanche* of 1825, in collaboration with Scribe, was, after a fashion, Walter Scott set to music: the operatic historical novel, just as *Jean de Paris* (1812) had been an earlier musical interpretation of the 'troubadour style'.

The first real revolutionary was Méhul. In his work we can trace clearly the transition from the lyrical theatre of Gluck to the Romantic opera of Weber and Berlioz. In his conception of opera which he envisaged above all as dramatic action, and in his desire to achieve expressiveness at every level, Méhul presaged the creation of the 'total' masterpiece, that was the dream and ambition of every dramatist of the time. Berlioz certainly understood this and said so in the homage that he paid to Méhul (*Les Soirées de l'orchestre*, a 'biography of Méhul'). Méhul's first work, *Euphrosine* (1790), was one of great dramatic power and sincerity. His later choice of subject matter denoted his tendency towards Romanticism: *Joanna* (1802) and *Helena* (1803) celebrated the troubadour style, *Uthal* (1806) drew on Ossianism, and *Joseph* (1807) pointed towards the picturesque and exoticism. Beyond the titles, it is interesting to note that

Wilhemine Schroder and Cornet in *La Muette de Portici* by Auber

Méhul set his librettists dark and intricate plots, and that the musical language was an attempt to reach the level of such dramatic preoccupations: for example, the instrumentation for strings in *Uthal* consisted solely of violas and basses, which gave it a more melancholy tone.

Lesueur and Auber can be placed into the same category, but only for very specific works. As early as 1803, *Ossian ou les Bardes* by Lesueur endowed opera with new colour. As for *La Muette de Portici* by Auber (1828), Wagner explained its modernism: 'Rarely has an artistic event borne a closer relationship with a universal fact: the spirit of 1830! It surprised one as something that was absolutely new. One had never before seen an opera that was so alive. Auber's score succeeded in maintaining a glowing heat like a flow of lava ... For the first time a crowd actually took part in the action ... Not a trace of hollow pathos ... A sonority of such striking quality that no theatre orchestra had ever been heard to perform anything to compare with it.'

Thus, between the first and the second Romantic generations, there was a group of Parisian composers of opera who, with a few specific works, served as catalysts in the Romantic movement. Spontini, Boieldieu, Méhul, Auber and Lesueur influenced the work of Rossini, Weber, Wagner, Berlioz and perhaps even Schubert.

Marie and Paul Taglioni in the ballet *La Sylphide* by F.G. Lepaulle, 1834

The second and third Romantic generations should be considered almost simultaneously. The second generation could be defined as that of the composers who were born in the years immediately before or after the turn of the century, and whose names only became known after 1830. It would include Meyerbeer, born in 1791, whose great successes took place in Paris after the July Revolution (*Robert le Diable* dates from 1831, *Les Huguenots* from 1836); Berlioz, born in 1803, who shot to fame with the *Symphonie fantastique* of 1830; Donizetti, born in 1797, whose first work of note was *Anna Bolena* in 1830; and Bellini, who was born in 1801 and died in 1835.

It is tempting to describe this as a 'Parisian' generation, as it was in Paris, or through Paris that these composers sought and achieved success. Meyerbeer came to live in Paris in 1826, and firmly insisted that all his new productions should be staged at the Académie de Musique. He cultivated Hugo, Dumas, Musset and George Sand in order, so to speak , to earn his credentials as a Romantic. Bellini arrived in Paris in 1833; his last work, *I Puritani*, was staged there and met with triumphant success, while his earlier works were equally triumphantly revived at the Théâtre des Italiens. He was emulated by Donizetti who came to Paris in about 1840. Donizetti adapted his *Poliuto* for production in Paris as *Les Martyrs*, wrote a new opera in French, *La Fille du Régiment*, and then *La Favorite* and *Don Pasquale* for the theatres of Paris. The differences he had with Victor Hugo over the staging of his opera *Lucrezia Borgia*, based on the latter's work, are also well-known.

This generation was also 'Parisian' in that since it essentially consisted of opera composers, its theatrical style was formed under the influence of Romantic drama. 'Grand' opera also sought to mix the registers, drew on local colour and favoured subjects borrowed from contemporary literature or fashion (*I Puritani* and *Lucia di Lammermoor* were inspired by Walter Scott, *Les Huguenots* was based on Merimée, *Lucrezia Borgia* on Hugo). Above all, grand opera sought to be supremely expressive and endeavoured to be a complete entertainment in itself; this was the case of *Robert le Diable* on which Scribe collaborated with Deschamps and Meyerbeer with Ciceri, because all the arts, and all the registers had to be used. The problem of the relations between word and sound, text and music preoccupied Bellini, Meyerbeer and Berlioz: works such as *Norma*, *Les Huguenots* and *Faust* (1829–1845) provide as many different answers to the question. But, on the whole, there was a chronological, and to some extent aesthetic and geographical homogeneity, in the second generation of Romantic composers.

The third generation consists of composers born around 1810: Mendelssohn, who was born in 1809, Schumann and Chopin, born in 1810, Liszt, born in 1811, and Wagner and Verdi, born in 1813. This generation perhaps represents the apotheosis of the Romantic movement in music. It certainly benefited from the militant efforts of its immediate predecessors, grew up in their shadow, often admired them, and sometimes even collaborated with them. But above all, this third generation strengthened and secured all that had hitherto been uncertain or tentative. It was undoubtedly the most famous generation in the eyes of posterity; but it might perhaps fairly be described, after the manner of its senior member, Mendelssohn, as a Romantic 'Classicist' generation.

This generation produced what are remembered as the purest masterpieces: the compositions for piano by Chopin, Schumann and Liszt, the symphonies and symphonic poems of Mendelssohn, Liszt and Schumann, the oratorios of Mendelssohn and Schumann, and the operas of Wagner and Verdi. They were achieved at the price of some modifications in relation to the work of the preceding generations.

For example, it might justifiably be said that in the years from 1830 to 1840, the piano and the concerto for piano held pride of place, and produced great variety: Schumann's *Car-*

Robert le Diable by Meyerbeer, cloister scene, Act III, scenery by Ciceri

nival and the beginning of Liszt's *Années de Pélerinage* date from 1835, 1838 saw the *Transcendental Etudes* by Liszt and Schumann's *Kreisleriana*, and 1839 Chopin's *Preludes*. The years from 1840 to 1850 were those of the *Lieder* and of chamber music: Schumann's *Frauenliebe und Leben* dates from 1840, Mendelssohn's *Trio* in C minor from 1845, his Quartet in F minor as well as Schumann's Fourth Quartet from 1847. The symphonies of Schumann and the symphonic poems of Liszt range from 1841 onwards (1841 being the date of Schumann's First Symphony). At the same time, in the field of opera, Wagner set out by placing himself in relation to Meyerbeer, and Verdi in relation to Donizetti. Each of these two great composers was initially feeling his way in a phase which did not produce what we would regard as characteristic works, before they defined a true style of their own: *Lohengrin* dates from 1850, *Tristan* was completed in 1858, while *Rigoletto*, *Trovatore* and *Traviata* date from 1851–1853.

The fourth generation, if one can so describe it, was that of the descendants and followers of Romanticism. It would encompass primarily the leaders of the national schools or the principal initiators of a trend: Bruckner (born 1824, died 1896) and Wolf (born 1860, but stopped writing in 1897) who proceeded from Wagnerism and illustrate Austrian music; Brahms (born in 1833) whose Romanticism flowed from Beethoven and ´Schumann; Tchaikovsky (born 1840, died 1893) who was the most Westernised of the Russians; Grieg (born in 1843), the leader of the Norwegian school; Smetana and Dvořák representing the Czech school; Gounod and Bizet, Reyer and Saint-Saëns, all these were in their different ways

Il Trovatore by Verdi, scene of the challenge

marked by the influence of Liszt, Wagner and Berlioz.

A motley gathering? No, because these composers knew the great masters of Romantic music personally, attended their schools and developed the forms that their masters had created. Thus the symphonic poem of Saint-Saëns or Smetana flowed directly from Liszt, Bizet's operas would not have existed had it not been for Berlioz, and all the works of Brahms would be inconceivable without Schumann.

It would be a mistake to think that these heirs of the Romantic movement squandered their inheritance in any way. On the contrary, they brought it to fruition; either by bringing Romanticism back to national roots which rejuvenated the movement, as was the case with the Czech composers; or by taking each form to its furthest limits as Brahms did in his last piano compositions (op. 116/9), as Wolf did in his *Lieder*, and Bruckner in his cyclical symphonies. As a result, there was a clear need for a revolution of tonal language. Even in opera, where the global Romantic heritage (and not just that of Wagner) was greater than in any other genre, the representatives of the fourth generation, to their great credit, created works that were not only vivid but truly original: one has only to think of *Carmen* (1875) or of *Eugene Onegin* (1878). In the field of opera, there was still formidable competition from the third generation, since Wagner was composing until 1882 (*Parsifal*) and Verdi until 1893 (*Otello* dates from 1887, *Falstaff* from 1893).

Harmony and melody

The most basic characteristic of classical melody was its metre, that is to say its division into segments of two, four or eight bars. This structure, which was almost always apparent o perceptible in the themes of classical music, acquired the force of law in musical doctrine Romanticism, while not abandoning it, blurred and softened its edges to replace it with a more flowing line. Beethoven had already, when necessary, taken this liberty, in the Adagio of hi twelfth quartet, for instance, but the Romantic composers increasingly used this practice: the most striking is perhaps that of the introductory theme to the *Symphonie fantastique* in which Berlioz wanted to evoke the candour of adolescence. Other examples are the introduction to the *Fourth Symphony* by Schumann, the *Benediction of God in the Wilderness* by Liszt, and the *Lullaby* by Chopin; while the dreamlike opening of Mendelssohn's *Scottish Symphony*, while observing traditional metre, seems to flow almost infinitely.

In addition to the principle of metre, was the exclusive division in classical composition into common, or four-four time, and three-four time. To this, the Romantics added, albeit rarely, five-four, and even seven-four time. The first exponent was probably Reicha who wrote choruses in five-four time; Boieldieu imitated him in the theme of Georges in *La Dame blanche* while Chopin adopted five-four time in the Larghetto of his First Sonata in C minor.

In contrast to this new freedom which made musical structure more supple by extending the flow of the romantic melody, another trend appeared, which probably emerged from the increasingly predominant symphonic style, especially that of Beethoven, in his last sonatas the caesura. This is the charm of Schumann's pieces for piano (*Kreisleriana*, *Papillons*) where the melody sparkles in a thousand different styles, before it disappears.

As well as strictly observing metre, classical melody also firmly adhered to tonality. With out abandoning it altogether, Romanticism tended to break away from it, either by inflection or by frequent modulations. Fétis was the first to point out this phenomenon in the style c Chopin; but the best example was that of Wagnerian chromatism.

It is worth noting briefly that this liberation of melody corresponded exactly to what wa happening in the field of lyricism. The work of the artist was becoming more and more subjec tive. These features were particularly characteristic of German Romanticism, and of Berlioz Italian music, which was exclusively theatrical, seemed initially to fight shy of them; the Italian opera of the Romantic years (up to the time of Verdi's *Trovatore*) preserved the metr and the character of melody intact. Its success can largely be attributed to this faithful adher ence to tradition. However, if one compares the operas of Rossini, Donizetti and Bellini with the older Italian opera as characterised by Cimarosa, Paesiello, Paer and Mayr, there is in fac a distinct evolution. The musical language shines with new fire: there is a tenderness in th melody that was unknown in the preceding period. While it still flattered the instrumenta agility of the singer, it also demanded more of the sensual quality of the human voice. It wa dedicated, above all, to the expression of love, multiplying those passages in thirds and sixth in the duets, tender interludes of which Balzac, in *Massimilla Doni*, praised the expressiv power, the symbol of two hearts beating as one. Such pieces have remained legendary: 'Cast diva' from *Norma*, the Quartet from *I Puritani*, the sextet from *Lucia di Lammermoor*. They ar often criticised today, but one should remember that, as early as 1808 in a report to th Académie des Beaux-Arts, Méhul prayed for the infusion of warmer and younger blood int the barrenness and pallor of French music. It was Italy that provided this revitalising force.

Because of the many correlations of nature and usage between harmony and melody, on would expect them to progress along parallel lines. There are two features which could sum marily define the harmony of classical music: on the one hand, strict observation of mode and key and on the other, the clear contrast between consonance and dissonance. Classical melody was always hinged on the keynote, while Romantic melody happily moved further away from it. The common chord was the basis of classical harmony; but it was so no longer, or certainly less so, in Romantic music. There are two famous examples of this in Beethoven's work: the return to the first theme in the *Eroica Symphony*, and the transition between the second scherzo and the finale of the *C minor Symphony*. The Romantic composers also liked to use modulations to distant keys: there are many examples in Schumann and in the *Symphonie fantastique*. Yet another feature of Romantic harmony was the more frequent use of sequences, namely harmonic phrases which were repeated first in one key, then in another, preferably in an ascending scale. Fine, and particularly expressive, examples are provided by the last finale of *Norma*, and the finale of the third act of *Tristan*, just before the death of Isolde.

Although the schools continued to teach the same rules of harmony, this new characteristic of Romantic harmony was noted by the theoreticians. Harmonic 'restlessness', if one can call it that, began to appear in the musical literature, which no longer considered music simply as a mathematical science. Lacépède, a composer himself, wrote a *Poétique de la musique* in 1785, in which he refused to accept emotion alone as a musical rule. In 1816, Monsigny, a very curious man in many respects, advocated the acceptance of chromatism, even though diatonism was the very foundation of all classical harmony. Monsigny asserted that chromatism belonged, *de facto* and *de jure*, to the scale and to pitch. Reicha, in 1818, in his *Cours de composition musicale ou Traité complet d'harmonie pratique*, moderated the absolute proscription of parallel octaves and fifths: he wanted to admit only that which was pleasing to the ear. Twenty years later, Colet, in his *Panharmonie musicale* (1839), recommended the use of consecutive dissonances to depict 'the disorder of passion'.

Counterpoint

Counterpoint, which is the art of playing two, or even several, themes simultaneously, and which finds its application in the fugue, was also a particular feature of Romantic music. The composers of the time adored the fugue. Examples in Beethoven's work are the monumental fugue that ends the Sonata op. 106, the fugue for quartet later published separately under the number op. 137, and, in the *Ninth Symphony*, the passage in the final movement when the chorus divides to sing simultaneously the two clear and contrasting themes ('Freude, schone Götterfunken' and 'Seid umschlungen'). Fugatos abounded in the last Sonatas and Quartets.

This example was to become widely copied in the Romantic movement. Berlioz gave a dazzling illustration of it in the last movement of the *Symphonie Fantastique*, when the round-dance of the witches' Sabbath and the 'Dies Irae' are heard together. Liszt was to do the same in *Tasso*, in the *Faust Symphony*, in the *Preludes*, and in the *Battle of the Huns*. There are reminders of it in Wagner too, early on in the overture to *Tannhäuser*, and later in the overture to *Die Meistersinger von Nürnberg* and the finale of *Götterdämmerung*.

This infatuation with counterpoint found its way into musical education. The great Reicha, professor at the Conservatoire, who died in 1836, trained Berlioz, Liszt, Onslow, Gounod and Franck in the rules of counterpoint. Based on thirty-six fugues that he himself had written, Reicha taught a freer and more modern doctrine than that of classical fugue and counterpoint.

Thus, from this brief outline, it will be clear that the aim of the Romantic movement, its teachers and its pupils alike, was to create music of maximum influence and effect, and to allow greater freedom of invention; to concentrate on the power of music to move the listener, rather than on the observance of purely formal procedures.

From this point of view, a form like that of the variation must almost have been the 'smash hit' of the time. Previously, the variation was a game in which the ornamentation always remained superficial; it was simply a question of displaying one's agility. But now emotion was introduced into an operation which, in form, seemed more akin to metamorphosis or alchemy than to hide-and-seek. Beethoven particularly, in his *Variations on a waltz by Diabelli* (1822), showed the way towards the dislocation of the initial theme. He adopted this form of development in several of his late works: the Andante of the *Ninth Symphony*, the Arietta of the Sonata op. 111, the Andante of the Quartet in C sharp minor. Now at last, music became as contemplative and thoughtful as it was, on the level of form, abundantly inventive.

The Romantic composers followed along the way that Beethoven had shown them, and none of them shone more brightly than Schumann. In his youth, he raised this thematic dislocation to an almost defiant level with his improvisations and variations, taking as his themes series of notes dictated by allusions from outside the field of music (*Variations on the name of Abegg*, variations on Asch in *Carnaval*). In so doing, he introduced a whimsical element that was far more spontaneous than the *Variations on a thème by Diabelli*, in an intentional analogy with the capricious and whimsical outbursts of Jean-Paul Richter, whom he greatly admired. Later, in 1834, Schumann, who was then twenty-four, composed the *Symphonic Studies* on a theme by Baron von Fricken. This work was an exercise of musical rhetoric that was far from being scholastic, for Schumann, adding to the title *Symphonic Studies* the words 'in the form of variations', was warning his audience that he had taken liberties with form. The successive pieces were ornamental and decorative without completely altering the original theme. He displayed greater audacity with his *Symphonic Variations* for two pianos, in which he proved himself a worthy successor to Beethoven in the field of the amplifying variation. Brahms in his *Variations on a theme by Handel* (1861) and his *Variations on a theme by Paganini* (1863) exploited the same possibility, whereas the *Variations sérieuses* by Mendelssohn (1841) were more akin to the decorative style of the *Symphonic Studies* by Schumann. Many more examples can be found among the works of Brahms, Schumann, Mendelssohn and Liszt, including variations for the piano as well as orchestral variations. One extreme example is the *Sonata in B minor* by Liszt. In this colossal work, which dates from 1853 and frees the sonata form from its traditional constraints, the multiple transformations of the three main themes within a half-an-hour performance represent a true musical feat.

Thus the Romantic period's love of the variation undoubtedly springs from the fact that it is a form particularly apt for the expression of contrasting emotions, while at the same time representing a perpetual renewal of creative imagination.

Instrumentation

Instrumentation is the last area in which we owe the creation of new effects to the Romantic movement. This was not a matter that was of interest only to the experts: contemporary audiences were aware that they were witnessing an evolution in the use of the orchestra. As early as 1813, the unusual impetuosity of the brass in *Tancredi* earned the young Rossini the nickname of '*signor vacarmini*'; Bertram's trombone call in the cloister scene of *Robert le Diable* by Meyerbeer imprints its stamp of terror on the whole opera. Contemporary caricatures of

'*Il Signor Tambourossini or the new music*'

Berlioz all depict him at the head of his musicians, whipping up storms of brass and thunderous bursts from the orchestra. The development of the orchestra in many respects reflected that of the Romantic era. Moreover, if the preceding periods had accumulated treatise upon treatise on counterpoint, harmony and acoustics, it was the Romantic era that inspired the first *Traité d'instrumentation*, by Berlioz, the most passionate of Romantics.

The innovations of the Romantic orchestra were perhaps less manifest in the pure symphony (with the exception of Berlioz), where it claimed – in the work of Weber, Schubert, Mendelssohn and Brahms – only to succeed to the Beethoven symphony, than in programme music, and, above all, in the theatre. Moveover, problems of orchestration have to be seen in relation to the purely technical problems of the manufacture of musical instruments, and even the invention of new products. All the instruments, apart from the strings, benefited from technical progress which increased their power ten-fold and facilitated virtuosity. One has only to think of the piano, modified by Erard, the harp, the whole range of brass instruments which were studied, in particular, by the famous Mr Sax, the cor anglais (invented in the 18th century), or of the bass clarinet. At the same time, there was a temptation to increase considerably the effects, power, and number of musicians of the orchestra.

'*A Concert in the Year 1846.*' Caricature of Berlioz conducting a concert

These changes had a two-fold effect. They brought some bright or deep new colours to the range, and intensified the power, density and balance of sound. The elements of middle tessitura were developed; the strings benefited from a counter-balance that was advantageous to the whole orchestra. In the theatre, the orchestra grew richer not only in brilliancy, but also in range and intensity; best illustrated perhaps by the Wagnerian orchestra, with effects such as those of the cor anglais at the beginning of the third act of *Tristan und Isolde*, or by the famous trumpets in Verdi's *Aida*. There is perhaps a parallel between this evolution of musical sound and the evolution of language which, in literature, was adding flesh to its bones and growing ever more vigorous.

At the same time as it was enriching the ensemble, the orchestra also threw into relief and accentuated the expression of the particular timbre of some of its individual instruments. Whereas the symphony had favoured thematic exchanges, Romanticism set up a dialogue between instruments, and played with contrasts of timbre far more than with contrasts of musical subject. Even Boieldieu in his overture to *Le Petit Chaperon rouge* (Little Red Riding Hood) indicated in a note to the score that Red Riding Hood's conversation with the wolf was to be evoked by a dialogue between instruments (the wolf being represented by the bassoon and

Red Riding Hood either by the flute, or by the violins). And one could cite a great many other examples; composers such as Weber, Rossini, Meyerbeer and Berlioz, when they wanted to emphasise the action or the emotions of a particular character, would underline his theme by doubling it with a solo instrument that would detach itself from the body of the orchestra: for example, the viola in *Harold en Italie* by Berlioz.

One could perhaps argue that these instrumental solos were not infrequently found in classical religious or dramatic music. But there are two major differences: firstly, the orchestra as a whole had not developed to anything approaching the same extent, and secondly, such solos always and only took on the concerted character of *obbligato* instruments. By contrast, with Weber, Rossini, Meyerbeer and Berlioz, the isolation of the soloist, and the timbre of his instrument, adopted a completely new dramatic character. It was part of the 'programme' or the 'staging' of the musical work. The Romantic conception of the concerto, namely as a work of oppositions rather than of unison, can be seen in the same light.

Composers of the Romantic movement had marked preferences for certain instruments. There was the horn, used by Weber (the first chords of *Freischütz*, the three first notes of *Oberon*), Boieldieu (voices taking up the harmonies assigned to the horns in *La Dame Blanche*), and Mendelssohn (in the beautiful nocturne of *A Midsummer Night's Dream*, developed like a vocal lied, in which the solo horn represents the voice of Nature). The clarinet was another favourite, for which there were some illustrious Mozartian antecedents. Weber wrote concertos for the instrument, and the clarinet played the central theme of Max in the overture to *Freischütz*, and that of Huon in the overture of *Oberon*. Later, Wagner gave it the Tannhäuser theme in the overture to *Tannhäuser*; and, recognising the instrument's mysterious and lyrical sonority, Brahms composed his Quintet with clarinet and his sonatas for clarinet and piano. Finally, there is the clarinet call at the end of Schumann's *Manfred*: the instrument rises, out of a diminuendo of horns, like a voice crying out alone in the desert.

Another favoured instrument was the cor anglais, which strengthened the penetrating timbre of the oboe with a kind of trembling stricken weight. Berlioz used it in *Rob Roy*, in the overture to *Carnaval romain* (Cellini's theme), and in *La Damnation de Faust* (the ritornello of the abandoned Marguerite). It appears in Schumann's *Manfred* and in Wagner's *Tristan*. Deeper wind instruments, such as the bass clarinet, double-bassoon and tuba were to bring more profound expression to more severe or menacing emotions, in the work of Meyerbeer in particular. Of the family of string instruments, the viola was accorded favoured treatment: *Harold en Italie* by Berlioz was, in fact, a concerto for viola; while Méhul in his opera *Uthal* did not use any strings higher than the viola, in order to convey a feeling of interiority to the musical sonority. Marschner followed his example in the scene from the second act of *Hans Heiling*, where a mother, anxiously awaiting the return of her daughter who is late home from the forest at night, listens to the voices of the dark.

Needless to say, all these examples should not be taken in isolation. They merely illustrate the fact that the Romantic orchestra added to the consideration of musical enjoyment or balance, with which classical music was chiefly concerned, an expressive specification of instruments, either in groups or isolated, depending on the nature and effect of their tone. In every field and form, the Romantic movement seemed to be drawn towards two quite opposite poles. On the one hand, it wanted to use external effects to create the most striking impression possible, while on the other hand, it took great pleasure in meditation and introspection. The orchestra echoed these dual aims: at times it was fuller and more brilliant than that of previous periods, at times it ventured into as yet unexplored areas. The orchestra, more than the human voice or the piano, and instrumentation diversified and enriched as it was – more than

any other form of music, symbolised the Romantic movement, and is the field in which it ha
left us its most precious heritage.

The different musical genres

On the innovations of form that it was putting into practice, Romanticism imprinted it
own, new stamp of musical expression. First, it brought about radical changes to the sym
phony, which represented the flowering of classical art, and to the sonata, the quartet anc
related styles of chamber music. Emotion and dramatic expression increasingly became th
most important features of the symphony. Not that this emotion and expression were absolute
ly new, but it was Beethoven who, by his use of them, gave a radical and irreversible characte
to the course of musical development. The titles he gave to his symphonies, like *Eroica* anc
Pastoral bear witness to this, even though both Haydn nor Mozart had appreciated the value o
titles. But it was the very nature of Beethoven's inspiration and style that was so extraordinar
and hitherto unheard-of: the brusqueness of his themes, the clash of contrasts, and the press
ing density of his thematic work. For Tieck, Jean-Paul Richter and Hoffmann, Romanticism
had already reached its full realisation in the Fifth Symphony (1806). But the *Eroica*, whict
pre-dated the Symphony by three years, would be an equally conclusive example.

In the opinion of Weber, that most ardent of Romantics, the Seventh Symphony (1812)
overstepped all bounds and brought Beethoven's reason into question. The Ninth Symphony
which came three years after *Freischütz* and one year after *Euryanthe*, thus belonged clearly and
completely to the Romantic period. Its Romanticism perhaps resides less in the innovation
that the addition of a final chorus represented, than in the sense of tension, almost of distress
that permeates the whole of the first movement, and especially in the pregnant and moving
pauses when the themes of the first three movements are recalled, before the finale. Thes
pauses attest to the erosion of classical forms and the necessity for a renewal in symphon
ic music – whence the final chorus. Thus, with this symphony, Beethoven had provided a
terminus ad quem, beyond which the symphonic form could not go without disintegrating.

So it is that Beethoven's successors, when they composed symphonies, seemed so far
behind him. The symphonic development of Schubert, Mendelssohn, Schumann, and even o
Brahms, does not offer as tight or as solid a musical fabric; they did not reveal anything
approaching the same knowledge of musical limitations and the same desire to transcend
them. The solution was to be that of the Brucknerian symphony (or the Berliozian symphony
in France), namely the implementation of a cyclical form, to replace the sonata form, with two
themes.

Furthermore, the innovation brought about by Beethoven with the chorus of the Nintr
Symphony has remained unparalleled. There is no doubt that, in the *Faust Symphony* by Liszt
the final chorus is one of incomparable originality, but the symphony itself, divided as it is into
three sections each depicting one of the three principal characters, is more of a symphonic
poem than a symphony proper. It is perhaps the symphonies of Schumann and Brahms that
are the best illustration of the legacy of Beethoven in German music. These works are all of a
great lyricism of inspiration, beautifully and glowingly orchestrated, and they represent a
sincere attempt to conform to the traditional rules of development. In France, too, there were
many fine illustrations of the symphonic form. Names such as those of Gossec (who died in
1829, one year before the *Symphonie Fantastique*), Cherubini (for his overture to *Abencérages*),
Reicha, Onslow and Bizet should not be forgotten. Inheriting more perhaps from Haydn than

from Beethoven, the symphonies of these various composers are well constructed and well instrumented works; a convincing spirit flowed through them, even if it was not one of frenzied passion.

Frenzied passion serves well to define Berlioz. With the *Symphonie Fantastique*, he seemed to have reached the very peak of Romanticism. The confidentiality of Beethoven was succeeded by the exhibitionism or, to be kinder, the ostentation of *Lélio*. The opposition of themes followed a development based on the periodic return to what Berlioz called the 'idée fixe', which was treated either in the form of a sonata, or as a waltz, a pastoral, a march. Such a cyclical form had already been adopted by Franck in his *Symphony in D minor* (1886–1888), thus profiting from the examples of Liszt and Wagner.

In fact, the symphonic poem was the true orchestral style of the Romantic era. The *Symphonie Fantastique* was not yet a symphonic poem such as Liszt was to create and which Berlioz himself came closest to in *Harold en Italie* and in *Lélio*. But it was the *Symphonie Fantastique* which, with its 'idée fixe', inspired in Liszt what he would call the 'idée-force' of the symphonic poem. Liszt composed twelve symphonic poems. There is a unity in their diversity: they mark a progress from the concrete to the abstract, a flowering of the symbolism which animated them. The one that is closest to pictoral decription is the *Battle of the Huns*, for which Liszt was inspired by the painting by Kaulbach. The central idea is that of the victory of Christianity over paganism. *Tasso* (1849) evokes both a personal destiny and historical fact: the imprisonment of the poet because he was in love with the princesses of the house of Este. *Mazeppa* (1851) also evokes an individual fate in a historical setting, and follows the lines of Byron's poem: 'He runs, he falls, and rises up a king'. Liszt retained these three elements: the mad gallop, the fall and the triumph which returns at the end in a variation of the initial theme of heroism. An individual fate no less legendary is portrayed in *Hamlet* (1858) and *Prometheus* (1850); while the evocation of their misfortunes was complemented by the depiction of collective tragedy and of failed revolutions, as for instance in *Hungaria* (1854). Then Liszt rose to examine the universal problems of human destiny and the result was the *Preludes* (1854) which illustrated the words of Lamartine: 'Is our life anything other than a series of preludes to that unknown song of which death intones the first solemn note?' These preludes, for Liszt as for Lamartine, were love, consolation within the heart of Nature, and glory. Their musical realisation took the form of the amplifying variation – the development of a theme in more and more varied forms. The themes were clear and glowingly developed in a series of sumptuous sequences. In the *Preludes*, Liszt crowned his achievement with an undisputed masterpiece.

The Ideals (1857) followed a similar pattern although in a less convincing manner. Liszt provided subtitles for the three sections: 'launching, disillusion, activity', ending with an 'apotheosis'. Of equally lofty inspiration was *What One Hears on the Mountain*, based on the poem by Victor Hugo, in which two voices are mingled in song, over the sound of ethereal harps: the voices of Nature and the voice of Humanity. Liszt, who was less pantheistic than Hugo, concluded his work with a beautiful theme that was almost religious in tone. Finally, *Orpheus* (1854) seems the very symbol of the composer himself. Here there is neither contrast nor conflict, but a majestic and gentle effusion, and immaterial apotheosis of music, a work of sovereign amplitude. These then are the major symphonic poems of Liszt.

It is easy to see why they provoked so much criticism at the time: they represented the offshoot of a literary argument. Yet this is precisely why they are typical of an era that was advocating a convergence of the arts. It is nonetheless true that Romantic music ended up by abusing these 'programmes', in applying them to overtures of non-existent operas (which is the case with many overtures by Mendelssohn and by Berlioz), and by confusing them with the form of the symphony itself (like *Manfred* by Schumann) or of incidental music (the *Faust Symphony* and the *Dante Symphony* by Liszt). Be that as it may, programme music was an invaluable creation. It had its representatives in all the national schools: Franck, in France, with *Les Djinns* (1883), *Le Chasseur maudit* (1882), and *Psyché* (1887), together with Saint-Saëns whose only works still played today are *Le Rouet d'Omphale* (1871) *Phaeton* (1873), and *La Danse macabre* (1874). There was Smetana in Bohemia, with *Ma Vlast* (My Country, 1874), and Grieg in Norway with the *Peer Gynt* suite (1874). The career of programme music finally came to an end in the symphonic poems of Strauss, Dukas and Fauré, who belong to another era.

Halfway between opera music and the symphony lies the music of ballet, another domain in which we find clear illustrations of Romanticism. The alliance of dance and music was certainly not new: it had existed in all times and in all countries. During the Romantic era, popular, folkloric dances (Hungarian, Polish, Russian) were to enrich considerably even piano and orchestral music, but quite specific to this period was the fact that ballet began to take an autonomous form. It proceeded not so much from opera itself, although the operas of the time continued to provide a showcase for ballet (for instance, the famous ballet of the nuns in *Robert le Diable*) as from the opera-ballet, created at the beginning of the 18th century in France. The ballet of the Romantic era continued to be very largely of French origin.

It began with the exotic in *Paul et Virginie* by Gardel in 1806, and all the 'oriental' titles of the 1830s: *Dieu et la Bayadère*, *Ali-Baba*, *Les Révoltes du sérail*. Then, with Meyerbeer, ballet took on tones of the fantastic, or black Romanticism. This fashion produced the masterpieces of the genre: *La Sylphide*, choreographed by Taglioni, music by Schneitzhoefer, based on an idea by the tenor Nourrit, and staged in 1832; *Giselle*, story outline by Gautier, music by Adam, choreography by Coralli and Perrot, created in 1841. These two works gave rise to great rivalries between some of the famous ballerinas of the day: La Taglioni, Fanny Elssler, Carlotta Grisi. From now on, the prima ballerina became an important personality of the Romantic age and of theatrical life. Under the Second Empire, ballet and ballerinas even became more important than opera and opera singers; it was the time of *Coppélia*, *Sylvia* and *La Source* by Léo Delibes, and of Gounod's *La Reine de Saba*.

The whole of Europe followed the lead of French fashion. In Vienna, Johann Strauss and Suppé composed ballets, as did Grieg in Norway, and Dvořák and Smetana in Bohemia. The Russian school achieved unparalleled renown with the scores of Rimsky-Korsakov (*Scheherezade*, *The Snow Maiden*) and Tchaikovsky (*Swan Lake*, *The Nutcracker*, *The Sleeping Beauty*), and the choreographies of Petipa. Although we may find the ballet composers of the Romantic era weak today, they wrote very much in the tradition of music that, since Weber's *Oberon* and Mendelssohn's *A Midsummer Night's Dream*, aspired to evoke aerial spirits, fantasy and grace. Ballet embodied the dreams and enchantment that pervaded all the music of the time.

The Romantic era was also very fond of musical genres that featured the voice. Leaving aside opera, which has been described above, we shall look at the roles of the folk song, the love song or romantic ballad, and the lied.

In every country, folk song had benefited from the attention of writers and musicologists. In France, for example, George Sand devoted a large part of her novels to providing a setting for the songs of Berri: *la Mare au diable*, *la Petite Fadette*, *Jeanne*, and also *L'Histoire de ma vie*, the fictionalised memoirs of the author. Chateaubriand too, in the course of his travels, heard the traditional songs of different countries and devoted a chapter of his *Essai sur la littérature anglaise* to 'Ballads and folk songs', thus delving into musicography. Alexandre Dumas, in an article for the *Gazette Musicale*, declared that he had been 'very impressed' by a ballad by Bourbon l'Archambault, *le Mal du pays*, 'accompanied by a peasant's musette'. Balzac cited and commented upon various songs: in *Les Chouans*, it was the tune of 'Beau capitaine' 'that no peasant woman from the West of France can listen to without being moved', in *Les Célibataires* it was the 'Chanson de la mariée', 'that Breton love song that the young people of the villages come to sing to the bridal pair on their wedding day'. Gérard de Nerval made a collection of the songs of the Valois region; he published a number of them and devoted a whole article to them in *la Sylphide* (1842). And of course, there was Robert Burns, who drew so much of his early inspiration from the folk songs of Scotland. Romantic writers drew attention to a form of music that had until then been all but ignored. The folk song took its place in the music of the Romantic era, and became one of its most valued forms.

However, the love song was even more popular. It brought fame to poets and composers who, without it, would have been long forgotten. The first of them was undoubtedly Monpou, whom Théophile Gautier described as 'the Berlioz of the ballad'. Monpou has since been forgotten, but the other great exponents of the love song or romantic ballad included Berlioz (*la Ballade du roi de Thulé*), Niedermeyer (*Le Lac* by Lamartine, *Lenore* by Burger), Bizet and Gounod (who wrote four volumes of melodies, and settings for poems by many authors).

A clear distinction should be made between the love song and the lied. First, the love song had to deal with the subject of tender and unhappy love: 'some story of love, often tragic' as Rousseau said in his *Dictionnaire de Musique*. Secondly, love songs were characterised by a very simple style: they contained no ornamentation, and there was nothing mannered about them, just a sweet and natural, even rustic, melody which had the power to move the listener spontaneously, without the addition of a rich accompaniment. It was not necessary for the singing to be particularly engaging, as long as it was unaffected and did not obscure the words of the song. The love song had several couplets, each one of which added something to the effect of the preceding ones; the interest increased progressively until, by the end of the song, the listener should be on the verge of tears. There was a great fashion for love songs among society ladies and in the salons. They were sung in the salons of Marie Nodier, Delphine de Girardin, the Countess Merlin and many others. There were two distinct types of love song: one of them was lyrical in character, and was the type most often composed by the likes of Sophie Gay, Plantade and Pauline Duchambge. It was the song of the salons, and its subject was a tender love story. It filled the albums and the keepsakes of the time. The other type was the dramatic love song, as illustrated by Grétry, Méhul and Berlioz. These songs were intended more for the concert platform and normally represented only part of a larger musical work (like the *Ballade du roi de Thulé*, or the *Chanson Gothique*, in the *Damnation de Faust* by Berlioz). The subject was still one of love, but seen this time in its more tragic and more violent guises. This type of love song endured far longer than the first, which disappeared as soon as the German lieder were introduced in France, in around 1834. Within a tighter framework and with more limited means, the romantic lied, by comparison with the folk song or the love song, exhibited the same characteristics, brought about the same innovations, and contained the same revelations as German opera during the same period.

Like German opera, the lied gave prominence to the voice of the singer. But, also like opera, on the one hand it borrowed its themes from poetry (almost always from the work of the best authors: Goethe, Heine and Eichendroff are names that recur constantly in the lieder by Schubert, Schumann and Wolf); while on the other hand it rested on an instrumental, even symphonic, base that was of major importance. In most cases, the singer was accompanied by the piano, but the instrument was an equal partner in the song and Schumann and Liszt, particularly, demanded great virtuosity of the pianist.

In its form and content, the lied marked the same progression, vis-à-vis the folk song or the love song, as that of the opera of the Romantic era in relation to that of the 18th century. This was due primarily to the fact that rigorous strophic division was abandoned, a fact already perceptible in Beethoven's lieder. The lied did not preserve the arrangement into strophes; it consistently modified it to a greater or a lesser extent and even went as far as the *durchkomponiertes Lied*, namely one that developed a continuous line from beginning to end, of which Hugo Wolf represents the extreme illustration. Here, the lied adopted a triple-time form inherited from classical instrumental music. The Romantic movement seized upon the lied as a kind of emotional dialectic, which marked the awakening and momentary reign of a new sentiment (which was in evidence as early as *Gretchen am Spinnrade* by Schubert, which dates from 1814). Thus the lied became a lyrical drama in miniature. Moreover, the lied genre took on such great expressive value during the Romantic period that the name was carried over into instrumental music: Mendelssohn composed some *Lieder ohne Worte* (Songs without words) and most of Chopin's *Nocturnes* followed the design of the lied in triple time.

With time, the piano part, which had served as mere harmonic support in the love song, became more than just an accompaniment. In Schubert's lieder, it commented on the action and expressed what the words and the song itself did not suffice to say: the underlying areas of emotion, or evocations of the natural setting (as in *Die Schöne Mühlerin* and *Die Winterreise*). With Schumann, this instrumental element, whether expressive or suggestive in character, played the principal role, without eclipsing the vocal part. In this way, a true interpenetration of the two registers was achieved, and the piano transmuted into poetry a text which was often rather flat, as for example in *Frauenliebe und Leben* (after a poem by Chamisso), and in many of Brahms' lieder.

The eminently expressive quality of the Romantic lied, which aimed no longer merely to 'set to music' some couplets in an agreeable way but to express the most profound emotions of the heart, meant that each lied seemed to be an episode of a drama, so that composers would often write whole cycles of lieder: those of Schubert and Schumann are well known, but there were also those of Wolf (*Spanisches Liederbuch, Italienisches Liederbuch*), Wagner (*Wesendonk Lieder*) and Mahler, and even those of Richard Strauss and Berg which provide extreme illustrations of the post-Romantic lied.

Taken as a whole, the lied, with its diversity and perennial appeal, is perhaps the most exemplary form of Romanticism in music.

The role of music in the Romantic aesthetic

The 18th century had sought to keep each of the arts in its place, to assign each one to a particular area of application. Despite all the progress and successes of music during this period, it was the art of reason and of language (poetry and tragedy) which remained the model and the foundation of every aesthetic. This was the basis of 'Classicism'.

But gradually this position was altered. Rousseau in his *Essai sur l'origine des langues* connected music with speech and saw its beginnings in man's cry and his singing, namely in the expression of emotion. Almost imperceptibly, music began to recover its lost importance.

With the first truly Romantic writers, the Germans Tieck, Wackenroder, Arnim and Brentano, the art of sounds, or more precisely the power of sounds, became the ideal of all aesthetic emotion. An abundance of works was written about music: *Fantasies on Art* and *The Outpourings of the Heart* by Wackenroder, and *Kreisleriana* and various articles of criticism by

Hoffmann. Various poems, by their very titles (*Hymns to the Night* by Novalis, *Des Knaben Wunderhorn* by Arnim and Brentano) showed that music, the most secret of the arts, was serving as the model for a poetry that sought now to evoke the infinite, unreal, and ineffable. Bettina Brentano, who had stormy affairs with both Goethe and Beethoven, expressed how inadequate ordinary language was to describe the feelings of her heart. Now, poetry in particular and literature in general began to try with their feeble words to recapture the magical power of sound and tone. Poets envied the universal appeal of music and started to seek to convey in their work an equivalent level of emotion.

Henceforward freed of any complex about words or speech, instrumental music was to play a role of great importance in the history of music. The term instrumental is used here in its broadest sense, since no century has ever produced the equivalent of the Beethoven sonatas, of the piano works of Chopin, Schumann and Liszt. This had not been the case beforehand: a composer acquired fame and fortune for his opera music, or for his church music, but not for his symphonies or chamber music. The reason for this is probably that, if music is the first of all the arts, then of all the forms of music the instrumental lends itself best to a translation of the irrational, and of pure passion.

This is not incompatible with the tendency, already mentioned above, that led all music, gradually, towards a 'programme'. Although in reality, every era had its programme music (for example, the *Biblical Sonatas* by Kuhnau, *The Battle of Vittoria* by Beethoven), the innovation of Romanticism consisted in adopting a far more ambitious programme, more abstract or more poetic than it had been in the past. But it would be wrong to think that music became the slave of poetry, as the very opposite was true: the blending of the literary with the musical was effected to the greater glory of music alone, to the exclusive profit of the instrumental or symphonic forms. Liszt's *Preludes* have ensured the enduring fame of a text by Lamartine that would otherwise have long since been forgotten. Schumann's *Kreisleriana* are undoubtedly more famous than Hoffmann's work which bears the same name. The same process can be observed in the field of opera: it is, above all, through Wagner's adaptation that we conceive of the *Nibelungenlied* today. When they based their operas on the works of Walter Scott or the little-known Spanish or French playwrights, the Italians Donizetti, Bellini and Verdi conferred everlasting fame on works that were too marked by their own periods to stand the test of time.

The other consequence of this new idealism represented by music was the demand for complementarity in the arts: to put it another way, the artist wished to be at ease in several different modes of expression. The musician was also a poet. There were certainly cases of multi-talented individuals in earlier periods: Bach had a gift for drawing, Jean-Jacques Rousseau was also a composer and musicologist; and dozens of musicians left theoretical essays or important memoirs – Marcello, Gretry, Rameau. What was new and different was that, at around the turn of the century, artists started to hesitate between different careers. Weber bore testimony to this in his unfinished autobiographical novel *Tonkünstlers Leben* (Life of a Musician) which tells how a man of many talents, for drawing, literature and music, finally chose to express himself through sound. Another example is Hoffmann who was a poet as well as a composer, a conductor as well as a musicologist. It was also characteristic that Musset in *Le Poète déchu* (The Fallen Poet), an unfinished autobiography, described how he wavered between a career as a painter, a poet or a musician. The best example is that of Berlioz, who came late to music and who was truly both a writer and a musician.

This doubling of vocations had some happy and some regrettable consequences. There is no question that piano music gained considerably from the fact that the composers were also poets: Chopin had already drawn his inspiration for the *Ballades* from the work of Mickiewicz but when Liszt in the *Années de Pelerinage*, Schumann in his *Carnaval* and his *Fantasy* in C (which has as an epigraph four verses by Schlegel on the universality of music), Chopin in his *Prelude* or his *Nocturnes*, gave voice to their double nature and let both the poet and the musician speak, they produced some of the masterpieces of a new genre.

Thus, in the lied, word and sound, poetry and music were intimately merged in one work. And if Romanticism was indeed the golden age of the lied, it was precisely because Schubert and Schumann, to name its greatest exponents, were fundamentally just as much poets as they were composers.

It was a remarkable phenomenon, the consequences of which affected both the history of musical forms as well as literary evolution, and which translated a revolutionary state of mind, producing a radically new way of regarding and experiencing music. The last of Schumann's *Childhood Scenes* bears the title 'The poet speaks': where could one find better proof that poetry is inextricably linked with music?

As far as opera is concerned, it can simply be said that during the Romantic era, it became a total masterpiece, thanks on the one hand to improved dramaturgy, and on the other to a clearer conception of the integration ow word and sound, of speech and singing.

Opera thus arrived at a level of perfection unknown in preceding centuries. The opera we hear today still largely consists of the repertoire of the second half of the 18th century and of the Romantic period. Our opera houses are, in general, those that were built or modified in the 19th century.

On a more detailed level, it should be remembered that it was Romantic opera that rehabilitated the art of decor and scenery: Stendhal was the first to sing the praises of Ciceri, Sanquirico, Perega and others who, starting with La Scala in Milan, progressively imposed their style and standards on the whole of Europe. Theatre like that of Meyerbeer would be inconceivable without its original scenery (especially in the case of *Robert le Diable*) or at least without scenery that adhered to the same spirit. Romantic opera also succeeded in integrating ballet better than ever before. Never had the collaboration of different artists been pushed so far; Rossini not only created roles to match the ability of his interpreters, as had been the practice in the past, but he also planned his embellishments to suit their abilities. Relations between poets and composers had become so close that Wagner and Berlioz were their own librettists. Conversely, Bellini, before he composed a single note, immersed himself in the libretto, read it, re-read it out loud, observing the inflexions of sound, the speed of delivery, the accent and the tone of expression. Then he would translate this phonic pattern into his score: an aria such as the famous 'Casta diva' owes its effect entirely to a subtle rhythmic asymmetry of phrasing, an irregular, almost hesitant, melodic diction, that reflects the ambiguous passion experienced by the priestess Norma at that moment. In this case, music bows to poetry. And so the boundaries become blurred and the styles become confused, not only those of poetry and music, but also of music and painting. Philipp Otto Runge, who enchanted the Romantics with his symbolics, wrote a dialogue on the analogies between colours and sounds. William Blake personifies the blurring of definition: should he be placed among the painters, the poets, or the musicians? Under these conditions, it is hardly surprising that Hoffmann, himself a composer and a writer, should have clearly underlined the preeminence of music in the Romantic system of the fine arts, when he concluded his account of the great Fifth Symphony by Beethoven with the words:

'Music is the most romantic of all the arts – one could almost say: it is the only purely romantic art!'

AUBER Daniel François Esprit (Caen 29.1.1782 – Paris 13.5.1871). This obstinately Parisian composer liked to repeat that he had 'never had the time' to travel outside the capital. In any case, during his long life, he witnessed twelve different political regimes in the course of which his success never flagged. He belongs to the Romantic movement not only on account of the great success of his opera *La Muette de Portici* – better known abroad as *Masaniello* – in 1828, but also because of the praise that Wagner accorded his work.

A few dates highlight a life filled with honours. Grandson of a painter at the court of Louis XVI, son of a painter who became a shopkeeper under the Revolution, Auber wrote his first *opéra-comique* in 1805: *L'Erreur d'un moment*. In 1807, he received lessons from Cherubini; in 1829, he entered the Institut to replace Gossec; he was appointed Director of Court Music in 1839; in 1842, he succeeded his teacher and friend Cherubini as Director of the Conservatoire; Napoleon III conferred on him the title of master of his chapel in 1852; in 1861, he became a 'grand officier' of the Légion d'Honneur. His last *opéra-comique*, *Rêve d'amour*, dates from 1869.

Auber wrote thirty-six *opéras-comiques* and ten operas; the most famous are *Le Maçon* (1825), *Emma ou la promesse imprudente* (1821), *La Neige ou le nouvel Eginhard*, *Léocadie*, *Fra Diavolo* (1830) *Le Philtre* (1831), *Le Domino noir* (1837), *Les Diamants de la Couronne* (1841), *La Part du Diable* (1843), and others, including of course *La Muette*. He had the good sense to choose as his librettist the famous Scribe, who worked regularly for the French stage from 1811 to 1862. There is no doubt that a significant proportion of Auber's success must be attributed to Scribe, who was very much in tune with the bourgeois taste of the time. *La Muette de Portici* was, before *Hernani*, a triumph of Romanticism in the theatre; audiences were interested in a subject that brought something new to the repertoire by staging an episode from modern history; the revolution of 1647 in Naples, instigated by a fisherman. Moreover, the role of Fanella, the mute, offered the orchestra an opportunity to be the 'star' of the evening. The interpreters of the two other roles, Madame Cinti-Damoreau (Elvire), who came from Brussels especially to appear, and Adolphe Nourrit (Masaniello), both made their names with his production. Wagner, writing of the opera, draw attention both to its Romantic and revolutionary inspiration and to the modernism of its form. In this respect, *La Muette* entered the annals of history by instigating the Belgian revolt against the Netherlands in 1830. Auber also wrote religious music, cantatas and love songs.

BEETHOVEN Ludwig van (Bonn 17.12.1770 – Vienna 26.3.1827). Beethoven was born into a family of musicians. From 1792 to 1827, he lived in Vienna, where he was taught by Haydn and by Albrechtsberger, and became known among the artistic and cultured circles of the town, aristocratic as well as bourgeois. From the age of twenty-two until his death, Beethoven was Viennese, and conferred a real superiority on the Austrian musical school. 1801 was an important year in his life: it was the year that he went deaf and that he confided his tragic secrets to his friends Amenda and Wegerler, when he wrote the *Heiligenstadt Testament* and his famous letter to the *Immortal Beloved*. There were many sides to his personality: the social man, the invalid, the composer. Most of his biographers agree that the year 1800 was a crucial one in his career: the period of his finest work began with the 19th century. But in spite of a great deal of serious biographical work, the life of the composer still contains many areas of uncertainty that only go to increase his legendary aura. The most important question to be considered here is whether it is valid to speak of Beethoven's 'Romanticism'. By virtue of his artistic training and his

Portrait of Beethoven by K.J. Stieler

literary and philosophical tastes, he was a 'revolutionary', in the sense that the French Revolution fired him with enthusiasm. He admired Schiller and Bonaparte, but never overstepped the boundaries of classical art: even his most emotional and expressive works (the *Pathétique Sonata* of 1799, the *Kreutzer Sonata*, 1803, the *Eroica Symphony*, 1803–1804, and the *Appassionata Sonata*, 1807) kept to the traditional order of movements, and the boundaries of tonal language; the traditional ratios and balance of melodic arrangement were respected. However, there was a later turning point: between the eleventh and the twelfth Quartets, a long interval from 1810 to 1824, the moment when the writing became revolutionary stands out very clearly. As Beethoven grew older, his emotions gradually grew calmer, resignation took the place of stormy soul-searching; paradoxically, however, in his composition the classical forms were shattered. Works like the classical sonatas op. 106, 109, 110, 111 close with emotional serenity, but at the price of a revolution in the means of expression. This should perhaps be seen as a transition from a Romanticism of inspiration to a Romantic revolution of musical form.

For many of his contemporaries, Beethoven was a Romantic. Even if Goethe voiced some reservations about him, Bettina Brentano, her brother Clemens, Berlioz and Hoffmann held him in high regard. In *William Shakespeare*, Hugo praised the 'visionary' Beethoven and in her *Lettres d'un voyageur* George Sand described the 'poet' Beethoven, while Schumann, Schubert and Wagner all expressed their admiration for him. Where then was Beethoven's Romanticism? First, it resided less in his musical language than in his inspiration: according to his *Notes*, he planned a Tenth Sympony 'to reconcile the modern world with the ancient world, as Goethe attempted to do in his second *Faust*'. The influence of external events on his compositions was particularly romantic: the *Appassionata* and the letter to the *Immortal Beloved* are closely related. However, he did also introduce new stylistic elements: new rhythms, martial rhythms for example (in the *Second* and *Third Symphonies*); details of instrumentation (drum rolls and brass in the *Missa Solemnis*); and generally, in all his works, there is a will to use the language to his advantage, to bend the form to his personal design, of which eloquent examples are to be found in the twelth and subsequent Quartets, the ten last piano Sonatas, the *Ninth Symphony*, etc.

Finally, Beethoven sought to be a total artist, to evoke with his art the whole universe and all the emotions. This was not 'programme music' in the sense of Berlioz, but a music in which, according to intimates of Beethoven, every work has a tacit, underlying subject, not necessarily illustrated by a title, not necessarily very distinct, but alive, precise and powerful, to which everything is suborned – the pulsation of rhythms, the accent of the themes, the sequence of the developments. From this point of view, Beethoven's most Romantic works are both the 'symphonies with titles' which he himself gave them: *Coriolanus*, *Egmont*, and the *Leonore* overtures; and the works without specific titles in which nonetheless something 'is happening' to a point where, as with the *Fifth Symphony*, or the *Seventh*, titles were added to them (Berlioz called the *Fifth* the 'Shakespearean' *Symphony* and the *Seventh* was called the *Apotheosis of Dance* by Wagner). The constant desire to express himself and be himself was one of the forces behind the Romantic movement. Beethoven stood at the turning point of Classicism and Romanticism – of the 18th and 19th centuries – and

therein lies the impossibility of assigning him totally to a single aesthetic or single school.

BELLINI Vincenzo (Catania, Sicily 1.11.1801 – Puteaux, near Paris 24.9.1835). *Il mio Bellini*, as he was called by his many female admirers in Italy, had a very Romantic life. Even in childhood, he showed such remarkable talent that his native town awarded him a scholarship to go to Naples, where he was a pupil of Zingarelli. It was there that his early works, operas and cantatas, were performed. His first mature work, *Il Pirata*, was premiered at La Scala in 1827. The libretto was the fruit of a collaboration with Felice Romani which was, with the exception of *Puritani*, to continue. During his 'middle period', as the years between his time in Naples and his arrival in Paris are known, Bellini composed *La Straniera* (Milan, 1829). *I Capuletti e i Montecchi* (Venice, 1830). Then came European fame with *La Somnambula* (Milan, 1831), *Norma* (Milan, 1831), and *Beatrice di Tenda* (Venice, 1833); his last opera, *I Puritani di Scozia*, from the novel by Walter Scott, was premiered with immense success in Paris, in January 1835. Bellini had settled in Paris in 1833 and died there, of consumption, in the year of his greatest triumph. Bellini was the favourite composer of Chopin, Musset, Heine and many other Romantic artists. The purity and richness of his melody perfectly represent what is known as *bel canto*. In his fiinest work there is a unique fusion of words and music, for example in the famous aria 'Casta Diva' from *Norma*, which results in an expressive language that transcends both words and music. Bellini fully realised the creation of a total art which was the major preoccupation of the Romantic movement. Though still relatively unrecognised, he was one of the great composers of the Romantic era.

BENNET William Sterndale (Sheffield 13.4.1816 – London 1.2.1875). Bennet is probably one of the most remarkable English musicians of the Romantic era. He was a talented pianist and Schumann dedicated his *Symphonic Studies* to him. He wrote concertos and overtures (including *The Naiads* and *The Nymph of the Forest* *Parisina*.) These works were inspired by the styles of Schumann and Mendelssohn: the influence of the latter is particularly evident in the *May Queen* cantata and the oratorio *Woman of Samaria*). Bennet was also well known in Germany, thanks to Mendelssohn who invited him to Leipzig.

BERLIOZ Hector (La Côte-Saint-André 11.12.1803 – Paris 8.3.1869). According to a story which is most probably true, Berlioz' name was included in the list of people enrolled to ensure the success of *Hernani* alongside those of Gautier, Balzac, Petrus Borel, Gigous and Bouchardy. The composer of *Eight Scenes from Faust* was thus awarded his official 'diploma' of Romanticism. In fact, with Berlioz, the new spirit did not stop at the calculated audacity of Meyerbeer or Rossini; it was to cause an explosion. Berlioz was more than a Romantic musician: he was Romanticism personified, with all its qualities and all its faults.

Portrait of Berlioz attributed to Daumier

His life is familiar thanks to his *Mémoires*, his *Letters* and, in addition, his writings about music (*Les Soirées de l'orchestre*, *Les Grotesques de la musique*, and *A Travers Chants*). Born in the Isère, intended by his father for a career in medicine, he went to Paris in 1821, ostensibly to pursue his medical studies, but at the same time taking tuition in musical theory (he never played an instrument, apart from the guitar) from Lesueur. His first publicly performed work was a *Mass*, as early as 1825. Then came the tribulations of the Grand Prix de Rome, which Berlioz won at his third attempt, in July 1830. The same year, a few months earlier, he had composed his *Symphonie fantastique*, inspired by his love for Harriet Smithson, which

was premiered in December 1830. The composer married the actress on his return from Rome, on 3 October 1833. A son, Louis, was born in 1834 and appeared frequently in the pages of the *Mémoires*. From this point on, the course of Berlioz' life is well known: difficulties in getting his works performed, bread-and-butter work (criticism in the *Journal des Débats*), composing, and journeys all over Europe. Berlioz always met with only relative success in France: the scholars did not like him, and he was only admitted to the Institut on his fourth application, in 1856. All his life, he struggled with' the debts he incurred to get his music played. Historically, his importance is equal to that of Hugo. With his musical criticism, he introduced the finest Romantic music to France (that of Beethoven and Liszt), while in his compositions he introduced most of the innovations of Romantic style. For example, he created the symphonic poem, before Liszt, with *Harold en Italie* in 1834. The same applied to his opera: Berlioz, whose *opéra-comique Benvenuto Cellini* dates from 1838, was already in 1851 working on an epic subject. *Les Troyens* would, if he had completed it, have been the French equivalent of Wagner's *Ring* (in 1851, Wagner had completed only *Lohengrin*, a Romantic opera yet still in the spirit of Weber). In his style too, Berlioz was a pioneer of the most modern of music: in his *Grand Traité d'instrumentation*, he emphasized the essential values of rhythm and instrumental sonority. Stravinsky, Debussy and Richard Strauss rigtly regarded Berlioz as a more daringly inventive precursor and revolutionary than Liszt.

The body of Berlioz' work was not very extensive: besides the very famous *Symphonie fantastique*, in the symphonic genre he also work *Lélio* (1831), *Harold en Italie*, and the *Symphonie funèbre et triomphale*. He also wrote religious music: the *Requiem* (1835), *Te Deum* (1849), and the oratorio *L'Enfance du Christ* (1854), and admirable music for the stage: overtures (*Waverley, Rob Roy, Les Francs-Juges*), operas (*Cellini, Les Troyens, Béatrice et Bénédict*) the *Scenes from Faust, La Damnation de Faust* (1846), *Romeo et Juliette* (1839); not forgetting his melodies, particularly *Nuits d'été*, and cantatas.

Together with Liszt and Wagner, Berlioz is one of the greatest representatives of Romantic music.

BOIELDIEU François Adrien (Rouen 15.12.1775 – Jarcy 8.10.1834). Boieldieu is often regarded as the last exponent of the French *opéra-comique* of the 18th century; this is in part erroneous, since *La Dame blanche* (from two of Walter Scott's novels), created in 1825, unquestionably belonged to the first, and most temperate, French Romantic movement. Weber, in fact, praised the composer for this work as 'worthy of Mozart'. After having staged *La Fille coupable* at the age of eighteen, and *Rosalie et Mirza* at twenty, in his native town, Boieldieu went to Paris, to the house of Sébastien Erard, where, to his great good fortune, he met Méhul and Cherubini, before tack-

Portrait of Boieldieu by Boilly

sented two complementary aspects of Germanic Romanticism: contemplation and exaltation. Born in Hamburg into a family of modest means, the young Johannes was introduced to music at a very early age by his father, who was a double-bass player in various bands. At the age of eight, he started his serious musical education and performed in his home town for the first time when he was only fourteen. In 1853, Brahms became the accompanist to the violinist Remenyi, who made concert tours of northern Germany. It was on these tours that he met Joseph Joachim, Liszt, and above all Schumann, to whom he played his first piano compositions and who wrote a famous article about them in the *Neue Zeitschrift fur Musik*. As a result, Brahms was soon appointed director of concerts and of the choir of the Court of Detmold-Lippe. In 1859, he returned to Hamburg and directed the famous ladies' choral society of the city. In 1862, he settled in Vienna. From then on, this Hanseatic German

Portrait of Brahms, 1853

ling the Parisian stage. From 1803 to 1810 he lived in Saint Petersburg, after a brief and unhappy marriage. On his return to Paris, his series of *opéras-comiques* were performed, of which *Jean de Paris* (1812) was the first. In 1817, he succeeded Méhul as Professor of Composition at the Conservatoire, where he remained until 1829 and counted Auber, Adam and Fétis among his pupils.

Boieldieu wrote thirty-nine compositions for the theatre, of which only one opera, *Les Deux Nuits* (1829), was not successful. He sometimes collaborated with Méhul (*Le Baiser et la Quittance*, 1804), with Cherubini, Catel, Isouard (*Bayard à Mezières*, 1814) and with Berton (*La Cour des fées*, 1821) and Kreutzer (*Pharamond*, 1825). His most notable works were *Les Voitures versées* (1808), *Le Chaperon rouge* (1818) and, of course, *La Dame blanche*, which was admired by all the composers of the day, including Mendelssohn, Weber and Wagner.

BRAHMS Johannes (Hamburg 7.5.1833 – Vienna 3.4.1897). In his lifetime Brahms was frequently compared and contrasted with Wagner. In fact they repre-

found a second home in Austria where he held several official posts: first as director of the Singakademie, then, from 1872 to 1875, as conductor of the famous Gesellschaft der Musikfreunde, and finally simply that of a composer of international renown. He led a very orderly life, dividing his time between his friends, his composing, and travel (particularly to Switzerland, to the Salzkammergut and the Black Forest). He died peacefully in Vienna in 1897, at the end of an undramatic life (with only a few love affairs or grand passions, the most famous being that for Clara Schumann), but a life filled with his love of the German musical tradition, and devoted, above all, to his work.

The music of Brahms is well known today. It is essentially music for the piano: sonatas, variations, short pieces of admirable lyricism (intermezzi, rhapsodies, ballads), dances, waltzes for two pianos, pieces for four hands. His four symphonies, his concertos (one for violin, one double concerto for violin and 'cello, two vast piano concertos), and his rhapsody for viola and orchestra are all familiar. Less well known perhaps are the hundred or so admirable lieder which extended, and somewhat dulled, the spirit of the Volkslied, and some very poetic choruses (*Liebeslieder Walzer, Marien Lieder*). He also composed excellent chamber music: trios with piano, two sextets, quartets, quintets (one with piano, the other with clarinet), and sonatas (violin/piano, 'cello/piano, and viola/piano). In total, he produced a body of work of exceptional quality, which as far as the works for voice, solo piano, and small ensembles are concerned, has never been questioned.

Although Brahms revered the sonata form and the other classical moulds, he was a true Romantic nonetheless. Even leaving aside the lieder, where his Romanticism is clearly apparent, all his music has an underlying inner exaltation that passes from morbidity to enchantment. Op. 116, 117, 118 and 119 for piano illustrate this double aspect well; they are brief, at the limit of tonality and rich in extremely varied rhythms. Brahms' many variations (on a theme by Haydn, on a theme by Handel, and on the Paganini caprices) illustrate great diversity and a total freedom of inspiration.

gan to train pupils. Later he became a Professor at the Conservatory. He spent his old age safe from want, but subject to serious crises of doubt and depression. He died in 1896 and was buried according to his wish in the cloister of St Florian.

The music of Bruckner, who only started to compose seriously at the age of forty-one, includes several Masses, a *Te Deum*, a *Quintet* for strings, and, above all, nine *Symphonies* which have recently become very famous. The man and his work may have seemed anachronistic, in the apotheosis of perfect pitch, the profession of faith in Wagner's diatonic system, and the religious and pantheistic emotion he expresses. But the body of his work is essentially Romantic. The Brucknerian symphony corresponds exactly to the Wagnerian musical drama. His broad themes stem directly from Wagner's *leitmotive*. In addition, the religious principle, which is fundamental to the music, places Bruckner firmly in the German tradition of Romanticism. On the other hand, he was also the direct descendant of Schubert and of Austrian inspiration: his music contains the expression of pure joy and intense musical creativity, and a leaning towards making music without concern for systematic or metaphysical order.

This is true of his scherzos, the rhythm and character of which could be described as rustic. Because of this fusion of Wagnerian and Schubertian influence, Bruckner's symphonies may be regarded as the great achievement of orchestral music in the German Romantic movement.

BRUCKNER Anton (Ahnsfelden 4.9.1824 – Vienna 11.10.1896). The name of Bruckner is often associated with that of Wagner, although in fact everything about them seems contrasted. Bruckner led an unostentatious and unadventurous life and never inspired the passionate controversy that Wagner aroused. Yet his discovery of Wagner, eleven years his senior, was a real revelation for Bruckner, an inspiration which drew them closer together.

Above all an Austrian composer, Bruckner was first a chorister, like Haydn and Schubert. The son of a schoolmaster, like Schubert, he was educated at the choir school of the St Florian Abbey. It was there, in Upper Austria, far from the bustle of the world, that he became an organist. Later, he took lessons in theory with Simon Sechter in Vienna. Thanks to Kitzler, a conductor in Linz where Bruckner had been the organist since 1856, he discovered Wagner and became an ardent Wagnerian. It was as an organist that he first met with success, notably during visits to England and France. Bruckner was appointed as Sechter's successor in Vienna and be-

CHOPIN Frédéric (Zelazowa Wola, near Warsaw 1.3.1810 – Paris 17.10.1849). Chopin belongs, with Liszt, Schumann and Wagner, to the second, and most famous, generation of Romantic composers. It is only possible to trace briefly here the life and work of the man whom Liszt called 'a remarkable musician'. Born near Warsaw of a French father who had settled in Poland, Frédéric Chopin completed his secondary education at the Gymnasium. His musical training was brief and even unfinished: his piano tutor was Zywny, a Czech who admired J. S. Bach, while for composition he was taught by Joseph Elsner, a very nationalistic Polish musician. At the age of twelve, Chopin stopped taking lessons and went on to teach himself. These incomplete studies were certainly not synonymous with insufficient training. His first real success as a pianist came in Vienna in 1829, in particular with some *Variations on a theme from Don Juan*, very much in contemporary taste. On 1 November 1830, Chopin left Poland for a concert tour, not suspecting that it would be anything but normal, but the revolution broke a few weeks later, and Chopin, on his way to London via

Vienna and Paris, decided to stay, temporarily, in Paris. He was to live there for nineteen years, in the aristocratic society of the July Monarchy. In his own time, he was less a virtuoso pianist than a teacher, perhaps less a musician than an artist, the host of a salon where men of the world rubbed shoulders with writers and musicians. His friendship with Heine and Mickiewicz and his liaison with George Sand are well known, as are his rare and well attended concerts, his regular visits to Nohant and the ill-fated winter in Majorca. However, contrary to popular opinion none of this had any direct bearing on his work. When the 1848 revolution broke out, Chopin finally left for England, which was waiting impatiently for his arrival. He gave several remarkable recitals there, but died soon after his return to Paris of the consumption from which he had suffered for years.

Chopin's work is almost exclusively composed for solo piano (the two concertos, his early works, the Polish songs and the two chamber pieces are exceptions). Ballads, impromptus, scherzos, waltzes, études, nocturnes,

most grotesque piano forms of the time: paraphrases, or particular kinds of virtuosity, that were to be found as late as in Liszt. This gave Chopin's Romanticism a very special and very subtle inspiration. This perhaps explains his immense and enduring success.

Portrait of Donizetti

Portrait of Chopin by Marie Wodzinska

mazurkas, polonaises, sonatas, the *Barcarolle* and the *Lullaby* all met with immediate, and enduring, success.

The body of his work could be characterised by the fact that it was, at one and the same time, in the style and taste of the day (the waltzes and the nocturnes for example), and prophetic of modern piano technique: that the études and the nocturnes herald Debussy, for instance, has often been commented upon. Furthermore, his style was strongly influenced by the inspiration of Polish folklore (*Polonaises*, *Mazurkas*) and totally independent of the

DONIZETTI Gaetano (Bergamo 29.11.1797 – Bergamo 8.4.1848). Donizetti was to opera what Hugo and Dumas were to the theatre. A pupil of Simon Mayr, Donizetti's first publicly performed opera was *Enrico conte di Borgogna* (Venice, 1818). Others followed in rapid succession. In total, Donizetti composed seventy-two operas, twenty-eight cantatas, fifteen symphonies, thirteen string quartets, a hundred and fifty songs, not counting instrumental and sacred music; today, however, he is known only for about ten of his operas.

His first works were naturally marked by the influence of Rossini. *Anna Bolena*, after Shakespeare, (Milan, 1830) was the first score that bore something of his personal stamp: dramatic truth, resounding instrumentation and generosity of vocal treatment ensured Donizetti's international renown. From then on, he was to write for different European theatres, and in particular for those of Paris. *L'Elisir d'amore* is an important work in both Romantic and *comique* genres; it was first performed in Milan in 1832. *Lucrezia Borgia* (Milan, 1833) and *Lucia di*

Lammermoor (Naples, 1835) are probably the master-pieces of Donizetti's serious work. They are typical of Romantic opera before Verdi: their libretti were drawn from fashionable novels (Hugo and Scott respectively); they were concerned with historical accuracy and dramatic probability; and are characterised by the difficulty of the vocal parts which demand voices that are both agile and powerful, and by the emotion that the action arouses in the spectator.

The famous 'mad scene' (finale of Act II) and the sextet (II) of *Lucia* are good examples of Donizetti's at once efficacious and uncomplicated style.

Like Rossini and Bellini before him, Donizetti composed for the theatres of Paris. His five operas with French libretti include *La Fille du régiment* (opéra-comique, 1840), and *La Favorite* (1840). For Vienna, he wrote *Linda di Chamounix* (1842) and *Maria di Rohan* (1843). But his real masterpiece is probably the *opera-buffa Don Pasquale* (Paris, 1843).

GLINKA Mikhail (Novospasskoye 1.6.1804 – Berlin 15.2.1857). Born in the region of Smolensk, Glinka studied music under the violinist Bohm, then under Field and Carl Mayr. His delicate health led him to seek southern climes. From 1829 to 1834, he was in the Caucasus, then in Milan, Rome, where he met Bellini and Donizetti, and Naples. In 1844, in Paris, he met Berlioz, who wrote about him in elegiac terms. From 1845 to 1847, Glinka was in Madrid and in Seville; he brought back from Spain the *Jota aragonese* and *A Night in Madrid*. The turning point in his life was in 1834 when, on a visit to Berlin, the composer Dehn suggested that he should write real Russian music. This was the genesis of his operas, of which only two were completed. They were *A Life for the Tsar*, or *Ivan Susanin* (1836) which was, and has remained, a great success; and *Russlan and Ludmilla* (1842) from Pushkin's poem, which is more of a fantastic tale than a drama. By introducing folklore into Russian music, Glinka became the mentor of a whole school (Dargomizhsky, the 'Mighty Handful') which was somewhat removed from Romanticism because of its overly marked national character.

GRIEG Edvard (Bergen 15.6.1843 – Bergen 4.9.1907). Grieg is the principal representative of Scandinavian Romanticism. His whole life was spent under German rule, which explains why he came late to Romanticism. He studied music in Leipzig from 1858 to 1863, then under the Dane, Gade, in Copenhagen in 1864. In 1865, he visited Italy, and then spent most of the rest of his life in Norway. He founded a music school in Christiania, in 1867. He travelled again, to Italy and Germany, and retired to Bergen in 1880.

Grieg left a relatively small body of work: it includes lieder, pieces for piano, for piano and violin, a famous concerto for piano, orchestral suites (*Peer Gynt*, incidental music, *Holberg Suite*), quartets and other chamber music. Grieg was strongly influenced by Chopin, Schumann, his compatriot Kjelruf and also Liszt, of whom he was the brilliant pupil as witness his lyrical pieces for the piano. His great achievement was to evoke the Romanticism of the North, with its mists and folklore, by means of an individual style of harmony, audacious even in its floating tonality and chromatism.

Portrait of Glinka by Repine

HALÉVY Fromental (Paris 27.5.1799 – Nice 17.3.1862). Halévy was a brilliant individual. A pupil of Cherubini, he was appointed assistant professor at the Conservatoire at the age of seventeen. In 1829, he became Professor of Harmony, and in 1833 of Counterpoint and Composition. He was elected to the Institut in 1836, to succeed Reicha. His colleagues praised his elegant style and his dogged quest for the 'correct' expression.

His most famous work is *La Juive* (The Jewess, 1835), a grand opera typical of the French style prevalent after the July Monarchy. His other operas, *Guido et Ginevra* (1838), *La Reine de Chypre* (1841), Le Val d'Andorre (1848) and some thirty or more other titles are less well known.

Portrait of Fromental Halévy

LISZT Franz (Raiding 22.10.1811 – Bayreuth 31.7.1886) A child prodigy, born on the borders of Austria and Hungary, Liszt's first teacher was his father Adam, an official in the service of Prince Esterhazy. From 1821 to 1823 he took lessons with Salieri and Czerny in Vienna. It was there that he gave his first concerts with enormous success in 1823; his path seemed clear: he was to be a virtuoso pianist. In the autumn of 1823, he arrived in Paris with his family but was refused admission to the Conservatoire because he was a foreigner. So Liszt worked alone, with some help from Paer and Reicha. After playing for the Duchesse de Berry and for the Duc d'Orléans, he gave a triumphal concert on 8 March 1824 at the Opéra Italien. The royal Opéra then commissioned a one-act opera, *Don Sanche*, which was performed when Liszt was twelve years old! Obliged to earn his own living after the premature death of his father, he gave piano lessons, at the same time continuing to work tenaciously alone. He was already prone to fits of mysticism and even considered entering a Trappist order. The July Revolution shook him out of his lethargy for a while. He read voraciously and was subject to various influences: Berlioz and Lesueur, in addition to Beethoven and Paganini, for music; Lamennais for philosophy and faith; Lamartine and Hugo for literature; Lamartine again, and also Saint-Simon, for politics. Liszt had personal contact with most of these great minds; his relationships with the whole intellectual élite of the time were to form his cosmopolitan and authentically Romantic spirit.

His private life, too, was eminently Romantic, in the passions he aroused; in his innumerable journeys all over Europe in the middle period of his life; his liaison with Marie d'Agoult from 1835 to 1844; his visits to Italy and Switzerland, which gave rise to the *Années de pèlerinage*; and his liaison with Carolyne Sayn-Wittgenstein, which was to change the course of his life. The years from 1847 to 1856 were the period of his greatest activity, centred on the vast Altenburg house: he was engaged in composition (all the great symphonic poems date from this period, as well as the *Christus* oratorio and the two *Concertos*); conducting and 'promoting' the music of other composers, including performances at the opera and concerts at the Court of *Tannhäuser*, *Lohengrin*, *Benvenuto Cellini*, *Genoveva*, and the works of Beethoven, Mozart, Mendelssohn and Schumann.

In 1861, the last period of his life began; he divided his time between Rome, Budapest and Weimar, between composition, tuition, and even politics, since he undertook secret missions on behalf of Napoleon III. In Rome, particularly, he composed lofty and deeply spiritual works: the three *Legends* (Saint Elizabeth, Saint Francis de Paul and Saint Francis of Assisi), the *Mass*, and *Via Crucis*. He tempered his earlier bombastic style: the *Fountains of the Villa d'Este*, the last *Rhapsodies* (17 to

Portrait of Liszt by Lehmann

19), the individual pieces (*Grey Clouds*, *Czardas macabre*, *The Venetian Gondola*) are increasingly 'de-romanticised'. He acquired real fame throughout Europe: in Budapest, he was a royal adviser and Director of the Conservatoire, and in Weimar he was regarded as the master that the whole of Europe came to consult, including the great minds of the day: Nerval, Wagner etc. He died in Bayreuth where he had come to attend performances of

Tristan and *Parsifal* by his friend, and now son-in-law, Wagner. He is buried there in the garden of the Wahn-fried villa.

Liszt wrote in every musical style and left over twelve hundred compositions. Some of them have been all but forgotten, notably the *paraphrases*, and the religious music, which is hardly ever performed. On the other hand, all his symphonies and all his work for piano, from the *Sonata in B minor* to the *Preludes or Mazeppa*, from the twelve *Transcendental Studies* to *Grey Clouds*, and including the *Rhapsodies* and the *Années de pèlerinage*, are as popular and successful today as ever.

LOEWE Carl (Löbejün, near Halle 30.11.1796 – Kiel 20.4.1869). Loewe wrote five operas, only one of which was performed, and sixteen oratorios, as well as symphonies and concertos, but it is for his songs alone that he is remembered today. Loewe was the creator of the ballad in the sense that, by the reiterated use of a principal theme with fixed outlines, he gave his compositions for voice and piano a truly epic narrative style, in keeping with the subject. The most characteristic, and famous, is his setting for Goethe's poem *Der Erlkönig*, orchestrated by Loewe himself. All Loewe's ballads are perfect illustrations of Romantic poetic art, be it legend (*Heinrich der Vogelfänger*), drama (*Archibald Douglas*) or dreams (*Ondine*).

MARSCHNER Heinrich (Zittau 16.8.1795 – Hanover 14.12.1861). Marschner wrote nineteen works for the stage. He was encouraged by Weber who had one of his first operas, *Henry IV and Agrippa d'Aubigne* (1820) performed in Dresden. *The Templar and the Jewess* (1831, after Ivanhoe by Walter Scott) and particularly *The Vampire* (1828) and *Hans Heiling* (1833) were very successful and contributed to his appointment as Kapellmeister to the Court of Hanover, where he spent the best part of his life. He wrote about three hundred lieder and sixty or so pieces of chamber music.

In the evolution of Romantic opera, Marschner is a link between Weber and Wagner. *Hans Heiling*, for example, has a very dramatic subject, served by an expressive

musical score. *The Vampire* brought to the stage one of Romanticism's favourite legends: that of the man whom only a woman can save from damnation. A feeling for Nature and a sense of the dark forces that lie hidden in Man are evident in Marschner's always powerful music. His operas are still widely performed in Germany.

MÉHUL Etienne-Nicolas (Givet 22.6.1763 – Paris 18.10.1817). Nowadays, Méhul is merely a name associated with one of the most popular songs of the French Revolution: *Le Chant du depart*. This is not altogether fair, since he was one of the precursors of Romantic music.

Portrait of Méhul by Ducreux

The advice and example of Gluck decisively influenced Méhul's career, but he very quickly, and independently, found his own way. He made his debut with an *opéra comique*, *Euphrosine* (1790) which was a huge success: he was then twenty-seven. Posterity (Cherubini, Berlioz, Wagner) was to admire the work. Méhul then became a protégé of Napoleon and wrote thirty-five operas of which the most notable were *Stratonice* (1792), *Ariodant* (1799) and *Uthal* (1806). They have both dramatic power, inherited from Gluck, and an Italian melodic style. All the subjects were extremely melodramatic which identify him immediately as a Romantic.

Méhul's masterpiece was *Joseph* (1807), which was much admired by Beethoven. An *opéra comique* with alternating recitative and singing, it is grand opera in the French tradition. The borrowings from religious style are justified by the subject (the biblical legend of Joseph). Weber wrote in 1817, when it was performed in Dresden: 'The beauty of works of this order does not have to prove itself' and Wagner said that *Joseph* 'transported him into a higher world'.

Finally, the value of the four symphonies that Méhul wrote between 1808 and 1810 should not be undervalued: their firm accents and melodic inspiration are eminently Romantic.

Portrait of Mendelssohn

MENDELSSOHN-BARTOLDI **Felix** (Hamburg 3.2.1809 – Leipzig 4.11.1847). Mendelssohn, together with Schumann and Wagner who were born at approximately the same time as him, embodies the spirit of the second generation of German musical Romanticism. Theirs was the most famous, and occasionally infamous, Romantic generation.

Mendelssohn ws born into a Jewish family rich both in talent and in material wealth. His grandfather, the famous Moses Mendelssohn, was a highly respected thinker who was Lessing's collaborator and fought all his life for the integration of the Jews into the German society of the Enlightenment. His father, Abraham, a fine patriarchal figure, had his children baptised in the Lutheran faith. Felix's sister, Fanny, an accomplished pianist, always surrounded him with loving solicitude. He lived in perfect harmony with his wife, Cécile Jeanrenaud, the daughter of an emigré French pastor. Thus, it seems that, in his private life, Mendelssohn was a truly happy man. And the same was true of his career.

Eminently gifted, brought up in surroundings where all the arts and all the intellectual disciplines were held in high esteem, Mendelssohn could just as well have been a painter or a writer as a musician. His musical studies were with L. Berger, for the piano, and Henning for the violin; Zelter, Goethe's musical adviser, taught him theory. At the age of nine, he gave his first concert of chamber music, at ten, he was playing the viola at the Singakademie, and at eleven, he performed for Goethe, who praised his talent. Mendelssohn's career was, to begin with, as a performer, even though he had been composing from a very early age. This first period, up to his establishing himself in Leipzig (1835), was marked by one great event: Mendelssohn's direction, on 11 March 1829 in Berlin, of the *St Matthew Passion* by Bach, its first performance since Bach's own time. He also travelled extensively: London, Berlin (1829–1830), Venice (1830), Paris (1831), and London again (1832). In 1833, he was called to Düsseldorf to direct the concerts and opera at the Gesangverein. In the same year, he founded a tri-annual Rhine festival in Cologne which was a great success. Finally, from 1835 until his death, he settled in Leipzig where he was musical director of the famous Gewandhaus and established a Conservatoire which gained great repute.

Mendelssohn left an abundant body of work which, paradoxically, was as formalistic as it was Romantic, and as full of genius as it was precocious. Whereas Mozart's first compositions were distinctly childish in character, Mendelssohn's were full of assurance from the very beginning, for example his *Sonata in G minor* or the *Capriccio* op.5 for piano, written in his twelfth year. The fabulous *Midsummer Night's Dream* overture, which was written at the age of seventeen (1826), embodies all the aspects of Mendelssohn's genius: respect for form, Romantic inspiration, melodic richness and expressive elegance. He also wrote symphonic music: symphonies, overtures (*Midsummer Night's Dream*, *Ruy Blas*, *Fingal's Cave*, *Calm Sea and Prosperous Voyage*), music for keyboard (organ, piano), either inspired by J. S. Bach as in the *Preludes and Fugues*, or free in form and spirit like the famous *Songs without Words*, the *Rondo Capriccioso* or the *Variations Sérieuses*. His finest work is perhaps to be found in his chamber music: the admirable *Trios* and *Quartets* with piano, the two *Sonatas for 'Cello and Piano* (op.45 and 58), the three *String Quartets* (op.44) and the astonishing *Octet* (op.20); and also in his dramatic music too – incidental music, cantatas, and oratorios: *Walpurgisnacht*, *St Paul*, and *Elijah* are among the most powerful works of German Romanticism. Often inspired by Handel's grandeur, they are a fine illustration of the synthetic nature of Mendelssohn's genius, which reconciled Classicism and Romanticism: their fairytale atmosphere is reminiscent of Tieck and, in fact, Mendelssohn's place in the history of music is every bit as important as that of Tieck in the history of literature.

MEYERBEER Giacomo (Berlin 5.9.1791 – Paris 2.5.1864) The son of a Jewish banker, the future author of *Robert le Diable* was actually called Jacob Beer: he Italianised his first name and added the name of his extremely rich maternal grandfather to his surname. Meyerbeer first studied piano with Lauska and Clementi and composition with 'Abbé' Vogler, where Weber was a fellow student. But the composer of *Freischütz* had ended his career before Meyerbeer's had really started. Meyerbeer's first ambition was to be a pianist, but he soon renounced it, though not before he had met with some success, particularly in Vienna. On the advice of Salieri, he

with the Italianism of Spontini and Rossini to create an art of synthesis, in which different modes of expression flowed together in a 'total' masterpiece (for example the scenery was by Ciceri and Scribe's libretto was a Romantic drama in itself). Six years later, also in collaboration with Scribe, he staged *Les Huguenots* (1836), another resounding success, which seemed to his contemporaries to have attained all the possibilities of all the Romantic arts put together. As a result of this triumph, Meyerbeer became a sort of dictator of opera; he was made a chevalier of the Légion d'Honneur, and *maître de chapelle*.

Nevertheless, he went back to Prussia; in 1842, he succeeded Spontini as Director General of Music in Berlin. To this period belong *Le Prophète* (1849), his last 'French' work, and German operas (*Ein Feldlager in Schlesien*, performed in Paris as *L'Etoile du Nord* in 1844, and *Struensee* in 1846). *Le Prophète* was also a decisive work. Composed with great decorative scope, full of colours and striking effects, it probably marked the high point of grand opera in the French style. *L'Africaine* on which Meyerbeer worked for five years and went on adapting until his very last day, was only performed a year after his death, simultaneously in Paris and Berlin.

Portrait of Meyerbeer by Maurin

MUSSORGSKY Modeste (Karev 9.3.1839 – St. Petersburg 16.3.1881). Modeste Mussorgsky was descended from a very old Russian family. He received a good all-round education and initially intended to make his career in the army, but later became a clerk in the service of the Tsarist government. His curiosity and natural inclinations impelled him towards music. After meeting Cui and Balakirev he decided, like them, to study the fundamental musical disciplines, learning techniques of harmony, counterpoint and orchestration. Together with Balakirev, Cui, Borodin and Rimsky-Korsakov, he was one of the famous "Mighty Handful" of Russian composers. The rest of his life was spent in St Petersburg, divided between his administrative work and his artistic vocation. Mussorgsky did not compose very many works: he wrote melodic compilations (*Songs and Dances of Death*, etc), chamber music and operas (*Khovanshchina, Sorochinsky Fair, The Marriage Salammbo*, and *Boris Godunov*). Only *Boris* was entirely completed by the composer: after all kinds of difficulties and adaptations, it was very successfully staged in 1874. Mussorgsky's aesthetic is founded on 'artistic truth'; for him, art was a means of communication with his fellow men and, above all, of singing the praises of Russia, whence his scorn for the rules and an expressiveness in which the inflections of speech are translated into melody without concern for traditional harmony and instrumentation. This made his music very direct, especially as many of his themes were taken from national folklore or orthodox religious songs.

Mussorgsky's masterpiece is, of course, *Boris Godunov*, based on the play by Pushkin. Mussorgsky succeeded in

went to Italy to complete his musical education. In Venice, he made contact with Rossini, who had just written *Tancredi* (1813). Meyerbeer then composed some Italian operas, exemplifying his early manner (*Emma di Resburgo, Il Crociato in Egitto*). 1826 marked the beginning of his French period, which lasted until 1842. Invited by Charles X to stage *The Crusader in Egypt* (*Il Crociato*) he soon returned with the idea of creating *Robert le Diable* in Paris (1830). It is an opera that one could describe as frenzied, absolutely in tune with the taste of the time for wild Romanticism. It was a huge success and from the very first performance, it was obvious that something had changed in grand opera: Meyerbeer was breaking

preserving the Shakespearean spirit of the historical play by using a very free dramatic structure.

ONSLOW Georges (Clermont-Ferrand 1784 – Mirefleurs 1853). Posterity can often be very unjust: though now neglected, Onslow was one of the most popular composers of chamber music during the Romantic period. Of British descent, he was born in the Auvergne, where his father had come to live upon his marriage. His father sent him to London where he studied the piano with two artists of repute, Dussek and Cramer. Back in the Auvergne, he also studied the 'cello. After a journey to Germany and Austria, he decided to start composing: his first known work was a string quintet in 1806. It met with success, so much so that he decided to undertake serious study and became a pupil of the famous Reicha. Onslow was a prolific composer: his operas (*Les Etats de Blois*, for example) were only relatively successful; his symphonies were sometimes simplistic; but he was above all a chamber musician. His most commonly cited work is the famous fifteenth quintet, which was inspired by a hunting accident in which he almost lost his hearing. His worth was soon recognised abroad: the Philharmonic Society in London, Mendelssohn, who invited him to Leipzig, and Schumann in his articles, all recognised him as a great musician. In 1842, he was elected to Cherubini's chair at the Institut, in preference to Berlioz who was competing for the position. Onslow spent the last years of his life in a château in the Puy-de-Dôme, correcting his scores and composing new ones.

PAËR Ferdinando (Parma 1.6.1771 – Paris 3.5.1839). Naturalised as a Frenchman at the time of the Restoration, Paër began his career in Vienna. It was there that the French invasion found him in 1809; Napoleon, who had liked his opera *Achilles*, brought him to Paris. There he became an official figure, as private music director to the Emperor, and then choir master to Louis-Philippe; he directed the Théâtre des Italiens for a while, then became a member of the Institut (1831).
Paër composed an astonishing total of forty-three operas! Notable among them were *Camilla* (1801), written for Vienna, *Sargino or the Pupil of Love* (1803), created in Dresden, and above all *Le Maître de Chapelle* (1831), a charming work, imbued with a subtle lyricism that is reminiscent of Mozart or the best of Rossini. Paër was one of the kings of music at the time of the Empire and the Restoration, and for this reason can be called a Romantic.

PAGANINI Niccolo (Genoa 27.10.1782 – Nice 27.5.1840). Paganini's father was a modest, and slightly musical, tradesman. Although various teachers may have given him some lessons as a child, for the most part Paganini was self-taught. From early on, he led an eventful life, the facts of which have been embellished by legend. His public appearances were followed by strange retreats, which gave rise to gossip. As he was deformed, miserly, rather secretive, and, above all, supremely gifted, rumour had it that he had made a pact with the Devil.
On a tour of northern Italy – Lucca, Milan, Venice and Rome – Paganini triumphed over all the rivals set up against him, and put Rossini's glory in peril. Pauline Bonaparte, princess of Lucca, became his official protector. It was only in 1828 that he first performed in Vienna, after a tour of northern Germany. In 1831, he began his concerts in London and in Paris, to which he returned regularly (1831, 1834 and 1836). We know from Liszt's letters and from Berlioz' *Mémoires* what secret generosity and magnificent musicality he was capable of on occasion. When he died, he left what was for the time a colossal fortune. During Paganini's lifetime, the works that appeared, apart from the famous *Caprices*, were twelve *Sonatas* for violin and guitar (op. 2/3), and three *Quartets* with guitar (op. 4/5), written before 1805. The works published after his death include two *Concertos* for violin (op. 6 in which one violin has to be tuned a semi-tone higher than the other instruments and op. 7 with the famous rondo *La Campanella*), an *Allegro de concert* (op. 11), and *Variations* (among others *Carnival in Venice*). Paganini's mysterious life and virtuosity make him a highly Romantic figure – though apparently when he took part in a trio or a quartet, he became a very average violinist. His opus 1, *24 Caprici per il violino solo* (1831) was extremely influential: Schumann, Liszt and Brahms transcirbed it for piano.

ROSSINI Gioacchino (Pesaro 29.2.1792 – Paris 13.11.1868). For a long time, it was denied that an Italian Romanticism had even existed. But it did exist, in literature as well as in music, and Rossini is one of the leading figures of the movement.
The son of a town clerk who was also the trumpeter in the municipal band, and of a singer, Rossini received a somewhat mediocre musical education in Bologna. But his precocious genius was revealed very early: at the age of twelve, he played a child's role in Paër's *Camilla*, at fourteen he was playing the harpsichord in an amateur ensemble, and at eighteen had his first work performed:

La Cambiale di matrimonio (1810). From then on, Rossini's career was one long series of triumphs; from 1810 to 1820 he was in Italy, and principally in Naples, where, financed by the impresario Barbaja, he took over from Cimarosa and Paesiello and made the San Carlo theatre and company, which included Isabella Colbran and the tenor Davide, into a remarkable centre of opera. From 1815 to 1820, he moved on with Barbaja to fresh triumphs at La Scala in Milan; and from 1820 to 1823 he lived in Vienna where, to the great detriment of German musicians, his glory reached its apotheosis. From 1823 until his death (1868) Rossini lived almost exclusively in Paris: he was director and then inspiring force of the Théâtre Italien and of the Opéra where *William Tell*

Portrait of Rossini by J Meyendorff, 1849

was to be his last work (1829) before an illustrious retirement.

Rossini was a prolific composer: between 1810 and 1823 he produced no less than thirty-four works of which some have been successful ever since, either in the *buffa* genre (*La Scala di seta*, *L'Italiana in Algeri*, *The Barber of Seville*, written for the carnival of Rome in 1816, *La Cenerentola*, and *La Gazza ladra*) or in the *seria* or *semiseria* vein much prized at the time (*Otello*, *Elisabetta Regina d'Inghilterra*, *Mosé*, *La Donna del Lago*), and above all the famous *Tancredi* which brought Rossini international fame in 1813. After leaving Italy, Rossini composed less, but he did still write some very great successes such as *Comte Ory* (1828), *Le Siège de Corinthe* (1826) and, of course, *William Tell*, for the Paris Opéra.

In his *Vie de Rossini*, an interesting and often neglected biography, Stendhal took stock of the composer's Romanticism. It is apparent in his choice of subjects bor-

rowed from Shakespeare (*Otello*) or from Walter Scott (*Tancredi, La Donna del Lago, Elisabetta*); in his way of evoking melancholy (very clear in *Elisabetta* and in *Mosé* which describes the captivity of the Jews in Egypt); and finally in his writing, what Stendhal called his imitation of German composers (namely the pursuit of contrapuntal writing, or the pursuit of rich harmony, at the expense of typically Italian melodic simplicity and generosity). His concern to find new means of expression is very evident, even though we are used to hearing better examples in Verdi, Wagner or Donizetti.

Thus in *Otello*, there is a vehement theme during the duet between Iago and Othello so stirring that Verdi was to incorporate both its rhythm and melody, almost note for note, in the stretto of the duet between Rigoletto and Gilda (Act III of *Rigoletto*). This abundance of life is typical of Rossini who produced from his orchestra previously unheard of brilliancy, notably in his use of the brass. In the thread of the music itself, he began to weave elements unusual for their time: in *Tancredi*, for instance, he introduced, in place of the *recitativo secco* of the old *opera seria*, the continuity of an *obbligato* recitative more accented and more dramatic, and commented on by the orchestra.

With hindsight, none of these innovations may seem particularly audacious, but it should be remembered that Rossini belonged to the generation of the founders of European Romanticism, which, between 1813 and 1820, was still a restrained and hesitant movement.

SCHUBERT Franz (Lichtental, near Vienna 31.1.1797 – Vienna 19.11.1828). Schubert only lived for thirty-one years, but that brief lapse of time saw the flowering of all musical Romanticism. The son of a schoolmaster, he had several brothers and sisters and learned the joys of music at home, where he and his family formed a quartet. He also very soon became aware of the difficulties and exigencies of the professional artist, when he became a choir-boy in the Court chapel and received an advanced musical education at the *Stadtkonvikt*, Vienna's leading boarding-school. For three years (1813–1816), he was a teacher at his father's school in the suburbs, then, from 1817, he made a living, modest though it was, from music. He taught in Count Esterhazy's household, worked as an organist, but most of the time he was composing. In post-Congress Vienna, Schubert led the austere but exciting life of an impoverished but esteemed artist, a life of authentic and confirmed Romanticism.

He was highly regarded by the celebrities of the day,

which heralded Wagner's chromatic research (aspects of *Lazarus* largely anticipate and outstrip Mendelssohn and Schumann, presaging the typical forms of post-Romantic modulation). All Schubert's work has its roots in popular art, an inspiration that is at once close to Nature and fantastic, even hallucinatory (in the *Winterreise* lieder for example).

Schubert was, in many respects, more Romantic and more rounded than Weber, and his *Schöne Müllerin*, *Winterreise*, *Trout Quintet*, *Impromptus*, and *Unfinished Symphony* have remained recognised masterworks of Romanticism.

Portrait of Schubert by Léon Noël, 1824

such as Grillparzer and the singer Vogl, and met with unfailing success in the enlightened bourgeois salons where his genius as a composer for the voice was much appreciated. Nowadays, we admire all Schubert's work – his lieder as well as his symphonies, his masses as well as his oratorio *Lazarus* and his chamber music. However, for over a century, Schubert was appreciated above all for his lieder and for his Romanticism. He was never really a martyr or even a misunderstood artist, but he died in poverty during a typhoid epidemic, in the prime of life.

He left a vast body of work (forty volumes in Mandyczewsky's first edition) which includes music for piano with works for two and four hands, in particular *Sonatas*, *Impromptus*, *Musical Moments*, *Dances*; chamber music with well-known *Trios*, *Quartets* and *Quintets*; eight *Symphonies*; over six hundred Lieder; about twenty works for the stage, including six operas and the famous *Rosamunde*, incidental music for a drama by Helmine von Chezy, mistress of Chamisso and Weber's librettist; and finally religious music (including ten masses). He was responsible for the birth of the Romantic lied (which could be for several voices and orchestral accompaniment, like the magnificent *Song of the Spirits on the Waters*, 1820, and *Nocturnal Song in the Forest*, 1827) which eliminated certain genres like the French 'romance' and the ballad. He also created other, freer, styles of instrumental music, like the piano impromptu.

Schubert represented the southern, Austrian, branch of German Romanticism, which was to give rise to Bruckner and the first Viennese school (Berg, Webern), and

SCHUMANN Robert (Zwickau 8.6.1810 – Endenich, near Bonn 29.7.1856). Although Schumann did not have the elegance of Mendelssohn, nor the passion of Berlioz, he was reticent and aristocratic like Chopin, full of enthusiasm and imagination like Wagner. He should perhaps be compared with Schubert: although their music has little in common, they shared a taste for reticence and simplicity. Schubert and Schumann are fine examples of the 'idyllic' and bourgeois aspect of German Romanticism, in complete contrast to the horrific and fantastic elements found in the tales of Hoffmann, the ballads by Burger or the novels of Jean-Paul Richter.

Schumann's life took a straightforward course, though he was always haunted by the underlying fear of insanity. From his earliest childhood, Schumann, the son of a Zwickau bookseller, had been strangely prone to reverie; he lived his life in fantasies, and indeed his initial ambition was to be a writer.

A student of law in Leipzig (1828) and then in Heidelberg, he revealed a sensitivity that verged on the ridiculous and on mawkishness, particularly in the way he courted his first fiancée, Ernestine von Fricken, whom he left from an excess of scruples. The important stages of Schumann's life were often marked by the initiatives of others which forced him to make decisions, and to make precipitate and extreme choices: his meeting with Professor Wieck who decided for him that he should become a pianist, and his love for Clara Wieck, are famous in the annals of music. In August 1837, she wrote to him: 'Nothing in the world will make *us* go back', thus forcing Schumann into a battle and a commitment, even though it was what he himself wanted. Similarly, his acceptance of a post in Düsseldorf, about which he was apprehensive ('because there is a lunatic asylum in the town') gradually led to his mental decline, to hallucinations and to his desire to put an end to it all by throwing himself into the Rhine on 27 February 1854. He was rescued and finally committed to the asylum at Endenich, where he died two years later.

His delicate mental balance and depressive tendencies did not prevent Schumann from working tenaciously.

Portrait of Schumann

Having lost the use of one hand through paralysis, he gave up his career as a virtuoso to devote himself to composition: *Etudes* after Paganini, *Papillons, Toccata, Intermezzi, Impromptus,* and *Symphonic Studies.* In 1834, he founded a musical review, the *Neue Zeitschrift fur Musik,* to defend 'good' music. During the tormented period of the refusal of Clara's father to agree to their marriage, he composed the *Carnaval, Phantasiestücke Novelettes,* and *Kreisleriana* as well as the *Sonatas,* eventually finding true happiness in 1840, the year of their marriage, which is marked by over two hundred lieder, settings for texts by Goethe, Heine and Schiller, *Frauenliebe und Leben, Dichterliebe,* and also a *Quintet,* three *String Quartets,* a *Piano Quartet,* and the *First Symphony.*

SMETANA Bedrich (Litomysl 2.3.1824 – Prague 12.5.1884). Smetana was, in the Romantic era, the founder of the modern Czech school (Dvořák, Suk, Fibich). Heir to a magnificent artistic tradition that moved Burney to call Prague in the 18th century the 'Conservatoire of Europe', Smetana musically deepened the influences of Liszt, Berlioz and Weber (all of whom had made famous visits to Prague).

This great musician was, tragically, to die deaf and insane. It was not until he was nineteen that he was able to devote himself to musical studies. He worked with Liszt, thanks to whom he founded a School of Music in Prague. Having spent some time in Sweden as a conductor, he returned home to undertake a variety of activities: as a pianist, conductor, composer and critic.

He wrote eight operas in Czech, of which several have remained very popular: *The Brandenburgers in Bohemia* (1863), *The Bartered Bride* (1866), *Dalibor* (1867), *Libussa* (1872), *The Two Widows* (1874), *The Kiss* (1876), *The Secret* (1878), and *The Devil's Wall* (1882); three *Quartets,* a *Trio,* various pieces for orchestra, twelve *a capella* choruses, and piano compositions.

Particularly memorable are the opera *The Bartered Bride,* with its vigorous popular rhythms and its fresh bubbling gaiety; and, of course, the six-part symphonic poem *Ma Vlast* (My Country) which evokes the history of Bohemia and its picturesque landscapes. This last work is particularly Romantic not only in its national feeling, but also in its atmosphere and very real feeling for Nature.

SPOHR Ludwig (Brunswick 5.4.1784 – Cassel 22.10.1859) 'Spohr is an excellent and worthy man; he is now seventy-five years old and, of all the musicians of his period, I consider him as the most valid, by far. His double career as a virtuoso and a composer is equally honorable; but both one and the other lacked that element of the extraordinary which is, quite simply, genius' Liszt wrote to a friend in 1855. Choirmaster at Cassel for a long time, Spohr wrote more than one hundred and fifty works in various forms, most of which have been consigned to oblivion: they include thirty-four quartets, nine symphonies, oratorios and operas. He was not fond of modernist music, particularly that of Wagner, to whom he recommended moderation in his writing (even though he conducted *The Flying Dutchman* and *Tannhäuser* in Cassel). His best-known opera is probably *Jessonda* (1823), which was was very successful, but in his *Faust* (1816), he opened the way for Weber, with his feeling for Nature and quest for a musical expression of the hero's inner life (an explanatory note was attached to the opera programme). Spohr's overflowing sentimentality is most evident in his oratorios: *The Last Judgement* (1812), and *Germany Liberated* (1819).

TCHAIKOVSKY Peter Ilych (Votkinsk 7.5.1840 – St. Petersburg 6.11.1893). There are few remarkable facts about Tchaikovsky's life: born in eastern Russia, his first musical education was at the hands of his mother. His father was an engineer and the family followed him in his various posts all over Russia. In 1847, Tchaikovsky started to study piano seriously; later he trained at the St Petersburg Conservatoire, founded by the illustrious Anton Rubinstein. At the same time he was studying law. In 1852, after a performance of Mozart's *Don Giovanni*, he decided to become a musician. His first attempts at composition date from 1863–1864. In 1866, he became a teacher of composition at the Moscow Conservatoire. From then on, he spent most of his life there, interspersed with visits and concert tours abroad.

Tchaikovsky's work includes operas, the best-known of which are *Eugène Onegin* (1877), *The Queen of Spades* (1890) and *Iolanthe* (1892); six symphonies of which the 4th, 5th and 6th (*Pathétique*) are the most famous; many ballets (*The Nutcracker, The Sleeping Beauty*, and *Swan Lake*); overtures and symphonic poems (*1812, Manfred, Hamlet, Francesca da Rimini*); two piano concertos, one violin concerto, chamber music (string quartets, trio), piano pieces and melodies. The works that are best known outside Russia are the concertos, the symphonies, *Onegin, The Queen of Spades* and the ballets.

Tchaikovsky belongs to the Romantic movement by virtue of his training, which was very much influenced by German music, his poetic and literary inspiration, his artistic approach, and his love of folklore, of the fantastic and of pathos. Though this may seem excessive at times, his sincerity cannot be doubted: despite a melancholy which can at times be mawkish, and a lyricism that is often facile, Tachaikovsky almost always dominated his subject. In his work, the commonplace becomes the heartfelt cry of a desperately lonely personality. Whether or not this resulted from his homosexuality, we have no way of knowing, but it remains true that Tchaikovsky, in many ways, personifies the accursed Romantic artist. Onegin and Hermann in *The Queen of Spades*, are his alter egos.

Portrait of Tchaikovsky

VERDI Giuseppe (Le Roncole, near Parma 10.10.1813 – Milan 27.1.1901). The story of Verdi's life is inextricably entwined with that of his work. Born in the same year as Wagner, he was educated in Busseto, in the province of Parma, and initiated to music by the organist Baistrocchi and by Ferdinando Provesi. Through the intermediary of the Philharmonic Society of Busseto, he also had contact with the 18th century musical tradition of old Italy. The Society, and especially its director Antonio Barezzi, a wealthy merchant, determined Verdi's musical career by sending him to Milan for more advanced musical studies.

But the Milan Conservatoire refused to admit him and Verdi had to train alone, with private tuition from Vincenzo Lavigna. This self-taught character was to remain with him all his life and he was always stubbornly determined to achieve success.

Like all young composers, he was approached by an impresario (operas were in such great demand in Italy at the time that it was not difficult to obtain commissions) and Verdi worked on his first opera for a long time. Started in 1836, it was almost complete under the title of *Rochester*, when Verdi reworked it completely and then was lucky enough to have it accepted at La Scala, where it was premiered on 17 November 1839, with the new title of *Oberto, conte di San Bonifaccio*. The melodramatic and patriotic aspects of the opera found favour with the Italian nationalist audience (a large part of Italy was occupied by Austria at the time). Favoured by the Risorgimento, he appeared as the champion of liberal ideas and a career as a committed composer opened up before him: *Nabucco* (1842) was a huge success: soon the cry was taken up of 'Viva Verdi' or Viva V (ittorio) E (mmanuele) R(e) d' I(talia). Verdi was now in a position to dictate his own terms to the impresarios: *I Lombardi* (1834), *Ernani* (1844) transposing Hugo's hero into the character of an Italian patriot, *I Due Foscari* (1844), *Giovanna d'Arco* (1845), another heroine adopted by the Risorgimento, *Alzira* (1846) and *Attila* (1847), all added to the glory of the young composer.

From 1847 to 1850, he dealt with loftier subject matter, in particular with *Macbeth* (1847), and *I Masnadieri* (1847) and *Luisa Miller*, both inspired by the works of Schiller. It was during this period that his fame spread further abroad and that he started to write for theatres outside Italy.

Portrait of Verdi

The years 1851 to 1853 saw the birth of the 'trilogy' that are still Verdi's best known and best loved works today: *Rigoletto* (1851), after *Le Roi s'amuse* by Hugo, *Il Trovatore* (1853), from a melodrama by the Spaniard Guttierez, and *La Traviata*, from *La Dame aux camélias* by Dumas fils. The initial failure of *La Traviata* led Verdi gradually but profoundly to modify his style. His major preoccupation was no longer immediate profitability, but the best way to validate his works: by the choice of an attractive theatre, the choice of a good librettist, particular singers for particular roles, and a 'specialist' conductor. In paral-

lel, Verdi's musical language was changing: there were, for instance, fewer 'Italian style' arias, and the symphonic orchestration became stronger, was more in evidence. This may, as has been suggested, have been the effect of rivalry with, or the example set by, Wagner. In any event, from the *Sicilian Vespers* (1855) to *Aida* (1871), Verdi took pains to 'compose' and to allow his works to mature more fully: the operas of this period include *La Forza del destino*, from the horrific melodrama by the Spaniard Rivas, composed for the Imperial Theatre in St Petersburg, *Don Carlos*, written for Paris (1867) and *Aida* for Cairo (1871). His mature operas, *Un ballo en maschera* (1859), *Don Carlos*, and *Simon Boccanegra* (particularly in the revised version for La Scala in 1881) exemplify Verdi's Romanticism well. It can be defined by the choice of a 'Romantic' subject, drawn from fashionable theatre (Shakespeare, Scribe, Hugo or Schiller); the balance between singing and symphony; the gradual disappearance of a tried and tested format in favour of a continuous musical dialogue; and recourse to more and more particularised voices, all in the service of a true *theatre* of music.

He also continued to use his art to serve his ideas, notably in composing his *Requiem* in memory of Manzoni (1874), another key figure of Italian Romanticism. Verdi's later work can perhaps be described as purified Romanticism. *Otello* (1887), *Falstaff* (1893), and the *Pièces sacrées* (1898) are like the wings that transported his art to the highest peaks. There is no more melodrama, but instead an inner drama (*Otello*) which leads to tragedy, or a comic plot (*Falstaff*) with a moralising aspect; the vocal richness is set now in an equally rich orchestral context; fashion is spurned in favour of the meditation of a patriarch of Romanticism on the human condition. In his last years and late masterpieces, Verdi is reminiscent of Hugo: both of them became more true to themselves, casting off artifice and fashion. Verdi died at the age of eighty-seven, Italy's greatest composer.

WAGNER Richard (Leipzig 22.5.1813 – Venice 13.2.1883) Wagner's father died six months before his birth, and soon after his mother was married again, to the actor and painter Geyer, who lived in Dresden and died there in 1821. The young Wagner thus grew up in a town rich in art. He leant initially towards poetry and it was not until his mother had returned to Leipzig, where her sister was an actress, that he began to take an interest in music. While he was a student at the University, he learned piano with the organist Müller and counterpoint

Scene from Tannhäuser after T. Piris

where he met Liszt, then settled in Zurich with his friends, the Wesendonks. During his exile, Wagner went to London in 1855 to conduct some concerts, formulated the first of the theoretical writings on which his work was based, and started work on a series of operas based on the Nibelungen legend. These years were also those of his love for Mathilde Wesendonk, which ended in painful separation and to which *Tristan und Isolde* (1859) bears poignant testimony.

In 1861, he returned to Paris for a production of *Tannhäuser*, which caused a sensational scandal. In 1864, Wagner received a message from the new king of Bavaria, Ludwig II, inviting him to come to Munich and offering to stage his operas. It was there that *Tristan, The Flying Dutchman* and *Tannhäuser* were performed, under the direction of Hans von Bülow, whose wife was already Wagner's mistress. His scandalous private life, the hostility of his political enemies, his extravagance and accumulated debts forced him to leave Munich. He settled in Switzerland, in Triebschen, with Cosima von Bülow (Liszt's daughter) whom he married in 1870.

In 1871, the dream of Bayreuth began to take shape,

The Death of Tristan after G. Goldberg

with a famous teacher, Theodor Weinlig. In 1834, he became musical director of the Magdeburg theatre. There he married the actress Minna Planer, and accompanied her to Koenigsberg where she had accepted an engagement, although the theatre went bankrupt two months later.

In 1837, Wagner was musical director of the theatre in Riga. In 1839, forced to flee from his creditors, he and Minna, trying to make their way to Paris, were smuggled aboard a ship bound for London. The ship was blown off course by violent storms, an experience that Wagner was to draw on later when he composed *The Flying Dutchman*. They finally reached Paris, where Wagner hoped, in vain, to find fame and fortune. To earn money, he wrote articles on German Romanticism for the *Revue musicale*, 'arranged' operas for the piano or the cornet, and even sold the libretto of *The Flying Dutchman* to the Opéra, where it was staged with music by the conductor Dietsch! He left Paris for Dresden where *Rienzi* (1842) was successfully performed and where he was appointed Kapellmeister to the Saxon court (1843). *The Flying Dutchman* was produced in 1843 without great success. He then completed *Lohengrin* (1845), and started work on *Die Meistersinger*. Meanwhile, enthused with revolutionary ideas, he took part in the uprising of 1849. With a warrant out for his arrest, he left Dresden for Weimar,

with its State inauguration in 1876, and the financial disappointments that followed. It was there that *Parsifal* was created, composed exclusively for the *Festspielhaus*, and there that the *Ring* cycle was performed again, this time in accordance with the composer's wishes. Wagner, who usually wintered in Italy, died in Venice on 13 February 1883.

Wagner's Romanticism is apparent at every level: in his life, his constant recourse to Nordic and Germanic mythology for inspiration, his perpetually contradictory philosophy which exalted sometimes worldly happiness and sometimes the joys of self-denial, and finally his technique which made him one of the great reforming forces in music. 'No musician' said Baudelaire, 'excels like Wagner at painting material and spiritual space and

depth. He possesses the art of translating by subtle de-
grees all that is excessive, immense, and ambitious in
spiritual and natural Man'.

WEBER Carl Maria von (Eutin 18.11.1786 – London
5.6.1826). Born in Holstein into a family ennobled in the
16th century, Carl Maria was educated in drawing,
painting and music amid a select company of distinguished minds. His father, Kapellmeister to the Bishop of
Lübeck at Eutin, was the director of a travelling theatre
company, so the rudiments of Weber's art were learnt
haphazardly on tour. His first important music teacher
was Michael Haydn, in Salzburg, with whom he studied
for a year (1797–1798). In Munich, his father had his *Six
Fuguettes* printed, by way of encouragement, while Carl
Maria was learning four-part composition from the
Court organist, Kalcher. It was under Kalcher's direction that he composed his first opera, *Die Macht der Liebe
und des Weines* (The Power of Love and Wine). He then
went to Freiberg, in Saxony, intending to perfect the
technique of lithography, but he also took the opportunity of having *Das Waldmädchen* performed. The work was
about a mute girl who lived in close communion with
Nature and its mysteries, and met with great success.
Weber returned to Michael Haydn in Salzburg and
wrote *Peter Schmoll und seine Nachbaren*, an *opéra comique*
which was performed without much success in Augsburg
in 1801.
However, in 1802, Weber's career turned definitively towards music when, accompanied by his father, he made
a concert tour of Germany. The success of the tour determined his future. He went to Vienna, where he met
Joseph Haydn and Vogler, then to Karlsruhe, Stuttgart,
Mannheim, Munich and Berlin. From 1813 to 1816, he
was director of the Prague Opera where he staged the
works of Spontini, Mozart, Cherubini, Mehul, Boieldieu
and Spohr, in other words, the whole Romantic repertoire of the day. In 1817, he became Director of the Dresden Opera and revolutionised German opera. Aristocratic, brilliantly gifted, as talented with the conductor's
baton as he was with the pen, as excellent a pianist as a
musical director, Weber personifies the complete artist of
whom the Romantic era dreamed. This final period saw
the composition of *Der Freischütz* (completed in 1820),
and the famous *Konzertstück* for piano and orchestra. He
was in demand throughout the whole of Europe. It was
largely for Paris and London, where Weber had decided
to go in person, that he composed *Oberon*. But he died of
consumption in London, shortly after its Covent Garden
premiere. His remains were only returned to Dresden in
1844.
Weber composed works of equal importance in every
genre. They include some very successful works for piano
(*Invitation to the Waltz*, for example), cantatas, masses,
and operas of which *Freischütz*, *Oberon*, *Euryanthe* and *Pre-
ciosa* are the most justly famous.
Weber was a Romantic in his life as well as his work, in
his many talents, enthusiasms, and the nature of his

music. His operas were often composed from libretti of
quality (thus Weber approached the Romantic poetess
Helmine von Chezy for the libretto of *Euryanthe*) in which
the miraculous and Nature always play an essential role.
Works of fairytale enchantment, the operas are distinguished by their melodious inspiration as well as by their
powerful symphonic score.

WOLF Hugo (Windischgraz, Yugoslavia 13.3.1860 –
Vienna 22.2.1903). Wolf is often considered, like Bruckner, a very late Romantic. In fact, it was he who
perfected the lied at a time when the form was tending
towards a proliferation and exaggeration of acoustic
material. He too was a Wagnerian, with an aggressive
side not evident in Bruckner. His literary inspirations
and unhappy life were very Romantic. He transformed
the Wagnerian declamatory principle into what was
perhaps the most intimate form of Romantic music, the
lied. For Wolf, it was no longer a question of putting
poetic language to music in order to create, in the manner of Schubert, Schumann and Brahms, a new formal
entity; his aspiration was to create a new musical language, to fulfil it and surpass it at the same time. He
exhausted all poetry, principally German, from Goethe's
Prometheus to the religious lyricism of the *Spanisches Liederbuch*, from the sombre confessions of Michaelangelo to
the pale and playful tones of Eichendorff and of the *Italienisches Liederbuch*. The importance of the piano part in
these lieder is worthy of note: it plays a role as important
as that of Wagner's orchestra: Wolf, in fact, entitled
these works 'Lieder for voice and piano' and not 'with
piano accompaniment'. This proud and solitary composer produced the main body of his work over a very short
period of time: the Mörike settings; the Goethe cycles
that cover both the vast poems of the poet's first period
and the cycles of *Mignom* and the *Divan*; and finally the
collections of Italian and Spanish poetry translated by
Geibel and Heyse.
Late in his life, Wolf turned to opera with *Der Corregidor*
and *Manuel Venegas*, but the förmer was very coolly received and the latter interrupted by the attacks of insanity to which Wolf had been prone since 1897.

List of Illustrations

Sur la jaquette sont reproduits les tableaux suivants : première page de haut en bas et de gauche à droite : Caspar David Friedrich *L'Arbre aux corbeaux.* 1822 - Eugène Delacroix *La Mort de Sardanapale* (détail). 1827 - Heinrich Füssli *Didon sur le bûcher.* 1781 - Philipp Otto Runge *Nous Trois.* 1805 - Dernière page : Francisco Goya *La Charge des Mamelouks* (détail). 1814 - John Constable *La Cathédrale de Salisbury.* 1829 - Gustave Courbet *La Rencontre.* 1854 - Théodore Géricault *Officier de chasseur à cheval chargeant.* 1812

Index